IT Strategic and Operational Controls

IT Strategic and Operational Controls

JOHN KYRIAZOGLOU

IT Governance Publishing

IT Governance Publishing
IT Governance Limited
Unit 3, Clive Court
Bartholomew's Walk
Cambridgeshire Business Park
Ely
Cambridgeshire
CB7 4EH
United Kingdom

www.itgovernance.co.uk

First published in the United Kingdom in 2010
by IT Governance Publishing.

978-1-84928-061-7

FOREWORD

For the past 40 years or more, the use of information technology in and between organisations has become increasingly pervasive in the developed and developing world. Yet how many large-scale information technology initiatives can claim to have been fully successful? Although numbers vary, most commentators agree that a majority of projects fail to meet end users' expectations; in many cases, projects may be completed but are over time, over budget and provide fewer features than promised, while between 20% and 30% have so many issues that they have to be cancelled. Highly publicised cases which spring to mind include public sector projects, such as the UK Passport Office project, the Child Support Agency project and the NHS's National Programme for IT; while in the private sector, Heathrow's Terminal 5 launch and J Sainsbury's write-off of millions of dollars invested in an automated supply chain management system are shining examples where taxpayers and shareholders have lost out.

Top management, not surprisingly, while aiming to realise the significant benefits of information technology, is, at the same time, also seeking to better understand and control concomitant risks arising from the organisation's often critical dependency on its systems. Recently, top management's attention has been enhanced with the corporate governance pronouncement that Boards are now tasked to provide assurance that all systems of control are robust, reliable and effective.

This book, in an attempt to address problems raised by organisations' extensive use of information technology, contains practical advice and illustrates solutions to the tremendously complicated problems of designing, implementing and auditing new and existing systems by taking as its focus the key area of strategic and operational controls.

John Kyriazoglou has written a comprehensive account illustrating how information technology controls enable and support management, at all levels, in their efforts to achieve the strategic and operational goals of the organisation, as delivered through the technological systems. In addition, for each aspect of control covered within individual chapters, he has provided audit programmes and checklists to help management and both internal and external auditors carry out reviews and audits. As an additional aid, he has provided an appendix to the book comprising guidelines through examples of 'how to enhance' IT security, IT policies, ethical code, etc.

I wholeheartedly recommend this book to senior and operations managers who are the ultimate users of IT and who need to ensure that the information they receive is relevant, accurate, timely and, more importantly, the result of systems which are well controlled. Both internal and external auditors will find reference to a large number of very relevant tools for use in auditing and reviewing IT operations. I also highly recommend this book to any students studying for a degree that includes an auditing and IT module as part of their programme.

Professor Georges M Selim
Emeritus Professor and Former Head of the Faculty of Management
Cass Business School
London, UK

PREFACE

It is possible to fail in many ways, while to succeed is possible only in one way.

Aristotle (384–322 BC)

The most critical assets, in the 21st Century, for the private and public enterprises, for organisations in general, for the global society, and for the economy (local, national, international) are not of a physical nature (equipment, machines, installations, plants), or of a financial nature (money, credit or other financing instruments), or of a computer software nature.

The most critical assets are knowledge (facts, experience, raw data, etc.) and ideas (concepts), which are stored in computerised systems (personal and corporate), in the modern business environment.

The computer technology and related infrastructure, the information systems, the network backbone (intranet, extranet, metropolitan, Internet, etc.) and related media technologies give everyone in a social context, and managers within a given organisational environment, direct access to what is going on: within the given organisation, in the industrial sector to which the company belongs, and in the general economy and market in which the organisation operates.

All these technological components, broadly termed Information Technology (IT), and the related Information Systems (IS) which operate within its realm, enable the modern private and public corporation and/or organisation to accrue the following benefits (indicative only): quicker and more effective information for decision making at all levels; increased competition in all services of the firm; improved production processes and procedures; and higher quality in products and services offered by information systems to customers (and citizens) and society in general.

Given the rate of development of the information processing and computer manufacturing technologies and processes, a rate without a precedent in the history of mankind, it is possible now for organisations to transfer almost all of their daily business operations to be carried out by integrated information systems.

These systems are like medical drugs, either strengthening the organisation, or enabling it to cure or resolve a particular problem or operating malfunction.

However, continuing the drug analogy, if these systems are not used in a disciplined manner, they can create havoc and frequently bring about unexpected results and even catastrophe.

These integrated information systems must, therefore, operate within a business environment which is ruled by the rules, policies, regulations and instructions of a corporate governance and risk framework and a related information technology governance framework.

As Negroponte has said: 'The next decade will see cases of intellectual property abuse and invasion of our privacy. We will experience digital vandalism, software piracy and data thievery'.[1]

---

[1] See *Being Digital*, Negroponte, N, Alfred A. Knopf, New York, USA (1995).

This has definitely been proven correct. Security incidents and other acts of electronic and computer-based crimes are on the rise (as per *www.cert.org* and other security-related sites).

Kevin David Mitnick, a computer security consultant, author, and convicted of various computer-related crimes in the USA in the late 1990s, has said: 'Valuable information must be protected no matter what forum it takes or where it is located. An organisation's customer list has the same value whether in hard-copy form or an electronic file at your office or in a storage box. Social engineers always prefer the easiest to circumvent, least defended point of attack. A company's off-site back-up storage facility is seen as having less risk of detection or getting caught. Every organisation that stores any valuable, sensitive, or critical data with third parties should encrypt their data to protect its confidentiality'.[2]

IT auditing will enhance the qualities of information (effectiveness, efficiency, confidentiality, integrity, availability, compliance, reliability) according to ISACA (*www.isaca.org*).

The answer for managers and leaders of organisations is to plan for this new operating environment with the proper tools, methodologies and resources.

This is, therefore, the rationale for writing this book. Namely to offer a comprehensive, practical and convenient (in style and content), yet conceptually clear book on the subject of IT Controls and their design, implementation, monitoring, review and audit issues.

---

[2] See *The Art of Deception*, Mitnick KD and Simor WL, Wiley (2002).

In almost all types of organisations, both private and public, corporate controls denote the set of policies, procedures, techniques, methods and practices to manage and control their business operations.

Within this corporate controls framework, Information Technology controls (or IT controls) are specific actions, usually specified by policies, procedures, practices, etc. performed by persons, hardware or software with the main objective to ensure that specific business objectives are met.

The overall guiding aim of IT controls relates to the secure processing, confidentiality, integrity and availability of data and the overall management of the IT function of the organisations.

They aim to enable, facilitate and support a knowledge management framework of the organisations, as IT systems and related organisational, administrative and infrastructural components (databases, data warehouses, networking, knowledge acquisition and analysis tools, etc.) are the main contributing factors to this framework.

IT controls are commonly described in two categories according to various sources:[3] IT general controls and IT application controls.

IT general controls are those controls that are applicable to all IT activities (systems, services, issues, processes, operations, etc.) and data for a given organisation or IT systems environment. They include controls over such areas as the strategy for IT, systems development, data centre operations, database and data communications infrastructure, systems software support and maintenance,

---

[3] www.isaca.org, www.theiia.org, www.itpi.org.

IT security, and ready-made application systems acquisition, development and maintenance.

IT application controls are those controls that are appropriate for transaction processing by individual computerised subsystems, such as financial accounting, personnel administration, customer sales, inventory control, payroll or accounts payable, etc.

They relate to the processing and storing of data in computer-based files by individual IT applications and programs and help ensure that business transactions occurred are authorised, and are completely and accurately recorded, stored, processed and reported.

IT general controls are the subject matter of Chapters 1 to 8. IT application controls are the topic of Chapter 9. Various case studies are included in Chapter 10.

The approach taken in this book is that of setting up and operating any business entity or function, like sales, production, IT, etc. and the required controls (plans, policies, procedures, practices, etc.) to manage and operate them better. It is a practical book, based mostly on practical, on-the-job experience of the author, complemented with research, in some cases.

First you establish the IT entity or function and its controls (*Chapter 1: IT organisation controls*).

As the second action you design and implement the basic administration policies and procedures for IT to obtain the requisite resources (*Chapter 2: IT administration controls*).

As the third activity you design a new, or improve your existing, business architecture to enable the IT strategic process (*Chapter 3: Enterprise Architecture controls*).

After the IT function is set up with a structure, personnel, administration and Enterprise Architecture, you craft an IT strategy and align it with the business functions of the organisation (*Chapter 4: IT strategic controls*).

Now you are ready to create secure and quality products and services by putting your IT strategy into action. To do this you develop and design IT application systems (*Chapter 5: System development controls*), and devise and implement security controls (*Chapter 6: IT security controls*).

To run these IT application systems and provide services across all levels and locations of the organisation and the wider community, including other interconnecting parties, you need to create and operate a physical infrastructure and obtain services from specialised external providers (*Chapter 7: Data centre operational and support controls*).

As these IT application systems are made up of application software which cannot be run alone but must have system software upon which they achieve their tasks, you need to install and configure specific systems software and technological platforms, such as database management systems, data communications and network software, etc. (*Chapter 8: Systems software controls*).

Last, but not least, all IT application systems are made up of individual programs that receive data of occurring business transactions, check them for errors, process and store them in computerised files, and provide reports and results to all approved users of these systems. As these programs need to accomplish their tasks with the highest level of accuracy, quality and safety, specific controls at the level of the individual program or subsystem must be applied (*Chapter 9: IT application controls*).

Moreover, several case studies on using the IT controls presented in all these chapters are outlined in Chapter 10 (*Using IT Controls in audit and consulting assignments*).

All the chapters contain examples of various plans, policies, procedures, methodologies, forms, performance measures and other controls (e.g. audit programmes and checklists), and are complemented and supported by an appendix, which contains various tools, (policies, forms, audit methodology, etc.).

Each chapter has a scope, the description of the main control types of the particular area (e.g. IT organisation, IT administration, etc.), an example of performance measures (strategic and operational), several audit programmes and checklists and a set of review questions.

Strategic and operational performance measures monitor the implementation and effectiveness of an organisation's IT strategies, determine the gap between actual and targeted performance and determine organisation effectiveness, quality of products and services, and operational efficiency.

Performance measurement may be deemed as: (a) the calculation of achievement used to measure and manage project quality, (b) the level of attainment of an objective in comparison to a given effort, and (c) the act of measuring or the process of being measured.

A key performance indicator or measure is a description of what is measured to determine the extent to which objectives and outcomes have been achieved and to what level.

A compliance indicator or measure denotes: (a) whether plans, policies, procedures, etc. exist or not, (b) whether these are followed or not, and (c) whether the organisation complies or not with the specific state laws, industry standards, ethics codes; such as SOX Act, Data Privacy Laws, Banking Regulations, ISO Standards, etc.

Examples of performance and compliance measures are included in Chapters 1 to 9.

Customisable IT audit programmes and checklists are provided in a separate volume, *Addendum to IT Strategic and Operational Controls* in Word format, which is available at *www.itgovernance.co.uk/products/3143*.

The potential audience of this book includes IT management, IT auditors, IT project managers, IS auditors, systems development and software support staff, e-crime experts, fraud examiners, security and risk professionals, IT consultants, students of accounting, finance, internal auditing and business administration, all management levels of private and public organisations, external auditors, corporate performance experts, Board members, human resources advisors, and anyone interested in how IT operations, activities and investments of organisations may be managed and controlled better. The material, concepts, ideas, plans, policies, procedures, forms, methods, tools, etc. presented, described and analysed in all chapters and appendices, are for educational and training purposes only. These are based on the experience of the author and on the resources identified in the notes as well as in the bibliography.

These may be used only, possibly, as an indicative base set, and should be customised by each organisation, after careful and considerable thought as to the needs and requirements of each organisation, taking into effect the implications and aspects of the legal, national, religious, philosophical, cultural and social environments, and expectations, within which each organisation operates and exists.

It is hoped that this book may assist you in executing management activities more efficiently and in understanding and controlling organisations in a better way.

John Kyriazoglou, CICA, MS, BA (Hons)

jkyriazoglou@hotmail.com

ABOUT THE AUTHOR

John Kyriazoglou obtained a certificate in computer programming and data processing from a technical college in Hamilton, Canada, a BA (Honours) in Computer Science and with a minor in Economics from the University of Toronto, Canada, also earning the 1975 Scholastic award for Academic Excellence in Computer Science, and a MS in Data Processing from the Pacific University, USA. John has worked in Canada, Europe (England, Switzerland, Luxembourg, Greece, etc.) and the Middle East for over 35 years as a senior IT manager, IT auditor, Group EDP Internal Audit Manager and senior management consultant, for a variety of clients and projects, in both the private and public sectors. John has published over 20 articles in professional publications, has served on numerous scientific committees, is a member of ISACA, the Institute for Internal Controls, Inc. (USA), and other professional and cultural associations, and provides courses in IT Auditing, Security and Electronic Crime Prevention.

John has authored five books: (a) *EDP/IT Auditing*, published in 2001 by Anubis Publications, and listed in the international website of ISACA www.isaca.org/bookstore, (b) *Performance Measurement for Private and Public Organisations*, co-authored by Despina Politou, and published in 2005 by ION publishers, (c) *Thoughts on Love and Friendship*, published in 2009 by YADES Publishers, (d) *Ancient Greek Maxims*, published in 2010, and offered free at: www.free-ebooks.gr, and (e) *Corporate Strategic and Operational Controls*, published by the Institute for

Internal Controls in 2010, co-authored by Dr. F. Nasuti and Dr C. Kyriazoglou.

John's recent control-related articles (last 10 years) include: (1) 'IT security', *TechBusiness*, Greece, 11/2000, (2) 'IT strategy', *TechBusiness*, Greece, 12/2000, (3) 'Contingency Planning & Business Continuity', *TechBusiness*, Greece, 2/2001, (4) 'Database systems implementation' in *TechBusiness*, Greece, 4/2001, (5) 'Ethical and Professional Code', pp. 67–74, *Hellenic Bank Association Magazine*, Athens, Greece, No. 40, Jan/March 2005, www.hba.gr, (6) 'Strategic Controls and the Balanced Scorecard Framework', *Archives in Economic History*, Vol. XVII, No.1, 1-6-/2006, Greece, (co-authors: Prof. Curtis and D. Politou), (7) Greek translation of the English Standard on 'Risk Management', www.theirm.org, England, 6/2007, (co-authors: Dr C. Kyriazoglou, and Dr R. Sygkouna), (8) 'Performance Measurement Audit programme and Checklists', www.auditnet.org, 12/2008, (co-author D. Politou), (9) Greek translation of the Code of Ethics of The Computer Ethics Institute, 2010, *www.computerethicsinstitute.com/listoflanguages.html*, and (10) Greek translation of the Code of Ethics of ISACA, 2010.

His voluntary efforts include mentoring, coaching, and founding and supporting cultural societies.

John can be contacted at: *jkyriazoglou@hotmail.com.*

ACKNOWLEDGEMENTS

I'd like to thank the following experts and professionals who had the disposition and stamina to go through my first draft and provide very helpful comments and improvements. I'm most grateful to Professor P. Georgiadis (National University of Athens, Department of Informatics and Telecommunications, Greece), Y. Charalambous (ex-Vice President of the Athens Stock Exchange Supervisory Committee, and ex-Deputy Senior Partner of KPMG Athens, Greece), Ms. A. Triantafylli, PhD (Lecturer in Management Accounting at Manchester Business School, The University of Manchester, England), and Dan Swanson (Health Information Security Officer, Manitoba eHealth, Canada and former Director of Professional Practices at the IIA), for their excellent review comments. I'm also thankful to several other academics and professionals, with whom I have had discussions and communications regarding the application of controls, and who have inspired me, in general: Professor G. Selim (CASS Business School, London, England), Dr. Marylin M. Helms, Sesquicentennial Chair and Professor of Management (Dalton State College, USA), Dr. Frank Nasuti, PhD, CPA, CICA, CFE (Chairman – Institute for Internal Controls, Dissertation Chair and Committee Member – Nova Southeastern University, USA), Professor A. Ballas and Professor D. Hevas (Athens University of Business and Economy, Greece), G. Raounas (Partner, KPMG Consulting, Greece), K. Georgiou (former Director of several private companies), and Professor B. Filios (University of Ioanina, Greece), and S. Missirlis (President, POSTIT, Inc., Canada). My sincere thanks also go to several of my professional associates: Ms. D. Politou (IT Management Consultant), Michael Hadjiefthymiou, CISA, CISM (IT Auditor at a major Bank), C. Faltsetas (Acting General Manager of KPMG Consulting), A. Thomopoulos (Partner, DIADIKASIA SA), John Anagnostou (Managing Partner, CLARUS Advisory SA), Dr. G. Boukis (International IT Projects

Manager), all my previous employers and associates, and to the many IT and senior management staff of my clients for their assistance and support and for making it easy for me to support them in various projects on IT, internal audit and e-Crime training issues. I offer my sincere thanks to the staff of the publisher: Alan Calder, Angela Wilde and Vicki Whitney, for their undivided attention and spirit.

We are grateful to the following for their generous time spent in reviewing the manuscript of this book and for their pertinent comments: Yiangos Charalambous FCCA, Associate Director; EuropeanProfiles SA Consulting Company and Technical Advisor of UHYAxon Certified auditors, Greece; Professor Panagiotis Geordiadis, PhD, National and Kapodistrian University of Athens, Informatics and Telecommunications Department and Androniki Triantafylli, Lecturer in Management Accounting, The University of Manchester, Manchester Business School, Accounting and Finance Group.

I'm most obligated to my Canadian Alma Mater, Woodsworth College of the University of Toronto, Canada, my inspirational beacon, nourishing source and fostering mother of my knowledge and intellectual base.

I'd like to thank my family for bearing with me during this wonderful but very long and enduring task. My wife Sandy, for her full understanding, support, patience, love, motivation and friendship. My wonderful Chris for his most inquisitive mind, love and support. My lovely princess Miranda and her Dimitri, for their supportive affection and love, humorous spirit and positive persistence in the journey of life. And last, but not least, to the seventh gift bestowed upon me by the Almighty, my always exquisite and supreme Queen of my life, my grand-daughter, the blue-eyed, lovely and admirable, Melina.

John Kyriazoglou

CONTENTS

CHAPTER 1: IT ORGANISATION CONTROLS

The right ruler should himself obey the law.

Architas (428–347 BC), ancient Greek philosopher, mathematician, astronomer and military leader

1.1 Scope

Organisations invest funds and effort, hire and use people and commit other critical resources for developing the information systems they need. They need an IT organisation (unit or function) and a set of required controls for this purpose.

IT organisation controls establish the good operating environment for IT (infrastructure and systems) and ensure the successful execution of the daily activities and operational transactions of the IT systems of the organisation.

A set of main IT organisation controls, with examples, are provided: IT department functional description controls, IT organisational controls, IT vision, mission and values statements, IT control frameworks, monitoring and review controls, and IT organisation performance measures. In addition to these, a set of audit programmes and checklists are presented to support the IT manager, the IT practitioner, the systems development and support staff, and other professionals (IT auditors, internal auditors, IT consultants, external auditors, compliance officers, etc.) in executing and improving their duties and responsibilities to the fullest possible level.

1.2 Purpose and main types of IT organisation controls

The direction for overall organisational control comes from the general strategic goals and strategic plans of the organisation. General strategic plans are translated into specific performance measures, such as share of the market, earnings, return on investment, budgets, customer or citizen satisfaction, benefits to society, etc. These corporate strategic plans (whether formal or informal) define and establish the framework within which other operational business functions, such as IT, production, finance, sales, marketing, etc. are organised and operate.

In terms of organising the IT activities, the purpose of IT organisation controls is to ensure, enable and facilitate (a) the establishment of the entire IT control framework, (b) the continuous support of IT on a formal basis by management (top, middle, lower), and its enforcement with proper policies, standards and procedures, registers, tagging and locks, including internal and external audits, (c) the management of the input, processing, and output functions of computerised application systems in recording, maintaining and processing the computerised transactions of the organisation, (d) the development, management and maintenance of IT infrastructure and application systems, and (e) the protection and safeguarding of the IT infrastructure, equipment, facilities and data of the organisation. These controls may overlap the usual corporate administration, human resource, financial, production and other similar controls.

The main types of IT organisation controls are:

- IT department functional description controls
- IT organisation controls
- IT vision, mission and values statements

- IT governance and control frameworks
- Monitoring and review controls
- IT organisation performance measures.

Establishing each of these controls, to serve the needs of the given organisation, may be carried out by the formal IT committee, or the IT management and its senior staff, or some other corporate work team or group, or a combination of these. It would be useful, however, as it has been proved in practice, to have these controls ratified by the Board or senior management executive committee of the organisation.

In addition, the audit programmes and checklists described in Paragraph 1.9 may be used to support the design, implementation and post-implementation review of the IT organisation controls.

1.3 IT department functional description controls

Defining what the IT function does, whether in a written formal statement or on an informal basis, depending on the culture of the organisation and its management, is the main task of these controls.

The main controls in this area are:

- IT department overall objectives
- IT department overall terms of reference
- Detailed IT department terms of reference
- IT department job description controls
- Other IT roles at the senior management level.

1.3.1 IT department overall objectives

The overall objectives of the IT function for any organisation may be described in terms of three types:

- Operational: the efficient, economical and effective day-to-day operation of the IT systems and related infrastructural components (communication systems, office information systems, networking equipment, etc.) to enable and effect the delivery of accurate and timely processing of data to all levels of the organisation
- Tactical: the efficient, economical and effective allocation of resources, obtaining and acquiring ready-made IT systems and services, and monitoring
- Strategic: the effective deployment of IT systems throughout the organisation and the provision of information and related services (e.g. content management) to all internal and external IT users.

The IT function is considered, in normal operating conditions, as responsible for:

- the accurate processing and reporting of the information contained in these systems
- ensuring that the software operates without errors and according to the business requirements and needs specified and agreed by the users of these IT systems, and the management of the organisation.

The IT function is not usually responsible, however, at least in the modern online operating environment, for the correct entry of data and the accurate inputting of all the information required by each IT system.

1.3.2 IT department overall terms of reference

The IT department is designed to be responsible for the provision of IT services, and managing the information and knowledge content of the corporate entity to which it belongs.

These services are extended to:

- all internal staff of the organisation
- all levels of management
- the Board of Directors or the top executive committee of the organisation, all stakeholders and other users, such as: unionised employees, shareholders, public organisations regulating the particular entity, vendors, customers, etc. of the IT systems
- all external organisations, in the case that the given corporate entity is connected to other corporations via inter-organisational systems, such as B2B networks, etc.

A typical example of the terms of reference of an IT function may be:

IT department overall terms of reference

The IT department provides technology and services that fulfil the organisation's broad-based IT strategic and operational needs. The department has the responsibility for planning that commits resources and provides a stable direction for the future. Duties include the responsibility and authority for review, control and improvements in such areas as computerised application systems, database management systems, office automation, desktop computers, networks, application servers and data communications. Other duties include:

Developing and implementing computerised information systems for the business needs of the organisation.

Developing and implementing office automation systems.

Ensuring the security of all data.

Carrying out the data centre operations.

Designing and managing data communications and telecommunications networks.

Developing and controlling all electronic forms.

Developing information processing policies and procedures.

Conducting feasibility studies of new automated systems.

Researching potential systems, methods, or equipment that could improve cost-effectiveness or enhance productivity.

Providing an organisation-wide IT training function, which includes training classes, answering help desk calls, support documentation and managing a training facility.

Designing, development and implementation of communications systems and related infrastructural components.

Operation, support and maintenance (preventive, corrective, etc.) of the IT systems running for the given organisation and providing continuous support of the users that interact with and depend on these systems.

Management of the information and knowledge content of the organisation, which is based on (a) the organisation's IT systems and (b) data and information provided by external sources. Such information and knowledge content could be residing in the IT systems of the organisation, such as main computers, minicomputers, professional systems, desktops, laptops, CAD systems, personal devices, application and other database servers, etc.

Support of the IT equipment of the organisation (computers, servers, cabling, computer room, peripheral equipment, networking, user-located equipment, etc.) to ensure that it always remains in good, safe and secure operating order for all its users. This may include support for outsourcing of the maintenance function of the organisation's IT equipment, which means managing and monitoring by the IT unit of the outsourcing entity to ensure that it provides the specific support function for the organisation.

Development, operation, maintenance, support and improvement of the organisation's management information systems (MIS). This MIS may be based on the corporate legacy systems as well as the knowledge-based, decision-support, data-warehousing, ERP (Enterprise Resource Planning) systems, in order to provide to all levels of management the required information for running, efficiently and effectively, the given corporate entity.

Design, development, implementation, operation and support of an enhanced IT governance framework. This framework consists of the continuous management of: aligning the IT strategy to corporate strategy within the framework of the Enterprise Architecture of the organisation, managing human and other resources, quality management, performance management, IT standards, policies, procedures, practices and methods for the safe, efficient, effective and cost-beneficial running of all ITC systems and infrastructural components for the good of the given organisation and greater society.

1.3.3 Detailed IT department terms of reference

Further to the IT department overall terms of reference, detailed IT department terms of reference may be required for some organisations.

A typical IT function may be made up of:

- IT management
- Information systems development
- Computer operations
- Technical support
- IT quality assurance standards.

IT management

The typical IT manager of a corporate entity appointed to head, organise and run the IT function, has the following duties and responsibilities:

IT governance strategy: Ensuring that the governance, strategic and tactical IT needs and requirements of the organisation are fully covered within the framework of the Enterprise Architecture.

User support: Ensuring that adequate, efficient and effective technical support is provided to the users of the organisation's Information Systems (IS).

Training: Ensuring that both IS personnel and users are trained to use and operate, at the most optimum level, the IT equipment and related IT resources (Corporate Information Systems, external databases, networking systems, computer and networking rooms, etc.).

Quality: Ensuring that the quality, integrity, validity and accuracy of raw data, processed information, IT equipment and computer software are maintained to the best professional standards and according to the organisation needs, standards of operation and business requirements.

Management: Managing and controlling all aspects of the IT organisation, its units and its related resources (human, financial, software, installations, etc.) according to corporate, professional and industry standards and guidelines.

Maintenance: Managing all the activities (including external vendors) to ensure that all IT equipment and software (operating system, database, application, etc.) are properly maintained, improved, supported and operated at all agreed time-frames and response windows.

IT project management: Managing all aspects and ensuring that all IT projects undertaken, whether within or external to the organisation, are completed within the budget, time, quality and other conditions, constraints and requirements set by and agreed with top management, stakeholders, users, IT personnel, external providers and the Executive Board of the organisation.

IT risk management: Managing all phases of the risk process related to IT projects to ensure that all risks are managed and minimised to delay, if not avoid, the occurrence of the given dangers, to the benefit of the organisation and users of the given IT projects implemented.

Database management: Managing, organising and ensuring the good and effective operation of the corporate databases (including data warehouses, data marts, knowledge bases, decision support systems, etc.) and related technical infrastructure (data dictionary, query facilities, data management specialised utilities and tools, etc.).

IT security: Managing, organising and ensuring the safe, secure and proper security controls are designed, implemented and monitored for all Information Systems managed by the IT function, all equipment and software maintained by outside entities, and all user data existing in computerised systems within the organisation.

Problem management: Ensuring that all user problems, whether technical, requirements for future systems, production of information reports, etc. are properly supported, improved, satisfied, etc. and elevated to Board management (if large resources are required for the provision of a specific and satisfactory solution).

IT systems recovery: Ensuring that all IT systems and related infrastructural components are designed, planned and tested continuously so that the most critical IT systems are recovered and normal business operations are resumed, in case of failures of any kind, thus avoiding any business disruption of normal operation and any potential loss of revenue, harm, abuse, service inadequacies, or fraud occurrences.

IT standards: Ensuring that the IT standards, policies and procedures are planned, implemented, monitored and improved upon, on a continuous basis for all IT systems, user training, equipment, infrastructure, etc.

IT reporting: Managing and ensuring that all user problems, application errors, data errors, equipment faults, security incidents (real or attempted or probable), human resource issues, vendor problems, governance issues (e.g. ethics, fraud controls, etc.), etc. are reported to the higher levels of the organisation (including executive Board management) for subsequent review, resource resolution and effective implementation to the stated problems.

IT procurement: Ensuring effective participation, as required by corporate rules, guidelines and standards, in the procurement process for IT solutions, IT projects and other related tasks and activities (e.g. building a computer room by outside vendors).

IT audit: Ensuring adequate participation and provision of information on controls, development process, security incidents, production issues, etc. to all audit activities related to the IT systems and the IT environment of the organisation.

Information systems development (ISD)

The ISD unit is charged with the main responsibility of developing the best Information Systems (IS) for the specific corporate entity it serves, its users, its management, its external stakeholders and partners, and, in the case of public sector organisations, to society at large.

Within this frame of reference, the ISD unit has the following duties and responsibilities:

IT project management: Analysis of the project objectives, requirements and needs, commitment of the required resources for the specific project, assessment and priority-setting of the projects portfolio components, risk assessment and resolution, and management of the specific IT project.

IS analysis: Analysis of the user requirements and needs for information collection, security, integrity and privacy aspects, maintenance, reporting and connectivity regarding the given IS under consideration.

General system design: Preparation and completion of the general specifications of the IS in technical terms for the architecture of the system, its filing and security mechanisms, its databases, and its computer programs, controls, etc.

Detailed system design: Production of documentation of the computer program specifications of the required logic, the structures of the files and the databases of the system, the security and data integrity and privacy aspects, the general and specific controls, etc.

Software development: Writing, coding and testing the computerised application programs of the system as specified in the previous analysis and design stages.

Integrated testing: Testing, with the full participation of the users of the IS developed, the subsystems first, and the fully fledged IS later, using real-life data and actual business operation conditions.

IS installation: Transferring the IS into the production environment enabling access to the users of its services according to corporate security and other governance guidelines, and turning over the specific system to the Computer Operations unit for the task of its daily operation.

IS quality assurance: Reviewing all the products and deliverables of the IS going into live production mode and recommending and ensuring that the IS is of the highest quality.

Application system maintenance: Supporting the running of the IS especially when errors appear within the application software that must be fixed, special problems on data and files must be corrected, new requirements in the user function and external (regulatory) environment must be accommodated, etc.

System documentation: Preparation, completion, issuing and maintaining all the required documentation of the specific application system supported by the IT function according to corporate and IT policies and standards.

User training: Preparation of all the needed documentation, technical instructions, environment, etc.

and enabling the training process for all the functions of the implemented IS. Conducting the training (if in-house) and acting in a coaching capacity in case of online and remote (Internet) facility training.

Computer operations (CO)

The CO unit is responsible for running the Information Systems installed in the main computer or data centre of the given organisation on behalf of the users of these systems, the management of the specific corporate entity, and, in the case of public organisations, of society at large.

The CO unit, within this frame of reference, has the following duties and responsibilities:

Production co-ordination and control: Co-ordination and control of all tasks, activities, resources and means required for running all computerised information systems in the computer centre (or data centre) of the organisation. This task is critical for systems running in the batch processing mode. In running online systems this may entail setting priorities for response-time windows, controlling the operation of any systems affected (really or potentially) by electronic crime, planning the execution of massive-report-generating mechanisms and of data collection systems for feeding the corporate data warehouses of the organisation, etc.

Operation of systems: Execution of computerised information systems in batch, online or other mode (e.g. dedicated data transfer operations, in off-line mode, stand-alone operations when the data centre is in a recovery mode, etc.). Execution of the massive-report-generating mechanisms, report distribution (as required), executions of the data collection systems feeding the corporate data warehousing facilities, running the back-up, recovery and archival procedures, etc. In batch processing mode this includes the data inputting and data control phases before the execution of the update and reporting phases.

Operation of equipment: Operation of the computer, network and related equipment in the computer (or network) room of the data centre of the organisation. The equipment located in the user areas is normally operated by the users themselves, even though they are supported by the technical support unit of the IT function.

Security and protection: Administration of the policies, procedures and controls regarding the protection and physical access to the data centre's facilities, such as computer and network rooms, cabling installations, stock inventory areas, rooms where specialised forms are kept (e.g. bank cheques), on-site storage areas (e.g. back-up media archival), etc.

Inventory control: Management and control of all the consumables, paper, magnetic media, etc. necessary for the good operation of the computerised information systems in the data centre, etc.

Equipment maintenance management: Administration, control, monitoring and follow up of all aspects related to the maintenance, normally undertaken by outside contractors, of the computer and network equipment of the organisation, regardless of where this equipment is located (computer room, user area, etc.).

Technical support (TS)

The TS unit is responsible for supporting all the other IT departments in their daily duties and tasks, the Information Systems installed and running in the main data centre of the organisation and the user areas, and ensuring that all operating systems, network and database management software operates in the best possible order.

The TS unit, within this frame of reference, has the following duties and responsibilities:

Installation support: Technical support of all the technical, physical and installation infrastructure (computer rooms, network rooms, cabling installations, etc.) of the areas under the management and control of the IT function.

User equipment support: Technical support and interfacing with external maintenance contractors of all the IT and related equipment (e.g. modems, routers, etc.) located in the user areas and offices and used to access corporate or other information systems. This also includes office automation systems running in the personal computers, printers and special devices attached to personal computers, personal devices, mobile devices, etc.

Systems programming: Generation, installation, testing and transfer into production mode of the operating system software, database management system software, networking software, compilers and computer languages, standard ERP-type or other packaged systems, etc. and in general terms all software running in the main data centre of the organisation. Maintenance and technical support of this environment and interface control with any external vendors on maintenance, changes, improvements, new versions and releases, and error resolution issues.

Information systems support: Technical support of the information system running for production purposes in the main data centre and the systems under development.

Development of operational procedures: Design, development and testing of all the computer operations procedures necessary to run the main data centre and the technical environment in which Information Systems and networks operate.

Database management: Design, development and preparation of all the technical aspects, files, procedures, data dictionary, etc. necessary to run information systems based on standard database management systems software (supplied by an outside vendor). Monitoring and reviewing any database performance and integrity issues and recommending changes and improvements in the logical design of the specific database system.

Training: Undertaking the training for all IT staff on the issues related to the operating system, database management, and other software running in the main data centre.

Security administration: Administration, control, monitoring and follow up of all the security aspects (access by main users, administrators, external users, outside maintenance contractors, etc.) of the central computer systems, networking systems, etc. This also includes monitoring of and reporting on the computer security incidents (real and potential).

IT quality assurance standards

The IT quality assurance standards unit has the following duties and responsibilities:

Standards development: Research, design, test and develop standards (quality, design, operation, security, privacy, etc.) on IT systems and related aspects (IT governance) and customise to the particular corporate environment in which the IT function operates and supports all the information requirements and needs of the organisation.

Quality assurance: Review the system testing procedures, products, services, and the results of testing of Information Systems, and recommend changes, improvements and new techniques to the staff of all the other IT units.

Standards compliance: Audit and review compliance of the approved IT standards within the IT organisation, for all staff, information systems, products and services offered by the IT function to the specific organisation.

Standards maintenance: Maintenance, review of the standards library and issuing of standards, policies and guidelines to all units of the IT function.

1.3.4 IT department job description controls

The IT units of the IT function need personnel to perform the duties described previously. These personnel must be hired and organised. Organisation of human resources is a large part of personnel administration of the typical organisation. The 'job description', whether written (usually preferred) or informal is the instrument used to assign duties and responsibilities to IT personnel. For the management and support of the IT development, security and operational activities of the organisation the following roles, duties and responsibilities are usually assigned and executed: Chief Information Officer (CIO), business systems analyst, application systems analyst, computer programmer, computer operator, systems programmer, web applications developer, network support analyst, IT security project manager, security test designer, security tester, security system test administrator and security system accounts administrator (*see Chapter 2*).

1.3.5 Other IT roles at the senior management level

In order to protect the corporate assets from potential harm and abuse of any kind, and to manage the risks and opportunities resulting from IT activities, initiatives and operations, senior management of organisations need to play an important role in setting objectives, reviewing performance, monitoring risks, resolving problems, supervising activities and approving critical issues related to IT.

Specific roles, duties and responsibilities may be assigned and executed by the following: Board of Directors, audit committee, benefits and personnel committee, business continuity issues committee, finance committee and corporate compliance officer. In some large organisations (e.g. banks) the Chief Risk Officer (CRO) also has a role in IT controls.

Board of Directors

In terms of IT, the Board's general responsibilities, may be to:

- Ensure that an effective Board of Directors is in place and that the Board possesses within its membership the appropriate skills, know-how and dexterities (governance, internal control, risk, IT, etc.) to enable it to fulfil its duties and responsibilities.

- Ensure that IT controls as part of an effective internal controls system is established, reviewed and improved.
- Elect the IT Executive Officer (CIO) on the recommendation of the Chief Executive Officer.
- Review the IT audit reports as requested, and monitor and evaluate the IT strategic plan and the IT capital and operating budgets on a monthly basis.
- Approve critical decisions not delegated to management, such as major IT acquisitions, IT capital investments, IT systems, etc.
- Monitor and evaluate the IT activities monthly, quarterly, annually, etc. to determine whether IT is functioning effectively, and according to plans and objectives.

Audit committee

The primary purpose of the audit committee is to assist and support the Board of Directors in fulfilling its duty and responsibility to oversee management's conduct of the company's corporate performance, financial management and reporting process.

This includes monitoring, supervision and review of:

- Financial reports, including financial information provided by the company to any governmental or regulatory body, the public or other persons and stakeholders who may use this financial information.
- The company's systems of internal corporate, asset, information technology, security, administrative, accounting and financial controls.

- The annual independent audit (usually external) of the company's financial statements.

In terms of IT:

- Confirm the scope of IT audits to be performed by the independent IT auditors, monitor progress and review results and review fees and expenses.
- Review significant findings or unsatisfactory internal IT audit reports, or audit problems or difficulties encountered by the independent auditor.
- Monitor management's response to such findings.

Benefits and personnel committee

The primary purpose of the benefits and personnel committee is to review, report and approve the compensation and other benefits of the employees of the organisation, including IT staff.

In terms of IT, the main responsibilities of this committee are:

- Approve and oversee administration of the company's executive compensation programme for the CIO and other IT managers of the organisation.
- Review, as appropriate, any changes to compensation matters for the officers listed above with the Board.
- Oversee the establishment and administration of the company's benefit programmes and severance policies, including review and approval of IT-related benefit plans, employment agreements, etc.

Business continuity issues committee

The primary purpose of the business continuity issues committee is to provide guidelines, review and approve the critical business continuity issues including critical IT applications and their budgets, plans, etc.

In terms of IT, the main responsibilities of this committee are:

- Review all the critical business functions, identify the critical ones, and submit recommendations to the Board, so that they will be included in the business continuity planning process and the IT disaster plan of the organisation.

Finance committee

The primary purpose of the finance committee is to provide guidelines, review and approve the critical strategic financial issues (IT systems, plans, budgets, etc.) of the company. The duties and areas of responsibility of the financial issues committee, in terms of IT, are:

- Oversee the IT budget and accounting guidelines in order to maintain the standards for the audited financial statements and reports.
- Provide financial expertise to all levels of IT management of the organisation.
- Ensure that the financial accountability of the IT management of the organisation is improved.

Corporate compliance officer

A corporate compliance officer generally deals with any day-to-day compliance issues that arise during financial transactions, trading, or the handling of client accounts.

In terms of IT, the main responsibilities of this officer are:

- Develop, initiate, maintain and revise policies and procedures for the general operation of the compliance programme and its related activities to prevent illegal, unethical or improper conduct.
- Manage the day-to-day operation of the programme.
- Develop and periodically review and update Standards of conduct to ensure continuing currency and relevance in providing guidance to management and employees.
- Collaborate with other departments (e.g. risk management, internal audit, employee services, etc.) to direct compliance issues to appropriate existing channels for investigation and resolution.
- Monitor and, as necessary, co-ordinate compliance activities of the IT department to keep abreast of the status of all compliance activities and to identify trends.
- Identify potential areas of IT compliance vulnerability and risk, develop and implement corrective action plans for resolution of problematic issues, and provide general guidance on how to avoid or deal with similar situations in the future.

1.4 IT organisation controls

Further to the general and detailed responsibilities specified for IT departments and the roles at senior management levels, an organisational structure is needed so that the IT function can operate effectively.

Organisations abound in today's socio-economic context. Groups of people, such as entrepreneurs, investors, researchers, other stakeholders, private individuals, etc. constantly join forces to accomplish general common goals and specific time-bound objectives. Sometimes the goals and objectives of these corporations are for profit. Other times, the goals are more altruistic and humane, such as non-profit churches, professional associations, chambers of commerce, industry associations, state universities, or public hospitals and schools. Regardless of what their general and specific objectives are, all these organisations share four things: people, structures, policies and procedures. These may be thought of as the four elements, or pillars, upon which an organisation is based: people (committees, staff, etc.) are doing the work, certain individuals are appointed to be in charge of these people (the managers), and people (Board, managers, etc.) establish organisational structures and institute policies and execute procedures to carry out their plans and reach their targets. This is usually the case at both the overall organisational level and at the functional or departmental level, within the frame of reference of an organisation.

Typical examples of these IT organisation controls are:

- IT committee
- Organisational structure of the IT department
- IT business policy.

1.4.1 IT committee

In the IT function, the primary expression of the first element or pillar of an organisation (people) is the IT committee. Its primary purpose is to provide guidelines, review and approve the IT critical strategic issues (systems, plans, etc.) of the company.

IT committee charter – example

Main Responsibilities

Oversee the Enterprise Architecture, IT strategic planning and execution process.

Approve and oversee the execution of the IT budget.

Approve the feasibility of new IT investments.

Approve the IT personnel hiring and training plan.

Determine and set operating and development priorities on existing and future IT projects.

Oversee the progress of IT projects and take appropriate actions.

Monitor IT security and the good resolution of IT security related incidents.

Oversee the maintenance and future development of all IT systems of the organisation.

Plan the development of the skills of its members.

Supply competent expertise to all levels of management of the organisation in the areas of IT technology.

Supply the membership with timely information regarding IT technology.

Membership and Organisation

Depending on the organisation size, structure and culture, the IT Committee may consist of the IT manager, and one member from each major department of the organisation, regardless of whether IT application systems or personal computers operate or are being developed and deployed.

1.4.2 Organisational structure of the IT department

Organisational structure is the second element or pillar of an organisation. The primary purpose of this is to facilitate the allocation of responsibilities for individuals working in the various units making up the IT function (systems development, computer operations, technical support, etc.) regardless of the type of the structure (hierarchical, network, etc.) of IT.

The organisational structure of the IT department and its position in the hierarchical tree within the specific company varies depending on conditions and factors, such as:

- The type of data processing operational model (batch, online, mixed, etc.)
- The type of organisational structure required (centralised, decentralised, etc.)
- The type and number of critical and regular Information Systems developed and operated in the corporate data centre
- The volume of data processed
- The user requirements in terms of time, integrity, security, etc. of the information requested by the IT Department
- The operating model of the organisation (cost centre, profit centre, etc.) within which the IT department operates.

The most prevalent types (excluding outsourcing of IT services and facilities management) of organisational structures for the IT department, considering all of the above, are as follows:

Type 1: Centralised IT organisation and batch processing

In this organisation type and data processing mode, end-users collect all the business data recorded in specially designed forms by following very strict and disciplined business procedures, and subsequently send these data in batches to the centrally located IT department.

The IT department enters, verifies, corrects and processes these data by using the equipment and systems located within its premises, by running the specific Information Systems corresponding to the business function being served and by updating the computerised files maintained by these Information Systems.

All the results of the data entered and processed, files updated, reports, etc. are sent back to the originating end-users by IT, usually within the next business day.

Type 2: Centralised IT organisation and online processing

In this organisation type and data processing mode, end-users collect all the business data recorded in specially designed forms for each business transaction by following very strict and disciplined business procedures, and subsequently enter these data immediately (online mode) by using the facilities (screens, etc.) and equipment located within their premises, and connected to computerised Information Systems and services of the centrally located IT department.

The end-users are fully responsible for entering, verifying and correcting these data by using the equipment and systems located within its premises, by running the specific Information Systems corresponding to the business function being served, and by updating in an immediate mode the computerised files maintained by these Information Systems.

The IT department is fully responsible for ensuring that the processing of these data and the updating of the files is carried out on the basis of the best quality and integrity aspects.

All the results of the data entered and processed, files updated, reports, etc. are immediately available, both to the originating end-users and to all valid and approved stakeholders.

Type 3: Decentralised IT organisation and online processing

In this organisation type and data processing mode, the end-users interact the same way as the Type 2 model. The only difference is that IT personnel are split into smaller units so that they reside within the end-user premises in order to serve them better.

Type 4: Mixed IT organisation and online processing

In this organisation type and data processing mode, the end-users interact the same way as the Type 2 model. The only difference is that IT personnel are both based centrally as well as within the end-user departments.

Conclusion

Each organisation will set up its own IT organisational structure considering one or more of the above elements, customising and establishing an IT structure that serves its own particular purposes.

1.4.3 IT business policy

Business policies and procedures make up the third and fourth elements or pillars of an organisation. In terms of the IT function, the primary expression of this organisational element is the IT business policy.

IT business policy – example

'The Company' is committed to safeguarding its IT assets and their strategic and operational use. The Company's IT strategy will provide the guidelines for the future of IT activities. IT operations will refer to the production of IT systems and services to provide value to the organisation by its IT processing operations. To this end it seeks to ensure the integrity of corporate data and information systems, the availability of service and the confidentiality of computerised data and information.

When introducing new corporate computer systems or major changes to existing corporate IT systems 'The Company' ensures these are developed and implemented in a controlled manner within the framework of the company's Enterprise Architecture and that appropriate controls are built into the application software.

While 'The Company' uses the Internet and electronic mail to conduct its business, it prohibits its improper use for downloading or transmitting (without appropriate authorisation), for example, offensive material or confidential information. In support of this a fuller set of IT policies and procedures are established and communicated in order to provide awareness and direction throughout the corporate environment of 'The Company'.

Its primary purpose is to state the commitment of the organisation for the most effective management of the IT assets and activities, and therefore provide the best service and quality of processed information to all levels of management and stakeholders.

1.5 IT vision, mission and values statements

Organisations, their functional units or departments, and their people, do not exist in a vacuum. They usually work within a specific frame of reference (optimal use of several resources for a general and specific purpose, creation of value, benefits, etc.) and socio-economic context. To this purpose they may need various guidelines and roadmaps to motivate them to better actions.

Motivation may be achieved by an envisioning process. The envisioning approach usually ensures that the achieved result matches the expected result. In a corporate environment, the main expressions of the envisioning process are vision, mission and values declarations.

More specifically, the purpose of the vision, mission and values statements, in an overall corporate framework, is to guide the organisation for the future (where it wants to go), to define more specific ways to accomplish that and to set ethical standards for all parties (Board, executives, management, staff, etc.) in order to carry out their daily activities and interactions. Defining the corporate vision, mission and values statements is usually done once. These, however, may be updated, depending on various circumstances and conditions, during the strategic planning process of the specific organisation.

Some of the benefits that can result from establishing corporate vision, mission and values statements are: greatly improved organisational image and focus on what is critical and important; enhancing the professional perception of the organisation; fostering a team-oriented ethical culture; and improving communication among all stakeholders.

The concepts of vision, mission and values can be, and sometimes are, propagated down to all critical functions of an organisation, such as IT, sales, marketing, production, etc.

IT vision, mission and values statement – example

The vision of the Department of Information Systems is to provide customers (external, internal), stakeholders, management and staff of the organisation with technological resources and information which support the strategic and operational objectives of the organisation. The mission of the department is to manage the efficient flow of data and electronic information throughout the organisation as well as to and from external parties (customers, banks, vendors, suppliers, etc.) and government authorities and regulatory agencies. This involves training, support and maintenance of existing information systems, critical application systems disaster recovery, and implementation of new information technologies and systems. These services will be provided with the highest values of quality, security, integrity of data, and with the most efficient and effective application of corporate and national codes of moral and professional conduct, rules and regulations. These rules of conduct may be based on The ACM Professional Code, The ISACA Code, The BCS Code or The (USA) Computer Ethics Institute Code, etc.

1.6 IT governance and control frameworks

Further to the above controls, organisations may also need, in actual practice, governance and internal control frameworks to operate in an optimal way.

Internal control, according to COSO (*www.coso.org*), is broadly defined as a process, effected by an entity's Board of Directors, management and other personnel, designed to provide reasonable assurance regarding the achievement of objectives in the following categories: effectiveness and efficiency of operations; reliability of financial reporting; and compliance with applicable laws and regulations.

The control environment sets the tone of an organisation, influencing the control consciousness of its people. It is the foundation for all other components of internal control, providing discipline and structure. Control environment factors include the integrity, ethical values and competence of the entity's people; management's philosophy and operating style; the way management assigns authority and responsibility, and organises and develops its people; and the attention and direction provided by the Board of Directors.

Internal control, in the area of IT and within the frame of reference of an organisation, is usually expressed by an IT governance and control framework.

In terms of the IT function, it is the job of IT management to design, develop, implement, operate and support an enhanced IT governance framework for its own purposes. This framework may consist of the continuous management of:

- aligning the IT strategy to corporate strategy within the framework of the Enterprise Architecture of the organisation
- managing human and other resources
- quality management
- performance management
- IT standards, policies, procedures, practices and methods for the safe, efficient, effective and cost-beneficial running of all ITC systems and infrastructural components for the good of the given organisation and greater society.

The IT governance and control framework may be published and communicated through the organisation and may also be established within the Enterprise Architecture framework of the organisation, and could be based on professional control standards, such as COBIT, ITIL, ISO/IEC 38500,[4] The Calder-Moir IT Governance Framework,[5] etc. It may also include the organisational knowledge management framework.

1.6.1 COBIT Control Framework

COBIT (Control Objectives for Information and Related Technologies) is a framework that is managed by the Information Systems Audit and Controls Association (ISACA: *www.isaca.org*[6]). It consists of 34 high-level processes that cover 210 control objectives categorised in four domains: Planning and Organisation, Acquisition and

---

[4] *www.iso.org, www.38500.org.*

[5] *www.itgovernance.co.uk/calder_moir.aspx.*

[6] This publication incorporates references to COBIT 4.1 © 1996–2007 ITGI. All rights reserved.

Implementation, Delivery and Support, and Monitoring and Evaluation. COBIT provides benefits to managers, IT users and auditors.

'Plan and Organise' Domain (PO Activities)

The activities of this domain are: Define a Strategic IT Plan and direction, Define the Information Architecture, Determine Technological Direction, Define the IT Processes, Organisation and Relationships, Manage the IT Investment, Communicate Management Aims and Direction, Manage IT Human Resources, Manage Quality, Assess and Manage IT Risks, and Manage Projects.

'Acquire and Implement' Domain (AI Activities)

The activities of this domain are: Identify Automated Solutions, Acquire and Maintain Application Software, Acquire and Maintain Technology Infrastructure, Enable Operation and Use, Procure IT Resources, Manage Changes, and Install and Accredit Solutions and Changes.

'Deliver and Support' Domain (DS Activities)

The activities of this domain are: Define and Manage Service Levels, Manage Third-party Services, Manage Performance and Capacity, Ensure Continuous Service, Ensure Systems Security, Identify and Allocate Costs, Educate and Train Users, Manage Service Desk and Incidents, Manage the Configuration, Manage Problems, Manage Data, Manage the Physical Environment, and Manage Operations.

'Monitor and Evaluate' Domain (ME Activities)

The activities of this domain are: Monitor and Evaluate IT Processes, Monitor and Evaluate Internal Control, Ensure Regulatory Compliance, and Provide IT Governance.

1.6.2 ITIL Framework

The Information Technology Infrastructure Library (ITIL) is a set of concepts and policies for managing IT infrastructure, development and operations. ITIL (*www.itil-officialsite.com*, *www.ogc.gov.uk*[7]) is published in a series of books, each of which covers an IT management topic.

ITIL gives a detailed description of a number of important IT practices with comprehensive checklists, tasks and procedures that can be tailored to any IT organisation.

The current version includes five core texts: Service Strategy, Service Design, Service Transition, Service Operation, and Continual Service Improvement.

Service Strategy: Service strategy is shown at the core of the ITIL v3.1 lifecycle but cannot exist in isolation to the other parts of the IT structure. It encompasses a framework to build best practice in developing a long-term service strategy.

Service Design: The design of IT services conforming to best practice, and including design of architecture, processes, policies, documentation, and allowing for future business requirements.

---

[7] ITIL® is a Registered Trade Mark of the Office of Government Commerce in the United Kingdom and other countries. IT Infrastructure Library® is a Registered Trade Mark of the Office of Government Commerce in the United Kingdom and other countries.

Service Transition: Service transition relates to the delivery of services required by the business into live/operational use, and often encompasses the 'project' side of IT rather than 'BAU' (Business As Usual). This area also covers topics, such as managing changes to the 'BAU' environment.

Service Operation: Best practice for achieving the delivery of agreed levels of services both to end-users and the customers (where 'customers' refer to those individuals who pay for the service and negotiate the SLAs). Service Operations is the part of the lifecycle where the services and value is actually directly delivered. The monitoring of problems and balance between service reliability and cost are considered.

Continual Service Improvement (CSI): Aligning and realigning IT services to changing business needs (because standstill implies decline) by identifying and implementing improvements to the IT services that support the business processes. The perspective of CSI on improvement is the business perspective of service quality, even though CSI aims to improve process effectiveness, efficiency and cost effectiveness of the IT processes through the whole lifecycle. In order to manage improvement, CSI should clearly define what should be controlled and measured.

There must be upfront planning, training and awareness, ongoing scheduling, roles creation, ownership assignment, and activities identified in order to be successful. CSI must be planned and scheduled as a process with defined activities, inputs, outputs, roles and reporting.

1.6.3 ISO/IEC 38500:2008: Corporate governance of information technology

ISO/IEC 38500:2008 provides guiding principles for directors of organisations on the effective, efficient, beneficial and acceptable use of IT within their organisations.

ISO/IEC 38500:2008 applies to the governance of management processes (and decisions) relating to the information and communication services used by an organisation, and is applicable to organisations of all sizes, including public and private companies, government entities and not-for-profit organisations.

The framework comprises definitions, principles and a model. It sets out six principles for good corporate governance of IT that express preferred behaviour to guide decision making:

- Ensure that IT responsibilities are clearly established.
- Corporate and IT strategy should be clearly aligned.
- Acquire IT acquisitions and investments in a proper and valid way.
- Ensure performance of IT is delivered when required.
- Ensure compliance with rules for all IT activities.
- Ensure respect and consideration for human factors in IT policies and practices.

1.6.4 The Calder-Moir IT Governance Framework

The purpose of the Calder-Moir IT Governance Framework[8] is the implementation of ISO/IEC 38500 standard, the first international standard providing guidelines for IT governance. The Calder-Moir IT Governance Framework provides a way of organising IT governance issues and tools to support the Board, executives, managers, stakeholders and practitioners. The framework is divided into six segments:

- Business Strategy (business model, business environment, business strategies, strategic plans, business plans, BSC, etc.)
- Risk, Conformance & Compliance (governance, conformance compliance, enterprise risk management, controls, audit, frameworks: COSO, COBIT, SOX, ISO38500, BSC, etc.)
- IT Strategy (information strategy, business and IT architectures (TOGAF, Zachman Framework, BSC), IT principles, etc.)
- Change (readiness, projects, programmes, methods (PRINCE2, PMBOK, MSP, CMMI, etc.), alignment, benefits)
- Information & Technology Balance Sheet (human, structural and market capital, organisation, data, applications, business and IT processes, technologies, Zachman Framework, BSC, ISO38500, etc.)
- Operations (business operations, IT operations, IT asset management, security, COBIT, ITIL, Data Protection rules, etc.).

---

[8] Permission provided by IT Governance Institute, UK.

Each segment is further divided into three layers:

- The innermost representing the Board
- The middle representing executive management
- The outermost representing IT and IT governance practitioners.

Starting at the Business Strategy, each segment is executed in clockwise order in an end-to-end process. In the first three segments the Board establishes directions and business strategies. These need to be compliant to corporate governance regimes (e.g. Basel II) and risk assessed. In the last three steps, architectures and plans are developed to meet business strategies through IT. After these plans are approved by the Board, they will be implemented through a series of change projects.

The three main tasks for directors in IT governance, according to ISO/IEC 38500, which are evaluate, direct and monitor, are present in this framework. The Board evaluates business conditions and strategies, directs by IT principles and monitors all processes in the framework. Executive managers also evaluate, direct and monitor processes carried out by practitioners.

Furthermore, the Calder-Moir Framework implements a PDCA (Plan, Do, Check, Act) Cycle at two levels. At a high level, spanning across the entire hexagon (*see Figure 1*), and at a more detailed lower level in each of the six segments (*see Figure 2*).

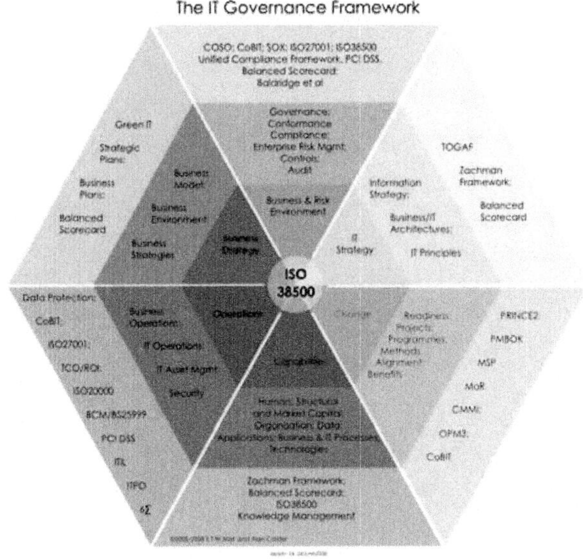

Figure 1: Calder-Moir Framework – high level

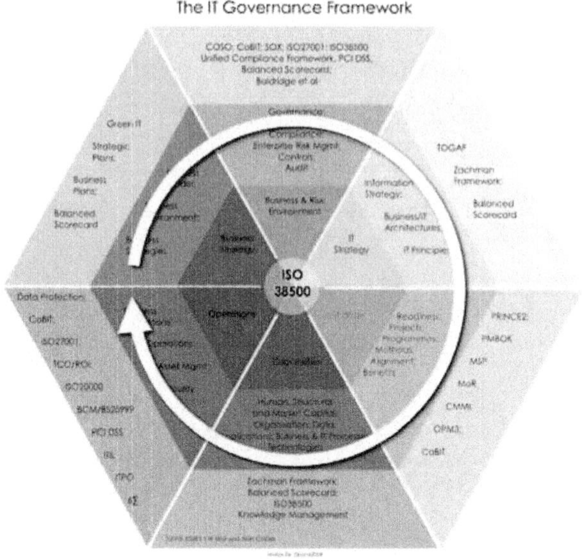

Figure 2: Calder-Moir Framework – lower level

Conclusion

The standard frameworks, described above, provide the general guidelines for IT management for setting up their own IT governance framework.

It is usually the job and responsibility of IT management to design, develop, implement, operate and support an enhanced IT governance framework for serving the information needs and business requirements of the organisation.

1.7 Monitoring and review controls

Controls specified previously must be monitored to ensure that they operate as planned, and must be reviewed to improve them.

Monitoring, according to COSO (www.coso.org) applies to all components of internal controls: risk assessment, control environment, control activities, and information and communication. Controls that are not monitored and reviewed are not improved, and deteriorate, as a result, over time. When monitoring is designed and implemented properly, organisations benefit as they are more likely to: identify and improve control problems on a timely basis; prepare accurate and timely performance management reports; collect, process and produce more accurate and reliable information for decision making on strategic and operational issues; and assure all stakeholders of the organisation of the efficiency and effectiveness of internal controls.

Establishing IT monitoring and review controls may be accomplished by a monitoring and review activities management plan.

Monitoring and review activities management plan

The first action after you set up the basic organisational elements of an IT function is to ensure that all IT controls are monitored and reviewed by a disciplined method:

Step 1: Set up the IT performance team (staff, leader, terms of reference, budget).

Step 2: Assess IT performance reporting needs and design which IT performance data and compliance measures will be monitored and collected.

Step 3: Create the IT performance reporting system. This could be based on a mixed system with two components: an IT BSC (Information Technology Balanced Scorecard) Measurement System (*described in Chapter 4*), and a Compliance Monitoring System for monitoring compliance to policies, procedures and related matters (e.g. budget issues).

Step 4: Design IT management report and obtain senior management approval.

Step 5: Train all staff in the IT performance reporting process.

Step 6: Collect the IT performance and compliance data.

Step 7: Review IT performance and compliance data with relevant officers, as needed at the particular reporting time (e.g. critical users, compliance officer, risk committee, internal audit, etc.).

Step 8: Prepare IT management report (IT performance and compliance data and analysis, etc.).

Step 9: Issue IT management report to all approved levels of management.

Step 10: Monitor and improve the system.

Implementing this plan will require the functioning of three contributing elements: (a) the IT management reporting procedure with the IT management report, (b) the performance measures in each IT area, and (c) the audit review tools and techniques.

IT management reporting

Developing an effective IT strategic plan to carry out IT operations is only part of the story of the IT strategic planning process. Getting the designed IT strategy implemented is generally the more difficult part. And an important part of IT strategy implementation is reviewing and monitoring it, and ensuring that it has the intended results for the organisation and its stakeholders.

Reviewing and monitoring the implementation of the IT strategic plan and the IT operations of the organisation is important for a number of reasons. First, it helps to assure that all efforts conform to the plan. Second, it ensures that results achieved align with the specific business objectives, and that corrective actions are taken when necessary. Finally, and most importantly, monitoring provides the essential link between the written plan and the day-to-day operation of the business the organisation is carrying out.

In addition to the corporate procedures on management reporting, the IT department may report to upper levels of management the IT-related performance issues. These reports usually contain:

- Changes, problems, errors, security incidents and backlog of requests
- Help desk related issues
- Online access issues
- Technical performance issues
- Back-up and recovery issues
- Transactions and jobs processed
- Development issues of new applications
- IT project milestones
- Project actual costs (against budgets)

- Post-implementation review issues
- Critical performance measures per IT area
- Compliance issues
- Industry trends and developments.

It is the job of the CIO to establish this reporting mechanism, and ensure that it works properly.

1.8 IT organisation performance measures

The main objective of any performance measurement and reporting system is to provide feedback relating to the specific objectives of an organisation. Performance measurement gains real value when it is used as the basis for timely decisions by management. In terms of the particular function, the purpose of performance measures is to provide the basis for performance management, review and improvement of the area being examined. The ultimate aim of implementing a performance measurement system is to improve the performance of the given organisation. If management can get the performance measurement of the organisation right, the performance data generated will tell management and stakeholders where the organisation is and where it is heading.

These performance measures could be based on a mixed system with two components: Component 1 would be an IT BSC (Information Technology Balanced Scorecard) Measurement System, described in Chapter 4 (IT strategic controls), and Component 2 would be a Compliance Monitoring System for monitoring compliance to policies, procedures and related matters (for more information on compliance see: Society of Corporate Compliance and Ethics, USA: *www.corporatecompliance.org*).

In the area of IT organisation, the typical performance measures are shown in Table 1.

Function	**Measures**
IT Finance	Adherence to budget, expenditures on maintenance vs. new development, expenditures on preventative maintenance, return on IT Investments, ratio of administrative (staff) costs to production (line) costs
IT Human Resource Management	Turnover ratios, training per employee (amounts, hours), average tenure within the company
IT System Development	Functions developed worth to users, number of lines coded/tested/changed, number of applications supporting critical business functions, hours spent on maintenance (person, program)
IT Operations	Timely delivery of reports to users, average response time, average availability time, volume of data stored, mean time between failures, number of lines printed, volume of data maintained, number of shared applications, number of shared databases, number of online transactions processed
IT Compliance	IT departmental terms of reference not followed, IT vision, mission and values statements not crafted, IT governance framework not instituted

Table 1: IT organisation performance measures

The IT management of the company may analyse all this performance and compliance monitoring information to review, assess and improve the IT organisational elements of the IT function.

1.9 Review and audit tools and techniques

Setting up and improving IT organisation controls is not an easy task. This task requires envisioning skills, business and IT knowledge, corporate and IT resources, a change management culture and a set of review and audit tools. The review and audit tools that may support IT managers and other professionals (IT auditors, IT consultants, internal auditors, external auditors, compliance officers, etc.) in establishing, evaluating and improving the IT organisation controls described in this chapter, and which are offered for potential use, are: IT terms of reference checklist, IT organisational assessment audit programme, IT functional assessment audit programme, IT vision, mission and values checklist, IT technology coverage checklist and IT business improvement checklist.

These may also determine the quality and effectiveness of the IT organisation controls and ensure that these specific controls are properly and effectively established to serve the control needs of the specific IT corporate entity.

These audit programmes and checklists are not intended to be a complete IT management or audit guide. IT managers and other professionals may choose to use only certain components based upon the size, complexity, business and IT maturity needs and expectations, and nature of the organisation's business and levels of deployment and utilisation of IT systems.

Other relevant guidelines and audit tools that might be found valuable and which support the IT management, evaluation and auditing processes are described in Appendix 3 (Monitoring IT controls checklist), Appendix 4 (Examples of IT forms), Appendix 5 (IT audit methodology), Appendix 6 (IT audit areas) and Appendix 7 (Internal audit report example).

1.9.1 IT terms of reference checklist

The objective of this checklist is to support the process of establishing, reviewing, evaluating and improving the controls identified in Paragraph 1.3 'IT department functional description controls' and Paragraph 1.4.2 'Organisational structure of the IT department'.

1 Is the CIO/IT manager reporting to the official/organisational responsibility centre of the IT unit?
2 Are the terms of reference detailed enough and tailored to the specific activities of each IT function/department and responsibility centre?
3 Are the Board members and/or executive management of the company/organisation familiar with these terms of reference and have they been ratified at the appropriate executive/Board level?
4 Are the IT department managers familiar with these terms of reference?
5 Are the IT department personnel familiar with these terms of reference?
6 Are the IT user managers familiar with these terms of reference?
7 Are the IT users familiar with these terms of reference?

8 Are these terms of reference aiding the IT managers and staff in discharging their duties?

9 Are these terms of reference known to the external stakeholders of IT (maintenance vendors, society interest groups, community groups, regulatory agencies, etc.)?

10 Is the IT function structured effectively to serve the organisation and its divisions/functions:
- o as a separate division, or as a part of another division?
- o interfacing with an outsource entity?
- o shared service among several departments?
- o a combination of the above?
- o a separate company, with its own Board of Directors?
- o at the right organisational and responsibility level?

1.9.2 IT organisational assessment audit programme

The objective of this audit programme is to support the process of reviewing, evaluating and improving the controls identified in Paragraph 1.3 'IT department functional description controls' and Paragraph 1.4 'IT organisation controls'.

1 Assess organisational responsibility of the IT unit

2 Obtain IT terms of reference and description of department and organisational chart

3 Assess IT organisational chart and IT department description with IT management

4 Review how the IT unit is structured to serve the company and its divisions/functions:
- o as a separate division
- o as a part of another division
- o interfacing with an outsource entity
- o shared service among several departments

   - a combination of the above
5. Obtain re-structuring plan of IT department
6. Review re-structuring plan of IT department with IT Management and with the Chief Information Officer (CIO).

1.9.3 IT functional assessment audit programme

The objective of this audit programme is to support the process of reviewing, evaluating and improving the overall performance of the IT function and the controls identified in Paragraphs 1.4 'IT organisation controls', 1.6 'IT governance and control frameworks' and 1.7 'Monitoring and review controls'.

1. Define, review and agree on what constitutes performance for the IT function, which may include the following:
   - IT personnel are talented and have modern skills
   - Customers expect and require IT departments to provide 'dial tone' levels of service
   - Competitive superiority must be an objective
   - Quality and productivity as parallel objectives within an IT function.
2. Assess whether various key performance indicators for IT may be monitored, such as:
   - Development activity
   - Operational performance
   - Financial performance
   - Human resource management.
3. Assess whether the primary IT service responsibilities are discharged:

- o Timely delivery of complete, accurate and relevant information (through both online and batch)?
- o Adequate separation of duties exists?
- o Custodian responsibilities properly carried out?
- o Change control procedures (test, production) exist?
- o Physical security measures carried out well?
- o Controls over work are adequate?
- o Management has enough information to manage data centre effectively?

4 Assess the system development methodology. Consider:
- o Timely development of computer systems
- o Is the methodology formally approved?
- o Is the methodology adhered to in all cases?
- o Are systems developed as per IT strategic plan?
- o Is the methodology accurate for the data and database needs of the enterprise?

5 Assess the systems testing methodology. Consider: does it contain performance, user testing and acceptance, meeting design specifications?

6 Assess the maintenance policy and procedures of existing computer systems. Consider:
- o Is it done in a timely way?
- o Do change control procedures exist?
- o Is a prioritisation process used (test vs. production)?
- o Do conversion procedures exist?
- o Do source/object maintenance and control procedures exist?
- o Is authority taken for all changes?
- o Are program change forms used for all changes?
- o Do quality control procedures exist?

7 Assess forms management. Consider: Is effective custody of all forms containing data (business, system, administrative) executed at all times?
8 Assess security issues. Consider:
   - o Do physical and logical security procedures exist?
   - o Is a contingency planning procedure in place?
   - o Do adequate back-up and recovery procedures exist?
   - o Is system software adequately protected?

9 Review key IT performance indicators

1.9.4 IT vision, mission, and values checklist

The objective of this checklist is to support the process of creating, reviewing, evaluating and improving the controls identified in Paragraph 1.5 'IT vision, mission and values statements'.

1 Are there overall corporate vision, mission and value statements?
2 Are the IT vision, mission and value statements in alignment with the overall corporate vision, mission and value statements?
3 Are all IT staff aware of the IT vision, mission and value statements in carrying out their duties?
4 Are all IT staff aware of the corporate vision, mission and value statements in carrying out their duties?
5 Are all the stakeholders and their staff aware of the entity's corporate vision, mission and value statements in carrying out their duties?
6 Are all the stakeholders and their staff aware of the IT vision, mission and value statements in carrying out their duties to the entity's IT function?

7 Is the IT function aligned with the corporate vision, mission and value statements?
8 Is the IT function aligned with the IT vision, mission and value statements?
9 Are the corporate vision, mission and value statements kept up to date and tied to the overall strategy?
10 Are the IT vision, mission and value statements kept up to date and tied to the overall strategy?

1.9.5 IT technology coverage checklist

The objective of this checklist is to support the process of reviewing, evaluating and improving the controls identified in Paragraph 1.3.2 'IT department overall terms of reference', and ensuring that the IT function is organised to cover and support all known IT technology elements, within the context of the specific organisation.

1 Does technology coverage include items and issues, such as:
   - Mainframe, mini/microcomputer hardware platforms?
   - operating systems and database management technologies?
   - information systems?
   - data centre?
   - personal computers and office systems and applications?
   - electronic mail and related aspects?
   - electronic data interchange (EDI) and Internet?
   - networking (cabling, hubs, WAN, LAN, intranet)?
   - data transmission with external parties and protocols?
   - voice communications?

- o advanced systems, knowledge systems, competitive intelligence applications and decision support systems?
- o other special systems (e.g. security , building management, embedded systems etc.)?

2 Is the issue of technology coverage adequately dealt with (i.e. there are no missing items)?

3 Is technology coverage included in the IT vision, mission and value statements?

4 Does the CIO have the official responsibility for the technology issues?

5 Are all the IT staff kept up to date on all technological issues by training, seminars, web-based tuition, etc?

6 Is the technology coverage issue adequately managed in the IT restructuring plan and/or other business process re-engineering/improvement in progress?

7 Is there a short-term as well as a long-term technology plan in place for the organisation?

8 Is the technology plan reviewed annually, improved (according to the firm's needs and new business requirements and processes, and with the participation and commitment of all parties), and communicated to all stakeholders and relevant parties?

9 Is adequate documentation maintained properly on all technological changes?

1.9.6 IT business improvement checklist

The objective of this checklist is to support the CIO and the IT Committee in the process of reviewing, evaluating and improving the IT function in terms of restructuring, if the need arises, and with the main aim to provide better value to the organisation regarding its information needs.

1. Is the IT restructuring plan and/or other business process re-engineering/improvement in progress?
2. Is the restructuring/improvement process/effort managed, sponsored and guided by the CIO and aligned with the Enterprise Architecture framework of the organisation?
3. Are all the IT managers aware of the restructuring/improvement process and plan?
4. Are all the IT staff aware of the restructuring/improvement process and plan?
5. Are all the IT users aware of the restructuring/improvement process and plan?
6. Is there a change management plan in place for the process improvement effort?
7. Is a standard re-engineering/improvement methodology used?
8. Is the restructuring/improvement process/effort managed, sponsored by the Board and guided by the CIO?
9. Is the restructuring/improvement process/effort measured by appropriate metrics and performance system?
10. Is the IT function restructured effectively to serve better the company and its divisions/functions?

1.10 Conclusion

Knowledge, in the modern 21st Century, is a critical issue for the survival of organisations in all world markets. Knowledge usually includes experience, facts, rules, data, assertions and concepts about subject areas crucial to the organisation, such as customers, markets, processes, regulations, etc. As knowledge is critical, it must be managed efficiently and effectively by a knowledge management framework, and related controls, in order to create value for the organisation.

This framework may, conceptually, have four supporting pillars:

- Processes: Organisational structures, methods, tools, techniques and system procedures to create, apply, exploit, disseminate, capture, record, analyse, maintain, locate and enable learning.
- Culture: Establish and maintain a culture of knowledge management and use at all levels of the organisation by all levels of management, and also by enabling all staff to participate in the knowledge management process.
- People: the human resource management policies and procedures should contain appraisal and reward systems which enable and facilitate knowledge sharing and dissemination.
- Systems: Corporate and IT controls should be enacted, and IT systems and repositories should be developed and deployed within the organisation for the easy and quick access and distribution of knowledge to all authorised levels of the organisation.

This framework should cover of all processes of knowledge management: Knowledge creation, knowledge application within the organisation (e.g. decision making by management), exploitation outside the organisation (e.g. in selling intellectual work, patent, etc.), dissemination, capturing, recording (by information systems), maintaining (by information systems), locating personnel skills, analysing, and learning (applying knowledge and reflecting on what could be done better).

A knowledge management framework is usually enabled and supported by IT systems and related organisational, administrative and infrastructural components (databases, data warehouses, networking, knowledge acquisition and analysis tools, etc.).

The main IT organisation controls and the audit and review programmes and checklists, identified and presented in this chapter may be deemed as the initial supporting structure that has to be erected for the creation and deployment of a knowledge management framework for the better operation of organisations.

IT organisation controls may be achieved probably more efficiently and effectively, by implementing a suitable set of controls, such as the ones described in this chapter by reviewing, changing, adding, deleting, customising them, etc., to meet the needs, demands and operating mode of the given organisation, and operating them with continuous diligence. These controls, as we have seen, may include policies, practices, procedures, organisational structures and other tools. These controls will need to be established to ensure that the specific IT organisational objectives of the specific corporate entity can be met.

1.11 Review questions

This set of questions may be employed by those using the controls identified in this book to assess and double-check their own conceptual understanding and practical knowledge contained in this chapter.

1. What is the purpose of IT organisation controls?

Reference: Paragraph 1.2 'Purpose and main types of IT organisation controls'.

2. Which are the main types of IT organisation controls?

Reference: Paragraph 1.2 'Purpose and main types of IT organisation controls'.

3. Which are the main IT department functional description controls?

Reference: Paragraph 1.3 'IT department functional description controls'.

4. Which are the five departments of a typical IT function?

Reference: Paragraph 1.3.3 'Detailed IT department terms of reference'.

5. What are the main duties of the IT quality assurance standards department of a typical IT function?

Reference: Paragraph 1.3.3 'Detailed IT department terms of reference'.

6. Which is the primary purpose of the IT committee?

Reference: Paragraph 1.4.1 'IT committee'.

7. Who should develop and ratify the IT business policy?

Reference: Paragraph 1.4.3 'IT business policy'.

8. What is a typical definition of a values statement for an IT function?

Reference: Paragraph 1.5 'IT vision, mission and values statements'.

9. Which roles and responsibilities should be formally assigned for the management and support of IT security?

Reference: Paragraph 1.3.3 'Detailed IT department terms of reference'.

10. To which components of internal controls does 'monitoring' apply according to COSO?

Reference: Paragraph 1.7. 'Monitoring and review controls'.

11. Which are the three contributing elements that must be functioning in implementing the monitoring and review activities management plan?

Reference: Paragraph 1.7. 'Monitoring and review controls'.

12. What types of issues are included in and reported by an IT management report?

Reference: Paragraph 1.7. 'Monitoring and review controls'.

13. What types of skills, knowledge, resources, culture and methods are required in setting up and improving IT organisation controls?

Reference: Paragraph 1.9. 'Review and audit tools and techniques'.

14. Which are the two major IT control frameworks?

Reference: Paragraph 1.6 'IT governance and control frameworks'.

15. Which are the four domains of the COBIT framework?

Reference: Paragraph 1.6 'IT governance and control frameworks'.

16. What is the purpose of the ITIL framework?

Reference: Paragraph 1.6 'IT governance and control frameworks'.

17. What items and issues should IT cover?

Reference: Paragraph 1.3 'IT department functional description controls'.

18. Which are some of the various IT organisation performance measures?

Reference: Paragraph 1.8 'IT organisation performance measures'.

19 Which are some of the various structural models for an IT unit?

Reference: Paragraph 1.4.2 'Organisational structure of the IT department'.

20. What does knowledge usually include?

Reference: Paragraph 1.10 'Conclusion'.

CHAPTER 2: IT ADMINISTRATION CONTROLS

Cities, as we know, when they give public notice of intent to let contracts for the building of temples or colossal statues, listen to the proposals of artists competing for the commission and bringing in their estimates and models, and then choose the man who will do the same work with the least expense and better than the others and more quickly.

*Plutarch (*Plutarch: Moralia, *Helmbold WC, London, William Heinemann Ltd (1970))*

2.1 Scope

Once you have established an IT organisation and its controls, you design and implement the basic IT administration policies and procedures for IT to operate and accomplish its mission. IT administration controls are designed and deployed with the main purpose of facilitating and enabling the proper execution of all the other IT controls.

Establishing these controls to serve the needs of the given organisation may be done by the formal IT committee, or the IT management and its senior staff, or some other corporate work team or group, or a combination of these. It would be useful, however, and as it has been proved in practice, to have these controls ratified by the Board or senior management executive committee of the organisation.

In addition to these, a set of audit programmes and checklists are presented to support the IT manager, the IT practitioner and other professionals (systems development and support staff, IT auditors, internal auditors, IT consultants, external auditors, compliance officers, etc.) in executing and improving their duties and responsibilities.

2.2 Purpose and main types of IT administration controls

Administration controls, in the general corporate sense, are the non-financial, non-IT and non-production controls that usually encompass the following activities of the organisation: human resources, marketing, sales, customer support, forms and records management. These are usually concerned with operational efficiency and with adherence to organisational policies and compliance rules and guidelines.

The purpose of IT administration controls is to enable and facilitate (a) the activities that manage the input, processing and output functions of computerised application systems in recording, maintaining and processing the computerised transactions of the organisation, (b) the developing, management and maintenance of IT infrastructure and application systems, and (c) the protection and safeguarding of the IT infrastructure, equipment, facilities and data of the organisation. These controls may overlap the corporate administration, human resource, financial and production controls, as well as other IT controls.

The main types of IT administration controls are:

- IT standards, policies and procedures
- IT budget
- IT asset controls
- IT personnel management controls
- IT purchasing controls

- IT office administration controls
- Monitoring and review controls
- IT administration performance measures.

2.3 IT standards, policies and procedures

A standard is an established norm of behaviour or technical performance. It is usually a formal document that establishes uniform human, engineering or technical criteria, methods and techniques for developing products, systems and delivering services.

Policies establish what should be done, usually according to a standard. Procedures denote how the policies should be carried out. More specifically, administrative procedures are precise, predetermined, step-by-step methods for conducting routine tasks in an organisation in an efficient manner.

Procedures are what operational and administrative staff use to accomplish their day-to-day work. Procedures are normally documented in detailed procedures manuals. In terms of the IT function, IT standards, policies and procedures should be identified and established, whether in a written formal statement or on an informal basis, depending on the culture of the organisation and its management, and the maturity of its IT systems.

They are usually part of an IT standards, policies and procedures manual, and cover all aspects of IT (organisation, administration, systems development, asset management, security, disaster recovery, systems software support, etc.). As an example, the following may be the contents of this manual:

- the full system development cycle (analysis, development, design, implementation and evaluation)
- the linking process of IT systems with the Enterprise Architecture framework of the organisation
- the IT strategic process (*see also Chapter 4*)
- IT personnel issues including working conditions handbook requirements
- IT performance issues
- forms management
- the IT security process (*see also Chapter 6*)
- the back-up and recovery process (*see also Chapter 7*)
- the documentation process (*see also Chapter 5*)
- the disaster recovery aspects for critical computerised applications
- computer availability management
- data centre operations
- service level management
- customer service support
- vendor and external parties management
- computer insurance
- legal issues (licences, application source code ownership, data privacy compliance, website, etc.)
- capacity management
- software control and distribution
- change management
- help desk
- personal computers support
- configuration management
- IT budget and cost management.

All these standards, policies and procedures may be complemented and supported by IT forms (*see Appendix 4*).

2.4 IT budget

The 'budget' can be considered as a tool for the strategic management control system and an integral part of the performance management process of the organisation. A budget generally refers to a list of all planned expenses and revenues. In summary, the purpose of the budget is to provide a forecast of revenues and expenditures, i.e. construct a model of how the business might perform financially speaking if certain strategies, events and plans are carried out, and enable the actual financial operation of the business to be measured against the forecast.

In terms of IT, all management decisions, activities, actions, system development projects, application maintenance, IT solutions procurement and deployment, computer system support, outsourcing and offsourcing activities, are ultimately reflected and contained in the IT budget of the given organisation.

The IT budget is a control tool for IT items and is an integral part of the corporate budgeting process. IT budgets, viewed as cost control procedures, are absolutely necessary if organisations are to control, manage, allocate, evaluate and monitor their resources and maintain their level of profitability and service. In public and non-profit organisations, IT budgets define the most optimal use of resources in order to provide the best service to the public.

Regardless of the type of organisational structure (private, public, etc.), there are two main types of IT budget approaches: 'top-down' budget and 'bottom-up' budget.

Top-down approach: the IT budget is based on the long-term organisational and IT strategy and in meeting the corporate strategic objectives of the enterprise. Once these are known and communicated to all levels of management, the IT budget follows.

Bottom-up approach: The IT budget is based on the needs and requirements of each department, function, business unit, etc. and the sum of all these budgets makes the overall IT budget.

NO	DESCRIPTION (of expenses)	AMOUNT (Currency)
1	Hardware (main severs)	xxxx.xxx
2	Operating System Software	xxxx.xxx
3	Database System Software	xxxx.xxx
4	Networking System Software	xxxx.xxx
5	Application Systems Software	xxxx.xxx
6	Personnel Payroll	xxxx.xxx
7	Personal Computers	xxxx.xxx
8	Office Equipment	xxxx.xxx
9	Security Administration	xxxx.xxx
10	Data Centre Administration	xxxx.xxx
11	Education and Training	xxxx.xxx
12	Computer Insurance	xxxx.xxx
	Total	xxxx.xxx

Table 2: IT budget – example

The typical IT budget will contain annual amounts for hardware, software, etc. and other IT items shown in Table 2. This budget is drafted by the CIO, and approved by the usual corporate budget procedures.

IT budgets should be monitored and reviewed and their progress (actual expenses, potential income, revisions, etc.) included in the IT management report.

2.5 IT asset controls

All assets (buildings, land, ledgers, records, files, media, films, DVDs, hardware, systems, data, manuals, procedures, contracts, patents, research work, etc.) of the organisation are usually protected by the appropriate policy and procedures. The responsibility for the protection of the assets should be separate from the function maintaining the documents and systems of the organisation. When assets must be destroyed, this may be done by an approved committee process and reported to the highest level of management of the organisation.

IT asset controls may include:

- a hardware and software inventory (*see Chapter 6 and Appendix 4*)
- an information asset register describing the types of information existing and maintained in all files (*see Appendix 4* 'Information Asset Register Form')
- a consumables inventory
- maintenance registers for systems and application software, and hardware
- visitors logs (*see also Chapter 7 and Appendix 4*) for both offices and computer rooms
- hardware locks

- hardware tagging (*see also Chapter 7*) with property labels, serial numbers, etc.

IT management will need to consider the needs and demands of their organisation in deciding their roles in protecting the IT assets which have been assigned to them for productive use and protection.

2.6 IT personnel management controls

The purpose of the corporate personnel management controls is to assist and support the management of the people within the organisation. Developing and implementing the human resource systems to support personnel management controls may be done by the personnel administration or human resource management director with the assistance and support of the personnel and benefits committee, and ratified by the Board. These may be supported and implemented by the IT function, especially when some of these are computerised.

In addition to whatever general personnel controls are exercised, the additional management controls for IT personnel include:

- Personnel administration controls
- IT personnel job descriptions
- IT personnel education and training controls.

2.6.1 Personnel administration controls

Particular IT personnel administration controls that may be useful, depending on the conditions of any given organisation, include the following:

- **Screening**: Screening of IT personnel during the hiring process should be careful, meticulous and thorough. Screening should be followed by initial orientation, the necessary periodic internal and external training, and the periodic progress review on tasks and jobs completed.
- **Employment contracts and job descriptions**: All IT personnel should have valid employment contracts and job descriptions, which should always reflect the current job assignment. Examples of various IT job descriptions are contained in Paragraph 2.6.2.
- **Supervision**: Supervision of IT personnel involves not only direction and progress review for the jobs and tasks assigned, but the monitoring of other aspects of their professional conduct within the work environment, paying particular attention to deviations from expected behaviour and performance results.
- **Segregation of duties**: Segregation of personnel duties as a control measure is very important in the IT area, basically to safeguard the organisation from fraud, crime and abnormal actions on IT systems and infrastructure. It should not be the sole responsibility of one person to authorise transactions, execute transactions, record transactions and safeguard resources resulting from consummating transactions. This means that systems development, technical support services and operations should be carried out by separate units or separate individuals.
- **Rotation of duties**: Rotation of duties, done periodically, prevents personnel from becoming bored and vulnerable to fraud, abuse and system tampering as a form of challenge.
- **Vacation**: The taking of vacations is also very important especially for IT personnel working in financial and

other critical systems as various abnormal and potentially illegal actions may be discovered.

- **Professional code adoption**: Adoption of professional ethical standards for system development and other IT professionals is also a good control measure as it instils a set of values which IT personnel will have to comply with and apply to their everyday work activities. Such standards are the ACM professional code, the ISACA Code, etc. The Computer Ethics Institute Code, as a good example for potential adoption depending on the organisation's needs and requirements, is provided in Appendix 2.

Selecting one or more of the above, customising, improving and implementing them in their IT function is the job of the IT manager with support from the human resources function of their organisation.

2.6.2 IT personnel job descriptions

Job descriptions are useful because they define the duties, responsibilities and performance specifications of all job holders in a corporate environment.

Likewise IT personnel job descriptions may be found to be needed, in the modern-day business operating environment. These job descriptions should be identified and formally established. Examples of some of the main IT jobs are:

- Chief Information Officer (CIO), full example
- Business Systems Analyst, summary only
- Application Systems Analyst, summary only
- Computer Programmer, summary only
- Computer Operator, summary only
- Systems Programmer, summary only

- Web Applications Developer, summary only
- Network Support Analyst, summary only
- Security roles.

The Enterprise Architecture development roles are described in Chapter 3.

Chief Information Officer (CIO): job description

Summary of responsibilities

The Chief Information Officer (CIO) will provide technology vision and leadership in the development and implementation of the Information Technology (IT) investments of the organisation.

The CIO will lead the organisation in planning and implementing enterprise information systems to support both distributed and centralised production and business operations and achieve more effective and cost beneficial enterprise-wide IT operations.

Additionally, the CIO:

- Provides strategic and tactical planning, development, evaluation and co-ordination of the information and technology systems for the business within the Enterprise Architecture framework of the organisation.
- Oversees the IT portfolio and manages the whole process of IT assets, such as software, hardware, middleware, an IT project, internal staff, an application or external consulting.
- Designs and implements the controls for the management of the IT function, including policies, procedures, methods and practices.

- Facilitates communication between staff, management, vendors and other technology resources within the organisation.
- Oversees the back office computer operations of the affiliate management information system, including local area networks and wide area networks.
- Responsible for the management of multiple information and communications systems and projects, including voice, data, imaging and office automation.
- Designs, implements and evaluates the systems that support end-users in the productive use of computer hardware and software.
- Develops and implements user-training programmes.
- Oversees and evaluates system security and back-up procedures.
- Supervises the Database and Network Administrators.

Qualifications

Minimum of 10 years' experience with increasing responsibilities for management and support of the information systems and information technology of the industry in which the organisation belongs.

The ideal candidate will also have:

- Familiarity with desktop, notebook, handheld and server computer hardware.
- Familiarity with local and wide area network design, implementation and operation.
- Familiarity with operating systems (for mainframes, minicomputers, personal computers, etc.).
- Knowledge of various office productivity software programs, such as word processing, database and spreadsheet programs, and communications software.

- Familiarity with various computer peripherals, such as printers, monitors, modems and other equipment.
- General knowledge of business processes and their interrelationship gained through 10 or more years of related experience.
- Ability to analyse and resolve complex issues, both logical and interpersonal.
- Effective verbal and written communications skills and presentation skills, all geared towards co-ordination and education.
- Ability to negotiate and defuse conflict.
- Ability to act in a self-motivating, independent, co-operative, flexible and creative way.
- Ability to drive with access to reliable transportation.
- Ability and willingness to travel when necessary.
- Requires a bachelor's degree in Computer Science, Business Administration or a related field or equivalent experience. A master's degree in Business Administration or a related field is highly desirable.

Knowledge

Comprehensive knowledge of:

- Business principles and techniques of administration, organisation and management to include an in-depth understanding of the key business issues of the organisation. These include, but are not limited to, knowledge of strategic and operational planning, economics, personnel administration, federal, state and local laws, marketing, financial and cost analysis, and trends in the industry.
- Data processing methods and procedures, and computer software systems.

- Business office operations as it pertains to third party billing and reimbursement activities in a managed environment.
- Systems design and development process, including requirements analysis, feasibility studies, software design, programming, pilot testing, installation, evaluation and operational management.
- Business process analysis and redesign.
- Design, management and operation of managed IT systems.

Skills and dexterities

Proven skills in:

- Negotiating with vendors, contractors and others
- Budget preparation and monitoring
- Planning and organising
- Management and leadership
- Communication
- Relating to all levels of the user community
- Being a team player who motivates and educates other team members
- Planning, implementing and supporting systems in a complex environment
- Setting and managing priorities
- Comprehending complex, technical subjects
- Translating technical language to lay audiences
- Linking and applying complex technologies to business strategies.

Working conditions

Working conditions are normal for an office environment. Work may require occasional weekend, and/or evening work, and some out-of-town and out-of-the-country travel (not more than 20% of work).

Business Systems Analyst: job description

Summary of responsibilities

- Study the overall business and information needs of the organisation, in order to develop solutions to business and related IT technology problems.
- Work closely with users to identify business needs and the costs and benefits of implementing computerised solutions.
- Build information technology (IT) definitions based on identified needs of the organisation.
- Work with other IT experts to address application software and hardware needs of the organisation.

Application Systems Analyst: job description

Summary of responsibilities

- Develop, install, maintain and modify advanced business and/or engineering application and/or other integrated systems and packages.
- Identify and analyse business user requirements and recommend appropriate applications or modifications.
- Investigate user problems and needs, identify their source, and determine possible solutions.
- Analyse user project proposals including identifying potential problem areas and recommending optimum approaches for project path.
- Participate in the development, implementation, installation and testing of applications software.

- Contribute, through code development and other means, to the development of tools and interfaces between application programs and for the development of debugging programs.
- Participate in the development of training materials and assist in conducting training and workshops.
- Document programming problems and resolutions for future reference.
- Assist personnel of other departments as a computer resource.

Computer Programmer: job description

Summary of responsibilities

- Perform a variety of programming assignments requiring knowledge of established programming procedures and data processing requirements.
- Code, test, maintain, modify and troubleshoot programs utilising the appropriate hardware, database and programming technology.
- Make approved changes by amending flow charts.
- Develop detailed programming logic and coding changes.
- Test and develop program modifications.
- Write new program code using prescribed specifications.
- Analyse performance of programs and take action to correct deficiencies based on consultation with users and approval of manager.
- Discuss with users to gain understanding of needed changes or modifications of existing programs.

- Resolve questions of program intent, data input, output requirements, and inclusion of internal checks and controls.
- Write and maintain programming documentation.
- Analyse client/server and microcomputer-based software solutions compatibility with company requirements.
- Document programming problems and resolutions for future reference.
- Assist personnel of other departments as a computer resource.
- Perform other relevant duties as assigned by IT management.

Computer Operator: job description

Summary of responsibilities

- Monitor console control panels and make procedural and/or operational corrections as necessary.
- Operate and monitor mainframe and mid-range computer and peripheral equipment to include printers, tape and disk drives.
- Monitor operation of equipment, control panels, error lights, verification printouts, error messages and faulty output.
- Research error messages and manipulate console to re-sequence job steps after a job is interrupted.
- Monitor console control panel for faulty output or machine stoppage.
- Make procedural and/or operational corrections as necessary.
- Contact appropriate personnel to rectify console control panel errors.

- Determine source of computer problems (hardware, software, user access, etc.).
- Remove and distribute computer output.
- Clear equipment at end of operating run and review schedule to determine next assignment.
- Document computer problems and resolutions for future reference.

Systems Programmer: job description

Summary of responsibilities

- Provision of system-level support of multi-user operating systems, hardware and software tools, including installation, configuration, maintenance and support of these systems.
- Identification of alternatives for optimising computer and network resources.
- Undertaking research, planning, installing, configuring, troubleshooting, maintaining and upgrading operating systems, network and database software.
- Writing and maintaining system documentation.
- Conducting technical research on system upgrades to determine feasibility, cost, time required, and compatibility with current system.
- Documenting system problems and resolutions for future purposes.

More details are also provided in Chapter 8 (Systems software controls).

Web Applications Developer: job description

Summary of responsibilities

- Design, create, produce and maintain web pages using relevant software packages.
- Develop the website content of the organisation.
- Manage the image and copyrights of the organisation on the Internet.
- Maintain the website once it is completed by adding new content, icons, illustrations or features and co-ordinate other people, such as programmers and analysts, to help maintain the website.

More details are also provided in Chapter 8 (Systems software controls).

Network Support Analyst: job description

Summary of responsibilities

- Plan, design, analyse, and provide technical support for data communications network or group of networks.
- Conduct research and evaluation of network technology and recommend purchases of network equipment.
- Analyse and resolve technical problems for established networks.
- Plan, test, recommend and implement network, file server, mainframe, and workstation hardware and software.
- Install, upgrade and configure network printing, directory structures, user access, security, software and file services.
- Establish user profiles, user environments, directories and security for networks being installed.

- Document network problems and resolutions for future reference.

More details are also provided in Chapter 8 (Systems software controls).

Security personnel roles

For the management and support of the IT security activities of the organisation, the following roles and responsibilities should be formally assigned:

IT Security Project Manager: Overall responsibility for managing and organising testing; obtaining, co-ordinating and allocating the required resources for IT security; providing technical guidance; performing quality reviews and inspections; managing risks; and maintaining the security library.

Other more specific responsibilities are:

- Develop and administer system and information ownership, information and data classification guidelines, standards and procedures.
- Develop, establish and maintain standards, procedures and guidelines to promote the security and uninterrupted operation of computer-based application systems.
- Identify and address exposures to accidental or intentional destruction, disclosure, modification or interruption of information that may cause serious financial and/or information loss to the organisation.
- Be responsible for the protection of the organisation's IT assets and information which are processed by or stored in the organisation's computerised information systems.

Security Test Designer: Produces, categorises and files security test scenarios.

Security Tester: Executes security test scenarios, documents the results and documents any required changes.

Security System Test Administrator: Establishes and maintains the required technical environment for security application testing.

Security System Accounts Administrator: Establishes and maintains the accounts of all users.

In closing, IT job descriptions may be found useful because they define the duties, responsibilities and performance specifications of all IT job holders in a corporate environment.

Selecting one or more of the above job descriptions, customising, improving and implementing them in their IT function is the job of the IT manager with support from the human resources function of their organisation.

2.6.3 IT personnel education and training controls

Education in the wider context is any act or experience that has a crucial effect on the character, mind, physical or technical ability of an individual. Training refers to learning or improving special skills and techniques by individuals. In a corporate environment, education refers to university education obtained by personnel, while training is the process by which the organisation provides the means for its personnel to obtain specialised skills and techniques to be applied to the tasks assigned to them.

Education and training are deemed to be investments in human capital, by most modern organisations. It is, therefore, paramount that organisations manage and enhance this process, so that they may achieve better results.

For IT systems, communications systems, equipment, professional systems and office automation systems to operate in the given corporate environment, special technical skills and dexterities may be required of the IT personnel, such as:

- Technical knowledge of the computer and communications technologies.
- Technical knowledge of the database management systems and software development technologies.
- Technical knowledge of application development in classical (COBOL, PL/I, etc.) as well as the latest languages (C++, Visual Basic, etc.) for web applications.
- Practical (on-the-job) experience in all above.
- Adequate knowledge of several business functions for which IT systems are being.
- Adequate (if not expert) knowledge in methodologies for systems analysis, systems design, systems testing, security, etc.

As the IT environment is evolving on a continuous basis, with more and more trends and techniques researched and put into practice, the work environment, within which the IT personnel are working, may demand the following:

- Continuous updating and effective application of all the new features identified for IT, communications, database management, systems design, etc.
- Continuous and effective support, both technical, business and psychological, to all users (internal and

external) of the ITC systems operating or being developed in the organisation.

- Efficient and effective use of corporate resources (time, effort, money, equipment, personnel) in the IT projects under development.
- Continuous problem solving for issues and matters of both a procedural (business) and logical (computerised processing) nature for developing, maintaining, supporting and running the specific IT systems of the organisation.

On the basis of the above analysis, the required IT personnel education and training controls will need to be identified and formally established. This is usually the job of both the IT committee and IT management. These organs need to ensure that a budget containing an itemised listing of each amount for all scheduled seminars, conferences and specialised IT courses for each IT resource, for the next time period, usually a year, and a programme to carry these out should be formulated and executed.

It may also be the job of senior corporate management to ensure that these take place as planned, and make the necessary improvements if these do not happen, or the expected results are not obtained in the long run.

2.7 IT purchasing controls

Purchasing refers to the corporate process used to obtain primary resources and acquire goods or services to accomplish the general goals and specific business objectives of the organisation. Though there are several organisations that attempt to set standards in the purchasing process, processes can vary greatly between organisations.

The purpose of purchasing controls is to minimise or avoid any potential cases of corporate fraud and to increase effectiveness, efficiency, transparency, accountability and the best use of corporate and societal resources. In terms of IT, and because IT may obtain goods and services of a highly technical nature, sometimes beyond the knowledge set of the usual corporate purchasing department, additional IT purchasing controls may be required.

Developing these IT purchasing controls may be done by the IT committee in conjunction with the corporate purchasing function, and are usually, as a good practice, ratified by the Board or the senior management committee.

These controls are usually the same controls which apply for all purchases of the organisation, but with specific emphasis on IT. In some large organisations an IT procurement function may be set up.

The strategic objectives of the IT procurement function are:

- Fast and effective processing of IT procurement services.
- Highest quality in IT products, solution and services obtained.
- Best pricing arrangements.

This procurement process may be made up of the following actions:

1 Establishment of the whole IT procurement process.
2 Setting up an IT budget for procurement.
3 Executing the IT procurement procedure.
4 Considering infrastructural issues.
5 IT vendor management.
6 Undertaking effective project scoping.
7 Maintaining documentation control.

Action 1: Establishment of the whole IT procurement process

This is usually the job of the executive Board of Directors of the company or organisation. The IT procurement process may be assigned to an IT procurement committee, the Finance Department, a user department, or a combination of these, depending on the corporate needs, geographical and national factors of the economy in which the organisation and its IT department function.

Establishing the IT procurement process entails the following:

- Describing the strategic objectives of the IT procurement process.
- Planning, designing and ratifying the procurement procedure.
- Instituting the proposal evaluation criteria, the management controls and budget approval level for IT goods, items services, etc.
- Setting the scope of the IT procurement process and what issues it will pertain to: purchase of ready-made IT systems, computer, hardware, networking, cabling installations, etc. contracting for system development services, maintenance for systems and hardware, outsourcing and offshoring operations and services, retiring of software and equipment, etc.

Action 2: Setting up an IT budget for procurement

An IT budget for procurement purposes may be required, either on an annual basis, or on a project-by-project basis. This budget could be split on the basis of:

- Capital funds for major IT systems
- Annual maintenance (hardware, software)
- Annual IT consumables and minor expenses
- Outsourcing and offshoring (operations and services).

Action 3: Executing the IT procurement procedure

The IT procurement procedure, at least in some large multinational enterprises or organisations, may be supported by a corporate computerised purchasing or logistics system, and may be made up of the following steps:

Step 1: Purchase requisition

A purchase requisition describes the form completed and signed by an authorised corporate official and describing the IT goods, systems or services required. Purchase requisitions may be triggered by the IT procurement committee, the IT steering committee, or other executive committee for IT issues, completing a purchase requisition form and sending to the organisational function charged with this role.

An IT purchase requisition is required for all IT items: computer hardware, software of any kind, personal computers and office automation applications, mobile devices, consumables, ready-made packages, application software, services for consulting, outsourcing, offshoring, preparation of computer and network rooms, computer hardware and facilities maintenance, etc.

Attached to this document there should also be exact specifications for hardware, user needs and requirements for application systems, designs and drawings for computer rooms and, in general, specific requirements for the IT item, product or service to be purchased.

Further to this, a list of previous IT suppliers should be noted as well as any new ones with their full details.

The IT purchase requisition should be signed by the authorised officers (signatories) and ratified by a supervising body (IT procurement committee, IT steering committee, CEO, etc.).

Step 2: Market research

The objective of this step is to research the IT market, both local and international, and obtain at least three complete proposals for the IT items requested.

Proposals are obtained from the IT vendors suggested by the requesting party as well as other vendors known or identified during the research process.

If there is a need for information only (RFI) then the obtained vendor information is returned to the requester, and the procurement process is terminated.

In cases where proposals are requested from the specific IT vendor, these proposals should contain the following parts: technical specifications, commercial issues, legal aspects and evaluation criteria.

This way, all IT vendors are aware of all the needs, requirements, specifications and conditions that will be followed by the organisation to award the particular items offered to the best bidder.

The IT vendor proposal may contain two sealed parts, one for the technical aspects and another for the financial issues.

In cases of small consumable items of low value or items of a repeated nature (for bulk orders) of some value according to a set of limits, the proposals may not be sealed. This, however, is defined by the procurement policy established prior to the initiation of IT purchases.

Step 3: Proposal evaluation

When all the IT proposals are received they are forwarded to the IT evaluation committee.

The vendor proposals for consumables or other items that do not require specific technical assessment are not reviewed by this committee, but they are ordered with the pre-selected vendor on the basis of the lowest price for the approved technical and other quality specifications.

In the case of IT vendor proposal evaluation the procedure is the following:

- The technical evaluation is completed first.
- The financial evaluation is completed next and only if the technical evaluation results in one or more potential IT vendors.
- The final evaluation and selection of vendor is a combination of both technical and financial evaluations, depending on the weighting of each part.

One method for proposal evaluations for IT systems containing hardware, operating system and application systems software, and project implementation services may be the following:

- Create a Technical Evaluation Table (TET) for each major component: infrastructure and equipment, software, support and services, project management, etc.
- Review the vendor proposals in comparison to the technical and other terms of the purchase request and request for proposal (RFP). Reject any proposals that do not fully meet these pre-stated requirements and specifications.
- Assign a weight factor in each part of the major component of the TET Table. For example, for the component of project management assign a weight factor to each of: quality, project manager skills, methodology, team, tools. Do the same for the other major components.
- Review the technical part of the vendor proposals and complete the TET accordingly. Run any performance benchmarks and/or computer simulation workloads on the vendor equipment and systems, if they have been specified in the RFP. Visit any client sites of the IT vendors, if required, before completing the TET (especially for the top two best technically evaluated vendor solutions).
- Review and finalise the TET.
- Perform a financial evaluation for all valid proposals.
- Establish an IT vendor evaluated list: Vendor X is the best (technically), Vendor Y next and document all findings and results.

Step 4: Expenditure approval

Following the evaluation of the IT proposals and before placing a purchase order with the selected vendor, the expenditure must be approved by the appropriate corporate management levels.

This expenditure approval could be obtained on the basis of an IT approved budget, or of a user department approved budget, etc. Expenditure approval describes the approvals required by authorised corporate officers according to the funds control approvals scheme of the organisation for the specific IT goods, items, services, etc. required to serve some purpose of the business function.

Management controls must be appropriately exercised to ensure that the IT system or services ordered are in alignment with the strategic objectives of the corporate entity which IT serves, and also that the required funds are available at the time needed for vendor payment.

If there are no problems arising, the expenditures for obtaining the IT system or services are approved and noted on specific documentation (as per corporate approvals standards or procedures).

Step 5: Placement of order

After the expenditures have been reviewed and approved, a written order is placed with the approved vendor.

For IT systems and services of large values or of strategic importance to the organisation, a contract is signed between the two parties (organisation and IT vendor).

Step 6: Expediting and final delivery

Once the purchase order has been placed and a contract has been agreed and signed, a final time schedule for the delivery of the IT goods and services ordered is forwarded to the authorised official (e.g. the IT manager) for management control purposes.

This official will follow all steps of this process to ensure that all items and services are delivered as per the terms and conditions of the purchase order, the IT vendor proposal and the signed contract.

This official is supported also by specific corporate and IT staff and the IT acceptance committee for IT projects or systems which are to be implemented by the external vendor. If any testing for the ordered computerised application system is to take place, then the procedure for system testing, described in Chapter 4, is also followed.

Step 7: Vendor payment

If all the previous steps have been executed fully and there are no outstanding issues of any consequence to be resolved, then the vendor is given the approval to issue the final invoice.

This final invoice should be settled on the basis of a final review by a member of the executive Board of the organisation to ensure that all ordered IT goods, systems and services have been delivered, as per the purchase order, the corporate needs, the IT vendor proposed, the signed contract, and the identified results.

A copy of this invoice should be kept by IT for management purposes.

Action 4: Considering infrastructural issues

Before an IT system becomes fully operational all the required infrastructural components must be in place. These may be: computer rooms, network rooms, cabling installations, telecommunication lines, physical security access controls, building management system (e.g. air-conditioning, heating, etc.) and other installations (e.g. warehouse facilities), etc.

Appropriate management controls must be exercised to ensure that the IT system purchased and to be installed, does not enter into a conflict situation, especially when the other required infrastructural components do not exist or are being prepared by other parties (within or external to the organisation).

Action 5: IT vendor management

All IT vendors, whether regular suppliers to the organisation or not, should be treated on the same basis of fairness, objectivity, ethics, corporate governance, and agreed industry and professional standards.

All agreements are usually in writing. The information provided by both parties should be accurate, timely and of the highest quality.

The corporate and IT management of the organisation must exercise the appropriate measures and controls that these criteria are applied throughout the whole IT procurement process.

Action 6: Undertaking effective project scoping

The scoping of an IT project is the sine qua non for its absolute success. This is because when the IT project is very open (a large number of unidentified users, many geographical locations, user needs and requirements not well defined, etc.) various risks and factors creep in and make the IT project prone to failures and other design and installation problems.

Appropriate scoping involves: (a) adequate specifications, well documented, agreed with the end-users and other corporate stakeholders, (b) agreed timetable for implementation, (c) agreed project milestones and deliverables, (d) agreed quality standards, (e) agreed and well-documented acceptance criteria and procedures, (f) agreed and well-documented error correction and resolution procedures, (g) agreed grievance settlement procedures, and (h) top management sponsoring on the behalf of the organisation.

Action 7: Maintaining documentation control

The IT organisation should keep files for all work, IT projects and purchase orders placed with external IT providers, as this may be necessary for fraud control, vendor control, approval of maintenance and other needs, such as vendor invoices payments control, auditing, etc.

In conclusion, IT management, depending on their experience, needs and nature of their organisation, may use or customise the above steps and actions, or even develop a different purchasing procedure to satisfy the organisation's IT needs for systems, hardware, software and services.

2.8 IT office administration controls

In addition to any corporate level administration controls, the IT function will probably need its own office administration controls, such as:

- physical security controls
- mail controls
- EDI controls
- facsimile transmission controls
- policies, procedures and forms controls.

Physical security controls

Physical security controls for all IT assets (ledgers, records, files, media, films, DVDs, hardware, systems, data, manuals, procedures, contracts, patents, research work, etc.), IT personnel and IT premises should be implemented. These controls may include:

- security guards, especially for computer rooms and data centres
- locked IT storerooms and offices
- safety and fire-proof vaults for IT assets (like back-ups, original vendor software, etc.)
- fire detection system for IT offices
- television and microwave surveillance for sensitive IT areas
- locked offices for personal computer locations
- computerised access-controlled doors
- visitor entry and exit controls
- close security events monitoring
- restricted access to valuable records, files, facilities and systems

- waste management for all reports, correspondence, digital media, diskettes, tapes, DVDs, ribbons, special forms, etc. via the use of paper shredders, incinerators, media crunchers, software degaussing and binary zero creation for all destroyed computerised data files.

Strict security rules should also apply for rooms and spaces containing PBX (telephone) equipment, cabling, etc. Thus PBX attendant console rooms, telephone wiring closets, telephone equipment rooms, and Local Exchange Company (LEC) demarcation rooms should always be locked and secured.

IT management should ensure on a periodic basis that these controls are in full force.

Mail controls

All outgoing mail (regular mail transmitted by national post or specialised courier, electronic messages, fax or Telex messages, hand-delivered correspondence, etc.) from the IT department, should be properly authorised before its transmission, and an electronic and printed copy should be maintained on file.

The same should apply for all incoming mail, i.e. it should be reviewed by authorised staff, replied to and filed in the same way.

Both incoming and outgoing mail should be recorded in a log, both at the IT department level and the level of the corporate headquarters.

EDI controls

When IT uses Electronic Data Interchange (EDI) systems and technologies to communicate with another business and transmit via computers and communications business data, documents and transactions they need a set of specific controls. These controls are necessary in order to improve accuracy, reduce errors and avoid potential fraud, and abuse, and avoid legal hassles.

These controls are both administrative and IT-oriented controls.

The administrative controls pertain to: whether the data, documents, transactions, etc. sent were received correctly by the other party; who is responsible for the integrity of the information; who implements security mechanisms; how errors are corrected; what are the penalties for non compliance, etc.

These types of issues are described in Chapter 8 Systems software controls.

Facsimile transmission controls

IT sensitive information should only be transmitted via a secure fax system (e.g. encrypted or via a protected network). Each IT office and facility of the organisation should develop procedures to protect privacy while transmitting information via fax.

This procedure must:

- Ensure that a proper cover letter is the first page of each fax.
- Limit use to urgent situations.

- Ensure appropriate and secure location of fax machines.
- Assign accountability for managing each fax machine.
- Ensure that all transmissions are recorded in a fax log.
- Define appropriate rules to ensure transmissions are sent to the appropriate individual.
- Define procedures for cases of misdirected transmissions and receipts.
- Not allow autofaxing (i.e. automatic facsimile transmission of reports).
- Manage the instances when a site is notified that a fax was received by other than the intended recipient.
- Assign responsibility regarding the transmittal and receipt of facsimile documents to a specific set of staff.
- Assign the monitoring activity of the fax machines to a manager.
- Arrange for secure delivery of the documents.

Policies, procedures and forms controls

The design, writing and implementation of the policies, procedures and forms of an organisation should be controlled by a central administration function.

The same should also apply to IT-related policies, procedures and forms, as IT systems support a business function which has policies, procedures and forms to execute its transactions.

The following controls may apply in this area:

Register: There should be a register for each of the policies, procedures and forms of both the IT department and the IT application. This must always remain current.

Numbering: There should be a unique sequence prefix and number for each of the policies, procedures and forms of both the IT department and the IT applications. For example, all policies may be prefixed and numbered POxxxx, all procedures PRxxxx and all forms FOxxxx (where 'xxxx' is a number from 0001 to 9999).

Corporate ID: All policies, procedures and forms of both the IT department and the IT applications should contain the same corporate ID (logo, name, address, signs, symbols, etc.).

Design: All policies, procedures and forms of both the IT department and the IT applications should be designed, written and maintained centrally, with the assistance and support of the business functions involved, as well as the sponsoring and guidance of the affected corporate committees and the Board.

Implementation: All policies, procedures and forms of both the IT department and the IT applications should be implemented by all departments (with no exception). All departments should send the required information about implementation and other problems regarding the policies, procedures and forms used by them to the central function for possible review and improvements.

Review and improvements: Both the central function and the IT department should review (at least annually) and improve all policies, procedures and forms of the organisation, on the basis of the experience and knowledge of all departments involved.

Forms stock control: All sensitive forms (e.g. cheques) should be issued to the IT department on an authorisation basis. All issued stock and returns should be recorded and accounted for.

In conclusion, IT management, depending on their experience, needs and aspects of their organisation, may use or customise the above, or even develop a set of different IT office administration controls to satisfy the organisation's needs for better IT office control.

2.9 Monitoring and review controls

These controls are required to ensure that all IT administration controls, described previously, operate as designed initially.

Establishing IT monitoring and review controls for the area of IT administration may be achieved by the IT management report, the performance measures of IT administration and the audit review tools and techniques described later in this chapter.

This may also be facilitated by following the monitoring and review activities management plan, presented in Chapter 1.

The following may be monitored, reviewed and included in the IT management report:

- purchases
- personnel issues
- daily visitors
- fax and other mail traffic
- critical performance measures of the IT administration area
- compliance issues.

It is the job of the CIO to ensure that the IT administration controls are followed and that the IT reporting mechanism is fed with the relevant data of this area.

2.10 IT administration performance measures

The main goal of these controls is to provide feedback relative to the specific time-bound objectives of IT administration. This would tend to increase the possibility of the organisation in achieving these objectives efficiently and effectively. Performance measurement gains real value when it is used as the basis for timely decisions by management.

In the area of IT administration, the typical IT administration performance measures are shown in Table 3.

These performance measures could be based on a mixed system with two components: Component 1 would be an IT BSC (Information Technology Balanced Scorecard) Measurement System, described in Chapter 4, and Component 2 would be a Compliance Monitoring System for monitoring compliance to policies, procedures and related matters (e.g. budget issues).

The IT management of the company, may analyse all this performance and compliance monitoring information to review, assess and improve the IT administration elements of the IT function.

Function	Measures
IT Finance	Adherence to budget, expenditures on maintenance vs. new development, expenditures on preventative maintenance, return on IT investments, purchases budget performance, ratio of administrative (staff) costs to production (line) costs
IT Human Resource Management	Turnover ratios, training per employee (amounts, hours), average tenure within the company
IT Compliance	IT corporate procedures not documented and kept current, IT corporate committee not established, IT corporate committee not functioning, IT personnel management controls not followed, IT procedures not followed, IT budget not followed, IT visitors not recorded, IT offices and premises not secured, IT problem solutions not recorded, IT computer jobs schedule not followed, security incidents not recorded, security reviews not performed, management reports not produced

Table 3: IT administration performance measures

2.11 Review and audit tools and techniques

Setting up and improving IT administration controls is usually a very difficult task. It demands excellent human skills, business and IT knowledge, corporate and IT resources, a change management culture, several methods and a set of review and audit tools. The review and audit tools that may support IT managers and other professionals (IT auditors, IT consultants, internal auditors, external auditors, compliance officers, etc.) in establishing, evaluating and improving the IT administration controls, and which are offered for potential use, are: IT personnel management controls audit programme, IT procedures audit programme, standards checklist and segregation of duties checklist.

It may be finally noted that IT managers and other professionals may choose to use only particular components of these audit programmes and checklists, depending on the size, complexity and nature of the organisation's business and deployment of IT systems and infrastructure.

Other relevant guidelines and audit tools that might be found valuable and which support the IT management, evaluation and auditing processes are described in Appendix 3 (Monitoring IT controls checklist), Appendix 4 (Examples of IT forms), Appendix 5 (IT audit methodology), Appendix 6 (IT audit areas) and Appendix 7 (Internal audit report example).

2.11.1 IT Personnel Management Controls Audit Programme

The objective of this audit programme is to support the process of establishing, reviewing, evaluating and improving the controls identified in Paragraph 2.6 'IT personnel management controls'.

1 Check to see that the following controls are executed effectively. Consider: screening, employment contracts and job descriptions, supervision, segregation of duties, rotation of duties, vacation, professional code adoption.

2 Examine personnel files to ensure that the appropriate job descriptions exist.
3 Examine personnel files to ensure that all IT staff have taken the appropriate on-the-job training and other relevant seminars.

2.11.2 IT Procedures Audit Programme

The objective of this audit programme is to support the process of establishing, reviewing, evaluating and improving the controls identified in Paragraphs 2.3 'IT standards, policies and procedures', 2.5 'IT asset controls' and 2.7 'IT purchasing controls'.

This audit programme covers the issues of: IT procurement policy and procedures review, customer service agreements review, vendor and external parties management review, computer insurance review, maintenance policy and procedures, forms management review, security procedures review, IT performance policy review, software licences review, data privacy act compliance review, employment contracts review, working conditions handbook, application programs review, and website review.

IT procurement policy and procedures review

1 Obtain copy of policy on IT equipment procurement (both hardware and software).
2 Assess both the hardware/software comparative selection methods and the commercial evaluations.
3 Ensure that IT purchases fall within the authority level of the IT manager and according to the IT budget.

4 Review the last two purchases for IT equipment and verify accuracy of method and ensure its usage (and up to what level).
5 Obtain copies of all original purchase contracts (including systems in production, development and supported) and for all types (such as lease, use, rent, outsource, latest software amendments, subscriptions) for all IT equipment and systems, computers, networking, personal computers and telecommunications.
6 Create a catalogue of all these entities (to be used as a reference table for auditing).

Customer service agreements review

7 Obtain customer list serviced by IT.
8 Obtain copies of all IT customer service agreements (in effect for period to be audited).
9 Obtain copies of all customer invoices for the same year.
10 Check invoices in conjunction with the usage statistics (computer and personnel) to assess whether all work is charged out according to the specific customer service agreements and record any variances.
11 Assess revenue sources of the IT function.

Vendor and external parties management review

12 Obtain copies of all maintenance contracts for all IT equipment and systems owned, used and supported (see original purchase contracts, leases, rentals, subscriptions etc.).
13 Obtain consultancy contracts for review purposes.

14 Check maintenance contracts to ensure that all IT resources (as per purchase contracts are covered), and assess the financial and technical capabilities of the maintenance providers.

15 Obtain copies of invoices (of last three months) and verify amounts charged by maintenance contractors.

16 Review contracts to ensure they contain the following clauses:

- description of goods and services
- specifications
- time and place of delivery (including any timetables)
- penalties for delays/defaults
- acceptance tests
- price, terms of payment and cost of living for increases
- duration of contract, termination and renewal terms
- warranties
- protection against copyright/patents infringement
- licensing (use by other Group companies, transfer rights)
- limitation of the supplier's liability
- actions to be performed by customer
- confidentiality/information disclosure protection
- security terms and conditions (also for remote access)
- escrow account requirements for source safe-keeping
- do not hire each other's personnel clause
- insurance (professional liability, civic damages)
- tax liability
- rights to new ideas/inventions
- disputes settlement procedure
- force majeure terms and conditions
- law applicable.

Computer insurance review

17 Obtain copies of all insurance contracts covering IT equipment and software, and create a reference table of the equipment and systems covered (ref. purchase contracts) by the insurance contracts.

18 Review and assess hardware, and software and systems insurance coverage to ensure that at least the following are covered: loss of equipment, reinstatement cost, additional processing costs, and loss of profits, as applicable.

Maintenance policy and procedures

19 Assess the maintenance policy and procedures of existing computer systems. Consider:

- Is it done in a timely way?
- Do change control procedures exist?
- Is a prioritisation process used (test vs. production)?
- Do conversion procedures exist?
- Do source/object maintenance and control procedures exist?
- Is authority taken for all changes?
- Are program change forms used for all changes?
- Do quality control procedures exist?

Forms management review

20 Assess forms management. Consider: Is effective custody of all forms containing data (business, system, administrative) executed at all times?

Security procedures review

21 Assess security issues. Consider:

- o Do physical and logical security procedures exist?
- o Is a contingency planning procedure in place?
- o Do adequate back-up and recovery procedures exist?
- o Is system software adequately protected?

IT performance policy review

22 Review IT performance policy.
23 Review key IT performance indicators.

Software licences review

24 Identify purchase documents used for each type of application.
25 Ensure valid contracts exist for each application.
26 Identify personnel responsible for licence control.
27 Review legal documents, and authorisation of purchases.
28 Determine if all licences (original documents) exist.
29 Determine if all documents are safely stored.
30 Determine if IT monitors licence use by the users and by the given IT system.
31 Determine if all licensed software exists on the computer (especially for 'demo' systems).
32 Determine if non-licensed software exists.

Data privacy act compliance review

33 Has the company registered with the authorities?
34 Review the procedure dealing with subject access.
35 Are all relevant systems noted in the registration?

36 Establish what personal data are held.
37 Confirm that the responsibility has been established within the company to ensure that personal data are only processed as registered.
38 Ensure that the principles of the Act are controlled (as per other sections: security, IT standards, back-up, destruction of personal data, software maintenance, etc.).

Employment contracts review

39 Ensure that employment contracts state that all property and moral rights of all works of programmers (code, documentation, designs) belong to the company.

Working conditions handbook

40 Confirm that a clause exists to handle the property rights issue (all property and moral rights of all works of personnel belong to the company).

Application programs review

41 Examine the application source documentation to ensure that in all critical programs there is a 'property label', hard-coded within the 'comments or object' parts of the software.

Website review

42 Who owns site and contents?
43 Examine how the web name will be protected.
44 Ensure that designs, images and logos from other sites are not copied or not linked to illegal sites.

2.11.3 Standards Checklist

The objective of this checklist is to support the process of establishing, reviewing, evaluating and improving the controls identified in Paragraph 2.3 'IT standards, policies and procedures'.

1 Are there formally documented standards and procedures covering all IT functions? Consider:
   - Scope and coverage, including systems development and maintenance, operation and maintenance of technical services, end-users as well as central IT services, organisation and personnel
   - Dates when documents were issued or last updated
   - Policy regarding hardware and software.

2 Do the standards on system development include all aspects of development? Consider:
   - Business analysis
   - Data processing analysis
   - System design
   - Specifications (system, program, forms, reports, screens)
   - Testing (system, program)
   - Programming (and coding)
   - Implementation
   - Conversion
   - User training
   - IT training
   - Documentation (technical and user)
   - Project management
   - IT personnel management.

3 Is there an application data retention policy in place? Consider: coverage of policy on data retention (and

deletion) for all application systems in production, length of time (years) data are kept in computer storage (both online and off-line) and how adequate those may be for each application system, deletion process for old data from the computer and back-up media, and whether the end-user management is aware and controlling this process.

2.11.4 Segregation of Duties Checklist

The objective of this checklist is to support the process of establishing, reviewing, evaluating and improving the controls identified in Paragraph 2.6 'IT personnel management controls'.

1 Is segregation of duties for staff, both within the IT department and between IT and user functions, adequate to prevent and/or detect errors and/or irregularities? Consider:
   - o responsibility for initiating or authorising transactions
   - o custody of valuable or moveable assets
   - o amendments to master files
   - o correction of input errors.

2 Is segregation of duties within the IT department appropriate for the size of the organisation? Consider: segregation of functions, e.g. number of IT staff, systems programmers, application programmers, database administrator, IT operations, data input, network security, reliance on key personnel and reliance on contract staff.

3 Are staff with programming expertise segregated from the users who are controlling the systems?

2.12 Conclusion

IT administration is necessary for the IT function to exist and for all its elements (staff, systems, management, etc.) to operate to the best of their ability. IT administration controls are the non-financial, non-technical and non-production controls that usually encompass the following activities of the IT organisation: human resources, marketing of IT services, IT customer support, forms and records management, etc. These are concerned with operational efficiency and with adherence to IT organisational policies.

IT administration controls provide detailed, procedural checks and balances to manage the files, documents, information and other assets of the organisation, to enable the standard management reporting process of the organisation, and to monitor and evaluate the performance of the IT organisation in this regard.

IT administration may be achieved probably more efficiently and effectively, by implementing a suitable set of controls which may include policies, practices, procedures, organisational structures and other tools (e.g. audit and review programmes and checklists). These controls will need to be established to ensure that the specific IT administration objectives of the organisation can be met.

IT administration controls add the necessary elements to complete the IT organisational support structure of the knowledge management framework of the organisation (*outlined in Chapter 1*), and create value for the organisations.

The following checklist may be found of some value, depending on the culture of the organisation, the socio-economic context within which it operates, its business model, its strategies and standards, the needs and expectations of its stakeholders, etc.

1 Policies and procedures should be formally established and communicated to all levels of the organisation.
2 An approved performance policy, system and evaluation process should be in place.
3 An approved IT human resources management policy, set of procedures, a system and an evaluation process should be in place.
4 An approved IT financial and cost management policy, and a set of related procedures should be in place.
5 An approved IT asset management, disposition and protection system must be established.
6 An approved IT policy and a set of related procedures covering all areas should be formulated.
7 An IT ethics policy should be in place.

2.13 Review questions

This set of questions may be employed by those using the controls identified in this book to assess and double-check their own conceptual understanding and practical knowledge contained in this chapter.

1. What is the purpose of IT Administration controls?

Reference: Paragraph 2.2 'Purpose and main types of IT administration controls'.

2. Which are the main types of IT Administration controls?

Reference: Paragraph 2.2 'Purpose and main types of IT administration controls'.

3. What are some of the areas that the IT standards, policies and procedures should cover?

Reference: Paragraph 2.3 'IT standards, policies and procedures'.

4. What should the IT asset controls usually include?

Reference: Paragraph 2.5 'IT asset controls'.

5. What are the usual IT personnel management controls?

Reference: Paragraph 2.6 'IT personnel management controls'.

6. What should the IT Manager consider in reviewing segregation of duties in the IT department?

Reference: Paragraph 2.6 'IT personnel management controls'.

7. Why is rotation of duties important?

Reference: Paragraph 2.6 'IT Personnel Management Controls'.

8. Who should develop and ratify IT personnel job descriptions?

Reference: Paragraph 2.6 'IT personnel management controls'.

9. Which are the main (summary) responsibilities of the Chief Information Officer (CIO)?

Reference: Paragraph 2.6 'IT personnel management controls'.

10. What are the main responsibilities of a business systems analyst?

Reference: Paragraph 2.6 'IT personnel management controls'.

11. What are some of the main responsibilities of a computer programmer?

Reference: Paragraph 2.6 'IT personnel management controls'.

12. What are some of the main responsibilities of a systems programmer?

Reference: Paragraph 2.6 'IT personnel management controls'.

13. What does the Security Test Designer do?

Reference: Paragraph 2.6 'IT personnel management controls'.

14. What does the Security Tester do?

Reference: Paragraph 2.6 'IT personnel management controls'.

15. What are the strategic objectives of the IT procurement function?

Reference: Paragraph 2.7 'IT purchasing controls'.

16. Which steps is the IT procurement procedure made up of?

Reference: Paragraph 2.7 'IT purchasing controls'.

17. What does project scoping involve?

Reference: Paragraph 2.7 'IT purchasing controls'.

18. What items and issues should an IT management report cover?

Reference: Paragraph 2.8 'IT Management Reporting'.

19. What are some of the various IT administration performance measures?

Reference: Paragraph 2.10 'IT administration performance measures'.

20. Why should the IT organisation keep files for all work, IT projects and purchase orders placed?

Reference: Paragraph 2.7 'IT purchasing controls'.

CHAPTER 3: ENTERPRISE ARCHITECTURE CONTROLS

Even when laws have been written down, they ought not always to remain unaltered.

Aristotle (384–322 BC)

3.1 Scope

After the establishment of an IT organisation and its administrative controls, you need to plan what you want IT to do.

To this purpose you design a new, or improve your existing, business or Enterprise Architecture to enable the IT strategic process.

Enterprise Architecture controls enable and support the alignment of IT (infrastructure and systems) with the business functions of the organisation, and support the successful execution of the daily activities and operational transactions of the IT systems.

A set of main Enterprise Architecture controls are explained with examples provided in some cases. These controls include: Enterprise Architecture frameworks, enterprise or operating model of the organisation, business process narratives, Enterprise Architecture repository, Enterprise Architecture business related controls and Enterprise Architecture performance measures.

In addition to these, a set of audit programmes and checklists are presented to support the IT manager, IT practitioners, and other professionals (systems development and software support staff, IT auditors, internal auditors, IT consultants, external auditors, compliance officers, etc.) in executing and improving their duties and responsibilities.

3.2 Purpose and main types of Enterprise Architecture controls

The ever-changing environment of modern organisations (private, public, non-profit, etc.) is currently affected by a set of social, political, economic, technological and scientific factors and conditions at a speed not foreseen even by the best minds. Even Alvin Toffler,[9] the most famous futurologist, did not foresee fully all the current problems (globalisation, terrorism, global financial crisis, political instability, poverty, mass immigration, regional wars, etc.) and their solutions that modern nations, societies and economies are faced with and must handle effectively.

This often presents new opportunities, challenges, threats and risks to all organisations across the globe. These must be managed and resolved accordingly by all organisations, in order to keep them operating to the best of their capabilities. The solution to dealing with the uncertainty of the future is the ability to sense the oncoming needs and apply the necessary changes in the functions of the organisation for its best survival.

The ability to implement all these changes can be described as 'flexibility' and is of the most strategic importance to modern organisations. For the last three decades, many methods and approaches have been introduced and used in order to attempt to achieve strategic flexibility for

---

[9] See his books *The Third Wave* and *The Future Shock*, published in 1991.

organisations, without very much success, due to various complications and disabling factors, beyond the scope of this book.

These methods and approaches include: Business process redesign, business process improvement, organisational design strategy, outsourcing, excessive use of ready-made software packages, ERP systems, the Henk Volberda Model,[10] the SOA Model[11] and the DEA Model.

One approach, however, that seems to bring forth better results to managing the 'flexibility' issue, is the 'Enterprise Architecture' approach, according to a latest study.[12]

The purpose of Enterprise Architecture controls is to ensure, enable and facilitate:

- the establishment of the entire IT governance framework (*see also Chapter 1*)
- the good alignment between the corporate strategy and the IT strategy
- the accomplishment of the strategic goals by the provision of optimal IT services
- the continuous support of the critical business functions by IT systems and infrastructure on an efficient and effective basis.

Establishing the Enterprise Architecture controls may be done by the Enterprise Architecture co-ordinator and his/her team, reviewed by the corporate and IT strategic committees and ratified by the Board. The audit

---

[10] *www.provenmodels.com.*
[11] *my.advisor.com.*
[12] See: Forrester Survey on Enterprise Architecture, September 2009, at *www.forrester.com.*

programmes and checklists described in Paragraph 3.10 'Review and audit tools and techniques' may be used to support the design, implementation and post-implementation review of the Enterprise Architecture controls for the specific organisation.

The main types of Enterprise Architecture controls are:

- Enterprise Architecture (EA) description controls
- Management plan for designing and implementing an Enterprise Architecture (EA) framework
- Organisational Structure
- Enterprise Architecture development roles
- Enterprise Architecture business related controls
- Enterprise Architecture IT-related controls
- Monitoring and review controls
- Enterprise Architecture performance measures.

3.3 Enterprise Architecture (EA) description controls

Before establishing an Enterprise Architecture for the needs of the given organisation the term of 'Enterprise Architecture' and what it entails will probably need to be described, clarified and understood by all relevant levels of both IT and business management.

3.3.1 Description of Enterprise Architecture

In the profession of managing organisations, the term 'Enterprise Architecture' refers to the art and science of designing an enterprise. An 'enterprise' may be defined as any business entity, a private listed or not listed corporation, a private for-profit organisation, a public services ministry, agency or organisation, a local or regional public government agency or organisation, a state regulatory authority, a non-profit organisation, etc.

One formal definition according to MIT is: 'Enterprise Architecture is the organising logic of business processes and IT infrastructure reflecting the integration and standardisation requirements of the firm's operating model'.[13]

Another definition, as per IEEE,[14] of an architecture used in ANSI/IEEE Standard 1471-2000 is 'the fundamental organisation of a system, embodied in its components, their relationships to each other and the environment, and the principles governing its design and evolution.'

The most comprehensive definition, probably, is offered by IFEAD (Institute for Enterprise Architecture Developments): 'Enterprise Architecture is a complex expression of the enterprise; a master plan which acts as a collaboration force between aspects of business planning, such as goals, visions, strategies and governance principles; aspects of business operations, such as business terms, organisation structures, processes and data; aspects of automation, such as Information Systems and Databases; and the enabling technological infrastructure of the business, such as computers, operating systems and networks.'

This definition, with the addition of performance management, system development methodologies, and other strategic management and audit tools, has been used

---

[13] For more on this, see MIT Centre for Information Research.

[14] See *standards.ieee.org*.

in various consulting projects by the author and other professionals very successfully.

Enterprise Architecture, however, needs a set of frameworks, methodologies and tools to bring forth their results. For this purpose there are several Enterprise Architecture frameworks, methodologies and tools offered for use by all organisations on a global scale.

An indicative list would include the following: EABOK, GERAM, RM-ODP, TOGAF, the Zachman Framework, CIMOSA, FEA, the NIST Framework, the US Department of Defence Architecture Framework, the NATO Framework, the Australia Government Enterprise Architecture, IDEAS GROUP, Integrated Architecture Framework, CLEAR Framework, OBASHI, Information Framework, AGATE, FDIC Enterprise Architecture Framework.

Various vendors (as an indication only), such as IBM, ORACLE and IDS offer a set of software tools, languages, etc. for Enterprise Architecture development and deployment.

3.3.2 Enterprise Architecture frameworks

Enterprise Architecture Body of Knowledge (EABOK)

This is a guide to Enterprise Architecture produced by MIT.[15]

---

[15] See MIT University, Centre for Innovative Computing and Informatics, *www.mitre.org*.

It treats Enterprise Architecture as not including merely diagrams and technical descriptions, but gives a holistic view that includes US legislative requirements and guidance, as well as giving technologists a better understanding of business needs on the basis of the value chain concept of Michael Porter.[16]

Generalized Enterprise Reference Architecture and Methodology (GERAM)

This is a generalized Enterprise Architecture framework for enterprise integration and business process engineering according to various sources.[17]

It defines the enterprise-related generic concepts recommended for use in enterprise integration projects.

These concepts include:

- a life cycle approach in identifying the life-cycle phases for any enterprise (from entity conception to its final end)
- enterprise entity types and enterprise modelling with business process modelling
- integrated model representation in different model views
- modelling languages for different users, such as business users, system designers and IT modelling specialists.

---

[16] As per *Competitive Advantage, Creating and Sustaining Superior Performance*, Porter M, Free Press (1985).

[17] Such as www.nist.gov; 'A framework to define a generic enterprise reference architecture and methodology', Bernus P and Nemes L in *Proceedings of the International Conference on Automation, Robotics and Computer Vision*, Singapore, November 10–12, 1994; and the Report on GERAM, Nell JG (2006) at www.mel.nist.gov.

Reference Model of Open Distributed Processing (RM-ODP)

This framework supports distribution, interworking, platform and technology independence, and portability, together with an Enterprise Architecture framework for the specification of open distributed processing systems. It provides five generic and complementary viewpoints on the system and its environment:

- enterprise viewpoint
- information viewpoint
- engineering viewpoint
- computational viewpoint
- technology viewpoint.[18]

The Open Group Architecture Framework (TOGAF)

This framework provides a comprehensive approach to the design, implementation and governance of an enterprise information architecture at four levels or domains:

- Business Domain (business strategy, governance, organisation and key business processes)
- Applications Domain (blueprints for the individual application systems to be deployed and their interactions)
- Data Domain (logical and physical data assets)
- Technology Domain (hardware, software and network facilities required to support the deployment of core and mission-critical applications).

---

[18] See 'Reference Model of Open Distributed Processing', *http://lams.epfl.ch/reference/rm-odp*, the ITU-TX.950, 952, 920, 931, 960, 910, 911, and corresponding ISO/IEC standards, and the ISO/IEC 19500-2:2003 ORB Protocol.

- Technology Domain (hardware, software and network facilities required to support the deployment of core and mission-critical applications).

In terms of the data domain there are three typical levels of data models which could be utilised: conceptual, logical and physical. The complexity increases from conceptual to logical to physical. This is why one always starts with the conceptual data model (which contains high level entities and their entity relationships), then moves on to the logical data model (which contains in addition to entities and their relationships, attributes, and primary and foreign keys of the data), and finally the physical data model (which contains primary and foreign keys, and their implementation particulars, such as table names, column names, and column data types, etc.), before the data model is implemented in a particular database.[19]

The Zachman Framework

This framework provides a formal and well-structured way of viewing and defining an enterprise on the basis of a two-dimensional classification matrix. Each row represents a type of stakeholder, these being: contextual, conceptual, logical, physical and detailed. Each column denotes the aspects of the architecture, such as:

- 'Why' (represents the motivation)
- 'How' (denotes the functional description)
- 'What' (represents the data description)

---

[19] For more on this framework, see TOGAF Introduction at www.opengroup.org, and the publication of the Department of Defence (1996), *Technical Architecture Framework for Information Management*, Vol. 4.

- 'Who' (represents the people)
- 'Where' (denotes the network)
- 'When' (defines the time).

The resulting matrix is a template that must be filled in by the goals, rules, processes, material, roles, locations and events specifically required by the organisation.[20]

The CIMOSA Framework

CIMOSA is a well-known framework which supports all phases of the CIM (Computer Integrated Manufacturing) system life cycle from requirements definition, through design specification, implementation description and execution of the daily enterprise operation.

CIMOSA incorporates an event-driven, process-based modelling approach with the goal of covering essential enterprise aspects in one integrated model. The main aspects are the functional, behavioural, resource, information and organisational aspect.[21]

---

[20] For more on this framework, see www.zachmaninternational.com; Roger Sessions, 'A comparison of the top four Enterprise Architecture methodologies', at msdn2.microsoft.com; and Inmon WH et al, *Data Stores, Data Warehouse, and Zachman Framework: Managing Enterprise Knowledge*, McGraw-Hill (1997).

[21] For more information on this framework, see: (1) AMICE Consortium, *Open System Architecture for CIM, Research Reports of ESPRIT Project 688*, Volume 1, Springer Verlag, Berlin (1989); (2) the references by Beeckman, Dirk, 'CIMOSA: Computer Integrated Manufacturing Open Systems Architecture', *International Journal of Computer Integrated Manufacturing*, Vol. 2, No. 2, pp. 94–105 (March–April 1989); (3) Jorysz HR and Vernadat FB, 'CIMOSA Part 1: Total Enterprise Modeling and Function View', *International Journal of Computer Integrated Manufacturing*, Vol. 3, Nos. 3 and 4, pp. 144–156 (1990); (4) Jorysz HR and Vernadat FB, 'CIMOSA Part 2: Information View', *International Journal of Computer Integrated Manufacturing*, Vol. 3, Nos. 3 and 4, pp. 157–167 (1990); and (5) Klittich M, 'CIMOSA Part 3: CIMOSA Integrating Infrastructure – The Operational Basis for Integrated Manufacturing Systems', *International Journal of Computer Integrated Manufacturing*, Vol. 3, Nos. 3 and 4, pp. 168–180 (1990).

Federal Enterprise Architecture (FEA) Framework

The FEA framework is a US Government standard which is used to facilitate shared development of common processes and information among US Federal agencies and other government agencies.

On the basis of this framework, a given architecture can be partitioned into:

- Business Architecture, which represents the business functions of the organisation and the information it uses
- Data Architecture, which defines how data are stored, managed and used in a system
- Application Architecture, which consists of the logical systems that manage the data in the data architecture and support the business architecture
- Technology Architecture, which describes current and future infrastructure (hardware and software) that supports the application systems in the application architecture.[22]

Other Government Enterprise Architecture Frameworks

There is a set of various other government-sponsored Enterprise Architecture frameworks, such as the ones listed below, which are beyond the scope of this book:

- Department of Defense (US) Architecture Model (see *cio-nii.defense.gov and architectureframework.com/dodaf/*).

---

[22] For more information on this framework, see *FEA Consolidated Reference Model Document*, Version 2.3, *www.whitehouse.gov,* and The US Federal Laws: GPRA 1993, PRA 1995, The Clinger-Cohen Act (CCA 1996), GPEA 1998, FISMA 2002, and E-GOV.2002.

- British Ministry of Defence Architectural Framework (see *www.modaf.org.uk*).
- The NATO Architecture Framework (see *www.nhqc3s.nato.int/architecture*).
- Government Enterprise (Australia, Queensland) Architecture (see *www.qgcio.qld.gov.au*).
- NIST (US) Enterprise Architecture Model (see (1) NIST Special Publication 500–167, September 1989, (2) *www.faa.gov* and *www.nist.gov*).

Every organisation and its authorised officers, if they decide to use the EA approach and attempt to achieve better alignment between IT and their business will need to select an enterprise framework, obtain the necessary expertise and required tools, and set up the Enterprise Architecture process accordingly in order to proceed on this issue effectively.

This is carried out by various activities, such as:

- setting up an Enterprise Architecture team
- formulating and executing a management plan for Enterprise Architecture, depicting the enterprise model of the organisation
- documenting its business processes and architectural information in an Enterprise Architecture repository.

3.4 Management plan for designing and implementing an Enterprise Architecture (EA) framework

An Enterprise Architecture (EA) is a conceptual tool that assists organisations with the understanding of their own structure and the way they work. It provides a map of the enterprise and is a route planner for business and technology change. Normally an Enterprise Architecture takes the form of a comprehensive set of cohesive models that describe the structure and the functions of an enterprise. Important uses of it are in systematic technology planning and architecture, and in enhanced decision making.

One way that this may be achieved in an organised and efficient manner is the use of a management plan.

Step 1: Form an Enterprise Architecture (EA) team by selecting an EA co-ordinator and the other required EA and support staff, appointing them on a formal basis, and with a charter and specific timetable, budget and responsibilities (*see Paragraph 3.5*).

Step 2: Plan communication methods.

Step 3: Create a list of questions, focusing on critical areas of business processes, information and data, and technology.

Step 4: Identify senior business and IT (technical) executives to gather knowledge about the strategic and operational needs and requirements of the organisation.

Step 5: Select an EA Framework by:

- studying the existing standards and the business and industry environments in which the particular organisation operates. One such example of an EA standard is the ISO19439:2006 Enterprise Integration Framework. This is an international standard for enterprise modelling and enterprise integration developed by the International Organisation for Standardisation. It specifies a framework conforming to requirements of ISO15704, which serves as a common basis to identify and co-ordinate standards development for modelling of enterprises, emphasising, but not restricted to, computer integrated manufacturing. The other EA frameworks presented in this chapter, as well as the Gartner EA Process Model (www.gartner.com), may be examined.

- examining the alternate EA frameworks in the market.
- obtaining an EA framework and the associated methods and tools (repositories, Architectural Description Languages, such as ArchiMate, UML, ADL, software like Casewise, IDS Scheer/Aris, Alfabet, IBK Rational, Oracle EA Tools, etc.) by following the procurement procedures of the organisation.
- trying the selected EA framework on a pilot basis for one part of the organisation following a proven and customised methodology.[23]

Step 6: Define the 'as-is' model of the organisation, by following Hamel's approach[24] or Linder's method,[25] or some other method available and tested in the market, in terms of:

- a business model
- processes
- data
- customers
- products and services offered
- financing sources
- applications

---

[23] One such example may be the methodology proposed by Jaap Schekkerman in his book *How to Survive in the Jungle of Enterprise Architecture Frameworks*, published by Trafford Publications, in 2004.

[24] See Hamel G, *Leading the Revolution*, Boston: Harvard Business School Press (2000).

[25] See Linder J and Cantrell S, *Changing Business Models: Surveying the Landscape*, Accenture Institute for Strategic Change (2000).

- system development methodology
- the way IT systems support the business processes
- the IT infrastructure.

For more on this see Paragraph 3.6 'Formulating and documenting the Enterprise Architecture elements'.

Step 7: Identify desired and necessary enhancements and obtain approvals from senior management.

Step 8: Define the 'to-be' model of the organisation (in terms of the points identified in Step 6). For more on this see also Paragraph 3.6 'Formulating and documenting the Enterprise Architecture elements'.

Step 9: Formulate the EA implementation plan (project team, risks, timetable, resources, tools, technologies, change plan, etc.).

Step 10: Execute the EA implementation plan (install EA software tools, populate EA asset repository, implement key EA technologies, communicate results, monitor changes and progress, assess, review and improve process, and manage EA environment, etc.).

Conclusion

Whether the IT and business management of the organisation decide to make use of or customise this plan, or use another formal or informal approach, depends greatly on various interacting factors and conditions, such as:

- the corporate culture
- the needs of the stakeholders
- the management style
- the risk appetite
- the change management techniques

- the sector to which the given organisation belongs.

3.5 Enterprise Architecture development roles

As described in Step 1 of the above-mentioned management plan, an Enterprise Architecture (EA) team and other support staff may be required for creating and supporting the EA process. Furthermore creating effective Enterprise Architecture solutions may require the careful management and fruitful use of several roles by a set of specific personnel of the organisation, such as:

- Enterprise Architecture Co-ordinator
- Enterprise Architect
- Technical Architect
- Other typical IT roles (e.g. system programmer, business analyst, computer programmer, IT manager, etc.).

3.5.1 Enterprise Architecture Co-ordinator (EAC)

The EAC is responsible for establishing the Enterprise Architecture (EA) team and acting as its main co-ordinator, guide and coach in the process of designing, developing and implementing an Enterprise Architecture for the organisation.

Job duties and responsibilities are recorded in a formal job description. Job descriptions are usually written statements that describe the duties and responsibilities, the most important results needed to be performed, the required skills and qualifications, the reporting relationships, and the specific management activities of the position. The specific duties and responsibilities of an EAC include the following:

- Selection of the staff and organisation of the EA team
- Analysis and assessment of how IT serves the needs of the organisation
- Defining the scope of work of the EA team
- Co-ordination of the team in its EA tasks, meetings and daily activities
- Obtaining other IT and business personnel to support the EA efforts and team
- Supervising all EA activities of the EA team
- Reporting on the performance of the EA project to higher management and obtaining their support and guidance on resolving any reported issues
- Communicating the EA project results to all authorised levels of management as well as stakeholders
- Closing out the EA project when the EA has been implemented successfully.

3.5.2 Enterprise Architect

The Enterprise Architect, under the guidance and supervision of the EAC, links the corporate vision, mission, values, strategy and processes of an organisation to its IT strategy.

He/she also documents this by the use of multiple architectural views that depict how the current and future needs of an organisation will be met in an effective and efficient manner.

Other specific responsibilities may also include:

- Responsibility for the organisation's long-term strategy of IT systems and infrastructure

- Support of the organisation's long-term strategic goals and ensuring alignment with the Enterprise Architecture, the IT strategy and project development action plans
- Optimisation of information management approaches by the understanding of evolving business needs and requirements and IT capabilities.

3.5.3 Technical Architect

The technical architect, under the guidance and supervision of the EAC:

- Supports the EA development methodology and recommends improvements, as needed
- Defines, analyses and reviews software architecture specifications
- Participates in the definition, design and review activities of software architecture, design, application frameworks and interfaces
- Leads the development and implementation of framework and application software, as required
- Supports and undertakes trials by installing, testing and troubleshooting software, as needed
- Supports the EAC and the team members in various technical implementation tasks, such as security, database design, testing, and problem debugging and resolution.

Conclusion

Whether the IT and business management of the organisation decide to make use of, or customise, these EA roles, or use other IT staff to do the work of EA, depends greatly on various issues, such as: the corporate culture, the needs of the stakeholders, the management style, the risk appetite of the organisation, etc.

3.6 Formulating and documenting the Enterprise Architecture elements

To support Steps 6 and 8 of the above-mentioned EA management plan, the EA elements will need to be formulated and documented by the following processes:

3.6.1 Organisational structure

The first process is analysing the organisational structure of the company. A typical hierarchical structure for a large organisation is:

- CEO (or Secretary, or Vice-minister, in charge of government function)
- Vice Presidents (or General Directors)
- Executive committees
- Lawyers, auditors, other professionals
- Decision support staff
- Management
- Employees.

The Enterprise Architecture (EA) team will have to work within the structure of the organisation for which it develops its Enterprise Architecture.

3.6.2 Enterprise or operating model of the organisation

An enterprise or operating model is a representation of the structure, activities, processes, information, resources, people, behaviour, strategic goals and constraints of a business, government or other enterprises.

This is usually depicted by a diagram supported by narrative text, showing the operating units of the organisation, the relationships between these operating units or business functions, and the decision and process flows between these units or functions.[26]

Another example of such an operating model in a diagram is contained in Figure 3:

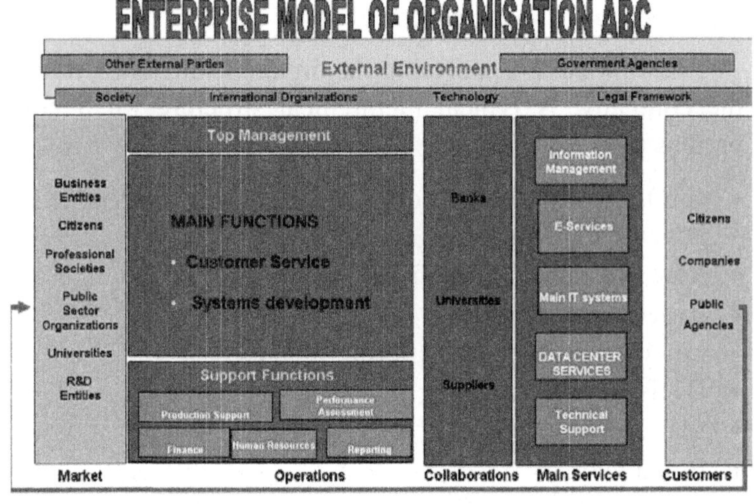

Figure 3: Business model example

[26] For a full example for a government treasury function, see Hashim A and Allan B, *Treasury Reference Model*, World Bank, 2001, www.worldbank.org, Report Number WTP505.

3.6.3 Business process narratives

Analysis of the business processes of the organisation is usually achieved by using 'business process narratives', which document all the processing logic for a business transaction. These narratives are also documented in the form of diagrams and are complemented by formal policies, procedures and forms.

Example of a business process narrative for a customer placing an order.[27]

Activity 1: Customer: places order.

Activity 2: Store: receives order. If customer has good rating, then payment by credit card is requested. Otherwise, cash payment is requested.

Activity 3: Customer: receives invoice. Settles payment.

Activity 4: Store: receives payment. Ships items ordered. Closes order.

Activity 5: Customer: receives items ordered.

3.6.4 Business strategic goals

Analysing the business strategic goals of the organisation is usually achieved by using various approaches and methods, such as:

- SWOT analysis

---

[27] A full example of process diagrams and narratives may be found in Hashim A and Allan B, *Treasury Reference Model*, World Bank, 2001, www.worldbank.org, Report Number WTP505.

- PEST analysis (also known as PESTLE Analysis)
- Gap analysis
- Portfolio analysis
- Value chain analysis
- Delphi Method
- Life cycle analysis
- Screening strategic options
- Financial analysis
- Scenario planning
- Critical success factor analysis
- The Five Forces
- Market segmentation
- Directional policy matrix
- Competitor analysis
- Change management methodology.

The first three are used most; the other methods are beyond the scope of this book.

SWOT analysis

The SWOT analysis (strengths, weaknesses, opportunities, threats) is one of the most popular. It involves looking at the strengths and weaknesses of a business's capabilities, and any opportunities and threats to the business. Once these have been identified, it is possible to assess how to capitalise on the strengths, minimise the effects of the weaknesses, make the most of any opportunities and reduce the impact of any threats.

It is important to remember that opportunities can also be threats; for example, new markets could be dominated by competitors, undermining the business position. Equally, threats can also be opportunities; for example, a competitor growing quickly could open up a new market for the business's product or service.

A SWOT analysis can provide a clear basis for examining the business performance and prospects. It can be used as part of a regular review process or in preparation for raising finance or bringing in consultants for a review.

Once the manager has collected information on the organisation's internal strengths and weaknesses, and external opportunities and threats, they enter this data into a simple table (*see Table 4*), for subsequent analysis.

	Positive	**Negative**
Internal	Strengths	Weaknesses
External	Opportunities	Threats

Table 4: SWOT analysis template

PEST analysis (also known as PESTLE analysis)

PEST analysis is concerned with the environmental influences on a business. The acronym stands for the Political, Economic, Social and Technological issues that could affect the strategic development of a business.

Some possible factors that could indicate important environmental influences for a business are: environmental regulation and protection, economic growth, income distribution, government spending on research, taxation, monetary policy, demographics, government and industry focus on technological effort, international trade regulation, government spending, labour and social mobility, new discoveries and development, consumer protection, policy towards unemployment, lifestyle changes, speed of technology transfer, employment law, rates of technological obsolescence, government organisation and attitude, exchange rates, education, energy use and costs, competition regulation, inflation, fashions, stage of the business cycle, health and welfare, impact of changes in IT, economic mood and consumer confidence, living and housing conditions, Internet, etc.

Gap analysis

Gap analysis is a method used extensively in the process of designing the strategy of an organisation. With the use of this method, the gaps between the present situation and the desired state are defined, in terms of processes, procedures, technology, systems, human resources, infrastructure and organisational structure.

The steps to achieve this are:

- Selection of basic quality and quantity criteria
- Definition of desired future performance position
- Measurement of current performance
- Recognition of the gaps between the existing and the future desired position
- Designing and executing a strategy to achieve the desired position by bridging all the defined gaps.

In conclusion, the manager may use only one method, or more than one, depending on their experience and situation. The products or outputs of these methods and tools are goals, objectives and strategies.

Strategies provide the roadmap for the future. Goals are typically timeless and less specific. Objectives are more specific and for a given time period. All these may also be funded via a budget.

To provide better understanding, an example of specific strategies, general goals and specific objectives for ABCX Airlines (a fictitious entity) is provided.

ABCX Airlines – examples of strategies

Overall corporate strategy: Our overall corporate strategy is to maintain and improve our position in the airline industry, to provide the most consistent service and of the highest quality to our customers, to improve the crucial elements of our services, to co-operate with other external entities while maintaining our quality, and to reduce our costs in providing our services and improve our profitability.

Operational service strategy: The service strategy of 'ABCX' begins by selecting the performance priorities by which the company will provide services to its customers.

These priorities include:

a. Treat the customer in a friendly, polite and helpful way.

b. Deliver our services in a quick and convenient way.

c. Price the offered services in a competitive manner.

d. Provide a variety of service-delivery mechanisms to suit customer needs and expectations.

Examples of general goals for ABCX are: Increase market share, improve customer satisfaction, improve profitability, increase sales, create better products and services.

Examples of specific objectives for ABCX are: Increase customer base by 5% in each year for the next five years, decrease production costs by 10% in the next two years, increase revenues by 20% in the next two years.

3.6.5 Vision, mission and values statements

A mission statement typically describes an organisation in terms of its:

- Purpose: why the organisation exists, and what it seeks to accomplish
- Business: the main method or activity through which the organisation tries to fulfil this purpose
- Values: the principles or beliefs that guide an organisation's members as they pursue the organisation's purpose.

Where the mission statement summarises the what, how and why of an organisation's work, a vision statement presents an image of what success will look like. The values statement provides the guiding principles to enable both the mission and the vision to be realised, such as promote client independence, expand cultural proficiency, collaborate with others, ensure own competence, etc.

An example of the mission, vision and values statements for ABCX Airlines (a fictitious entity) is provided.

ABCX Airlines

Vision: The vision of ABCX is to ensure that we are the customer's first choice in air travel around the world.

Mission: The mission of ABCX is to be the best and most successful company in the airline business, also to build the world's best global alliance in air travel, co-operating with similar corporate entities, with a presence in all major world markets.

Values: ABCX will provide services to the public to the highest quality, with honesty, fairness and integrity, and with value for money for all customers.

3.6.6 Corporate ethics and compliance rules

These are the principles of conduct governing an individual or group, a system or philosophy of conduct and principles practised by a person or group, the discipline dealing with what is good and bad and with moral duty and obligation, and a set of moral principles or values.

An example of a typical corporate ethics policy for ABCX Airlines (a fictitious entity) is provided.

Corporate Ethics Policy Example

1. The Ethics Policy of ABCX Airlines ('the Company') sets forth the values and ethics of service to guide and support all employees, Board members, management and external contractors in all their professional activities.

2. In carrying out the Company's business, all personnel, External Consultants and Maintenance Contractors often learn and have access to sensitive, confidential or proprietary data, information, trade secrets and transactions about the Company, its activities, customers, suppliers or joint venture and joint project partners. This Policy prohibits the unauthorised disclosure or use of sensitive, confidential or proprietary data, trade secrets and information about the Company, its customers, suppliers or joint venture and joint project partners.

3. No Board Director, Executive, Manager, Employee or External Contractor entrusted with, or otherwise knowledgeable about, information of a sensitive, confidential or proprietary nature shall disclose, give or use that data, trade secret, information or transactions outside the Company or for personal gain, either during or after employment or other service to the Company, without the valid and proper written Company authorisation to do so given by a Manager or Employee with the authority to release sensitive, confidential or proprietary information, data or transactions.

4. No Board Director, Manager, Employee or External Contractor shall disclose or use sensitive, confidential or proprietary information owned by someone other than the Company to anyone without Company written authorisation, nor shall any such person disclose the information to others unless a need-to-know basis is established and approved.

5. All staff are required to sign at the time of employment a proprietary information agreement that restricts disclosure of proprietary, trade secrets and certain other data and information about the Company, its joint venture partners, suppliers and customers. This Policy applies to all Board Members, Directors, Managers, Employees and External Contractors without regard to whether such agreements have been formally signed.

6. All Board Members, Executive Management, Middle and Lower Level Managers, Non-Executive Directors and Employees should not have private interests, other than those permitted by these measures, that would be affected particularly or significantly by actions in which they participate.

7. All Board Members, Executive Management, Middle and Lower Level Managers, Non-Executive Directors and Employees may engage in employment and business activities outside the Company only when they are specifically authorised to do so.

8. All Board Members, Executive Management, Middle and Lower Level Managers, Non-Executive Directors and Employees must perform all duties to the fullest extent of their capabilities, ensure that all confidential information that is made available to them by virtue of their position is not divulged without written permission, avail themselves of information and material that will improve their effectiveness for all matters relating to the business of the Company or their profession, and actively participate in all activities of their Professional Association.

9. Any Board Member, Executive Manager, Middle and Lower Level Manager, Non-Executive Director and Employee who wants to raise, inform, discuss and clarify issues related to this policy should first talk with his or her manager or contact the senior official designated by the Board for ethics issues, according to the procedures and conditions established.

10. All Board Members, Executive Management, Middle and Lower Level Managers, Non-Executive Directors and Employees shall report, in person or in writing, any known or suspected violations of governmental laws, rules and regulations, or this Ethics Policy to the Company's President, Chief Financial Officer or head of the Audit Committee.

3.6.7 EA management plan

Using the EA management plan is discussed in Paragraph 3.4 'Management plan for designing and implementing an EA framework'. Alternatively the EA Team may decide to use its own way based on either the plan mentioned above and customised to their unique purposes, or use a step-by-step informal approach, or some other method or technique, without being concerned about the strict rigours of a formalised approach.

3.6.8 EA team

The EA team should be involved in the whole process of designing and implementing an EA for the specific organisation.

Using the EA team is discussed in Paragraph 3.5 'Enterprise Architecture development roles'.

3.6.9 Enterprise Architecture Repository (EAR)

The Enterprise Architecture Repository (EAR) is a web-based Enterprise Architecture knowledge repository solution that provides top executives, managers, staff and authorised suppliers and system development contractors, and other external authorised parties with a common area (e.g. database) to access for purposes of design, documentation, capture, viewing and collaboration on all the elements and information (including models, etc.) that define and describe the Enterprise Architecture of the given organisation.

Several commercial software packages provide ready-made Enterprise Architecture Repositories (EAR).

An Enterprise Repository may provide an organisation, when used in a very disciplined way, with the basis for delivering governance throughout the service-oriented architecture (SOA) life cycle by acting as the single source for information surrounding SOA assets and their dependencies.

The typical EAR contains the following information on the Enterprise Architecture specifics of the organisation, such as:

- Strategic initiatives (operating model, vision, mission, goals, initiatives, performance measures, etc.)
- Stakeholders (internal and external customers, regulatory authorities, government auditors, external auditors, etc.)
- Business processes (lines of business, business rules, investment portfolio, IT projects, etc.)
- Information flows (knowledge warehouse, data flows, data dictionary, etc.)
- Systems and services (IT systems and services provided, front office systems, back office systems, e-mail and web systems, databases, etc.)
- Technology infrastructure (operating system, networks, database management software, buildings, equipment, etc.)

- Security (policies, data privacy rules, procedures, monitoring mechanisms, logging, etc.)
- IT asset management (IT inventory control, IT asset disposition, etc.).

3.7 Other Enterprise Architecture business-related controls

In addition to formulating and documenting the Enterprise Architecture elements of an organisation, there are also other main business controls related to Enterprise Architecture that may be relevant and which will probably need to be examined.

3.7.1 Corporate governance controls

- Vision, mission and values statements
- Corporate social responsibility policy
- Corporate ethics
- Board of Directors' charter
- Corporate committees (for strategy planning, audit, benefits and personnel, IT, financial issues and business continuity)
- Corporate policies (for financial accounting, customer relations, fraud and theft, community relations, human rights, health and safety, internal audit, asset management, security, quality, production process, IT and environment management)
- Corporate processes and plans (for performance management, internal audit, risk management, business continuity plan, transaction authorisation controls, Corporate Compliance Officer)

- Strategic plans
- Strategic budgets
- Strategy implementation action plans
- Performance management framework.

3.7.2 Administration controls

- Administrative organisational controls (corporate committees, personnel job descriptions and departmental terms of reference)
- Administrative procedures (procedures manual, files, documents and records management procedures, confidential information release procedures, management reporting procedures, asset protection procedures, legal procedures, etc.)
- Administrative office controls (physical security controls, mail controls, EDI controls, facsimile transmission controls, forms controls, daily activities controls, etc.)
- Personnel management controls
- Employee management policies and procedures handbook
- Human resources (HR) systems.

3.7.3 Financial management controls

- Financial organisation controls (financial issues committee, finance officers job descriptions and budget department terms of reference)
- Financial policies and procedures (financial accounting controls policy, financial accounting procedures, financial revenue procedures and budgeting procedures)

- General Ledger controls (chart of accounts, General Ledger, trial balance and financial statements)
- Computerised financial systems (General Ledger (GL) systems, Customer Invoicing (CI) systems, Accounts Payable (AP) systems, Customer Orders/Sales Processing (COP) systems and Payroll systems).

3.7.4 Production or output controls

- Operations policies and procedures (purchasing process and procedural controls, and inventory control procedures)
- Manufacturing process controls, (new product development controls, Bill of Materials (BOM) file, Master Production Schedule (MPS), Material Requirements Planning (MRP), Inventory Master Records (IMR) File, inventory transactions file, preventive maintenance controls)
- Computerised production information systems (Material Requirements Planning (MRP) System, Cost Accounting (CA) System, Production Planning and Control (PPC) system, Enterprise Resource Planning (ERP) system)
- Quality management controls
- Standardisation procedures
- Project management controls
- Performance management controls
- Production performance measures.

Out of all these controls, the most critical ones for Enterprise Architecture purposes are:

- Business strategic goals
- Vision, mission and values statements
- Corporate ethics and compliance rules.

The EA team will analyse all these policies, controls and procedures, and record in the EAR whatever information is required to complement the Enterprise Architecture of the organisation.

3.8 Enterprise Architecture IT-related controls

The main IT controls related to Enterprise Architecture are:

- IT organisation controls (*see Chapter 1*)
- IT administration controls (*see Chapter 2*)
- IT strategic controls (*see Chapter 4*)
- IT system development controls (*see Chapter 5*)
- IT security controls (*see Chapter 6*)
- Data centre operational and support controls (*see Chapter 7*)
- Systems software controls (*see Chapter 8*)
- Computerised application controls (*see Chapter 9*).

3.9 Monitoring and review controls

Establishing IT monitoring and review controls for this area may be achieved by the IT management report, the performance measures of Enterprise Architecture and the audit review tools and techniques described later in this chapter. This may also be facilitated by following the monitoring and review activities management plan, presented in Chapter 1.

In the area of Enterprise Architecture, the typical Enterprise Architecture performance measures are:

- Corporate vision statement not crafted and communicated

- Corporate mission statement not crafted and communicated
- Corporate values statement not crafted and communicated
- Corporate ethics programme not formulated
- Enterprise Architecture framework not implemented
- Enterprise architects and other team members not functioning
- Enterprise Architecture Repository not used
- Training for Enterprise Architecture issues not given
- Enterprise Architecture budget not followed.

These performance measures could be based on a mixed system with two components: Component 1 would be an IT BSC (Information Technology Balanced Scorecard) Measurement System, described in Chapter 4; and Component 2 would be a Compliance Monitoring System for monitoring compliance to policies, procedures and related matters (e.g. budget issues).

The EA team and the IT management of the company may analyse all this information to review, assess and improve the Enterprise Architecture of the specific organisation.

3.10 Review and audit tools and techniques

Setting up and improving Enterprise Architecture controls may prove to be a very difficult task to achieve. It may require excellent human skills, advanced business and IT knowledge, adequate use of corporate and IT resources, a change management culture, several methods and a set of review and audit tools. The review and audit tools that may support IT managers and other professionals (IT auditors, IT consultants, internal auditors, external auditors, compliance officers, etc.) in establishing, evaluating and improving the Enterprise Architecture controls, and which are offered for potential use, are: Enterprise Architecture framework checklist, corporate vision, mission, and values statements checklist, and corporate strategic plan checklist. These checklists are not intended to be a complete management review or IT audit guide. EA personnel, IT managers and other professionals may choose to use only certain components of the checklists based upon the size, complexity, business, EA needs and demands, IT maturity needs and expectations, nature of the organisation's business, and levels of deployment and utilisation of IT systems.

It may be finally noted that IT managers and other professionals may choose to use only particular components of these audit programmes and checklists, depending on the size, complexity and nature of the organisation's business and deployment of IT systems and infrastructure.

Other relevant guidelines and audit tools that might be found valuable and which support the IT management, evaluation, and auditing processes are described in Appendix 3 (Monitoring IT controls checklist), Appendix 4 (Examples of IT forms), Appendix 5 (IT audit methodology), Appendix 6 (IT audit areas) and Appendix 7 (Internal audit report example).

3.10.1 Enterprise Architecture framework checklist

The objective of this checklist is to support the process of constructing, reviewing, evaluating and improving the controls identified in Paragraphs 3.3 to 3.6 inclusive.

Business processes

1 How are processes executed?
2 What data do they use?
3 Where are these processes executed?
4 Who is responsible for the processes?
5 When are these processes used?
6 Why are these processes needed?
7 Do these processes support strategic and operational business plans?

Data management

8 What does the data represent?
9 How is the data processed?
10 Where is it used?
11 Who is responsible for the data?
12 When is the data used?
13 Why is the data needed?
14 Does this data support the strategic and tactical business plans?

Business strategy

15 What data do the business units need?
16 How are key processes executed in each business unit?
17 Where is each business unit located?
18 Who is responsible for the business unit?
19 When is the business unit involved in key events?
20 Why does each business unit exist?
21 Do the business plans for each business unit support the corporate strategic and operational business plans?
22 What data does each business event need?
23 Which processes are initiated by each business event?

24 Where do the business events occur?
25 Who is responsible for these business events?
26 When do they occur?
27 Why do they occur?
28 Do the business events support the strategic and tactical business plans?
29 What data do the business plans need?
30 How do processes support the business plans?
31 Which locations do the business plans apply to?
32 Who is responsible for these business plans?
33 When does each event that supports the business plans occur?
34 Do operational business plans align with the overall corporate plan?

Enterprise Architecture (EA) issues

35 Does the EA framework support future-state IT requirements?
36 Is the EA framework consistent with the enterprise position on technology and technology market trends?
37 Does the EA framework align IT and business strategies?
38 Are any technology requirements not met by the proposed technical infrastructure?
39 Was a gap analysis used?
40 Were all business requirements documented?
41 Were future-state specifications documented?
42 Were recommendations proposed?
43 Is there an EA team to manage all EA efforts?

3.10.2 Corporate vision, mission and values statements checklist

The objective of this checklist is to support the process of constructing, reviewing, evaluating and improving the controls identified in Paragraph 3.6.5 'Vision, mission and values statements'.

This checklist covers the issues of quality of vision, mission and values statements, whether these are known to all levels of the organisation, their connection to ethics and compliance, and their documentation requirements.

Quality of vision, mission and values

1 Vision: Does the vision statement have quality attributes? Consider:
   - o Conciseness
   - o Balanced between internal and external needs
   - o Inspiration
   - o Appealing to all stakeholders
   - o Consistent with the mission
   - o Verifiable?

2 Mission: Does the mission statement reply to questions, such as:
   - o Who are we?
   - o What social or political needs do we exist to meet?
   - o What problems do we exist to resolve?
   - o How do we respond to our key stakeholders?
   - o How do we resolve social or other problems?
   - o What is our guiding philosophy or culture?
   - o What makes us unique or distinctive?

3 Values: Has a values statement been formulated and communicated to all levels of the organisation?
4 Are vision, mission values and corporate strategy implemented down to all relevant organisational levels and all critical departments?

Knowledge to all levels of the organisation

5 Are vision, mission, values and corporate strategy understood by all organisational levels, such as staff, suppliers, subcontractors, customers, management and Board of Directors?
6 Are vision, mission, values and corporate strategy supported by all organisational levels?

Connection to ethics and compliance

7 Are all corporate vision, mission and values statements aligned with the corporate ethics and compliance codes?
8 Are all corporate vision, mission and values statements aligned with the functional vision, mission and values statements, where relevant?

Documentation requirements

9 Does the Enterprise Architecture Repository contain all elements of the corporate vision, mission and values?
10 Are all corporate and functional vision, mission and values statements documented in the appropriate business manuals to facilitate easy access and understanding by all personnel?

3.10.3 Corporate strategic plan checklist

The objective of this checklist is to support the process of creating, reviewing, evaluating and improving the controls identified in Paragraphs 3.3 to 3.6 inclusive.

This checklist covers the following issues: Enterprise Architecture process, strategic management process, strategic components alignment, education and training issues, and support activities.

Enterprise Architecture process

1 Has the Board established an Enterprise Architecture management programme. Consider: establishment of an Enterprise Architecture team, executing the Enterprise Architecture process, etc.

2 Does the executive and middle management of the organisation have a process, in operating mode, for managing, reviewing and improving EA and business strategy? Consider: all appropriate levels should participate, such as Board members, executive management, middle management, etc.

Strategic management process

3 Does the strategic management process include all aspects? Consider:

- o Aligning Enterprise Architecture to business strategy?
- o Monitoring performance against the corporate strategy?
- o Interpreting performance data in a collaborative way?
- o Developing new and innovative strategic ideas and insights?

- o Formulating new short-term and long-term strategic directions?
- o Reviewing the performance measures kept by the system?
- o Updating the performance measures kept by the system?
- o Reviewing and changing the budgets, as required?

4 Are all the results of the Enterprise Architecture and strategic management process properly documented?

5 Does the strategic plan of the organisation contain all required elements? Consider:

- o SWOT analysis
- o PESTLE analysis
- o Vision statement
- o Mission statement
- o Values statement
- o corporate strategy for the business affairs and activities of the organisation at the general and appropriate functional level
- o contingency planning, disaster recovery and business continuity plan.

6 Are there corporate plans and specific targets at the specific operational level of: manufacturing/production process, business unit, project and work team?

7 Are budgets, priorities and other resources assigned to corporate strategic objectives and down to which hierarchy/management level?

8 Is there a communication system in place, assisting dissemination of strategies, policies and goals to all levels of the organisation?

Strategic components alignment

9 Are all the essential strategic components aligned? Consider:
   - Corporate predefined objectives to objectives of business units, divisions, departments, functions and projects?
   - Executive team activities aligned to corporate strategy?
   - Monitoring and reviewing activities of the Board to corporate strategy?
   - Middle management activities aligned to corporate strategy?
   - Incentives and benefits plan to corporate strategy?
   - Alignment of the following strategies to corporate strategy: human resources, IT, communications technology resources, public relations, financial and budgeting, sales strategy, production (manufacturing), research and innovation, customer support, marketing, change management.

10 Do all personnel have a full understanding of the strategy, and its relevant co-ordination, alignment and co-operation activities required at all levels of the organisation? Consider: Board, executives, middle management, employees, and stakeholders.

Education and training issues

11 Are the pertinent personnel educated and trained on EA, strategy and related performance issues? Consider: personnel educated (taught how to increase their insight and understanding of the 'why'), and personnel trained (taught how to perform a particular task/job/process).

12 Is there trust and confidence throughout the organisation that the chosen education and training strategy will work and that it will improve the results for the organisation?

Support activities

13 Are the EA and strategy execution activities formally documented, discussed, reviewed and improved on a time-specific basis (e.g. month, quarter, year)?
14 Is there a strong and sponsoring-type support at the executive level for the selected strategy of the organisation?
15 Does the quality management system support the strategy of the organisation?
16 Does the customer support system provide performance feedback information to the strategic management process of the organisation?
17 Does the Enterprise Architecture Repository contain all elements of the Enterprise Architecture, such as vision, mission, values, business strategies, goals, IT systems, stakeholders, infrastructure, customer, products, services, etc.

3.11 Conclusion

Modern organisations must always seek ways to change and improve its functions, so that it satisfies its customers and its stakeholders and maintains its optimal survival and capability to compete in its own market and socio-economic environment. The design, development and deployment of an Enterprise Architecture enables the organisation to study all elements of its operational functions and align its IT systems and operations with its business processes in a more integrated way.

In a recent study of over 150 companies,[28] the authors and researchers found that many companies didn't have the architecture they wanted. According to this study and its findings, to get the right architecture, companies should focus on Enterprise Architecture, not IT architecture. Almost all of the companies surveyed had an 'architect', usually in IT, whose job was to design and improve the architecture of the company. Yet their efforts usually focused on IT architecture, and had little impact.

Top performing companies define how they will do business (an operating model), and design the architecture of the processes and systems critical to their current and future operations. They use this architecture to guide the evolution of their core foundation of systems and processes.

In a latest online survey of enterprise architects in large enterprises,[29] among several interesting findings, the following key drivers to Enterprise Architecture implementations were reported to be predominately strategic and business-focused ones.

These drivers were:

- 'enable better planning'
- 'improve business agility'
- 'enable better Business-IT alignment'.

---

[28] See *Enterprise Architecture as Strategy: Creating a Foundation for Business Execution*, Ross JW, Weill P and Robertson D, Harvard Business School Press (2006).
[29] See Forrester Research, September 2009, *Global Annual State of Enterprise Architecture Online Survey*.

The more technical and tactical ones were generally lower in priority.

It is clear that senior management should concentrate on introducing strategic flexibility in their organisations in lieu of the traditional focus on strategic fit which has tended to be rigid and inappropriate in the ever-changing business environment. Using the Enterprise Architecture to build a stable foundation gives a company greater agility, strategic flexibility, faster time to market, lower risk and lower costs.

Enterprise Architecture is the organising logic for business processes and IT infrastructure of a company. The Enterprise Architecture provides a long-term view of a company's processes, systems and technologies, so that individual projects can build capabilities, not just fulfil immediate needs. The Enterprise Architecture is the explicit design of the systems and processes in a company that help it fulfil its operating model.

Enterprise Architecture may be achieved probably more efficiently and effectively, by implementing a suitable set of controls, such as the ones described in this chapter by reviewing, changing, adding, deleting, customising them, etc. to meet the needs, demands and operating mode of the given organisation, and operating them with continuous diligence. These controls, as we have seen, may include policies, practices, procedures, organisational structures and other tools. These controls will need to be established to ensure that the specific Enterprise Architecture objectives of the organisation can be met.

Moreover, the main Enterprise Architecture Controls and the audit and review programmes and checklists identified and presented in this chapter, may be deemed as the initial envisioning process that enables the activities of aligning the IT strategy to the business goals, processes and systems of the organisation. This way they add strategic value to the information base of the knowledge management framework of organisations (*outlined in Chapter 1*), and create long-term value for organisations.

3.12 Review questions

This set of questions may be employed by those using the controls identified in this book to assess and double-check their own conceptual understanding and practical knowledge contained in this chapter.

1. Why is Enterprise Architecture important?

Reference: Paragraph 3.2 'Purpose and main types of Enterprise Architecture controls'.

2. What is the purpose of Enterprise Architecture controls?

Reference: Paragraph 3.2 'Purpose and main types of Enterprise Architecture controls'.

3. Which are the main types of Enterprise Architecture controls?

Reference: Paragraph 3.2 'Purpose and main types of Enterprise Architecture controls'.

4. What is one formal definition of the term 'Enterprise Architecture'?

Reference: Paragraph 3.3.1 'Description of Enterprise Architecture'.

5. Which are some of the most common Enterprise Architecture frameworks?

Reference: Paragraph 3.3.2 'Enterprise Architecture frameworks'.

6. On what basis does the Zachman Framework define the Enterprise Architecture?

Reference: Paragraph 3.3.2 'Enterprise Architecture frameworks'.

7. What types of architecture partitions does the Federal Enterprise Architecture (FEA) Framework contain?

Reference: Paragraph 3.3.2 'Enterprise Architecture frameworks'.

8. What do business process narratives document?

Reference: Paragraph 3.6.3 'Business process narratives'.

9. What types of information does the Enterprise Architecture Repository (EAR) contain?

Reference: Paragraph 3.6.9 'Enterprise Architecture Repository'.

10. What does the first step of the management plan for designing and implementing an Enterprise Architecture (EA) framework state?

Reference: Paragraph 3.4 'Management plan for designing and implementing an Enterprise Architecture framework'.

11. What are the main responsibilities of the Enterprise Architecture Co-ordinator (EAC)?

Reference: Paragraph 3.5 'Enterprise Architecture development roles'.

12. What are the main responsibilities of the Enterprise Architect?

Reference: Paragraph 3.5 'Enterprise Architecture development roles'.

13. Which are the main types of business controls related to Enterprise Architecture?

Reference: Paragraph 3.7 'Other Enterprise Architecture business-related controls'.

14. Which are some of the many approaches to formulating business strategic goals, strategies and objectives?

Reference: Paragraph 3.6.4 'Business strategic goals'.

15. What does a mission statement describe?

Reference: Paragraph 3.6.5 'Vision, mission and values statements'.

16. What is a definition of the corporate ethics and compliance rules?

Reference: Paragraph 3.6.6 'Corporate ethics and compliance rules'.

17. What are the three typical levels of data models?

Reference: Paragraph 3.3.2 'Enterprise Architecture frameworks'.

18. What is the ISO 19439:2006?

Reference: Paragraph 3.4. 'Management Plan for designing and implementing an Enterprise Architecture (EA) framework'.

19. What are job descriptions?

Reference: Paragraph 3.5.1 'Enterprise Architecture Co-ordinator'.

20. What are UML and ADL?

Reference: Paragraph 3.4 'Management plan for designing and implementing an Enterprise Architecture (EA) framework'.

CHAPTER 4: IT STRATEGIC CONTROLS

Give me a point to stand on and I will move the Earth.

Archimedes

4.1 Scope

After the IT function is set up with a structure, personnel, administration, and the Enterprise Architecture is designed or improved, an IT strategy is crafted and aligned with the business functions of the organisation.

Controls at this level enable and support the future roadmap for IT infrastructure and systems, and facilitate and support the successful execution of the daily activities and operational transactions of the IT systems of the organisation. These controls include: IT strategic process controls, IT strategy implementation and monitoring controls and IT strategic performance management controls, with examples provided in some cases.

In addition to these, a set of audit programmes and checklists are presented to support the IT manager, IT practitioners, systems development and software support staff, and other professionals (IT auditors, internal auditors, IT consultants, external auditors, compliance officers, etc.) in executing and improving their duties and responsibilities.

4.2 Characteristics of strategy

The word 'strategy' comes into the English language from the ancient Greeks – it meant the art of generalship, of devising and carrying out a military campaign. Strategy, in more modern terms, is defined by Andrews[30] as the pattern of objectives, purposes or goals, and the major policies and plans for achieving these goals, stated in such a way as to define what business the company is in or should be and the kind of company it is or should be.

Johnson and Scholes[31] define four types of strategy:

- Organisational strategy as the direction and scope of an organisation over the long term which achieves advantage for the organisation through its configuration of resources within a challenging environment, to meet the needs of markets and to fulfil stakeholder expectations.
- Corporate strategy as the strategy concerning the overall purpose and scope of the organisation to meet the expectations of owners or major stakeholders and add value to the different parts of the enterprise.
- Business unit strategy as the strategy of how to compete successfully in a particular external market for goods and services.
- Operational strategy as the strategy concerned with how to use the organisational resources, processes, people and their skills effectively to attain the corporate and business-level strategic direction.

Strategy, in game theory, is a prescription (model or metaphor) that tells us what to do as the game unfolds, and specifies a sequence of decisions in any possible situation. Models and metaphors enable us to see new connections and are most important in strategy and innovation.

---

[30] See *The Concept of Corporate Strategy*, Andrews K, Irwin, Homewood, IL. (1971).
[31] See *Exploring Corporate Strategy*, Johnson G and Scholes K, Prentice-Hall (1999).

A model may be a tentative ideational structure used as a testing device. Models include such things as recipes, maps, symbols, numbers, games, paintings and even metaphors (activators of a train of associations, connections, complicated interactions and interpretations).

To conclude, in practical business terms, strategy is usually about:

- **Future direction**: Where is the organisation trying to get to in the long run?
- **Markets**: Which markets (local, national, international) in a greater sense should the organisation compete in and what kind of activities should it be involved in?
- **Customers**: What are the values, needs and expectations of the customers of the organisation?
- **Competitive advantage**: How can the organisation perform better than the competition in those markets?
- **Resources**: What resources (skills, assets, finance, relationships, technical competence, facilities, etc.) are required in order to be able to survive and compete?
- **Rules and regulations**: What external, regulatory, legal and other environmental factors, rules, regulations and guidelines affect the organisation's ability to survive and compete?
- **Stakeholders**: What are the values, needs and expectations of the stakeholders (shareholders, employees, management, unions, regulatory authorities, citizens, community leaders, etc.) of the organisation?

Strategy may exist at different levels of an organisation, such as:

- **Corporate level**: This is usually called 'corporate strategy', and is concerned with the overall purpose and scope of the organisation to meet the expectations of its stakeholders. This is a crucial level since it is heavily influenced by external parties and acts to guide strategic decision making throughout the business. Corporate strategy goes well beyond giving directions for any particular business unit or function. It involves providing guidance and vision for the overall development of the organisation. It deals with industry developments, who to co-operate with and who to compete with. Finally, it gives, usually, more emphasis to overall innovation.

- **Business unit level**: This is usually called 'business unit strategy', and is concerned more with how a business competes successfully in a particular market. It concerns strategic decisions about choice of products and services, meeting needs of customers (including citizens), gaining advantage over competitors, exploiting or creating new opportunities and potential new markets, etc.
- **Operational or departmental level**: This is usually called 'functional or departmental strategy', and is concerned with how each part of the business (e.g. sales, marketing, finance, administration, IT, production, etc.) is organised to deliver the corporate and business unit level strategic direction. Operational strategy, therefore, focuses on issues of products, services, resources, processes, people, etc.

Each organisation and its senior management and Board of Directors (or executive committee), depending on the type of organisation, market, stakeholders and socio-economic context, will decide at which levels to formulate strategies, if at all.

The important point to be made here is that the strategy provides a 'compass' and may be needed to motivate and drive the organisation and its people. Without it, an organisation can and will probably function, and at times might even be profitable. Without the strategy functioning as a 'compass', organisations may not be so effective and efficient, in the long run, in both costs and benefits to its stakeholders and society at large.

Furthermore, it may be noted that the usual time-frame for the various strategic plans is, in most cases:

- Corporate strategic plan: 3–5 years.
- Business unit plan: 1–3 years.
- Operational or functional or departmental strategy, such as IT: 1–5 years (reviewed every year).
- Budget: 1 year (for operational purposes), 1–5 years (for strategic purposes).

The IT strategic process, elements and plans, the main components of IT strategy, fall within the realm of operational strategy and are governed by the same corporate strategic aspects noted before.

4.3 Purpose and main types of IT strategic controls

The direction for overall organisational control comes from the general strategic goals and strategic plans of the organisation. General strategic plans are translated into specific performance measures, such as share of the market, earnings, return on investment, budgets, customer or citizen satisfaction, benefits to society, etc. These corporate strategic plans (whether formal or informal) define and establish the framework within which other operational business functions, such as IT, production, finance, sales, marketing, etc. are organised and operate.

In terms of organising the IT activities, within the larger framework of the organisation, several controls, such as organisational, strategic, administrative, etc. may be instituted and executed.

The purpose of IT strategic controls is to define and establish the future IT vision and mission for the IT efforts (infrastructure and systems) of the organisation, and prepare the whole IT environment to accommodate such requirements and needs of the IT systems and IT operations of the organisation.

Establishing the specific IT strategic controls to serve the needs of the organisation may be done by the formal IT committee, or the IT management and its senior staff, or some other corporate work team or group, or a combination of these (e.g. IT committee and IT management, etc.). It would be useful, however, and as it has been proved in practice, to have these controls ratified by the Board or senior management executive committee of the organisation.

The audit programmes and checklists described in Paragraph 4.8 'Review and audit tools and techniques' may be used to support the design, implementation and post-implementation review of the IT strategic controls for the specific organisation.

The main types of IT strategic controls that may be designed and deployed are:

- IT strategic process controls
- IT strategy implementation controls
- IT strategic performance management controls
- Monitoring and review controls.

4.4 IT strategic process controls

These controls are required to formulate an IT strategic plan and to obtain the necessary funds to implement the IT strategy.

The main IT strategic process controls are:

- IT strategy analysis methodology
- IT strategic plan
- IT strategic resource plans
- IT strategic budgets
- IT strategic analysis tools.

4.4.1 IT strategy analysis methodology

A methodology, in a wider context, may be thought of as the system of working methods, principles, practices, procedures and rules used in a particular discipline, profession, etc. Its usual result is an output, product, service or process.

In IT terms, in executing the IT strategic process controls to craft and implement the IT strategy, an IT strategy analysis methodology may be used.

This methodology is usually employed, depending on the conditions prevalent in the given organisation and IT area, by the IT manager (CIO, etc.), or an external consultant, or a combination of both of these, etc. This methodology may also be overviewed by the IT committee and ratified by the Board, before its use in the environment of the organisation. The IT strategy analysis methodology is similar to the corporate strategy analysis methodology, except that it is targeted wholly at IT.

The main steps of this process are:

Step 1: Preparing for IT strategy

To prepare for IT strategic planning, an organisation and its IT management must first assess if it is in fact ready. While a number of issues must be addressed in assessing readiness, the determination essentially comes down to whether an organisation's leaders and IT managers are really committed to the effort, and whether they are able to devote the necessary resources and attention to the 'large picture', in terms of IT systems and services required.

The formulation of IT strategy requires, given the current socio-economic environment:

- rational decisions regarding the future of the organisation
- corporate experience and learning
- personal experience
- interpersonal intelligence
- intrapersonal intelligence and learning
- quick and effective responses to the requirements, needs and expectations of the complex world, taking into consideration the cultural conditions and factors both within the organisation and within society
- assessing the environmental, legal, economic and regulatory frameworks which impact the organisation.

An organisation that determines, therefore, that it is indeed ready to begin IT strategic planning, may perform the following six tasks to pave the way for an organised strategic process:

Task 1: Identify specific issues or choices that the IT planning process should address.

Task 2: Clarify management and support staff roles ('who' does 'what' in the process).

Task 3: Create an IT planning committee.

Task 4: Develop an organisational IT profile (current projects, systems, hardware, services, etc.).

Task 5: Identify the information and the detailed data that must be collected to help make rational decisions.

Task 6: Carry out an IT strategic cultural readiness check (*see Paragraph 4.8.1*).

Task 7: Obtain enough knowledge and expertise on using one or more strategic tools, such as SWOT, PEST, Value Chain Analysis, etc. (*see Paragraph 4.4.5*).

Step 2: Articulating IT vision, mission and values

An organisation's vision, mission and values statements depict where the organisation is going and how to get there. Likewise, within this corporate frame of reference, an IT vision statement presents an image of what IT success will look like, an IT mission statement lets all parties know where the IT organisation is going and how IT is getting there, and the IT values statement provides the guiding principles to enable both the IT mission and the IT vision to be realised.

To gain better understanding an example of the IT mission, IT vision and IT values statements of an airline company XYZWA Corporation (fictitious entity) are provided.

XYZWA Corporation

IT Vision: The IT vision of XYZWA Corporation is to ensure that the IT function provides the best IT services to all users and therefore to enable all customers to select it as a first choice in air travel around the world.

IT Mission: The IT mission of XYZWA Corporation is to design, develop and deploy the most secure, efficient and effective IT systems and services to enable XYZWA Corporation to be the best and most successful company in the airline business. To utilise the best IT technology in the market to support the strategic goals of XYZWA of building the world's best global alliance in air travel and co-operating with similar corporate entities with a good presence in all major world markets.

IT Values: The IT function of XYZWA Corporation will provide services to the Company's customers to the highest quality, with security, honesty, fairness and integrity.

Step 3: Assessing the situation

Once an organisation and its IT function are committed as to why they exist and what they want to do, they may take a clear-eyed look at their current situation. Assessing the current situation can be done by the use of methods, such as SWOT, PEST and other methods described in Paragraph 4.4.5 'IT strategic analysis tools'. Situation assessment usually means:

- obtaining current information about the organisation's strengths, weaknesses, opportunities and threats via SWOT analysis
- assessing the environmental influences on the specific business and on its IT activities via PEST analysis and other methods

- assessing performance information which will highlight the critical issues that the organisation faces in an overall context and in terms of IT, and that its corporate and IT strategic plans must address.

These could include a variety of primary concerns, such as funding IT projects, new business opportunities due to IT, changing regulations and rules, changing needs in the customer population, new market penetration opportunities, etc. The point here might be to choose the most important issues to address, in terms of the IT strategy. The Planning Committee, for reasons of better performance and control, will probably need to agree on no more than five to 10 critical issues around which to organise the IT strategic plan.

The products of Step 3 include: a file of quality information that can be used to make decisions, and a list of critical IT issues which demand a response from the organisation.

Step 4: Developing IT strategy, goals, objectives and budget

After the vision, mission and values statements of the IT function have been confirmed and linked to the corporate vision, mission and values, it may be prudent for IT management to consider how to use them. This may be done by crafting the broad approaches to be taken (IT strategies), and the general and specific results to be sought (the IT goals and objectives). The inspiring and motivating words contained in mission, vision and value statements represent very little unless they are accompanied by IT strategy, IT objectives, IT performance measures, IT targets and IT initiatives.

There are many approaches to IT strategy crafting, such as: SWOT analysis, portfolio analysis, scenario planning, etc. (*see Paragraph 4.4.5*).

IT goals are typically timeless and less specific. IT objectives are more specific and for a given time period. All these must be funded via an IT budget. Strategies, goals and objectives may come from individual inspiration, group discussion, formal decision-making techniques, etc. (*see also Paragraph 4.4.5*). The bottom line, however, is that the leadership agrees on how to address the critical issues.

The product of this step is (a) an outline of the organisation's IT strategic direction, IT long-range goals and specific IT objectives in responding to its IT critical issues, and (b) an IT budget.

Example of IT strategic direction

The IT service strategy of XYZWA Corporation begins by selecting the IT performance priorities by which the corporation will provide services to its customers. These IT priorities include treating the customer in a friendly, polite and helpful way, deliver IT services in a quick and convenient way, provide a variety of IT service-delivery mechanisms to suit customer needs and expectations, and provide IT services at the highest quality and at the minimum cost.

Example of general IT goals

Increase market share, improve customer satisfaction and increase sales by the design, development and deployment of specific IT application systems and services.

Example of specific IT objectives

Increase sales by 5% in each year for the next 5 years and increase revenues by 20% in the next two years by the design, development and deployment of specific IT application systems and services.

Strategic direction, goals and objectives must be monitored to ensure that they achieve their planned results. In practice, strategic direction, goals and objectives may be linked by the use of the Balanced Scorecard (BSC) model, in an overall corporate sense. Likewise for IT, the IT BSC model can link IT strategy, IT objectives, etc. with measures, targets and initiatives in a very efficient way (*see Paragraph 4.6.2*).

Step 5: Completing the written IT strategic plan

The IT vision, mission and values have been articulated, the critical IT issues identified, and the IT goals, objectives and strategies agreed upon. This step essentially involves documenting all that information. Usually one member of the IT Planning Committee, the CIO, or even an external consultant will draft a final IT planning document and submit it for review to all key decision makers (usually the Board and senior IT staff). This is also the time to consult with senior staff to determine whether the document can be translated into IT operating plans (the subsequent detailed action plans for accomplishing the goals proposed by the strategic plan) and to ensure that the plan answers key questions about IT priorities and directions in sufficient detail to serve as a guide. An example of an IT strategic plan in presented in Paragraph 4.4.2.

Step 6: IT strategy implementation

Most companies and organisations know their businesses, and the corporate and IT strategies required for success. However, many corporations may struggle to translate the theory that may be contained in an IT strategic plan into action plans that will enable the strategy to be successfully implemented and sustained. It may, therefore, prove necessary to have a disciplined methodology and management attitude to implement the crafted IT strategy. Such a methodology is offered in Paragraph 4.5.1.

Step 7: IT strategy evaluation

Measuring the effectiveness of the IT strategy is extremely important. This can be accomplished:

- by a SWOT analysis (and other methods described in Paragraph 4.4.5)
- by reviewing the actual results as per the performance measures defined in the IT BSC model (*see Paragraph 4.6.2*).

4.4.2 IT strategic plan

An IT strategy is a plan to meet the organisation's information needs over 3 to 5 years through the development of computer systems and related services, such as automation and technology.

This may be needed as many private and public organisations find it necessary for efficiency and effectiveness reasons, and for survival purposes, to have a model for the future of their information systems.

This is achieved by IT strategic controls, both in terms of assessing the present needs of the organisation in terms of data and IT infrastructure, and a plan for the future.

The IT strategy includes a computer systems development plan but also the business needs and goals that must be satisfied including the environmental issues that must be addressed in support of a primary process of the business delivered through IT.

This strategy should also enable and facilitate the knowledge management framework.

The objectives of the IT strategic plan are:

- Align information systems with the competitive strategy and the Enterprise Architecture of the enterprise to enhance the company's performance.
- Ensure that IT delivers effective solutions to business problems.
- Make certain that IT provides strategic advantage to the company through cost or price benefits, innovation, value of products or services offered.
- Target the customer, supplier, and competitor needs.
- Accurately target the corporate success factors to achieve, through the use of IT, the given business objectives.

This strategic plan should be reviewed at least every year, and it should be updated and re-issued every three to five years.

It should be linked to the master business plan of the organisation.

IT strategic plan – example

1. Executive Summary: A statement of organisational objectives, a summary of the strategic plan of the organisation and how the business objectives are related to the IT function and the IT strategic plan, and a set of proposed IT Projects (new and amendments to existing systems).

2. A statement of IT strategic objectives: A full description of IT systems, strategies, vision, mission, values, objectives and data maintained by these systems, and how these systems give the organisation a strategic advantage.

3. Future projection of the organisational environment: A statement of the needs of the organisation for the next 5 to 10 years in IT systems, infrastructure, telecommunications capabilities and data.

4. Future projection of the IT environment: A statement of the future (next 5 to 10 years) IT technological developments and how these might serve the organisation.

5. Current IT SWOT analysis: Description of the strengths, weaknesses, opportunities and threats of current IT systems. Other tools such as PEST, GAP, portfolio analysis, value chain analysis, Delphi Method, critical success factor analysis, etc. can be used to augment the strategy analysis process.

6. Current IT inventory: A description of the current IT systems and infrastructure and their problems in meeting the current and future business needs of the organisation.

7. Future acquisition of IT assets: Acquisition and development schedules and budgets for hardware, software and application systems to serve the current and future needs of the organisation.

8. IT regulations: Description of IT-related regulations, standards and guidelines, with which the organisation will have to comply,

such as Sarbanes-Oxley Act, Data Privacy Legal Framework, International Accounting Standards for financial systems, etc.

9. IT risks: Description of the process of identifying and managing the IT risks in the development and deployment of new IT systems and infrastructure.[32]

10. IT infrastructure plan: A general plan outlining the general architectural design of the computer systems, telecommunication network, databases and application systems of the organisation. This will have to be linked and connected to the Enterprise Architecture of the organisation (*see Chapter 3*), and the information management quality procedures (*see paragraph 4.5.2* 'Information quality management procedures').

11. Human resources plan: A specific plan outlining the skills and dexterities required in terms of both IT and end-user personnel for the next 5 to 10 years.

12. Budget: A detailed budget for all new acquisitions and updates of all IT assets of the organisation.

13. IT organisation: A plan for the required changes of the organisational structure of the IT function.

14. IT strategic action plan: A management action plan for the implementation of the IT strategic plan. Action specifications and statements (for hardware, software, communications, cabling, database platform, organisational changes, standards, methods, tools and techniques, costs, benefits, resources, training, conversion). Action plans (objectives, responsibilities and time elements) specify how the strategic goals and strategies will be carried out. Action plans often include various objectives to be reached while achieving each goal, who is responsible for achieving each objective and by when.

---

[32] For more on risks, see (a) www.theirm.org; (b) *Beyond Compliance: The Future of Risk Management*, www.conference-board.org; (c) *OECD Principles of Corporate Governance*, www.oecd.org; (d) www.frc.org.uk; (e) www.ccgg.ca; (f) ISO/DIS 31000 *Risk management – Principles and guidelines on implementation*, www.iso.org.

15. Changes policy: A statement on how this IT strategic plan will be reviewed and updated.

16. Appendices:

Appendix A: Description of IT strategic planning process used

Appendix B: IT strategic analysis data (External analysis: PEST, TRENDS, etc.)

Appendix C: IT strategic analysis data (Internal analysis: SWOT)

Appendix D: Goals for Board Committees and Chief Executive Officer

Appendix E: IT management team and IT staffing plans

Appendix F: IT operating budgets

Appendix G: IT investments financial reports (budgets, statements, etc.)

Appendix H: IT communicating the plan

Appendix I: Procedure for monitoring and evaluation of IT plan.

Implementing this plan requires, usually, strategic resources and a budget, plus very important factors, such as discipline, proper management culture, skilled staff, etc.

4.4.3 IT strategic resource plans

Implementing any strategy, including the IT strategy, is usually a very difficult and demanding task. The management of the IT function may, therefore, need to craft strategic resource plans with all the necessary and critical IT resources (human, systems, materials, funds, facilities, equipment, etc.) required to operate all IT critical systems, networks and equipment in all offices and locations of the organisation. This plan will probably need, as good practice, to be reviewed and evaluated annually and should remain current on a continuing basis.

4.4.4 IT strategic budgets

The 'budget' (*as explained in Chapter 2*) can be considered as a tool for the strategic management control system of the organisation, and an integral part of the performance management process of the organisation. A budget generally refers to a list of all planned expenses and revenues.

In terms of IT, all management decisions, activities, actions, system development projects, application maintenance, IT solutions procurement and deployment, computer system support, outsourcing and offsourcing activities are ultimately reflected and contained in the IT budget of the given organisation.

The budgets relevant to implementing the IT strategy of the organisation, may be: IT strategic initiatives budget, IT operational budget and IT BSC implementation budget.

IT strategic initiatives budget

In general, budgets are tools that promote decision making on the basis of a top-down approach and are used to assess financial and other corporate performance at all functional levels of an organisation. IT strategic initiatives budgets also play a crucial role in the strategic management process, especially when initiatives must be undertaken to improve IT performance for a given set of IT strategic objectives. These IT strategic initiatives must be funded and evaluated through the formulation and execution of an IT strategic initiatives budget.

IT operational budget for strategy execution

The IT operational budget consists of a forecast of the expected revenues from sales of IT goods and services offered and the expenses to be incurred in the provision of these goods and services to customers (external and internal). This budget is also linked to the overall corporate strategy as the expected performance of the organisation is accomplished via the infrastructure, operations, maintenance and enhancement activities, and with the resources funded by the operational budget of the organisation.

IT BSC implementation budget

The implementation of the IT BSC for the IT function comes with a definite financial price tag. The budget for building and implementing the IT BSC should be formulated taking into consideration the following issues: personnel time, training and communication, consulting, BSC software and off-site expenses.

4.4.5 IT strategic analysis tools

Crafting an IT strategy and documenting it in a plan to be implemented, requires a set of methods, methodologies and techniques.

Methods are processes by which tasks may be accomplished, methodologies may be defined as the system of working methods, principles, practices, procedures and rules used in a particular discipline, etc. and techniques may be deemed as procedures used to accomplish a specific activity or task.

The methods, methodologies and techniques that may be utilised for the analysis and evaluation of IT strategy of the organisation include:

- SWOT analysis (described in Paragraph 3.6.4)
- PEST analysis (described in Paragraph 3.6.4)
- Gap analysis (described in Paragraph 3.6.4)
- IT portfolio analysis
- IT value chain analysis
- Delphi Method
- Screening IT strategic options
- IT Financial analysis
- Critical success factor analysis.

The manager or IT strategy consultant may use only one method, or more than one, depending on their experience, corporate environment and situation.

IT portfolio analysis

Analysis of the balance and compatibility of an organisation's IT strategic process, options and systems within a larger corporate setting, in terms of market share, growth rate, investment, product growth, etc.

IT value chain analysis

A systematic way of examining all activities within and around the organisation, such as purchasing inputs, human resources, designing products, delivering and supporting products, and IT systems, and relating them to an analysis of the competitive strength and advantage of the organisation.

Value chain analysis describes the activities that take place in a business and relates them to an analysis of the competitive strength of the business. These activities are:

1 Primary activities: those that are directly concerned with creating and delivering a product (e.g. component assembly).
2 Support activities: while not directly involved in production, they may increase effectiveness or efficiency (e.g. human resource management). It is rare for a business to undertake all primary and support activities.

Which activities a business undertakes is directly linked to achieving competitive advantage.

Value chain analysis can be broken down into a three sequential steps:

1 Break down a market/organisation into its key activities under each of the major headings in the model.
2 Assess the potential for adding value via cost advantage or differentiation, or identify current activities where a business appears to be at a competitive disadvantage.
3 Determine strategies built around focusing on activities where competitive advantage can be sustained.

Delphi Method

Assessment of whether an IT strategy is likely to be correct or needs change/improvements on the following basis:

- A moderator crafts a questionnaire and submits it to a group of experts; the experts do not know the identity of the other experts in the group.
- Each expert responds individually, without the influence of the group or other dominating individuals.
- The moderator compiles the results, and formulates a new questionnaire that is submitted to the group again (three to four rounds is the usual case), until satisfactory results are achieved.

Screening IT strategic options

Evaluation of various IT strategic options by ranking them against the expectations of resources and stakeholders, and/or by decision tree analysis, and/or by scenario planning (i.e. matching options to different future scenarios).

IT financial analysis

Assessment of profitability and beneficial impacts likely to accrue from the IT strategies by the use of various financial measures and tools, such as: payback period, ROCE, Discounted Cash Flow analysis, Shareholder Value Analysis, funds flow analysis, break-even analysis, sensitivity analysis, cost-benefit analysis, etc.

Critical success factor analysis

A technique to identify the areas in which a business and its IT operations must succeed in order to achieve its objectives and outperform the competition.

4.5 IT strategy implementation controls

These controls are required to ensure that the crafted IT strategic plan of the organisation is implemented, as planned, so that the intended results are achieved for all users of the IT systems and services.

The main controls in this area are:

- IT strategy implementation action plan
- Information quality management procedures.

4.5.1 IT strategy implementation action plan

An IT strategy that has been crafted is of no value unless it is also implemented. Implementation in this context encompasses all the processes involved in the execution of the tasks and activities contained in the IT strategic plan (*see Paragraph 4.4.2*). Its implementation may require, for efficiency and effectiveness reasons, a methodology:

Action 1: Set up an organisational structure

Setting up an organisational structure usually includes:

- establishing an organisation and its constituent parts to implement the IT strategy (if one does not exist), or restructuring the organisation (if the structure is not deemed appropriate)
- establishing a chain of command or some alternative structure (such as cross-functional teams)
- having a highly motivated leadership and workforce.

Action 2: Allocate resources

This entails allocating sufficient resources (financial, personnel, time, technology support) and managing them.

Action 3: Fund the IT strategy

Organisations successful at the implementation of IT strategies are aware of their need to fund their intended strategies on a continuous basis. This is accomplished by linking IT strategy to the corporate strategy and to the annual budget process.

Action 4: Establish and execute IT action plans

Action planning means assigning responsibility of specific tasks or processes to specific individuals or groups on the basis of an action plan with:

- chronological lists of action steps
- assignment of responsibilities to individuals
- due dates
- estimation of the resources required
- progress reporting.

Action 5: Linking and aligning strategy

Many organisations successfully carry out the above steps, and yet still fail to successfully implement those strategies. The reason, most often, is that they may lack aligning and linking. Aligning and linking is simply the tying together of all the activities (e.g. primary, support) to the Enterprise Architecture to make sure that all of the organisational resources are focusing on achieving the same results.

Strategies require linking and alignment both vertically and horizontally. Vertical linkages and alignments establish co-ordination and support between corporate, divisional and departmental plans. Horizontal linking and alignment (across departments, across regional offices, across manufacturing plants or divisions) require co-ordination and co-operation to get the organisational units in harmony. For example, a strategy calling for the introduction of a new IT service or system requires the combined efforts of co-ordination and co-operation among all business functions that this system or service is supposed to support.

Action 6: Establish the performance management process

This action includes:

- formulating and setting up the performance measurement system (e.g. BSC at the corporate level, and IT BSC at the IT level)
- entering the performance data
- carrying out the required performance analyses
- setting up a corporate awards system.

A good performance system must communicate strategy, must measure performance in real time, must offer an integrated performance project management capability, and must acknowledge and enable emotional contracting with all staff, which is so vital for linking individual commitment and activity to the attainment of organisational plans and goals.

Emotional contracting (also referred to as 'the psychological contract') is the crucial and powerful link between the organisational performance intent, and the motivations, values and aspirations of staff. This emotional contracting element is sometimes overlooked by organisations, and this may explain why people have failed to do what the organisation expected and asked them to do.

Additional details are described in Paragraph 4.6 'IT strategic performance management controls'.

Action 7: Managing the IT strategy implementation process

Implementing the IT strategy also involves managing the process.

This usually includes:

- rolling out the plan to the whole organisation
- reviewing the IT strategy in monthly meetings
- monitoring results, at the overall or detailed level, depending on the conditions, cultural aspects and circumstances of the given organisation (*see also Paragraph 4.7*)
- comparing to benchmarks and best practices
- evaluating the effectiveness and efficiency of the process
- controlling for variances
- making adjustments to the process as necessary.

When implementing specific IT systems, this involves acquiring the requisite resources, developing the process, training, process testing, documentation and integration with (and/or conversion from) legacy processes. The use of a change management methodology (*see Paragraph 5.5.1*) might be required. In order for a policy to work, there must be a level of consistency from every person in an organisation, including the management and the Board. This is what is needed, probably, to occur on both the tactical level of management as well as the strategic level.

4.5.2 Information quality management procedures

An IT strategy plan is also concerned with what data are required to be collected, processed and managed by IT so that the crafted IT strategy achieves its mission and objectives.

This is because corporate data represent the ever-changing world in which organisations operate and survive. Business functions and transactions may change, customers may come and go, organisations may die, restructure and add, change or delete functions, etc. Therefore, the data recorded to document all these (both on a manual and a computerised basis) may become obsolete and out of date. Hardware and software vendors may change their products and supplies. Government and other international regulators often make changes which affect the rules of doing business.

Without a strategic commitment to continuous ongoing information management and data quality, an organisation's data may quickly become incorrect or invalid as incorrect or contaminated data reach mission-critical business applications.

Management may need to focus seriously on the issue of managing the quality of information and the underlying data. This may be achieved by the use of a data quality management procedure, giving organisations the tools they need to understand how and when their data changes significantly from its intended purpose.

With such a procedure in place, management can recognise data problems, inspect data sources and data processes, and implement process corrections to get the problems fixed.

Data management also helps identify and correct these inefficiencies through automated, ongoing enforcement of customisable business rules, and ensures that once data obtain the highest quality (i.e. they are consistent, accurate and reliable), they give confidence to management and professionals in their information-based decisions.

Organisations must also understand that the outcome of monitoring routines (reports, exception items, etc.) can provide important insight into the processes that create bad data. By studying this information, management can do more than correct the data. It can begin to improve the overall efficiency of the organisation.

Data quality may be improved, however, by the application of a data quality improvement methodology and the use of a data monitoring tool.

Data quality improvement methodology

A typical data quality improvement methodology[33] that is offered for potential use by managers of organisations (on an 'as is' basis or customised by themselves to their own needs and frame of reference) is made up of three major phases:

Phase 1: Analyse the problem

This involves discovering the root cause of the problem and defining a path to improvement. Some problems are the result of a bad business decision, such as one that cannot be substantiated with underlying data. Other problems may

[33] For more on quality, see: (1) *Juran on planning for quality*, Juran JM, Free Press, USA (1988), (2) *Juran on quality*, Juran JM, Free Press, New York, USA (1992), (3) 'The Quality Trilogy', *Quality Progress*, Aug 1986, pp. 19–24, Juran JM (1986), and (4) *Quality, Productivity and Competitive Position*, Deming WE, MIT Center for Advanced Engineering Study (1982).

continuously erode the organisation's effectiveness but never surface as identifiable problems. This initial analysis measures all aspects of data quality, including completeness, accuracy, consistency and duplication of the organisation's data. A data quality effort also measures business rule integrity as well as the deviation from corporate standards.

Phase 2: Fix the problem

Once specific data quality issues are identified, the next phase involves planning and executing processes for the improvement of the data. This is done by:

- ensuring that edits and validations occur during original data capture
- assigning clear procedures to improve data entry processes
- conducting intensive training and performance measure refinement
- performing data checks as information flows from application to application.

Phase 3: Control the problem

After data correction, the final step is to establish a control mechanism to ensure that high levels of data quality are maintained on an ongoing basis.

To monitor and control data effectively, organisations need to investigate:

- ongoing reporting and analysis of potential problem areas
- an alerting mechanism that recognises out-of-control data records and automatically flags the data owner or responsible party.

Data monitoring tool

A data monitoring tool (typically a computerised application) requires a repository (this may be a data dictionary, *see Chapter 8*, or an Enterprise Architecture repository, *see Chapter 3*) to store and manage all existing business rules. This repository should allow authorised users to track and note trends in specific rules and their violations. Business users can view rule exceptions and track violations over time. This system should provide a single view into how, and when, data are exceeding preset quality limits, and take the appropriate corrective actions.

4.6 IT strategic performance management controls

These controls are required to ensure that the results and benefits of the implementation of the IT strategic plan are properly evaluated and improved.

The main controls in this area are:

- IT performance management policy
- Design and implementation of the IT Balanced Scorecard.

4.6.1 IT performance management policy

The IT performance management policy describes what elements the IT performance process of the organisation should handle. A typical example of such a policy might be as follows:

IT performance management policy

Policy description: It is the policy of the 'The Company' that specific IT performance considerations will be communicated to all IT employees. Individual responsibility for accomplishing team and IT departmental goals will be identified, IT employees will be provided with feedback regarding performance, performance will be evaluated and improved, and performance results will be used as a basis for appropriate personnel actions. Communication between the IT manager and the employee is essential throughout this process. IT management and employees should work together to jointly clarify how competencies apply within the work environment so that there is a common understanding about the expectations for IT performance. In addition, there should be a discussion of the IT goals of the individual work unit and the employee's involvement/contribution to unit goals for the upcoming year. The manager of each IT business unit is ultimately responsible for setting performance targets. The Board of 'The Company' is responsible for setting overall performance standards.

IT performance planning process: IT planning performance is the process of developing IT performance work plans that align individual performance with IT organisational goals. The focus must be placed on accomplishments (i.e. end results) rather than on activities. Standardised performance elements have been established by 'The Company' and are available for use in developing IT performance work plans. If the IT employee refuses to agree with the performance work plan at the beginning of the appraisal period, the IT manager should note this in the employee's file. Lack of the employee's signature and date on the performance work plan does not negate implementation of the plan.

Monitoring and evaluating IT performance: The IT employee and his/her manager will meet periodically throughout the appraisal period to provide feedback relating to performance. This feedback will be accomplished through progress reviews and performance ratings. IT management is responsible for initiating communication with the employee about actual performance and ensuring that progress reviews are held. Open dialogue between the employee and the IT manager is crucial during these discussions. Progress reviews are conducted one or more times during a full appraisal period. Normally, these required reviews will be accomplished during the midpoint of the appraisal period. The manager should make written comments concerning the employee's performance on the appropriate performance form at the time of the progress review. The purpose of the written comments is to provide for a more formal identification of the employee's performance in relation to the performance work plan. Employees are also encouraged to provide written comments on the form at this time. The employee and the manager initial and date the appropriate blocks to indicate that the discussions were held. If a progress review is not conducted, the employee has the option of contacting the manager involved to enquire of the status. All IT employees must be issued a rating of their performance annually. IT employees who have not served under established standards for the minimum appraisal period must have the time-frame extended to meet this requirement. IT managers shall discuss and consider reasonable means by which to assist IT employees in improving performance. Such assistance may include training, closer supervision, revision of assignments, and coaching, etc. If the employee's performance is still not improved, the manager will contact the servicing human resources office to determine further action necessary, such as reassignment, demotion, or removal.

Training and development: The performance appraisal process may be used as a basis for identifying the training needs of employees. Additional performance elements are particularly useful for this purpose.

Program evaluation: Ongoing evaluation of the IT performance management programme will be conducted by the Board in order to identify continuous improvement opportunities and to make adjustments to the overall policy. The evaluation of overall organisational results, employee satisfaction and consistency with mission objectives will promote the continued enhancement of a performance management program supportive of critical organisational results.

4.6.2 Design and implementation of the IT Balanced Scorecard

The whole idea of the Balanced Scorecard is that it gives you a clear picture of how well you're doing. When it comes to IT, however, the rules for keeping score can get a little murky. IT departments frequently use a set of metrics to gauge their progress, but they track performance indicators (e.g. system availability and network uptime) that are unfamiliar to people in other areas of the business. So while IT may believe it's performing well, the rest of the organisation may be less convinced of its success. The traditional mind-set of IT personnel has been usually reactive, and their focus has been limited, many times, to putting out fires and answering distress calls. That kind of orientation doesn't lend itself to strategic thinking. If a company intends to develop strategic measures for IT, the function will likely need to be told what those measures should or might be. IT departments may need to align their strategic goals (via their own IT Balanced Scorecard) with strategic goals defined by business managers (in the corporate Balanced Scorecard) in order to deliver the best results.

According to Kaplan and Norton (BSC Thinkers)[34], the BSC implementation process should start with crafting strategy, and which objectives to establish. Objectives will lead to measures. Measures will lead to targets, and these will lead to the required initiatives. All these IT goals,

---

[34] For more on BSC, see: (1) 'Linking the Balanced Scorecard to Strategy', *California Management Review*, 1996, vol. 39, No. 1, pp. 53-79, Kaplan RS and Norton DP (1996), (2) 'Putting the Balanced Scorecard to Work', *Harvard Business Review*, September–October 1993, pp. 134–147, Kaplan RS and Norton DP (1993) and (3) 'The Balanced Scorecard – Measures That Drive Performance', *Harvard Business Review*, January–February 1992, pp. 71–79, Kaplan RS and Norton DP (1992).

objectives and performance measures are probably best managed by implementing the BSC framework for the IT department.

IT BSC quick implementation approach

Step 1: Preparation

Based on the overall corporate strategy for BSC, the IT committee decides to implement the BSC, appoints an IT BSC facilitator and informs the personnel of the IT units involved to participate and support the effort.

Step 2: Management workshops

The IT BSC facilitator conducts workshops with personnel of the relevant functions in which:

- the general BSC model is explained
- the IT-related performance perspectives, objectives, targets and measures are defined
- the IT vision, mission and strategy are reviewed to assess whether they align with the corresponding overall corporate vision, mission and organisational strategy
- the IT performance measurement process is defined and agreed with.

These workshops could be repeated, if necessary, after the first pilot runs of the IT BSCs in order for the IT BSC to be constructed and implemented in the best manner.

Step 3: Design, development and testing of the pilot IT BSC

Defining and selecting the users of the IT BSC which will be used on a pilot is very important. These users must be well trained, motivated, hard workers, and must be knowledgeable in the functional area(s) where the pilot IT BSC will be implemented. Defining and developing the performance measures for the pilot IT BSC is a crucial and important process. Initially very few measures must be defined and tried in order to gain experience of the process.

The pilot IT BSCs designed in this step should be tested for 1 to 6 months. This test process also executes the IT performance measurement procedures, while communicating and reviewing the performance results, both by the performance team, and by the top management of the organisation.

Step 4: Implementation of the IT BSC

The designed IT BSCs, after the successful operation on a pilot basis, are put into productive use, IT performance data are collected and analysed, and the results of the whole process are reported, reviewed and evaluated, in accordance with the specific IT performance management policy (*see Paragraph 4.6.1*).

Step 5: Project Closure

The IT BSC evaluator and the staff involved in the quick IT BSC implementation, review the whole process with the IT committee and upper level management in order for the organisation to examine whether the IT BSC framework produces the expected results, and whether changes to the overall implementation approach should be made.

A Balanced Scorecard for the IT function

This example is based on the Balanced Scorecard Model and it describes the strategic controls for an IT department, for the four BSC perspectives, as defined by Kaplan and

Norton, with the replacement of the Internal Process perspective with the IT Systems Development perspective. These perspectives are: Financial Results, Customer, IT Systems Development, and Innovation & Learning.

FINANCIAL RESULTS PERSPECTIVE	
Strategic Objectives	Strategic Controls (Measures)
Financial Efficiency	Monthly performance against the operating IT budget % of IT projects implemented within budget Return on IT Investments
CUSTOMER PERSPECTIVE	
Strategic Objectives	Strategic Controls (Measures)
Service	% of IT projects implemented within time Time spent on customer problem resolution Network availability
IT SYSTEMS DEVELOPMENT PERSPECTIVE	
Strategic Objectives	Strategic Controls (Measures)
Improvement of business functions	Number of projects with easily identifiable benefits Number of projects with economic benefits Number of projects with soft benefits

INNOVATION & LEARNING PERSPECTIVE	
Strategic Objectives	Strategic Controls (Measures)
Development	% of IT projects developed by Standard 'XX' Number of IT staff trained on the customer business functions Number of training hours by IT staff
IT Personnel Management	% IT staff resigned voluntarily % hours of unjustified absence

Table 5: IT BSC example

4.7 Monitoring and review controls

Establishing IT monitoring and review controls for this area may be achieved by: (a) the IT management report (*see Chapter 1*), (b) monitoring detailed implementation of the IT strategic plan, (c) the IT strategic performance measures and (d) the audit review tools and techniques (*see Paragraph 4.8*). This may also be facilitated by following the monitoring and review activities management plan, presented in Chapter 1.

4.7.1 Monitoring detailed implementation of the IT strategic plan

Management might decide that IT strategy must be monitored at the detail level, for a variety of reasons, such as:

- Developing an effective (results-oriented) IT strategic plan is only part of the story of the IT strategic process.
- Getting the designed IT strategy implemented is generally the tougher part.
- Monitoring IT strategy implementation ensures that it has the intended results for the organisation and its stakeholders.
- Monitoring the implementation of the IT strategic plan (along with the IT and Corporate BSC frameworks) helps to assure that all efforts conform to the plan, and that results achieved align with the specific objectives, and that corrective actions are taken when necessary. Corrective actions may be required also by unionised employees, shareholders, public organisations regulating the particular entity, vendors, customers, etc.
- Finally, and most importantly, monitoring provides the essential link between the written plan and the day-to-day operation of the business. In many cases, the given corporate entity is connected to other corporations via inter-organisational systems, such as B2B networks.

The actual detailed monitoring of the implementation of the IT strategic plan may be carried out by an officer reporting to the IT corporate committee, or the functional IT managers, or a combination of both, sometimes with external support provided. This whole process will probably need to be overviewed by the Chief Executive Officer, and all results reported and ratified by the Board.

Moreover, various IT forms that may be used for management control, monitoring strategy, and other monitoring and review purposes are included in Appendix 4.

It is the job of the CIO to ensure that the IT reporting mechanism is fed with the relevant data of this area.

4.7.2 IT strategic performance measures

Ensuring that the activities of IT strategy are achieved may be accomplished by establishing, monitoring and reviewing the IT strategic performance and compliance measures. These measures ensure that the formulated IT strategic plan has the required and expected performance, and to take the necessary improvement actions, as needed.

In terms of compliance measures the following may be monitored, reviewed and included in the IT management report:

- alignment with the organisational strategic objectives
- customer commitments and customer satisfaction
- cycle and delivery time
- quality and cost
- financial management
- IT infrastructure availability
- internal IT operations
- IT skill availability.

In terms of IT strategic performance the measures in Table 6 may be monitored, reviewed and included in the IT management report.

IT management will need to select one small set of performance measures from all these, initially, until they gain enough experience on performance measurement.

Strategic Goals	Measures
1. Strategic Alignment	% of active projects approved by senior management
2. Customer Satisfaction	% compliance with customer service level agreements
3. IT Business Performance	% computer and network availability
4. IT Staff Innovation & Learning	% of IT staff training plans executed
IT Key Performance Indicators	Functions developed worth to users, no. of lines coded/tested/changed, hours spent on maintenance (person, program), timely delivery of reports to users, average response time, average availability time, volume of data stored, mean time between failures, no. of lines printed, volume of data maintained, no. of online transactions processed, adherence to budget, expenditures on maintenance vs. new development, expenditures on preventative maintenance, ratio of administrative (staff) costs to production (line) costs, human resource management: (Turnover ratios, training per employee (amounts, hours), average tenure within the company).

Table 6: IT strategic performance measures – example

These performance measures could be based on a mixed system with two components: Component 1 would be an IT

BSC (Information Technology Balanced Scorecard) Measurement System, described in this chapter, and Component 2, a Compliance Monitoring System for monitoring compliance to policies, procedures and related matters (e.g. budget issues).

The IT management of the company, may, depending on various aspects of the organisation, analyse all this performance and compliance monitoring information to review, assess and improve the IT strategic elements of the IT function of the specific organisation.

4.8 Review and audit tools and techniques

Establishing and improving IT strategic controls may prove to be a very difficult task to accomplish. It may require excellent management and human skills, advanced business and IT knowledge, adequate use of corporate and IT resources, a change management culture, several methods and a set of review and audit tools. The review and audit tools that may support IT managers and other professionals (IT auditors, IT consultants, internal auditors, external auditors, compliance officers, etc.) in establishing, evaluating, and improving the IT strategic controls, and which are offered for potential use, are: IT strategic readiness checklist, IT strategic planning checklist, IT BSC implementation checklist, IT strategic controls implementation checklist, IT performance assessment audit programme, and CIO Business Plan Assessment Audit Programme.

It may be finally noted that IT managers and other professionals may choose to use only particular components of these audit programmes and checklists, depending on the size, complexity and nature of the organisation's business and deployment of IT systems and infrastructure.

Other relevant guidelines and audit tools that might be found valuable and which support the IT management, evaluation, and auditing processes are described in Appendix 3 (Monitoring IT controls checklist), Appendix 4 (Examples of IT forms), Appendix 5 (IT audit methodology), Appendix 6 (IT audit areas), and Appendix 7 (Internal audit report example).

The checklists and audit programmes presented in this paragraph are not intended to be a complete management review or IT audit guide. IT managers and other professionals may choose to use only certain components of the checklists and audit programmes based upon the size, complexity, business needs and demands, IT maturity needs and expectations, nature of the organisation's business, and levels of deployment and utilisation of IT systems.

4.8.1 IT strategic readiness checklist

The objective of this checklist is to support the process of constructing, reviewing, evaluating and improving the controls identified in Paragraph 4.4.1 'IT strategy analysis methodology'.

This checklist covers the issues of: overall corporate strategy, business unit strategy, risk management, human resources management and management procedures.

Overall corporate strategy

1 What should our direction be for the future, in terms of developing new IT systems to support existing or new

products, entering (or increasing share) of markets, and developing corporate competence and capability?

2 Does everyone in the organisation (management and staff) know what our direction is?

3 What assistance and support do all employees need in order to assist in the process of formulating IT strategy?

4 How much emphasis should be put on innovating and existing products and services provided by IT?

5 Does everyone in the IT function have a clear view of the future of the organisation in terms of vision, mission, values and industry direction?

6 Does everyone have a clear understanding who our potential partners are?

7 Does everyone know who our potential competitors are?

Business unit strategy

8 What IT resources should the organisation invest in innovation?

9 What types of IT innovations should we focus on (e.g. product innovation, process innovation, service innovation, features of existing products, features of existing processes and services)?

10 How will planned IT innovation fit in and align with our product and services strategy?

11 Where is IT strategy developed (e.g. headquarter level, department level, product/service level)?

12 Does the IT function have its own vision, mission and values statements?

13 Are the IT function statements of vision, mission and values well aligned with the corporate vision, mission and values statements?

14 Is the IT strategic process well understood and communicated at the IT functional level?

Risk management

15 How is market risk managed, assuming IT products and services are developed?
16 How is the risk of IT competition managed, assuming the products and services sell?
17 How is the internal capacity risk managed? (Do we have the capacity to develop the IT products and services?)
18 How is the IT technology cost risk handled? (Will we be able to produce the planned IT products and services at a reasonable cost?)
19 How is the IT partner and supplier risk managed? (Can the IT suppliers provide the required raw materials and components? Will materials and components supplied be cost-effective? Can our IT partners take away our profits?)
20 Will regulators allow the IT products and services to be sold as the organisation envisions?

Human resources management

21 Do we have the right mix of competences, skills and dexterities in the IT and user functions?
22 Do we know what competences, skills and dexterities exist in the IT and user functions?
23 Do we manage our IT competences, skills and dexterities efficiently and effectively?
24 Do we know what IT competences, skills and dexterities we are developing?

25 Can we transfer IT competencies, skills and dexterities, when needed, to more IT strategic products or developments?
26 How do we manage IT skills, competencies and dexterities? (Obtaining them from the market? Acquiring them from within the organisation? Performing a cost–benefit analysis in order to decide what should be done?)
27 Can we innovate more and improve our strategy by improving and enriching our mix of IT skills, competencies and dexterities?
28 Does the organisation motivate all IT and user staff to develop new ideas about IT products and services?
29 Are all IT development opportunities communicated effectively?
30 Do we offer and manage incentives effectively (monetary benefits, career incentives, social rewards, motivation, etc.)?
31 Do we know when to reward individuals and when to reward groups or functions?
32 Do incentives motivate and enable people to be innovators?
33 Does top management sponsor IT innovators?

Management procedures

34 Do evaluations of individual and IT team performance consider the full range of the individual's and team's contribution to the organisations (financial results? customer support? idea development? other members support?)?
35 Are IT performance targets agreed and set with all participants in a fair and balanced way?

36 Are IT and user policy and procedural errors and conflicts identified and corrected quickly?
37 Do individuals and teams get appropriate recognition on both successful and unsuccessful projects?
38 Are individuals and teams protected from undue and uncreative interference from the highest level of management?
39 Does management efficiently and effectively create and maintain contacts and communications with key external stakeholders?
40 Are the appropriate levels of management, both on a continuous and on an *ad hoc* basis, aware of key issues, problems and conflicts?
41 Are there effective communications in the organisation (internal communication to all staff and levels of management, external stakeholder communication, customers and partners, suppliers and chain value participants)?

4.8.2 IT strategic planning checklist

The objective of this checklist is to support the process of constructing, reviewing, evaluating and improving the controls identified in Paragraph 4.4 'IT strategic process controls'.

1 Does the chosen planning method (PM) involve detailed examination of all IT activities?
2 Does the chosen PM identify beneficial uses of IT?
3 Has an IT strategic planning project (PJ) been set up (with participants from both IT and users) and is it linked to corporate goals?
4 Is the PJ sponsored by the CEO, the IT committee and ratified by the Board?

5 Were meetings held with key IT users?
6 Were meetings held with business managers?
7 Were any external consultants used?
8 Are minutes of PJ meetings kept and circulated?
9 Have business plans been linked to IT systems?
10 Have IT benefits been identified in the organisation's business plan?
11 Have existing/new IT applications been identified in terms of strategic impact to the organisation?
12 Have new corporate data been identified?
13 Have present IT systems been examined in terms of shortfalls?
14 Has the hardware platform (present, future) been examined?
15 Has the application software platform (present, future) been examined?
16 Has the database software (present, future) been examined?
17 Are IT action plans agreed and signed off by key users?
18 Are IT action plans and report (as per deliverables) reviewed and ratified by CEO/Board?
19 Is PJ plan reviewed every six months?
20 Is there an IT budget prepared (short-term, long-term) for all required approved acquisitions, internal developments and enhancements?

4.8.3 IT BSC implementation checklist

The objective of this checklist is to support the process of constructing, reviewing, evaluating and improving the controls identified in Paragraph 4.6.2 'Design and implementation of the IT Balanced Scorecard'.

1. Is there guidance, support, participation and involvement by the senior IT management in IT BSC deployment?
2. Has senior IT management set a minimum set of key performance indicators (KPIs)?
3. Is senior IT management involved in IT departmental performance measurement and evaluation?
4. Do all senior IT executives fully understand the role of each IT unit and process as well as its performance link to the overall organisation performance measurement?
5. Do all senior IT executives have adequate skills, training and character attributes in IT BSC-related issues?
6. Are IT performance measurements related to senior IT management conduct?
7. Is there an IT BSC performance measurement implementation plan comprising the following: Team establishment, Project management structure, Milestones, Allocation and management of resources, Budgeting, Communication, Change and risk management?
8. Is there a progress audit and reporting system for IT BSC performance measurement?
9. Are there IT performance measurement procedures in operation?
10. Do the human resources of each IT department, project, unit and process have adequate skills, training and attributes in IT BSC performance-related issues?

4.8.4 IT strategic controls implementation checklist

The objective of this checklist is to support the process of constructing, reviewing, evaluating and improving the controls identified in Paragraph 4.5 'IT strategy implementation controls'.

1. Have general goals and specific (annual) objectives of the IT organisation been achieved or not?
2. Have the IT goals and objectives been achieved according to the time targets specified in the plan?
3. Were the deadlines for completion realistic or were they changed?
4. Do IT personnel have adequate resources (money, equipment, facilities, training, IT systems, etc.) to achieve the goals and objectives?
5. Are the IT goals and objectives still realistic?
6. Should IT priorities be changed to put more focus on achieving the goals and objectives?
7. Should the IT goals and objectives be modified for the best time period?
8. What can be learned from monitoring and evaluation of IT activities in order to improve future planning activities and also to improve future monitoring and evaluation efforts?
9. Have IT policies and procedures been written, approved and formally established?
10. Have IT policies and procedures been reviewed in the last year and improved or changed accordingly?

4.8.5 IT performance assessment audit programme

The objective of this audit programme is to support the process of constructing, reviewing, evaluating and improving the controls identified in Paragraph 4.6 'IT strategic performance management controls'.

1. Obtain a copy of the IT performance policy and review with IT management.
2. Assess the validity and usage of this policy and up to what level (criteria, user satisfaction etc.).

3 Obtain machine statistics for systems running in the data centre.
4 Assess how IT management records operational statistics on equipment and systems availability and down time, and how these processing problems (and their resolution) are communicated to end-user and top management.
5 Carry out, if possible, a comparison cost analysis of this IT department with other IT units.
6 Assess the computer performance and capacity planning process, especially for computer hardware upgrades.
7 Review key performance indicators and their effectiveness for the particular IT function audited. Consider the following IT performance measures:
   - Development/maintenance activity: functions developed worth to users, no. of lines coded/tested/changed, hours spent on maintenance (person, program).
   - Operational performance: timely delivery of reports to users, average response time, average availability time, volume of data stored, mean time between failures, no. of lines printed, volume of data maintained, no. of online transactions processed.
   - Financial performance: adherence to budget, expenditures on maintenance vs. new development, expenditures on preventative maintenance, ratio of administrative (staff) costs to production (line) costs.
   - Human resource management: turnover ratios, training per employee (amounts, hours), average tenure within the company).

4.8.6 CIO business plan assessment audit programme

The objective of this audit programme is to support the process of constructing, reviewing, evaluating and improving the controls identified in Paragraph 4.6 'IT strategic performance management controls'.

1. Obtain the formal (or informal) company business plan for the whole group and for each company or function supported by IT.
2. Assess this business plan for each company/function that it covers, for both long-range and short-range time-frames, in terms of IT activities and projects.
3. Obtain the CIO business plan both for the group as a whole and for each company and function covered by the IT department.
4. Examine the CIO business plan to ensure that it covers both long-range and short-range time-frames, all companies detailed in the group business strategic plan, and the application systems, technology and personnel sectors.
5. Obtain the IT customer list describing which departments and functions are serviced by IT and what type of service is given.
6. Examine this customer list to ensure compatibility with the companies detailed in the business plan.

4.9 Conclusion

IT strategy may be achieved probably more efficiently and effectively, by implementing a suitable set of controls, such as the ones described in this chapter by reviewing, changing, adding, deleting, customising them, etc. to meet the IT needs, demands and operating mode of the given organisation, and operating them with continuous diligence. These controls, as we have seen, may include policies, practices, procedures, organisational structures and specialised tools. These controls will need to be established to ensure that the specific IT strategic objectives of the organisation can be met.

The main IT strategic controls and the audit and review programmes and checklists identified, and customised accordingly, may be deemed as the final envisioning and mission-setting process that prepares the whole IT environment (applications, data, infrastructure, etc.) to run IT activities and operations to support the business goals, processes and systems of the organisation. This way they add strategic value to the information processing capability and storage base of the knowledge management framework (*see Chapter 1*), and create additional long-term benefits and value for the organisation.

The 'glue' that binds the design and implementation of IT strategy, as analysed previously, is the IT Balanced Scorecard Model. This is probably one of the most used and most effective performance frameworks, achieving balance between strategy and tactical operations in private and public organisations.

According to a Canadian Study,[35] the BSC framework:

- is an effective communication tool that translates the organisational vision, mission and strategy and links them to objectives and performance targets

[35] See 'The Balanced Scorecard', *CA Magazine*, Steven Salterio & Alan Webb: (www.camagazine.com), 2003.

- assists managers in predicting and managing financial and non-financial performance better
- can facilitate and enable the review, feedback, innovation and learning process of the organisation.

The beneficial impacts of using the BSC Framework, reported by several organisations, are: financial impacts (e.g. improvement of profit, reduction of costs, etc.), and non-financial impacts (e.g. customer satisfaction, maintenance of market share, customer retention, alignment with corporate strategy, etc.).

Strategy drives the BSC and the IT BSC. The BSC drives the budget process which is also interacting with operations (inputs and results). Reporting and reviewing financial and non-financial results drives and affects the budget, the BSC and the strategy. All elements in the process are, therefore, continually interlinked and aligned in order to make the organisation better.

The process and implementation approaches for implementing IT strategic controls via the BSC framework are the instrument by which the achievement of the IT goals and the critical and significant facts, IT strategies, policies, procedures and results are disclosed to all stakeholders of private and public organisations, on a timely, open and simultaneous basis. When these IT strategic controls are exercised and executed in the best way, organisations are more efficient and effective, and in the end, more profitable and beneficial to its stakeholders, to society at large, and to the national and international economy.

4.10 Review questions

This set of questions may be employed by those using the controls identified in this book to assess and double-check their own conceptual understanding and practical knowledge contained in this chapter.

1. What is the purpose of IT strategic controls?

Reference: Paragraph 4.3 'Purpose and main types of IT strategic controls'.

2. What are the main types of IT strategic controls?

Reference: Paragraph 4.3 'Purpose and main types of IT strategic controls'.

3. What is the primary purpose of the IT committee?

Reference: Paragraph 4.4 'IT strategic process controls'.

4. Who develops and ratifies the IT policy?

Reference: Paragraph 4.4.1 'IT strategy analysis methodology'.

5. How is a typical IT mission statement described?

Reference: Paragraph 4.4.1 'IT strategy analysis methodology'.

7. What are the main steps of the IT strategic process?

Reference: Paragraph 4.4 'IT strategic process controls'.

8. What are some of the objectives of the IT strategic plan?

Reference: Paragraph 4.4.2 'IT strategic plan'.

9. How often should the IT strategic resource plan be reviewed?

Reference: Paragraph 4.4.3 'IT strategic resource plans'.

10. What issues should the IT BSC implementation budget consider?

Reference: Paragraph 4.4.4 'IT strategic budgets'.

11. Which types of controls should be included in IT strategy implementation and monitoring controls?

Reference: Paragraph 4.5 'IT strategy implementation controls'.

12. What are some of the actions of the IT strategy implementation action plan?

Reference: Paragraph 4.5.1 'IT strategy implementation action plan'.

13. How is monitoring the implementation of the IT strategic plan carried out?

Reference: Paragraph 4.5.1 'IT strategy implementation action plan'.

14. Why is a strategic commitment for ongoing information management and data quality required?

Reference: Paragraph 4.5.2 'Information quality management procedures'.

15. Which are the three major phases of a typical data quality improvement methodology?

Reference: Paragraph 4.5.2 'Information quality management procedures'.

16. Which controls are included in IT strategic performance management controls?

Reference: Paragraph 4.6 'IT strategic performance management controls'.

17. Which steps does the IT BSC quick implementation approach include?

Reference: Paragraph 4.6.2 'Design and implementation of the IT Balanced Scorecard'.

18. What are the perspectives of the Balanced Scorecard for the IT function?

Reference: Paragraph 4.6.2 'Design and implementation of the IT Balanced Scorecard'.

19. What are some of the operational IT performance measures that should be considered in assessing IT performance?

Reference: Paragraph 4.7 'Monitoring and review controls'.

20. What are the two beneficial impacts of using the BSC Framework?

Reference: Paragraph 4.9 'Conclusion'.

CHAPTER 5: SYSTEM DEVELOPMENT CONTROLS

We are what we repeatedly do. Excellence, then, is not an act, but a habit (defined as the intersection of knowledge, skill and desire).

Aristotle

5.1 Scope

After the IT function is set up with an organisational structure, personnel, administration, a well-linked Enterprise Architecture for IT systems and an IT strategy, it is ready to create quality IT products and services, by developing IT application systems.

Controls at this level establish a good operating environment for the development of IT systems and ensure the successful testing and preparation of these systems for serving the business purposes of the organisation. They also facilitate and support the successful execution of the daily activities and operational transactions of the IT systems.

A set of IT system development controls are described and include: application development controls, IT systems testing methodology, end-user application development controls, audit trails, software package controls and system development quality controls. Examples are provided in some cases.

In addition to these, a set of checklists are presented to support the CIO, the IT manager and other professionals (system development staff, end-users, IT auditors, internal auditors, IT consultants, external auditors, compliance officers, etc.) in executing and improving their duties and responsibilities.

5.2 Purpose and main types of system development controls

Designing and developing efficient IT application systems may no longer be adequate enough. To survive in today's competitive market and IT environment, both the organisation and the IT functions will probably need to perform at higher levels of excellence.

To reach these levels of excellence, an organisation and its management may need to concentrate on all functional parts of the organisation, optimising the use, efficiency and effectiveness of all of its resources, methods and systems.

In terms of IT system development, practice may show that the IT function and its system development staff or external software providers, will, likewise, need to reach higher levels of performance, by focusing on managing the following five major components of application systems development:

- Use of application systems development methodology and related products and tools
- Managing the quality of systems development
- Management of changes
- Managing systems development personnel
- Monitoring and reviewing all development activities.

All five components will need to be managed in parallel. It may be the job of senior IT management to keep all of them at a predefined level of performance, at the same time. To concentrate on one or two of them and let the others fall behind may prove disastrous in the long run.

All of these components of system development will therefore need to be controlled, for efficiency and effectiveness reasons. This is the task of System Development Controls.

The specific purpose of these controls is to ensure the safe and secure development of computerised information systems and the protection from harm or other potential damage of the organisation's information and data maintained by these systems.

The main types of system development controls are:

- Application systems development process controls
- System development quality controls
- Change management controls
- Systems development personnel controls
- Monitoring and review controls.

5.3 Application systems development process controls

Application systems basically process and store data in electronic mass storage files, devices, etc. produce reports and provide processed information to all authorised end-users and systems.

These are usually carried out by application software developed in a certain way, and in accordance with a disciplined process. A software development process is an approach used in developing application software. Application software can be developed either internally (within the organisation by staff of the IT function, or external contractors working under the management and standards of the organisation) or externally (by the provision of a standard application package provided by a software vendor).

The application systems development process controls of an organisation may be developed and implemented by the IT manager, or other officer in charge of IT (e.g. CIO), overviewed by the IT committee, and ratified by the Board. The audit checklists provided in Paragraph 5.9 may be used to support the design, implementation and post-implementation review of the application development controls for the specific organisation.

The typical application systems development process controls are:

- IT systems development methodology
- System development products
- IT systems testing methodology
- End-user application development controls
- Audit trails
- Software package controls.

5.3.1 IT systems development methodology

There are several software development models available for designing, developing and implementing IT (or application) systems. Some of these are: Waterfall model, V-model, spiral model, process improvement models (CMMI, ISO9000, ISO15504,[36] etc.), formal mathematical methods, development models (object-oriented, iterative,

---

[36] For more on CMMI, see www.sei.cmu.edu/cmmi. For more on ISO standards, see www.iso.org.

incremental, agile, RUP, etc.), prototyping, etc. All these models describe the software development processes as a set of different tasks or phases to be accomplished in order to create and deploy an IT system for an organisation.

A typical software development process that may be used, for both internal and external development, extending the aspects of the first model (waterfall model), is usually made up of the following phases:

Phase 1: Planning of system

The activities of this phase are:

- determine the feasibility of whether the application project should proceed or not
- produce a high-level overview document of the project which relates to the application system project requirements and scope.

The product of this phase is an IT System Feasibility Document (*see Paragraph 5.3.2* 'System development products').

Phase 2: Definition of system

The activities of this phase are:

- define 'what', 'when', 'who', and 'how' the application project will be carried out
- expand on the high-level project outline
- provide a specific and detailed project definition
- prepare and issue an RFP (if system is obtained from the market)
- select a software project development team

- appoint an IT project manager for the particular system.

The products of this phase are: an RFP document (if appropriate), an IT project plan, a business requirement document and an IT requirements document (*see Paragraph 5.3.6*).

Phase 3: Analysis of system

The activities of this phase are:

- Enable the development team to understand and document the users' needs for the system, possibly using a variety of tools (such as interviewing the users, business focus group presentation, brainstorming, Delphi method, Strategic Questioning method, analysis of the present system in terms of data analysis, document analysis, operations observing, participation in the business processes, etc. critical success factors (CSFs) analysis, etc.).
- Document in detail the scope, business objectives and requirements of the system.
- Emphasise what the system is to do.
- Include analysis of what data needs should be replicated to the data warehouse.

The products of this phase are a systems analysis and design document, a business requirements document, and an IT requirements document.

Phase 4: Design of system

The activities of this phase are:

- Describe how the proposed system is to be built.

- Document the system design and the technical requirements required for the system to operate in and the tools used in building the system.
- Describe the movement of data between operational databases and the data warehouse.

The products of this phase are a Systems Analysis and Design Document (*see Paragraph 5.3.2* 'System development products').

Phase 5: Construction of system

The activities of this phase are:

- Deal with the development, program coding, unit testing and integration testing of the system modules, screens and reports and data replication to the data warehouse if required.
- Develop and complete the technical documentation, and the user procedures and user documentation for the system implementation phase.

The products of this phase are a system with software coded and tested, and the system-required documentation. Details on a testing methodology, procedure and plan that may be used are depicted in Paragraph 5.3.3 'IT systems testing methodology'. An (indicative) example of system-required documentation is presented in Paragraph 5.3.2 'System development products'.

Phase 6: Implementation of system

The activities of this phase are:

- Prepare the production environment for the system implementation and production data loading.
- Carry out the implementation of the developed system through final user acceptance testing (or parallel run) to full production and data warehouse population.
- Run the system in full production mode.
- Maintain the system and correct the processing errors due to the incorrect logic of software, or data inputs, or changes to business rules, etc.

The product of this phase is a full running system.

Phase 7: Post-implementation review of system

The activities of this phase are:

- Review the results and performance indicators of the system after the first full year (usually) in full production status.
- Carry out interviews with the main end-users to evaluate their perception and understanding of the results and effect of the system in their business operations.
- Assess whether the system has satisfied, and up to what level, the initial user and management specifications.
- Request, in some cases, a security penetration series of tests be executed by a specialist IT security group to evaluate the system's potential security gaps.

The product of this phase is a report for potential system changes and improvements, produced by a manager, auditor, analyst or consultant (*see Paragraph 5.3.6* 'Software package controls').

All these phases may make up a typical IT Systems Development Methodology. One example is the SSADM

Methodology[37] which is made up of seven stages (zero to six): feasibility, investigation of current environment, business system options, definition of requirements, technical system options, logical design and physical design. Methodologies usually provide guidance to IT project managers and development staff on all aspects of managing their IT development projects.

If IT management wishes to set up, for various management control reasons and cost–benefit purposes, an IT project for the development of a system, they may do so by using a classical approach. This typical approach may view an IT systems development project as made up of seven major stages:

- IT project proposal
- IT project initiation
- IT project planning
- IT project execution (feasibility, analysis, design, development, implementation, evaluation)
- IT project management
- IT project termination
- IT project closure.

A large variety of system development methodologies have evolved over the last 20 years, each with its own strengths and weaknesses. One system development methodology may not necessarily be suitable for use by all IT projects and all organisations. Each of the available methodologies is probably best suited to specific kinds of IT software projects, based on a various cultural, technological,

---

[37] SSADM® is a Registered Trade Mark of the Office of Government Commerce in the United Kingdom, www.ogc.gov.uk.

organisational, management, project and team considerations and conditions.

Every organisation and its IT management, therefore, may need to try and benchmark several, or get expert advice, before using one or more of these for one IT development effort, and before they adopt it as a standard for all their IT software projects.

5.3.2 System development products

As was outlined previously, each phase of the software development process creates one or more system development products.

These system development products usually include the following (as an indicative example only):

- IT system feasibility document
- IT systems analysis and design document
- software code (source listing, source code, object code)
- application documentation (e.g. programming and user guides).

Examples of other relevant documents, that may be used, are presented in Paragraph 5.3.6 'Software package controls'.

Feasibility study

The IT system feasibility document is the result of the execution of a set of procedures carried out during the feasibility study. Here, the systems outlined during the IT strategic planning process are analysed as to whether they are feasible or not, before approval is given by the management and the users of the organisation to develop and implement the systems.

The main steps to create the feasibility document include:

- determine the nature and extent of the problems to be solved by the IT system
- determine the feasibility of any proposed development (technical, operational, economic)
- propose a general plan of action to solve the problem
- create a detailed plan of action for conducting the analysis phase
- devise a summarised plan for the entire IT system development project.

IT system feasibility document – example

1. Executive summary: A summary of the findings of the feasibility phase for the proposed IT system and the recommendations of the analyst.

2. Problem description: A detailed description of the problems studied, along with a summary of the interviews, observations, current systems used, and related documentation describing the problems studied.

3. Solution specifications: A detailed statement of the objectives that a new or revised IT system is to achieve, and a statement of the constraints and restrictions placed on the development of the IT system. The description of a new or revised IT system's main characteristics.

4. Feasibility specifications: A detailed statement of the technical (can the problem be solved with the current technology), operational (does the organisation have the personnel, procedures and work methods to implement the proposed system), and economic feasibility (what are the costs and benefits of the proposed solution) of the proposed IT system.

5. IT system development plan: A detailed statement of the scope of the development, a complete list of tasks to be accomplished, a timetable for accomplishing the tasks, and a human resources plan (systems development users, outside consultants, etc.) for the next phase of the IT system to be developed.

6. Recommendations: A detailed statement by the analyst of the recommendations to the management of the organisation regarding the proposed IT system. These recommendations should depict both the documented opinion of the analyst whether the next phases of development should be approved (or not) as well as the strategy on how to proceed to the next phases.

7. Appendices: The appendices to the main feasibility document should contain all the documentation in a very analytical form regarding the activities of the analyst during the feasibility stage, such as schedules of the interviews, minutes of meetings, various memoranda and copies of all electronic messages, planning documents (GANTT, PERT, project schedules, etc.), documentation reviewed (list of procedures, systems, technologies, data flow diagrams, etc.) and detailed feasibility data (economic feasibility tables, such as NET PRESENT VALUE analysis, etc.).

Systems analysis and design

The IT systems analysis document (systems analysis and design document) is the result of the execution of a set of procedures carried out during the requirements analysis, where the systems analyst will set out in detail what the system will do. The main steps to create the Systems Analysis and Design Document include:

- gathering the user needs (via interviews, questionnaires, group reviews, brainstorming, use of the Delphi method, etc.)

- extracting the requirements from the existing information systems (via data analysis, document analysis, observation, participatory work, etc.)
- deriving the requirements from the business functions (via business systems planning, use of the critical success factors method, use of the decision analysis method, prototyping, etc.)
- describing the future 'logical' and 'physical' system (via the use of data flow diagrams (DFDs))
- documenting the data volumes, interfaces, outputs and the control requirements of the system.

IT systems analysis and design document – example

1. Executive summary: A summary statement of the costs, effectiveness, impact and other benefits of the proposed system.

2. Systems analysis and design summary: A summary statement of the facts and other data gathered during the systems analysis and design phase, the analysis performed and the overall design proposed.

3. User requirements of the proposed system: A detailed statement of the user requirements for the new (proposed) system in terms of: inputs of the system, processing steps (translate inputs into outputs), outputs (screens, reports, data to be maintained), volumes of data and databases, and performance requirements, interfaces required with other systems, and control measures specific to the system (such as transaction authorisation, access, data quality, security controls, back-up and recovery controls, etc.).

4. Future 'logical' system description: A detailed narrative of the future 'logical' system as well as the DFDs, data dictionary descriptions, and other documentation supporting the 'logical' system, and a summary statement of the improvements brought about by the 'logical' system design.

5. Future 'physical' system description: A detailed narrative of the future 'physical' system as well as the DFDs, flowcharts and other documentation supporting the 'physical' system, and a summary statement of the improvements brought about by the 'physical' systems design.

6. System constraints: A detailed statement of the constraints of the new (proposed) system at the level of hardware, software, interfaces, legal environment, contractual obligations, risks involved in system implementation and security conditions.

7. Programming phase budget: A detailed statement of the budget requirements for the programming phase of the new (proposed) system, and the requirements for personnel (both IT and user levels).

8. Appendices: All supporting documentation of the systems analysis and design phase, such as minutes of meetings, documentation review list, user approvals, summaries, tables, graphs, diagrams, charts, costs, effectiveness analysis, programming phase time schedule, etc.

Application documentation

The systems development methodology should include procedures to ensure that full and comprehensive documentation is developed for each application to enable the efficient, effective and best use, operation, maintenance and technical problem support of the application.

Application documentation – example

1. Application system documentation: The system's purpose, system flowcharts, data flow diagrams, entity-relationship diagrams, narratives, etc.

2. Program documentation: The purpose of each program, program flowcharts, decision tables, structure charts, source code listings, description of inputs, files, databases and outputs,

test data and results, and the history of program changes and approvals to such changes. If spreadsheets are involved, these should also follow the same documentation principles.

3. Computer operations documentation: Input source, form and receiving instructions, output form and distribution instructions, computer operation instructions including set-up, required files, restart procedure and error handling.

4. End-user documentation: Application description, procedures for completing source documents, input screen, and how-to-do manual and automated processing, description of manual and computerised files, data and report descriptions, explanation of controls, error handling instructions and procedures for distributing output data and reports.

5.3.3 IT systems testing methodology

As IT systems testing is crucial to the application development process, it needs the effort, focus and disciplined attention of IT systems development staff for the development of better IT systems.

Testing of systems and applications is critical to the success of any IT development project. In order to attain a successful systems implementation, all aspects of the testing phase need to be reviewed to incorporate not only the software but also the IT elements. IT systems testing involves operation of a system or application under controlled conditions and evaluation of results. The controlled conditions should include both normal and abnormal conditions. Testing should intentionally attempt to make things go wrong to determine if things happen when they shouldn't or things don't happen when they should.

Testing should be performed through the system development process on the basis of:

- an IT testing standard and methodology[38]
- an IT application test plan and an acceptance procedure
- a set of testing tools (e.g. Assess Mate for Java, Automated Test Facility Packages, Bound Checkers for memory and queue problems, test applications written in the environments of Windows APIs with ActiveX, DirectX, Win32, X-Designer, Dumpbin, Netcat, Ethereal, Brutus, Whisker, Appscan, etc.).

The actual IT system testing controls may be developed and implemented by the IT manager, in charge, overviewed by the IT committee, and ratified by the Board. The audit checklists provided in Paragraph 5.9 may also be used to support the design, implementation and post-implementation review of the application development controls for the specific organisation.

Various IT forms that may also be used for management control, system development monitoring and other quality monitoring purposes are included in Appendix 4.

The main IT system testing controls are:

- IT application acceptance procedure
- IT application test plan.

---

[38] E.g. BCS standard for software testing, *www.testingstandards.co.uk*, USA Department of Health General Principles of Software Validation, *www.fda.gov/cber/guidelines.htm*, and *Risk-Based E-Business Testing*, Gerrard P and Thompson N, Artech (2002).

IT application acceptance procedure

The usual steps of a typical application acceptance procedure, executed by both IT staff and end-users, are:

1 Examination and review of all contractual arrangements, activities and deliverables in terms of what has been done up to now
2 Analysis and assessment of the risks to examine and establish what functions of the system should be tested further
3 Establishment of a dedicated test environment
4 Design of all tests
5 Execution of tests which should include: testing of system designs, testing of code as it is developed, testing of integration when components are ready, testing of interfaces, user acceptance testing, both 'black box' testing (testing from an external perspective) and 'white box' testing (testing from an internal perspective with access to source code and architecture documents), regression analysis and testing, negative testing (how a system responds to incorrect or inappropriate information) and testing of data conversion routines
6 Review and examination of all results
7 Documenting and filing the test process and results
8 Logging and resolving all issues and errors
9 Reporting all test results
10 Filing all intermediate and final test data and results.

IT application test plan

The contents of a typical application test plan are the following (as an indication only):

- Testing Strategy.

- Detailed testing design plan for each unit (program, subsystem, etc.).
- Clear definition of testing responsibilities and organisation.
- Components to be tested (function (system should meet specified business requirements), load stress, volume, hardware configuration and portability, database loading and data conversion, security, performance, availability, entering transactions out of sequence to identify whether software reacts correctly, recovery, hardware maintainability, interfaces, documentation, and human factors).
- Expected deliverables of tests.
- Formalised test procedures (including test scenarios, forms and test data). Procedures should include the following: preparing appropriate test data, ensuring availability and configuration of software under test, loading initial data, inputting test data, logging of issues, error resolution and comparison of results against those expected.
- Post-implementation review.

Examples of the forms to execute and document the tests, and other tools to aid this effort are given in Appendix 4.

5.3.4 End-user application development controls

An end-user is any person who interacts directly with a computer or a network system. This includes both those persons who are authorised to interact with the system and those people who interact without authorisation. Note that users do not include operators, system programmers, technical control officers, system security officers and other system support personnel.

These individuals must be controlled as they may cause damage to the organisation beyond repair (sometimes).

The actual end-user application development controls may be developed and implemented by the IT manager in charge, overviewed by the IT committee, and ratified by the Board. The audit checklists provided in Paragraph 5.9 may be used to support the design, implementation and post-implementation review of the end-user application development controls for the specific organisation.

The main purpose of these controls is to ensure that the end-users, especially when they are using personal computers to do their daily business tasks, are protected from harm, damage and errors. The principal controls in this area include:

- Spreadsheet applications control. As computer-based spreadsheet applications proliferate, especially with personal computers, organisations must be very careful to implement controls that will preclude potential wrong decisions and fraud from using data produced by undocumented and untested spreadsheet applications. The usual controls may be standard a spreadsheet design template for all spreadsheets of the organisation, testing rules and strategies for each spreadsheet used, documentation for each spreadsheet, and complete list of spreadsheets used for management decision making.[39]

---

[39] For more on controlling spreadsheets, see: (1) 'Preventing Errors in Spreadsheets', *Internal Auditor Magazine*, Feb. 1988, p. 42–47, Kee RC and Mason Jr JO (1988); and (2) 'Building Structured Spreadsheets', *Journal of Accountancy*, Oct. 1989, p. 131, Stone, DN and Black RL (1989).

- Other end-user applications control. As with spreadsheet applications, all other applications developed by end-users (e.g. database system for office application) should follow the above-mentioned controls.

5.3.5 Audit Trails

The actual audit trail controls may be developed and implemented by the IT manager, in charge, overviewed by the IT committee, and ratified by the Board. The audit checklists provided in Paragraph 5.9 may be used to support the design, implementation and post-implementation review of the application development controls for the specific organisation.

Audit trails are specialised records kept for reasons, such as:

- monitoring of transactions
- updates of databases and files
- data recovery
- error analysis
- detection and resolution
- fraud detection
- security incidents monitoring.

The various audit trail types are: system software and hardware logs, application journal logs for updating databases and classical files, security monitoring logs for network traffic, etc.

Audit trails in application systems[40] record the activity by system or application process and by user activity.

In conjunction with appropriate mechanisms, software tools and procedures, audit trails provide a means to help accomplish several security-related and fraud-prevention objectives, including individual accountability, reconstruction of events, intrusion detection and problem identification.

An audit trail must include sufficient information to establish what event occurred and who (or what) caused them. The scope and contents of the audit trail will balance security needs with performance needs, privacy and costs.

At a minimum the contents of the audit trail record must contain:

- Type of event
- When the event or transaction occurred (time and day)
- User ID associated with the event or transaction
- Program or command used to initiate the event or transaction
- Copy of the transaction
- Copy of the database record before and after the update process.

---

[40] As per (1) 'IT Audit Basics: Auditing OS and Database Controls', *ISACA Journal*, Vol. 3, 2003, pp. 32–35, Sayana AS (2003), and (2) 'Information Quality Standards in Computerized Systems', *IDPM Journal*, Vol. 1/1, 1/1995, Kyriazoglou J, IDPM Society, England.

5.3.6 Software package controls

A software development process is an approach used in developing application software. Application software can be developed either internally (within the organisation by staff of the IT function, or external contractors working under the management and standards of the organisation) or externally (by the provision of a standard application package provided by a software vendor).

These actual software package controls that may be required to control this process better may be developed and implemented by the IT manager, in charge, overviewed by the IT committee, and ratified by the Board. The audit checklists provided in Paragraph 5.9 may be used to support the design, implementation and post-implementation review of the application development controls for the specific organisation.

The main objective of software package controls is to ensure that software packages to serve business applications are selected on the basis of approved predefined standards and to prevent the potential case of fraud and misuse of resources in the purchase process. The purchasing process for software packages should follow the steps identified in Chapter 2 (IT administration controls).

The main controls for software package purchases are:

- Software package project plan
- Software package feasibility study
- Software package vendor proposals evaluation
- Software package business requirements document
- Software package technical IT requirements document
- Software package testing plan
- Software package application documentation

- Software package post-implementation review.

Software package project plan – example

The contents of a software package project plan may be:

Project Structure

Project Management Methodology

Project Deliverables

Conditions for Acceptance of Deliverables

Milestone Decisions

Issue Escalation Procedure

Project Schedule

Project Cost Management Procedure

Project Cost Estimation

Project Cost Budget

Project Quality Plan

Project Quality Objectives

Project Quality Control Procedure

Project Organisation

Project Human Resources

Project Communication Plan

Project Communications Objectives

Roles and Responsibilities of Communications Staff

Risk Management Plan

Risk Resolution Procedure

Software package feasibility study – example

The contents of a software package feasibility study are:

Executive Summary

Organisational Needs

Proposed Solutions (at least two or three)

Solution 1 (Description, Benefits, Cost, Resources Required, Impacts, Risks, Constraints)

Solution 2 (Description, Benefits, Cost, Resources Required, Impacts, Risks, Constraints)

Solution 3 (Description, Benefits, Cost, Resources Required, Impacts, Risks, Constraints)

Overall Recommendations

Evaluation of Proposed Solutions and Comparative Analysis

Recommended Solution

Concepts and Definitions

Appendices

References

Software package vendor proposals evaluation – example

The contents of a software package vendor proposals evaluation are:

Executive Summary

Evaluation Criteria

Evaluation of Proposals

Proposed Solutions

Evaluation of Vendor Capability (by vendor)

Evaluation of Solution Suitability (by vendor)

Evaluation of Each Vendor (vendor profile, quality procedures, vendor organisation and personnel, turnover over the last 3 years, training, support, maintenance and development services provided, software development methodology, security issues coverage, etc.)

Evaluation of Development Plan (by vendor)

Financial Evaluation of Proposed Solutions (by vendor)

Evaluation Results for all Vendor Proposals and Solutions

Software package business requirements document – example

The contents of a software package business requirements document for a computerised application are:

Executive Summary

Business Strategic Objectives

General IT Strategic Objectives

Project/IT System Objectives

Project/System Constraints

Summary Description of Existing System

Model of Present System

Evaluation of Present System

Requirements and Needs of New System

Main Procedures of New System

Data Model of New System

Security and Control Requirements of New System

Performance Requirements of New System

Evaluation of Alternate Solutions

Recommended Solution

Draft Implementation Plan for Recommended Solution

Solution Summary Description

Forecasted Costs of Recommended Solution

Solution Constraints

Forecasted Benefits

Solution Deliverables Plan

Solution Milestones

Terms and Definitions

Appendices

References

Software package technical IT requirements – example

The contents of a software package technical IT requirements document for a recommended computerised application may be:

Technical IT Framework

Technical IT Specifications

Technical Constraints

System Standards

Architectural Framework

Evaluation of Present Architecture
Topology of Present Network
Present Hardware and Software
Specifications of Recommended Architecture
Topology of Recommended System
Topology of Recommended Network
Data Architecture of Recommended System
Hardware and Software Requirements of Recommended System
Interface Requirements of Recommended System
Security Requirements of Recommended System
Development Environment Specifications
Testing Environment Specifications
Implementation Environment Specifications
Architectural Environment Specifications
Technical Data Design
Database Design
Functional Requirements Specifications
Technical Requirements Specifications
System Resource Requirements
System Capacity Requirements
Contingency Plan
Data Conversion Requirements
Data Conversion and Data Loading Plan
Terms and Definitions
Appendices
References

Software Package Testing Plan

A software package testing plan might be created on the basis of the 'IT Application Test Plan' contained in Paragraph 5.3.3 'IT systems testing methodology'.

Software Package Application Documentation

A software package application documentation might be created on the basis of the 'IT Application Documentation' contained in Paragraph 5.3.2 'System development products'.

Software package post-implementation review – example

The contents of a post-implementation review for a software package computerised application may be:

Objectives and Scope of Review

Evaluation of System Functionality and Performance

Economic Evaluation

Findings

Conclusions and Recommendations

Evidence Collected

Appendices.

The implementation of ready-made software packages has proven to be quite a demanding task. The management of the organisation will have to consider very carefully the potential advantages, costs, benefits and disadvantages of this approach before they embark on the 'voyage' of ready-made solutions. In that case, the above-mentioned controls, as well as other resources and support techniques identified during the planning process, might prove very supportive and help them to get the job done in a better way.

5.4 System development quality controls

Quality controls, in general, are best carried out as close to where the activity takes place as possible, because in this way poor quality can be spotted quickly and rectified before it has progressed too far down the system. The same concept also applies to IT development activities in general.

This means that all system development activities may follow the IT quality principles[41] outlined next, in order to provide information systems, probably, of the highest quality.

The actual system development quality controls may be developed and implemented by the IT manager in charge, overviewed by the IT committee, and ratified by the Board. The audit checklists provided in Paragraph 5.9 may be used to support the design, implementation and post-implementation review of the application development quality controls for the specific organisation.

The IT quality principles are:

Integrity: The inputs, processes, interactions, processing rules, logical conditions and information presentations of the said information system should always, and without exceptions, be designed and executed in a systemic way so

---

[41] See also 'Information Quality Standards in Computerized Systems', *IDPM Journal*, Vol. 1/1, 1/1995, Kyriazoglou J, IDPM Society, England.

as to minimise the possibility of human and machine errors, and produce, always, the same results.

Accuracy: Processing rules and conditions of logic on single data validation and cross-data contextual validity should be well depicted, and documented within the given program as well as in the documentation.

Trustworthiness: The information collected, processed and presented should always be reliable. Procedures should exist to provide security and recoverability at all times.

Consistency: A set of inputs, given a specified state of the information system and the databases, should always result in the same set of processes and outputs.

Completeness: The particular information collected, processed and presented should be treated in a systematic way as a whole unit. Other hidden, embedded, indirect and assumed knowledge, effects or references should be totally avoided.

User-oriented ergonomy: The information collection, viewing, storing and reporting aspects must be fully tailored to the needs of the end-users.

Easy to use: All components of the information system (screens, reports, equipment, documentation, etc.) should be easy to use. Design and use standards should apply to all screens and reports of the system (e.g. company name, date, program name, time and date, help line, etc. should appear in a uniform way in all screens and reports, etc.).

Relevant: The information provided to the end-user should always be relevant, i.e. according to whatever he/she requires at the given time.

Timely: The information requested and provided to the end-user should always be given immediately (online systems), or within the time constraints specified at the given time (batch reports).

Understandable: The information presented to the end-user in terms of screens, reports, documentation, online help, etc. should always be immediately understandable.

Significant: The significance of the information provided must be immediately recognisable by the end-user. Non-significant data should never be collected, processed and presented.

As IT quality controls are best carried out as close to where the activity takes place as possible, the actual IT quality controls implemented will need to be identified at the application program level (*see Chapter 9*).

All these IT quality principles are usually contained in an IT quality policy or plan, and in the methodology, procedures, products developed and forms used.

5.5 Change management controls

Change management, in general terms, would typically be made up of identifying and recording of changes, assessing the impacts, costs, benefits and risks of proposed changes, developing business case justification and obtaining senior management approval for these changes, and managing and co-ordinating change implementation, monitoring and reporting activities.

The development and deployment of IT systems, in many organisations and operating environments, impacts (to a small or large level) the everyday business operating procedures and the jobs of the end-users themselves, requiring changes to both the impacted user operating procedures and the jobs themselves.

This may be best accomplished, depending on the characteristics of operation of the given organisation and its culture, by the use of a change management process.

This process may be made up of three parts:

- a change management methodology
- a communications policy
- an end-user awareness procedure.

5.5.1 Change management methodology

Change management, in IT system development terms, is typically be made up of the following activities:

- Identifying and documenting the required changes by examining the current IT environment with respect to organisation culture, communication, organisation design, job design, infrastructure, personnel, skills and knowledge, people/machine interfaces, and incentive systems
- Identifying the best approaches of implementing the changes
- Identifying a senior manager responsible for supporting and coaching the whole change implementation effort
- Identifying the level of change acceptance within the organisation, by interviews, surveys, group discussions and involvement of major key players in change implementation
- Identification of the various roles in managing IT changes

- Establishing and maintaining successful support for the IT change management project
- Establishing commitment from all staff involved via effective communication
- Identification and management of resistance to change
- Development of co-operation through team work.

The change management team responsible for implementing changes in a specific organisation will probably need to customise the above methodology to their needs and particular demands, or even add, delete or change one or more of its activities, or even use another methodology, in order to have the most optimal effect of implementing changes in their style and management culture.

5.5.2 Communications policy

An example of a typical communications policy may be:

> The Company communicates with those most directly affected first. Our organisation's first obligation is to the health, welfare, and safety of the people most directly affected, our employees, and the protection, restoration, and recovery of company operations and mission-critical IT systems. In terms of systems developed and deployed, we will: respond quickly, act conclusively, take appropriate responsibility, ask for help and understanding, inform company employees immediately, show concern, strive for transparent decision making, behaviour, and results, be open to suggestion, explain to the staff affected as soon as possible how their jobs may be affected by the said system, and use simple, direct and positive messages in implementing all approved changes.

5.5.3 End-user awareness procedure

The procedure for communicating information related to the activities of the changes to the organisation, should include, as a minimum, the following activities:

- Formulate and disseminate to all staff and levels of the organisation a communications policy. This policy should state what should be done in terms of communicating the relevant information to all stakeholders of the organisation.
- Keep an open environment in transmitting information and receiving feedback comments.
- Enable and facilitate mechanisms to allow the easy flow of information down, across and up the organisation.
- Enable ways to allow employees to recommend improvements in operations, strategy and other critical issues affected by the changes.
- Monitor the compliance of all communications activities for changes by the Board.

Change management may be the process of identifying, implementing and monitoring changes to organisational functions as a possible result of developing and implementing IT application systems. Because changes may be difficult and quite stressful, in some cases, to all staff of an organisation impacted by the IT application implemented, it may be most crucial to the change management team, to complete all identified and approved changes in the workplace in a disciplined, efficient and effective manner.

The main concept will probably need to be 'changes for the better', not just 'changes for the sake of changes themselves'.

5.6 Systems development personnel controls

Among the many challenges that organisations (private and public) face today is fraud, according to many sources.[42] Technological advances (computer and communications technology and infrastructure, IT systems, Internet, electronic business and immediate digital information provision channels, etc.) have probably made things worse in terms of committing fraud.

The various fraud types that may be committed by the use of computer-enabled technologies and IT systems include: manipulation of financial and other corporate records, theft of intellectual property, falsification of company records, performance and other results (research, corporate responsibility, human rights, etc.), manipulation of employee records, theft of equipment and software, misuse of the assets and resources of the organisation, etc.

This may make it imperative for organisations to find ways and means to counter this vice. These may include various anti-fraud measures, such as: corporate policies and procedures (financial management, asset protection, personnel management, ethics policy, etc.), IT policies and procedures, IT security measures, external audit, internal audit, etc.

The IT-related policies and procedures are dealt with in this book. The corporate policies and procedures are outside the scope of this book.

The Systems Development Personnel Controls may be required for mainly two reasons. The first reason has to do with management's desires, expectations and demands of

---

[42] *www.acfe.com, www.cifas.org.uk.*

the IT function to develop and implement better mission-critical IT systems. The second reason has to do with the direct involvement of system development staff in IT system development and maintenance, and the potential frauds committed by them or with their collaboration.

This is because these staff have access, sometimes at the complete level, to the most sensitive software and data of the organisation. And these same staff develop and maintain mission-critical IT systems that are used to process and store these critical corporate data in corporate-wide databases, either by themselves or sometimes by outside partners (hardware and software maintenance vendors, software contractors, etc.).

The main Systems Development Personnel Controls that may be found useful, depending on the conditions of any given organisation and its IT function, include the following:

- System Development Anti-Fraud Controls
- System Development Personnel Administration Controls.

Developing these controls may be carried out by the CIO, overviewed by the given IT or other corporate committee, and reviewed, improved, ratified by the Board, and communicated to all involved parties of the organisation.

The IT manager may use one, two, several or all of the described controls, or even devise their own set, depending on their personnel management experience, corporate environment, risk appetite, management style, and situation.

5.6.1 Systems Development Anti-Fraud Controls

These controls may be implemented by a system development anti-fraud policy and a system development anti-fraud monitoring procedure.

System development anti-fraud policy

> **System development anti-fraud policy – example**
>
> Organisation WXYZ (The Company) is committed to the prevention and detection of fraud, abuse and theft committed by system development staff, either by themselves or with their direct involvement and support, by either inside or outside people, parties, or any combination of these, within the business. In alignment with the corporate fraud and ethics policy, the management of the IT function of the Company is assigned with prime responsibility for this. In order to reduce the risk of its occurrence The Company maintains an appropriate system of internal corporate and IT controls, has established security measures and controls, conducts structured pre-employment screening, and has established a corporate ethics programme, policy and training. A corporate anti-fraud team exists to investigate any suspected fraud, abuse or theft, regardless of how they may be committed. In support of this a fuller policy document, incorporating a corporate ethics policy and an employee handbook are communicated in order to provide awareness, standards and direction throughout The Company.

System development anti-fraud monitoring procedure

All policies have no value unless they are implemented by procedures and monitored accordingly.

In terms of fraud control by system development personnel, IT management and senior executives of the organisation may need to ensure that all system development staff sign a statement, on a annual basis (possibly), declaring their compliance to the above-mentioned anti-fraud policy. Management will need to monitor the application and implementation of these fraud controls.

5.6.2 Systems development personnel administration controls

Particular System Development Personnel Administration Controls that may be found useful, depending on the conditions of any given organisation and its IT function, include the following (as an indication only): screening, employment contracts, job descriptions, supervision, segregation of duties, rotation of duties, vacation taking, professional code adoption, and signing an anti-fraud statement (*see also Chapter 2*).

5.7 Monitoring and review controls

Establishing IT monitoring and review controls for this area may be achieved by the IT management report, the performance measures of systems development and the audit review tools and techniques described later in this chapter. This may also be facilitated by following the monitoring and review activities management plan (*see Chapter 1*).

In addition, the following may be monitored, reviewed and included in the IT management report:

- Compliance to systems development standards
- Personnel issues (systems development personnel controls and systems development anti-fraud controls)

- Critical Performance Measures of the system development area
- Compliance issues (system developed according to privacy laws, etc.).

It is the job of the CIO to ensure that the IT reporting mechanism is fed with the relevant data of this area.

5.8 Systems development performance measures

To ensure that the systems development process produces the expected results, in addition to the monitoring and review activities discussed earlier, the following performance measures (*see Table 7*) may be used.

Systems Development Performance Measures
1. Delivered lines of code, Development time
2. Delivered vs. planned function points
3. No. of listed requirements not delivered on time
4. Actual development cost vs. budget
5. Average time to deliver an application
6. Planned value, earned value, cost variance
7. Schedule variance, cost performance index
8. Percentage of users satisfied with the delivered application
9. Percentage of users trained in new application

Table 7: Systems development performance measures – example

These performance measures could be based on a mixed system with two components: Component 1 would be an IT BSC (Information Technology Balanced Scorecard) Measurement System (*see Chapter 4*), and a Compliance Monitoring System for monitoring compliance to policies, procedures and related matters (e.g. budget issues).

The IT management of the company, may, depending on various aspects of the organisation, analyse all this performance and compliance monitoring information to review, assess and improve the systems development elements of the IT function of the specific organisation.

5.9 Review and audit tools and techniques

In order to ensure that the system development controls are properly and effectively organised to serve the control needs of the specific corporate entity, guidelines and other tools may be necessary to aid the manager and other professionals (auditor, system development staff, compliance officers, etc.) in discharging their duties.

The review and audit tools that may support IT managers and other professionals in establishing, evaluating and improving the systems development controls, and which are offered for potential use, are: IT data management controls checklist, documentation checklist, system development strategy checklist, system development and maintenance checklist, end-user application development checklist, software requirements specification checklist, and software feasibility approval checklist.

Guidelines and other tools are described in Appendix 3 (Monitoring IT controls checklist), Appendix 4 (Examples of IT forms), Appendix 5 (IT audit methodology),

Appendix 6 (IT audit areas), and Appendix 7 (Internal audit report example).

The checklists presented are not intended to be a complete management review or IT audit guide. IT managers and other professionals may choose to use only certain components of the checklists and audit programmes based upon the size, complexity, business needs and demands, IT maturity needs and expectations, nature of the organisation's business, and levels of deployment and utilisation of IT systems.

5.9.1 IT data management controls checklist

The objective of this checklist is to support the process of constructing, reviewing, evaluating and improving the controls identified in Paragraph 5.4 ('System development quality controls').

1 Do all IT systems provide data and reports for determining that the organisation is operating efficiently, effectively and in compliance with laws and regulations?
2 Are the data and the reports provided by the IT systems useful for making management decisions, i.e. complete, accurate, relevant, reliable and timely?
3 Does the organisation undertake testing (at least every one to three years on changes to the data or the systems) to ensure that all data and reports provided are correct?
4 Do the data provided show the 'red flags' when operations go outside of normal operating thresholds?
5 Do the data and reports provided allow for continuous timely monitoring of daily operations of the organisation?

6 Are managers able to obtain both operational and financial data from systems to determine whether they are meeting their strategic and annual performance plans and meeting their goals for accountability for effective and efficient use of resources?
7 Are reconciliations of data to get accurate reports done and are corrective actions taken when errors occur in data and reports?
8 Have managers and customers been asked in the last year (or every 6 months) if the data provided are useful or what changes they would like to have?
9 Does the organisation have sufficient back-up for all IT systems?
10 Do all IT systems guarantee the privacy of information?
11 Does the organisation have a system for collecting accurate data related to monitoring, tracking and auditing all IT and telecommunications systems and equipment?
12 Does the organisation have (built-in) software controls to ensure the security of data access and to guard against damage, abuse and loss of data?
13 Have adequate physical security controls been implemented that are commensurate with the risks of physical damage or access?
14 Have adequate 'logical' (computerised application) security controls been implemented that are commensurate with the risks of 'logical' or improper access?
15 Has an overall IT security review been performed in the last 1 to 3 years?
16 Are management controls built into systems through an internal software management control module (e.g.

within a database management system, such as ORACLE)?

17 Does the organisation have and keep in good operational state a complete disaster and business continuity plan for the critical IT applications, systems and data communications equipment?

5.9.2 Documentation checklist

1 Is systems documentation maintained, up to date and secured? Consider: system flowcharts, data flow diagrams, logical data structures, database dictionary, system specifications, program specifications, off-site storage of copies of essential documentation.

2 Are user manuals maintained, up to date and secured? Consider: user and IT department responsibilities, objectives and description of system, including coverage of input requirements, output report descriptions, control requirements, distribution of reports, availability of help functions, off-site storage, easy to read and well referenced.

3 Are operating manuals maintained, up to date and secured? Consider: flowcharts showing input and output files, output reports and files, job frequency, sequence and schedules, job control language statements, rerun, checkpoint, back-up and restart or recovery procedures, off-site storage.

5.9.3 System development strategy checklist

The objective of this checklist is to support the process of creating, reviewing, evaluating and improving the controls identified in this chapter.

1 Will the developed system support and drive our strategy?
2 Is there a business case for the system?
3 Does the feasibility study justify the development?
4 What are the benefits of the system?
5 What will the total capital cost be for the system?
6 What human resources are required for the system?
7 What will the annual operating costs be to run the system?
8 Will the system meet the security needs of the organisation?
9 When (time-frame) will the system be available for productive use?
10 Who has been involved (IT, business users, Board members, etc.) in the definition of needs and requirements?
11 What is the strategy for communication with all stakeholders regarding the system's implementation requirements?
12 Has the implementation plan been agreed with all levels of affected business management?

5.9.4 System development and maintenance checklist

The objective of this checklist is to support the process of creating, reviewing, evaluating and improving the controls identified in this chapter.

1 Does an IT Steering Committee (SC) function exist within the organisation? Consider: membership of SC, authorisation procedure for examination of all proposals, review process of project plans and budgets, review of costs and benefits for all IT projects.

2 Is a formal IT systems development methodology used? Consider: Which methodology is used by IT to develop or buy software applications (structured, other, etc.)? Are user needs written and approved by key users? Does the testing, implementation and data conversion process include planning, user participation and user acceptance, during the specifications, testing and training phases?
3 Is a resource planning procedure in operation? Consider: Are hardware and software upgrade plans completed? Are IT skills available? Are IT training plans in place? Are user training plans approved? Are any security requirements identified, in terms of procedures, personnel and systems for the best use of the system under review?
4 Is there an IT investments review process in place, at least annually?
5 Is there an error correction procedure and is this used effectively (i.e. Are all errors fixed? Are all solutions documented?)? Consider: emergency procedures for problem fixing for production problems and how these are both fixed and managed.
6 Is there a software package evaluation procedure and is this used effectively (i.e. Are evaluation criteria used? Are all solutions documented?)?
7 Are improvements and changes (of major and minor importance) originated and authorised by end-users, controlled formally by IT management?
8 Is there a formal system testing methodology? Consider: program testing, subsystem testing, system testing, parallel runs, documentation of testing results, conversion testing, user and IT sign-offs.
9 Are audit trails designed and used for critical applications?

10 Is the user documentation adequate? Consider: user (clerical procedures), functional description for each menu and sub-menu to the lowest level, files and data description, overall system diagram, reporting and queries (instructions), and samples of input forms and outputs.

11 Is the system documentation adequate? Consider: systems diagram (overall and at least down to third level of detail), cross-reference diagram between all system components and programs, security and control requirements, files and data description (including a technical data dictionary), systems changes log (including description of the change, origin, authorisation levels and acceptance criteria).

5.9.5 End-user application development checklist

The objective of this checklist is to support the process of creating, reviewing, evaluating and improving the controls identified in Paragraph 5.3.4 'End-user application development controls'.

1 Are there adequate controls as regards application development through end-user use of PCs, terminals, printers, and/or workstations? Consider: policy for end-user computing, security guidelines and responsibilities, authorisation rules, etc.

2 Have end-user application development guidelines been developed and distributed? Consider: security requirements, authorised software, authorised hardware, programming requirements, testing and documentation.

3 Are regular back-ups taken of the PC developed software? Consider: regular back-ups taken of key models and data, and a record maintained of back-ups.

4 Are installation standards in place to control the implementation of new software? Consider: maintaining records to ensure that all end-users are running standard configurations of general purpose software.
5 Are controls in place to monitor and/or authorise the development of spreadsheets, databases and applications?
6 Is the documentation for programs adequate? Consider: central guidelines, quality control or peer reviews, formula coding.
7 Is the documentation for models, spreadsheets, etc. adequate? Consider: central guidelines, quality control or peer reviews.
8 Is access to programming languages and tools controlled?
9 Are changes to programs authorised and controlled?
10 Are changes to models authorised and controlled?
11 Are models and programs sufficiently tested before going into production or 'live'?
12 Are procedures in place for the creation of secure models?
13 Can the various models, spreadsheets and databases interface satisfactorily with other software to avoid rekeying?
14 Are procedures in place to control the migration of programs from development on 'intelligent workstations' (e.g. PCs) to production?

5.9.6 Software requirements specification checklist

The objective of this checklist is to support the process of creating, reviewing, evaluating and improving the controls identified in this chapter.

1 Are requirements properly organised and complete? Consider:

- o Are all internal cross-references to other requirements correct?
- o Are all requirements written at a consistent and appropriate level of detail?
- o Do the requirements provide an adequate basis for design?
- o Is the implementation priority of each requirement included?
- o Are all external hardware, software, and communication interfaces defined?
- o Have algorithms intrinsic to the functional requirements been defined?
- o Does the specification document include all of the known customer or system needs?
- o Is any necessary information missing from a requirement?
- o Is the expected behaviour documented for all anticipated error conditions?

2 Are requirements correct? Consider:

- o Do any requirements conflict with or duplicate other requirements?
- o Is each requirement written in clear, concise, unambiguous language?
- o Is each requirement verifiable by testing, demonstration, review or analysis?
- o Is each requirement in scope for the project?
- o Is each requirement free from content and grammatical errors?
- o Can all of the requirements be implemented within known computer hardware and software constraints?

- o Are any specified error messages unique and meaningful?

3 Do requirements have quality attributes? Consider:

- o Are all performance objectives properly specified?
- o Are all security and safety considerations properly specified?
- o Are other pertinent quality attribute goals explicitly documented and quantified, with the acceptable trade-offs specified?
- o Are all requirements actually requirements, not design or implementation solutions?
- o Are the time-critical functions identified, and timing criteria specified for them?
- o Are all significant consumers of scarce resources (memory, network bandwidth, processor capacity, etc.) identified, and is their anticipated resource consumption specified?
- o Have internationalisation issues been adequately addressed?

4 Are requirements traceable? Consider:

- o Is each requirement uniquely and correctly identified?
- o Can each software functional requirement be traced to a higher-level requirement (e.g. system requirement, user case)?
- o Is an audit trail designed to be an integral part of the application?

5.9.7 Software feasibility approval checklist

The objective of this checklist is to support the process of creating, reviewing, evaluating and improving the controls identified in this chapter.

1 Is the computerised application feasible at the technical level? Consider: Is the application within the limits of:
   - Available hardware and software technology?
   - Corporate resources (IT, other)?
   - IT Security required technology?
   - Legal framework aspects?
   - Available database management and networking capabilities?

2 Is the computerised application feasible at the economic level? Consider:
   - Are the application development and maintenance costs less than the potential benefits (by the use of the application)?
   - Does the application improve the position of the organisation?
   - Does the application enhance the competitive image of the organisation?
   - Does the application improve the firm's quality of decision making (faster information, more accurate data)?

3 Is the computerised application feasible at the operational level? Consider: Does the application:
   - meet the user's information requirements (present and future?
   - meet corporate objectives?
   - improve customer relations?
   - improve the streamlining of operations?
   - resolve customer issues faster?

5.10 Conclusion

Systems development, as practice over the last 30 years and several studies have shown, may be quite difficult, laborious and error-prone.

For example, according to The Standish Group's recently released report *CHAOS Summary 2009*: 'This year's results show a marked decrease in project success rates, with 32% of all projects succeeding which are delivered on time, on budget, with required features and functions,' says Jim Johnson, Chairman of The Standish Group, '44% were challenged which are late, over budget, and/or with less than the required features and functions and 24% failed which are cancelled prior to completion or delivered and never used.'[43]

Other recent studies show even more disturbing statistics. For example, according to the data reported by a consulting company:[44]

- 51% of users, in one ERP project, reported that their implementation was unsuccessful (Robbins-Gioia Survey, 2001)
- 40% of the projects failed to achieve their business case within one year of going live (The Conference Board Survey, 2001).

Other failure data were also reported, which makes the picture even worse.

In closing, the system development controls and the audit and review programmes and checklists presented in this

---

[43] November 2009, at *www.standishgroup.com.*
[44] See IT CORTEX, *www.it-cortex.com.*

chapter may aid, support and facilitate the IT management of any organisation in their effort of achieving their IT goals in terms of developing and maintaining information systems in efficient and effective ways.

These may be reviewed, changed, added, deleted, customised, etc. to meet the needs, demands and operating mode of the given organisation, and must be operated and executed with continuous diligence. These controls, as we have seen, may include policies, practices, procedures, organisational structures and specialised tools.

Moreover, they give substance to the knowledge management framework of organisations (*outlined in Chapter 1*), as they provide data and systems, the life-blood of the modern organisation.

When these controls are exercised and executed in the best way, assuming all other factors and conditions are favourable, they may make the IT systems of the specific organisation probably more efficient and effective, and in the end, more profitable and beneficial to its stakeholders, to society at large, and to the national and international economy.

5.11 Review questions

This set of questions may be employed by those using the controls identified in this book to assess and double-check their own conceptual understanding and practical knowledge contained in this chapter.

1. What is the purpose of system development controls?

Reference: Paragraph 5.2 'Purpose and main types of systems development controls'.

2. What are the main types of system development controls?

Reference: Paragraph 5.2 'Purpose and main types of systems development controls'.

3. What are the major stages of a typical IT systems development project?

Reference: Paragraph 5.3 'Application systems development process controls'.

4. What are the usual system development products?

Reference: Paragraph 5.3.2 'System development products'.

5. What are the main contents of the IT system feasibility document?

Reference: Paragraph 5.3.2 'System development products'.

6. What are the main steps to create the systems analysis and design document?

Reference: Paragraph 5.3.2 'System development products'.

7. What are the main contents of the systems analysis and design document?

Reference: Paragraph 5.3.2 'System development products'.

8. What are the contents of end-user documentation?

Reference: Paragraph 5.3.2 'System development products'.

9. What basis should be used for testing an IT system?

Reference: Paragraph 5.3.3 'IT systems testing methodology'.

10. What are the contents of a typical application test plan?

Reference: Paragraph 5.3.3 'IT systems testing methodology'.

11. Which data fields should a test case execution log form include?

Reference: Paragraph 5.3.3 'IT systems testing methodology'.

12. What is the main purpose of end-user application development controls?

Reference: Paragraph 5.3.4 'End-user application development controls'.

13. What is the definition of an end-user?

Reference: Paragraph 5.3.4 'End-user application development controls'.

14. What are the usual spreadsheet applications controls?

Reference: Paragraph 5.3.4 'End-user application development controls'.

15. What are the various audit trail types?

Reference: Paragraph 5.3.5 'Audit trails'.

16. What are the minimum contents of an audit trail record?

Reference: Paragraph 5.3.5 'Audit trails'.

17. What are the main objectives of software package controls?

Reference: Paragraph 5.3.6 'Software package controls'.

18. What are the main controls for software package purchases?

Reference: Paragraph 5.3.6 'Software package controls'.

19. What is included in the dimension of 'integrity' of the system development quality controls?

Reference: Paragraph 5.4 'Systems development quality controls'.

20. What are some of the usual system development performance measures?

Reference: Paragraph 5.8 'Systems development performance measures'.

CHAPTER 6: IT SECURITY CONTROLS

Whatever is done for our security by people, even formal power and hegemony, is a natural good, supposing someone has enough means to acquire it (i.e. security).

Epicurus

6.1 Scope

The main aim of IT is, once it has been set up properly (structure, personnel, administration, strategy, etc.), to design and develop high-quality IT application systems, and protect both the systems themselves, as well as the data and the infrastructural elements upon which these systems operate, in the most secure and safe way.

Controls at this level establish the secure operating environment for the development and operation of IT systems and services, and ensure the safe processing of data and successful operation of these systems and services for serving the business purposes of the organisation.

IT security controls include: IT security governance guidelines, standards, and legal frameworks, IT security plans, policies and procedures, personnel security management controls, and specialised IT technical protection controls, with examples of controls provided in some cases (e.g. IT security management plan, systems development security plan, etc.).

In addition to these, a set of audit programmes and checklists are presented to support the CIO, the IT manager and other professionals (system development staff, end-users, IT auditors, internal auditors, IT consultants, external auditors, compliance officers, etc.) in executing and improving their duties and responsibilities.

6.2 Purpose and main types of IT security controls

IT security means protecting data, information, information systems and other IT-related assets and elements of an organisation from unauthorised access, use, deployment, ownership, disclosure, disruption, modification or destruction.

Furthermore, designing, developing and deploying efficient and results-oriented IT application systems across all locations and functions of an organisation, including external access points, demands a very secure system and environment. To survive in the current competitive and turbulent world, both at the business level and in the IT and communication environment, both the organisation and its IT management will probably need to perform to higher levels of safety and security.

To reach these levels of performance, an organisation and its IT management may need to concentrate on better protection of, at least, the following IT-related assets and elements of its IT operation, such as: data, software programs, personnel, hardware, documentation (plans, contracts, manuals, guides, licences, etc.), services and infrastructure (installations, offices, computer and network rooms, cabling ducts, etc.).

In terms of IT security practice, this may demand that the IT function and its management and technical (including external) providers, in order to reach higher levels of security performance, will need to focus on managing the following five major components of IT security and the main types of security controls:

- Component 1: IT security governance guidelines, standards and legal frameworks.
- Component 2: IT Security plans and policies.
- Component 3: IT Security procedures and practices.
- Component 4: Specialised IT security hardware and software protection controls.
- Component 5: Evaluation and management monitoring controls of IT security.

All five components will need to be managed in parallel. It is usually the job of senior IT management to keep all of them at a predefined level of performance, at the same time. To concentrate on one or two of them and let the others fall behind may prove very risky and disastrous, in the long run.

All of these components of IT security will therefore need to be controlled, to increase the effectiveness of the implementation of the security controls.

The specific purpose of IT security controls is to ensure that all IT assets, systems, facilities, data and files are protected against unauthorised access, potential damage and improper or illegal use, and that they are operable, safe and secure at all times. Information security protects information from a wide range of threats in order to ensure business continuity, minimise business damage and maximise return on investments and business opportunities. Information security can be characterised as the preservation of:

- Confidentiality: ensuring that information is accessible only to those authorised to have access.
- Integrity: safeguarding the accuracy and completeness of information and processing methods.

- Availability: ensuring that authorised users have access to information and associated assets when required.

6.3 IT security governance guidelines, standards and legal frameworks

These are concerned with the necessary guidelines and standards which need the concentrated effort, additional focus and disciplined attention of IT management, as well as of the IT systems development and technical staff.

Guidelines and standards, in general corporate terms, define and establish a set of uniform criteria, methods, processes and practices, within which organisations and their functions operate, and offer products and services.

In the IT functional area, likewise, IT security guidelines, standards and legal frameworks, enable the IT function to operate, and offer products (e.g. processed information) and services (access to corporate data, process business transactions, etc.).

Establishing the IT security guidelines and standards (within the existing legal frameworks) for the specific organisation may be done by the CIO with possible support by an external party, overviewed by the IT committee and for credibility and authority reasons, ratified by the Board or senior executive committee. These, specific to the organisation and IT function guidelines and standards, could follow international guidelines and frameworks issued by international organisations, such as OECD, NIST (USA), European Union, IATF, ISO (ISO/IEC 17799, ISO/IEC 27001, ISO13335, ISO15408), US Federal Information Processing Standard (FIPS 140), etc.

The more universal guidelines, standards and legal frameworks applicable, potentially, to devising the given organisation's specific guidelines and standards for security purposes are:

- OECD IT Security Guidelines
- NIST IT Security Guidelines
- Other IT Security Guidelines and Standards
- Legal Frameworks related to IT Security.

6.3.1 OECD IT Security Guidelines

The OECD Guidelines for Security of Information Systems and Networks[45] are based on the following nine principles:

PRINCIPLE 1. Awareness: Participants should be aware of the need for security of information systems and networks and what they can do to enhance security.

PRINCIPLE 2. Responsibility: All participants are responsible for the security of information systems and networks.

PRINCIPLE 3. Response: Participants should act in a timely and co-operative manner to prevent, detect and respond to security incidents.

PRINCIPLE 4. Ethics: Participants should respect the legitimate interests of others.

---

[45] *OECD Principles of Corporate Governance 2004*, see *www.oecd.org/daf/corporateaffairs/principles/text*, as per permission granted to the author.

PRINCIPLE 5. Democracy: The security of information systems and networks should be compatible with the essential values of a democratic society.

PRINCIPLE 6. Risk assessment: Participants should conduct risk assessments.

PRINCIPLE 7: Security design and implementation. Participants should incorporate security as an essential element of information systems and networks.

PRINCIPLE 8. Security management: Participants should adopt a comprehensive approach to security management.

PRINCIPLE 9. Reassessment: Participants should review and reassess the security of information systems and networks, and make appropriate modifications to security policies, practices, measures and procedures.

These guidelines are complemented by the 1980 OECD Guidelines Governing the Protection of Privacy and Transborder Flows of Personal Data, and the 1997 OECD Guidelines for Cryptography Policy, etc.

6.3.2 NIST IT Security Guidelines

NIST (National Institute of Standards and Technology, a USA Government Institution: www.nist.gov) has drafted a document containing the following eight principles to be followed by the US Federal Government community as a base on which to build their IT security programmes. These principles are intended to guide personnel when creating new systems, practices or policies.

PRINCIPLE 1. Computer security supports the mission of the organisation: The purpose of computer security is to protect an organisation's valuable resources, such as information, hardware and software.

PRINCIPLE 2. Computer security is an integral element of sound management: Information and IT systems are often critical assets that support the mission of an organisation. Protecting them can be as important as protecting other organisational resources, such as money, physical assets or employees.

PRINCIPLE 3. Computer security should be cost-effective: The costs and benefits of security should be carefully examined in both monetary and non-monetary terms to ensure that the cost of controls does not exceed expected benefits.

PRINCIPLE 4. Systems owners have security responsibilities outside their own organisations: If a system has external users, its owners have a responsibility to share appropriate knowledge about the existence and general extent of security measures so that other users can be confident that the system is adequately secure.

PRINCIPLE 5. Computer security responsibilities and accountability should be made explicit: The responsibility and accountability of owners, providers and users of IT systems, and other parties concerned with the security of IT systems, should be explicit. The assignment of responsibilities may be internal to an organisation or may extend across organisational boundaries.

PRINCIPLE 6. Computer security requires a comprehensive and integrated approach: Providing effective computer security requires a comprehensive approach that considers a variety of areas both within and outside of the computer security field. This comprehensive approach extends throughout the entire information life cycle.

PRINCIPLE 7. Computer security should be periodically reassessed: Computers and the environments in which they operate are dynamic. System technology and users, data and information in the systems, risks associated with the system, and security requirements are ever-changing.

PRINCIPLE 8. Computer security is constrained by societal factors: The ability of security to support the mission of an organisation may be limited by various factors, such as social issues.

6.3.3 Other IT Security Guidelines and Standards

Various other guidelines and standards available for potential use by organisations in the wider area of IT security are:

- The ISO standards (*www.iso.org*): (a) ISO/IEC 27002:2005, Code of practice for information security management, (b) ISO15443: *Information technology – Security techniques – A framework for IT security assurance*, (c) ISO20000: *Information technology – Service management*, and (d) ISO27001: *Information technology – Security techniques – Information Management Systems*.
- The standard for information security of the Information Security Forum (*www.isfsecuritystandard.com*).
- The security controls for system and network components offered by the Centre for Internet Security (*www.cisecurity.org*).

- The security guidance offered by the VISA credit card organisation ('The Digital Dozen').
- The control guidance (ITGI Control Objectives for Information and Related Technology) offered by the CobiT standard (*www.isaca.org*).
- The Generally Accepted Information Security Principles (GAISP) offered by the Information Systems Security Association (*www.issa.org*), etc.

6.3.4 Legal frameworks related to IT security

There are various legal frameworks applicable, possibly, to the wider area of IT security for organisations, public and private, such as:

- The Sarbanes-Oxley Act of 2002 (*www.theiia.org*), particularly sections 103, 802, 201, 301, 302 and 404.
- G8: International Principles for Computer Evidence (*www.unescap.org*, *www.interpol.org*, *www.fbi.org*).
- European Union Data Protection Laws (EC Directive 95/46/EC).
- Other Data Protection Standards (see *www.privacy.org*, *www.privacyexchange.org*, *www.istpa.org* and *www.privacyalliance.org*).
- Various USA Acts (e.g. GLBA, FERPA, HIPPAA, etc.).
- The Canada Evidence Act (*www.canlii.org*).
- Electronic Signatures Guide to Enactment of the UNCITRAL Model Law on Electronic Signatures 2001 (*www.uncitral.org*).
- Convention on Cybercrime Council of Europe November 2001 (*www.coe.int*).
- UNCITRAL Model Law on Electronic Commerce.

- Recommendation of the OECD council concerning guidelines for consumer protection in the context of electronic commerce, etc.

These guidelines, laws and security standards will establish the required security tone and the compliance frameworks, and may enable, facilitate and drive management to undertake further action by plans, policies, procedures, etc.

Taking into consideration all of the above, as well as other relevant corporate governance guidelines and Board instructions, enables the IT team (CIO, Compliance Officer, IT senior staff, external consultant, etc.) to select, customise and formulate the IT guidelines and standards that may be applied to the IT systems and infrastructure of the specific organisation.

6.4 IT security plans and policies

This component of IT security is concerned with the necessary security plans and policies. These may also need the concentrated effort, additional focus and disciplined attention of IT management for the development and deployment of safer and more secure IT systems.

Guidelines, laws and security standards necessitate the crafting of plans and roadmaps to reach the security goals. Plans document the actions to be taken to institute IT security, and plans and policies contain security architectural elements to enable the organisation to become more secure. They drive and complete the security implementation process and effort by the means of procedures, techniques and tools.

Security policies establish what is to be done in corporate terms for the specific environment of the organisation to improve its IT security. Procedures define how what has been defined in security polices are carried out by the use of people, practices, techniques, specialised systems (hardware, software, etc.) and tools.

Establishing the IT security policies and plans may be developed and implemented by the IT manager in charge, sometimes with external support, overviewed by the IT committee, and ratified by the Board. The audit checklists 'IT security policy checklist' and 'Logical security controls checklist' (*see Paragraph 6.9*) may be used to support the design, implementation and post-implementation review of the IT security policies and plans for the specific organisation.
The main controls of IT security plans and policies are:

- IT security management plan.
- IT security strategy plan.
- IT security awareness and training programme.
- System development security plan.
- IT security policy.
- Privacy of information policy.
- Information sensitivity policy.
- Password controls policy.
- Site security policies and procedures handbook.

6.4.1 IT security management plan

The primary objective of the IT security management plan is to provide guidelines for the implementing an IT security data programme for all the information collection, storing and processing activities of the organisation.

IT security management plan – example

This plan will usually, depending on the corporate environment, include:

Establishment of the IT Security Management Steering Committee.

Formulation of the IT Security Strategy for the specific organisation by crafting an IT Security Strategy Plan (*see Paragraph 6.4.2* 'IT security strategy plan').

Examining the various options and deciding on the security model of the organisation, such as Biba Model, Clark-Wilson model, Brewer-Nash model, La Padula model, etc. (see *Role-Based Access Controls,* Ferraiolo DF et al., Artech House (2003).

Establishment and implementation of security policies and procedures.

Establishment of the IT Security Organisation (manager responsible, type of organisation: unit, department, team, etc. appointment of security staff, security budget formulation and approval, procurement of other resources, etc.).

Description of the responsibilities, roles and work tasks of the IT Security Organisation (unit, department, team, etc.) and its dedicated staff.

Execution of the required activities to instil awareness and sensitivity on security issues to all personnel of the organisation (*see Paragraph 6.4.3* 'IT security awareness and training programme).

Documenting all the activities and transactions of the organisation where IT Systems are deployed and used.

Education and Training of the IT Security Team.

Implementation of the IT Security Plan.

Full operation of the IT Security Organisation.

> Monthly review and improvement of the functions of the IT Security Team on the basis of reported results, incidents (detected, reported and resolved) and resource utilisation.
>
> Monitoring, reporting and reviewing security issues, both every month and on an *ad hoc* basis (on urgent matters) at the top management level.

6.4.2 IT security strategy plan

The IT strategy of a specific organisation is documented in an IT strategy plan, the primary objective of which is to determine and document 'what' is to be protected, against 'what' and 'how'. It can be incorporated into the IT security management plan.

Formulation of the IT security strategy for the specific organisation could be achieved (as an example) by executing the actions identified in the following steps:

Step 1: Identifying what IT-related assets, processes, data, installations, premises, resources, etc. you are trying to protect.

Step 2: Determining what you are trying to protect them from.

Step 3: Examining the legal, statutory, regulatory and contractual requirements, and the principles, objectives and requirements of information processing that an organisation, its trading partners, contractors and service providers have to satisfy, and assessing by risk analysis and other relevant methods how likely the potential threats are for the particular organisation.

Step 4: Establishing security controls specific to your organisation on the basis of the security requirements that have been identified to ensure risks are reduced to an acceptable level, and with some IT security standards (*see Paragraph 6.3*).

Step 5: Implementing controls which will aim to protect your assets in a cost–benefit effective manner.

Step 6: Monitoring and reviewing the process continuously by the use of special procedures, tests and tools.

Step 7: Making the necessary improvements when security gaps or new goals are identified.

6.4.3 IT security awareness and training programme

Security awareness must be instilled in all users so that the organisation can improve the results of implementing security measures. An effective IT security awareness and training programme requires proper planning, implementation, maintenance and periodic evaluation. In general, such a programme should encompass the following:

- identify programme scope, goals and objectives
- identify training staff
- identify target audiences
- motivate management and employees
- administer the programme
- maintain the programme
- evaluate the programme.

6.4.4 Application system development security plan

The IT strategy of a specific organisation may include security controls at the application level. Application security, like other aspects of an IT system, is best managed if planned for throughout the IT system development life cycle.

There are many models available, but most contain five basic phases: initiation, development, implementation, operation and disposal. Organisations and IT managers will need to ensure that security activities are accomplished during each of the phases.

The primary objective of the system development security plan is to provide guidelines for security issues for all the phases of an IT system development life cycle.

Application system development security plan – example

Phase 1: Initiation

Step 1.1 Sensitivity Analysis: During the feasibility study phase, the need for a system is expressed, the purpose of the system is documented, and any security needs, expectations and specifications are noted. In addition, a sensitivity assessment may be conducted to look at the sensitivity of the information to be processed and the system itself.

Phase 2: Development

During this phase, the system is designed, purchased, programmed, developed, or otherwise constructed. This phase often consists of other defined cycles, such as the system development cycle or the acquisition cycle. The following steps should be considered during this phase:

Step 2.1 Determine security requirements: During the first part of the system development phase, security requirements should be developed at the same time that system planners define the requirements of the system. These requirements can be expressed as technical features (e.g. access controls), assurance statements (e.g. background checks for system developers), or operational practices (e.g. awareness and training). Special attention should be paid to the security aspects of web applications.[46]

Step 2.2 Include security requirements into specifications: Determining security features, assurances and operational practices can yield significant security information and often voluminous requirements. This information needs to be validated, updated and organised into the detailed security protection requirements and specifications used by systems designers.

Step 2.3 Monitor the system development activities: If the system is being built, security activities may include developing the system's security features, monitoring the development process itself for security problems, responding to changes and monitoring threats. Threats or vulnerabilities that may arise during the development phase include Trojan horses, incorrect code, poorly functioning development tools, manipulation of code and malicious insiders, etc. If the system is being acquired off the shelf, security activities may include monitoring to ensure security is a part of the design and implementation aspects of the acquired system, review of purchase or lease contract and evaluation of proposed systems.

Step 2.4 Develop operational practices: In addition to obtaining the system, operational practices need to be developed. These refer to human activities that take place around the system, such as contingency planning, awareness and training, and preparing documentation.

[46] For more on this issue, see (1) *Hacking Web Applications Exposed*, Scambray J and Shema M, McGraw-Hill (2002), (2) *Security and Control Over Intranets and Extranets*. Parts 1 & 2, pp. 1–12, and 1–20, Gallegos F, Auerbach Publishers, USA (2002), and (3) 'Common Web Application Vulnerabilities', *ISACA Journal*, Vol. 4, 2005, pp. 29–31, Kennedy S (2005).

Phase 3: Implementation

During implementation, the system is tested and installed. The following items should be considered during this phase:

Step 3.1 Enable security features: When acquired, a system often comes with security features disabled. These need to be enabled and configured.

Step 3.2 Conduct security testing: System security testing includes both the testing of the particular parts of the system that have been developed or acquired and the testing of the entire system. Security management, physical facilities, personnel, procedures, the use of commercial or in-house services (such as networking services) and contingency planning are examples of areas that affect the security of the entire system, but may have been specified outside of the development or acquisition cycle.

Step 3.3 Conduct external review: The security of the system may also be examined by outside experts in order to assure the management of the organisation that the information system is protected against potential threats, and that some risks may be accepted as unavoidable. It is usually supported by a review of the system, including its management, operational and technical controls.

Phase 4: Operation

During this phase, the system performs its work. The system is almost always being continuously modified by the addition of hardware and software, and by numerous other events. The following high-level issues should be considered during this phase:

Step 4.1 Security administration: Operation of a system involves many security activities, such as taking back-ups, holding training classes, managing cryptographic keys, keeping up with user administration and access privileges, and updating security software, and also examining whether the system is operated according to its current security requirements. This includes both the actions of people who operate or use the system and the functioning of technical controls.

Step 4.2 Security monitoring: To maintain operational assurance, most organisations use two basic methods: system audits and monitoring. A system audit is a one-time or periodic event to evaluate security. Monitoring refers to an ongoing activity that examines either the system or the users. More details on these are contained in Paragraph 6.7 'Evaluation and monitoring controls of IT security'.

Phase 5. Disposal

The disposal phase of the IT system life cycle involves the disposal of information, hardware and software. The following items should be considered during this phase:

Step 5.1 Information disposal: Information may be moved to another system, archived, discarded or destroyed. When archiving information, consider the method for retrieving the information in the future. While electronic information is generally easier to retrieve and store, the technology used to create the records may not be readily available in the future. Measures may also have to be taken for the future use of data that has been encrypted, such as taking appropriate steps to ensure the secure, long-term storage of cryptographic keys. It is important to consider legal requirements for records retention when disposing of IT systems.

Step 5.2 Media Sanitisation: The removal of information from a storage medium (such as a hard disk or tape) is called sanitisation. Different kinds of sanitisation provide different levels of protection. A distinction can be made between clearing information (rendering it unrecoverable by keyboard attack) and purging (rendering information unrecoverable against laboratory attack). There are three general methods of purging media: overwriting, degaussing (for magnetic media only) and destruction.

6.4.5 IT security policy

This policy explains the procedures to be executed for the protection of IT assets. The IT security policy may cover (as an indication only): access control standards, accountability, audit trails, back-ups, business continuity planning, disposal of media, disposal of printed matter, downloading from the Internet, information ownership, management responsibilities, modems and analogue lines, off-site repairs to equipment, physical security, portable devices, staff responsibilities, use of e-mail, viruses, workstation security, privacy, non-compliance, legislation, computer insurance policy, etc. (*see Appendix 1*).

6.4.6 Privacy of information policy

The primary purpose of the privacy of information policy is to provide guidelines for the privacy issues of information activities (collection, use, disclosure, monitoring, etc.) of the organisation.

The privacy of information policy should cover the following issues: collection of information, privacy of customer data, use of information, disclosure of information, monitoring activities, protection of information, the Internet, and the use of 'cookies' to monitor website user traffic patterns and site usage (*see Appendix 1*).

A cookie is a piece of information that is stored on your computer's hard drive and which records your navigation of a website so that, when you revisit that website, it can present tailored options to you based upon the stored information about your last visit.

6.4.7 Information sensitivity policy

The primary objective of the information sensitivity policy is to provide guidelines for the data classification issues of information collected and processed by information systems activities of the organisation.

The information sensitivity policy should cover the following issues: purpose, definitions of data classification, responsibility of personnel, the role of the manager, sensibility guidelines in protecting information, enforcement rules, management of business connections, and use of encryption rules (*see Appendix 1*).

Certain organisations, especially in the consulting and engineering areas, may cover the risk of the responsibility of their personnel by obtaining professional liability insurance.

6.4.8 Password controls policy

The actual detailed password controls may be developed and implemented by the IT manager in charge, sometimes with external support, overviewed by the IT committee and ratified by the Board. The audit checklists 'IT security policy checklist' and 'Logical security controls checklist' (*see Paragraph 6.9*) may be used to support the design, implementation and post-implementation review of the password controls for the specific organisation.

A password policy and associated compliance procedures should be established and put into operation by the organisation to handle the specific password control requirements. This password policy should include the following controls:

Structure of password: Acceptable passwords must include each of the following characteristics:

- Letters – upper or lower case letters (A, B, C, … Z, a, b, c, … z).
- Arabic numerals (0, 1, 2, … 9).
- Non-alphanumeric 'special characters'. For example, punctuation or symbols. ([};"!$=).
- At a minimum, user passwords must be at least nine characters long.
- The password must not contain the user's e-mail name, user ID or the full name as shown in the domain registry.
- New passwords shall never be the same as any of the last 12 passwords.
- The password must not contain dictionary words from any language because numerous password-cracking programs exist that can run through millions of possible word combinations in seconds. Simply adding a number onto the end of a word is not sufficient. The numeric and/or special characters should be integrated into the password. However, a complex password that cannot be broken is useless if you cannot remember it. For security to function, you must choose a password you can remember and yet is complex (e.g. password 'Mgd11!Yo' (My grand-daughter is 11 years old) or 'IriCf10yn' (I've resided in Canada for 10 years now) may be defined as strong passwords).

Storing of passwords: Passwords must be stored in irreversible encrypted form and the password file cannot be viewed in unencrypted form.

Password display: A password must not be displayed on the data entry/display device.

Default passwords: Operating systems, systems software and other systems (database, data communications, etc.) at high risk of compromise are sometimes installed with a standard set of default accounts and associated standard passwords. Like all accounts, these access routes must be protected by strong passwords.

Password disabling: Additional measures, such as disabling, renaming or decoying these standard accounts, should be employed.

First access: During the first instance of access with a new account, the initial password must be changed by the individual responsible for the account, in compliance with the password controls defined in this policy.

Password changes control: Each web user should periodically be prompted to change his or her password. The interval between password changes could be at 30, 60, or 90 days, etc. which is set at the level of the organisation.

Training: The proper and secure use of passwords must be included in user training.

The specific organisation and its management team may use these polices or customise these or devise their own, according to their needs. All these will need, however, for efficiency and effectiveness reasons, to be documented and maintained properly.

6.4.9 Site security policies and procedures handbook

The security procedures to implement the IT security policies of an organisation may include (as an indication only): security compliance policy monitoring, security assessment, IT systems risk assessment, IT security controls evaluation, information classification, logical access, physical access, access codes management, remote access, access by third parties, Internet and intranet management, e-mail management, and security incidents handling. these must be established, implemented and monitored, and improved after annual review and assessment.

Site security handbook – example

1 Introduction (1.2 Audience, 1.3 Definitions).

2 Basic approach to security (2.1 Risk assessment, 2.2 Identifying the IT assets, 2.3 Identifying the threats).

3 IT Architecture of the Organisation (3.1 IT infrastructure, 3.2 Computerised applications, 3.3 Network services).

4 IT security organisation, policies and procedures (4.1 Definition of a security policy, 4.2 Purposes of a security policy, 4.3 Contents of IT security polices, 4.4 Contents of IT security procedures, 4.5 IT security organisation and management responsibilities, 4.6 Security of back-ups and digital media).

5 Physical protection of IT site and network facilities (5.1 Objectives, 5.2 Security controls).

6 Security of computerised applications (6.1 General IT controls, 6.2 Application controls, 6.3 Specialised security applications).

7 Security of network services (7.1 Identify real needs for services, 7.2 Network and service configuration, 7.3 Protecting the network infrastructure, 7.4 Protecting the network, 7.5 Protecting the services, 7.6 Protecting the protection).

8 Security auditing (8.1 What to collect, 8.2 Collection process, 8.3 Handling and preserving audit data, 8.4 Legal considerations).

9 Security incident handling (9.1 Preparing and planning for incident handling, 9.2 Notification and points of contact, 9.3 Local managers and personnel, 9.4 Law enforcement and investigative agencies, 9.5 Affected sites, 9.6 Internal communications, 9.7

Public relations, 9.8 Identifying an incident, 9.9 Assessing the damage and extent, 9.10 Handling an incident, 9.11 Protecting evidence and activity logs, 9.12 Containment, 9.13 Eradication, 9.14 Recovery, 9.15 Follow-Up).

10 Ongoing security monitoring activities.

The security polices and procedures that an organisation is using are usually documented in a site security policies and procedures handbook.

The IT security team, taking into consideration all of the above, as well as other relevant corporate governance guidelines and Board instructions, may choose to use the above plans and policies or modify them to their needs, or even formulate another different set, to suit their purpose.

Security plans and policies, however, are implemented by security procedures and practices, tailored to the specific organisation.

6.5 IT security procedures and practices

This component is concerned with the necessary security procedures and practices, which may need the concentrated effort, additional focus and disciplined attention of IT management for the development and deployment of safer and more secure IT systems.

The main IT security procedures and practices are:

- Physical and logical access controls
- Identification and authentication controls
- End-user security administration procedures
- IT contingency planning procedures
- Computer operations controls
- Personnel security management practices

- Social engineering controls
- Security change management procedure.

6.5.1 Physical and logical access controls

IT security, at the procedural and practical level, is usually implemented by what are called 'physical' and 'logical' access controls.

Physical access controls are used to control physical access to offices, installations, computer rooms, network cabling and server rooms, etc. where IT systems and services are available. Logical access controls refer to the policies, procedures and technical controls used in computerised information systems.

The exercise of logical controls for IT security purposes is often administered separately from the implementation of physical security controls; but the requirements from a security architectural perspective are potentially the same, even subject to varied risks and authentication levels.

Physical access and environmental security controls refer to the control of the environment of the workplace and computing facilities, and may include monitoring and control access to and from such facilities (e.g. doors, locks, heating and air conditioning, smoke and fire alarms, fire suppression systems, cameras, barricades, fencing, security guards, cable locks, etc.).

An organisation's physical and environmental security programme should address the following topics: physical access controls, fire safety, failure of supporting utilities, structural collapse, plumbing leaks, interception of data, and mobile and portable systems. In doing so, it can help prevent interruptions in computer services, physical damage, unauthorised disclosure of information, loss of control over system integrity, and theft. Detailed guidelines for designing secure data centres are provided in Appendix 3 and see also Chapter 7.

Logical access controls, more specifically, refer to the collection of policies, procedures, practices, security organisational structure and other technical controls embedded within operating systems software, application software, specialised IT security packages, database management systems and data communication management systems.

Access is the ability to do something with a computer resource (e.g. use, change or view). Logical access controls are the system-based means by which the ability is explicitly enabled or restricted in some way. Logical access controls can prescribe not only who or what (e.g. in the case of a process) is to have access to a specific system resource, but also the type of access that is permitted.

Organisations may implement logical access controls based on policy made by a management official responsible for a particular system, application, subsystem or group of systems. The policy should balance the often-competing interests of security, operational requirements and user-friendliness.

In general, some organisations may base, for improved security reasons, access control policy on the principle of least privilege, which states that users should be granted access only to the resources they need to perform their official functions.

6.5.2 Identification and authentication controls

Identification and authentication is a critical building block of computer security since it is the basis for most types of access control and for establishing user accountability. Identification and authentication is a technical measure that prevents unauthorised people (or unauthorised processes) from entering an IT system.

Access control usually requires that the system be able to identify and differentiate among users; for example, access control is often based on least privilege. User accountability requires the linking of activities on an IT system to specific individuals and, therefore, requires the system to identify users.

These controls are usually established and implemented under the control of systems software (operating system, database management system, data communications system, etc.)

6.5.3 End-user security administration procedures

Organisations should ensure effective administration of users' computer access to maintain system security, including user account management, auditing and the timely modification or removal of access. The following should be considered, in terms of account management:

User account management: Organisations should have a process for:

- requesting, establishing, issuing and closing user accounts
- tracking users and their respective access authorisations
- managing these functions.

User-friendly terminations: Friendly terminations should be accomplished by implementing a standard set of procedures for outgoing or transferring employees. This normally includes:

- removal of access privileges, computer accounts, authentication tokens
- control of keys
- briefing on the continuing responsibilities for confidentiality and privacy
- return of property
- continued availability of data.

In both the manual and the electronic worlds, this may involve documenting procedures or filing schemes, such as how documents are stored on the hard disk, and how they are backed up. Employees should be instructed whether or not to 'clean up' their PC before leaving. If cryptography is used to protect data, the availability of cryptographic keys to management personnel must be ensured.

User-unfriendly terminations: Given the potential for adverse consequences, organisations should do the following in situations of unfriendly terminations:

- System access should be terminated as quickly as possible when an employee is leaving a position under less than friendly terms. If employees are to be fired, system access should be removed at the same time (or just before) the employees are notified of their dismissal.
- When an employee notifies an organisation of a resignation and it can be reasonably expected that it is on unfriendly terms, system access should be terminated immediately.

- During the 'notice of termination' period, it may be necessary to assign the individual to a restricted area and function. This may be particularly true for employees capable of changing programs or modifying the system or applications.

6.5.4 IT contingency planning procedures

IT contingency planning directly supports an organisation's goal of continued IT operations. Contingency planning addresses how to keep an organisation's critical functions operating in the event of disruptions, both large and small. This broad perspective on contingency planning is based on the distribution of computer support throughout an organisation. Contingency planning is part of the greater business continuity planning (BCP) effort of the organisation. In terms of IT, the BCP should contain a disaster recovery plan (DRP) which should be tested at predetermined time points, in order to ensure all stakeholders that the critical IT systems and infrastructure of the organisation can resume operational status very quickly. The detailed controls in this area are described in Chapter 7.

6.5.5 Computer operations controls

Computer support and operations refers to system administration and tasks external to the system that support its operation (e.g. maintaining documentation). Failure to consider security as part of the support and operations of IT systems is, for many organisations, a significant weakness. Computer security system literature includes many examples of how organisations undermined their often expensive security measures because of poor documentation, no control of maintenance accounts, or other shoddy practices. The following practices are an example of what an organisation's support and operation should include:

- User support: In general, system support and operations staff should provide assistance to users, such as via a help desk. Support staff need to be able to identify security problems, respond appropriately and inform appropriate individuals.
- Software support: Controls should be placed on system software commensurate with the risk. The controls may include:
  - Policies for loading and executing new software on a system. Executing new software can lead to viruses, unexpected software interactions, or software that may subvert or bypass security controls
  - Use of powerful system utilities. System utilities can compromise the integrity of operating systems and logical access controls
  - Authorisation of system changes. This involves the protection of software and back-up copies and can be achieved with a combination of logical and physical access controls
  - Licence management. Software should be properly licensed and organisations should take steps to ensure that no illegal software is being used. For example, an organisation may audit systems for illegal copies of copyrighted software
  - Configuration management. Configuration management should ensure that changes to the system do not diminish security. The goal is to know how changes will affect system security.

- Back-ups: It is critical to back up software and data. Frequency of back-ups will depend upon how often data changes and how important those changes are. Program managers should be consulted to determine what back-up schedule is appropriate. Back-up copies should be tested to ensure they are usable. Back-ups should be stored securely.
- Media controls: A variety of measures, such as marking and logging, should be used to provide physical and environmental protection and accountability for tapes, diskettes, printouts and other media. The extent of media control depends upon many factors, including the type of data, the quantity of media and the nature of the user environment.
- Documentation: All aspects of computer support and operations should be documented to ensure continuity and consistency. Security documentation should be designed to fulfil the needs of the different types of people who use it. The security of a system also needs to be documented, including security plans, contingency plans, and security policies and procedures.
- Maintenance: Procedures should be developed to ensure that only authorised personnel perform maintenance. If a system has a maintenance account, it is critical to change factory-set passwords or otherwise disable the accounts until they are needed. If maintenance is to be performed remotely, authentication of the maintenance provider should be made.
- Standard logon message: Prior to user authentication, the system should display a banner warning that use of the system is restricted to authorised people.

6.5.6 Personnel security management practices

According to a CSI/FBI report,[47] 80% of attacks on computer systems are carried out by internal users while 20% are done by external users of organisations.

These computer users, both internal and external, include (as an indication only) end-users, system designers, implementers and managers. A broad range of security issues relate to how these individuals interact with computers and the access and authority they need to do their job. No IT system can be secured without properly addressing these security issues, such as:

- staffing
- position definition
- separation of duties (for example, in IT systems, the system programmer should not write application software and should not have access, without explicit authorisation, to production data. The operators also should not be allowed to maintain application software, etc.)
- least privilege refers to the security objective of granting users only those accesses they need to perform their official duties. Data entry clerks, for example, may not have any need to run analysis reports of their database
- screening
- employee training and awareness in security issues, etc.

These are described in Chapter 2.

One latest control that is applied currently by many organisations is the requirement to employ security

---

[47] 2005: www.gocsi.com.

personnel who have professional security certifications (e.g. CISSP, CISA, ISSAP, ISSEP, ISSMP, CISM, etc.).

6.5.7 Social engineering controls

'Social engineering'[48] is a euphemism for non-technical or low-technology means (such as lies, persuasion, influence, friendly behaviour, impersonation, tricks, fax messages, e-mail messages, mobile telephone messages, bribes, blackmail, and threats, etc.) used to gain illegal access to sensitive assets, offices, information systems, etc. with intent to gain, damage or abuse them:

Data classification: All items (printed reports, typed reports, manuals, digital media, tape copies of computerised information, etc.) should be classified according to the data classification policy of the organisation (confidential, private, internal, etc.).

Data off-site storage: Valuable, sensitive or critical corporate data should be encrypted if stored off site.

Data release: All organisational data (e.g. printed reports, typed reports, manuals, digital media, tape copies of computerised information, etc.) should be released according to the information release authorisation policy of the organisation, or according to specific release instructions. All releases should be logged and reported.

Disclosing information over the phone: Sensitive information should not be disclosed over the phone to anyone. Verbal security codes should be used to identify

---

[48] For more on social engineering, see *The Art of Intrusion: The real stories behind the exploits of hackers, intruders, and deceivers*, Mitnick KD and Simon WL, Wiley, Indianapolis, USA (2005).

persons authorised and allowed to obtain sensitive codes, passwords, financial information, details of IT systems, software, networks, etc. of the organisation. Internal directory information should not be released over the phone. These requests should be recorded and handled either by the customer service function or the requested department. When disclosure takes place to authorised persons only, this should be logged and reported.

Documenting suspicious calls: All suspicious calls should be documented by the person receiving the call and reported accordingly.

Sending passwords to remote users: All passwords sent to remote users should be delivered by person and released upon the signature of the authorised users themselves. All these actions should also be logged and reported.

Personal identification: All employees should have badges with a large photo worn at all times. All visitors should also have badges worn at all times while in the offices or premises of the organisation. The visitors' personal data should be recorded in a visitors log and reported.

E-mail attachments handling: All electronic mail attachments should be handled and checked by a central administration function, and only released to the particular person when a security check has been performed.

Generic e-mail addresses: Generic e-mail addresses should be set up for business functions of the organisation communicating with external parties.

Fax relaying: Relaying of fax messages should not be allowed.

Domain registrations: When registering Internet domain names of the organisation, no personal contact details should be given. Only generic functional data (department name, address, etc.) should be recorded as contact data.

Personnel roaming: Unauthorised company employees should never be allowed to roam unescorted within any business areas containing sensitive information.

External contractors handling: Check the credentials and work orders of anyone performing technical work in or around your offices. Double-check and verify the work was actually requested and necessary. Have someone representing your interests accompany these visitors while on your property, and have them complete their work during normal business hours. Outside contractors should never be allowed to roam unescorted within any business areas.

Items left for pick up: Before releasing any item to be picked up by anyone (e.g. external messenger, another company employee), the person giving the item should record all personal and corporate details of the recipient.

Waste handling: All waste items (printed reports, work notes, company documentation of any kind, management reports, performance data, digital media, manuals, policies, procedures, printer cartridges, unused forms, etc.) should be destroyed completely, either by using a paper shredder (for paper waste) or a degaussing device (for digital media).

6.5.8 Security change management procedure

Security change management is a disciplined process for managing and controlling security modifications to the information processing environment. This includes alterations to the security-related issues of main computing systems software, the network, database servers and specialised security software, etc.

The objectives of security change management are to reduce the risks posed by modifications to the information processing environment, and improve the stability and reliability of the IT processing operations as changes are made.

The critical first steps in change management are, usually, the following:

- identifying the security changes
- defining the scope of the changes
- obtaining approval for the changes
- taking the proper back-ups before the changes are implemented
- implementing the changes
- recovering to the previous state if the changes fail
- reviewing and documenting all changes.

Various other IT forms that may be used for management control, system development and security monitoring and other security quality monitoring purposes are included in Appendix 4.

6.6 Specialised IT security hardware and software protection controls

This component is concerned with the necessary IT technical protection controls. These may also need the concentrated effort, additional focus and disciplined attention of IT management for the development and deployment of safer and more secure IT systems.

The actual detailed IT technical protection controls may be developed and implemented by the IT manager, in charge, sometimes with external support, overviewed by the IT committee, and ratified by the Board. The audit checklists in Paragraph 6.9 may be used to support the design, implementation and post-implementation review of the IT technical protection controls for the specific organisation.

The usual IT technical protection controls are:

- Computer security incident handling system
- Cryptography controls
- Other technical controls.

6.6.1 Computer security incident handling system

A computer security incident can result from a computer virus, other malicious code, or a system intruder, either an insider or an outsider. The definition of a computer security incident is somewhat flexible and may vary by organisation and computing environment. An incident handling capability (such as an Intrusion Detection System) may be viewed as a component of contingency planning, because it provides the ability to react quickly and efficiently to disruptions in normal processing. Incident handling can be considered that portion of contingency planning that responds to malicious technical threats.

This system should include for all incidents (potential and actual) the following stages:

- preparation
- detection
- containment
- eradication

- recovery
- follow-up and reporting
- feedback and review.

6.6.2 Cryptography controls

Cryptography is a branch of mathematics based on the transformation of data. It provides an important tool for protecting information and is used in many aspects of computer security. Cryptography is traditionally associated only with keeping data secret. However, modern cryptography can be used to provide many security services, such as electronic signatures and ensuring that data has not been modified (*see also Chapter 8*).

6.6.3 Other technical controls

These are hardware and software mechanisms for implementing security at the technical level, such as: firewalls, Virtual Private Networks, DMZ, IDS/IPS systems, website content filtering, gateway anti-virus, Email Server, DNS, VLAN, BACK-UP lines, WEB URL filtering, URL keyword blocking, database management system security parameters setting, database password profiles, digital certificates, honeypots and honeynets, etc.

Honeypots and honeynets are mechanisms (hardware, software) that create an environment where the tools and behaviour of 'blackhats' (the most dangerous hackers) can be captured and analysed further.[49]

6.7 Evaluation and monitoring controls of IT security

This component is concerned with the necessary evaluation and monitoring controls. These may also need the concentrated effort, additional focus and disciplined attention of IT management for the development and deployment of safer and more secure IT systems.

The actual detailed evaluation and management monitoring controls of IT security may be developed and implemented by the IT manager, in charge, sometimes with external support, overviewed by the IT committee, and ratified by the Board. The audit checklists in Paragraph 6.9 may be used to support the design, implementation and post-implementation review of the evaluation and monitoring controls for the specific organisation.

The usual evaluation and monitoring controls are:

- Audit and management reviews
- Audit trail controls
- Security monitoring controls.

6.7.1 Audit and management reviews

It is necessary to periodically review user account management on a system. Reviews should examine the levels of access each individual has, conformity with the

---

[49] For more on honeypots and honeynets, see (a) www.cert.org, (b) www.honeypots.net, (c) The Honeynet Project (http://project.honeynet.org), and (d) *Honeypots, Tracking Hackers*, Spitzner L, Addison-Wesley (2003).

concept of least privilege, whether all accounts are still active, whether management authorisations are up to date, whether required training has been completed, and so on. These reviews can be conducted on at least two levels: (1) on an application-by-application basis, or (2) on a system wide basis.

Mechanisms besides auditing and analysis of audit trails should be used to detect unauthorised and illegal acts. Rotating employees in sensitive positions, which could expose a scam that required an employee's presence, or periodic rescreening of personnel are methods that can be used.

6.7.2 Audit trail controls

Audit trails maintain a record of system activity by system or application processes and by user activity. In conjunction with appropriate tools and procedures, audit trails can provide a means to help accomplish several security-related objectives, including individual accountability, reconstruction of events, intrusion detection and problem identification (*see also Chapter 8*).

6.7.3 Security monitoring controls

To maintain operational assurance in terms of security, organisations can use two basic methods: audits and monitoring.

Audits

Audits can be self-administered or independent (either internal or external). Both types can provide excellent information about technical, procedural, managerial or other aspects of security. The essential difference between a self-audit and an independent audit is objectivity. An auditor can review controls in place and determine whether they are effective. The auditor will often analyse both computer- and non-computer-based controls.

Monitoring and review tools

There is a variety of monitoring and review tools, such as activity monitor software, automated tools, security checklists, penetration testing, etc. These are executed, usually, by an assigned IT manager or senior IT staff member.

Activity monitor software: This is software that runs on a firewall or network server which aims to prevent virus infection by monitoring for malicious activity on a system, and blocking that activity when possible.

Vulnerability automated tools: Automated tools can be used to support threat monitoring and to help find a variety of vulnerabilities, such as improper access controls or access control configurations, weak passwords, lack of integrity of the system software, or not using all relevant software updates and patches. There are two types of automated tools: (1) active tools, which find vulnerabilities by trying to exploit them, and (2) passive tests, which only examine the system and infer the existence of problems from the state of the system.

Security checklists: Checklists can be developed, which include national or organisational security policies and practices (often referred to as baselines), and used. The audit and review security checklists provided in this book can be used for the same purpose.

Penetration testing: This can employ many methods to attempt a system break-in. In addition to using active automated tools, penetration testing can be done 'manually'. For many systems, lax procedures or a lack of internal controls on applications are common vulnerabilities that penetration testing can target. Penetration testing is a very powerful technique; it should preferably be conducted with the knowledge and consent of both IT and end-user management.

Review of system logs: A periodic review of system-generated logs can detect security problems, including attempts to exceed access authority or gain system access during unusual hours, detect log clipping, etc.

Automated security checking tools: Several types of automated tools monitor a system for security problems. Some examples are virus scanners, checksumming, password crackers, integrity verification programs, intrusion detectors and system performance monitoring.

Configuration management: From a security point of view, configuration management provides assurance that the system in operation is the correct version (configuration) of the system and that any changes to be made are reviewed for security implications.

Trade literature review: In addition to monitoring the system, it is useful to monitor external sources for information.

Periodic re-accreditation: Periodically, it is useful to formally re-examine the security of a system from a wider perspective. The analysis, which leads to re-accreditation, should address such questions as: Is the security still sufficient? Are major changes needed? The re-accreditation should address high-level security and management concerns as well as the implementation of the security.

Site certification: Periodically, it is useful to formally undertake a comprehensive assessment of the technical and non-technical security functions of an IT system in its operational environment to establish the extent to which the system meets a set of specified security requirements, performed to support operational system accreditation.

Network taps review: Periodically, it is useful to formally examine the network cabling system to ensure that no network taps exist. Network taps are hardware devices that hook directly onto the network cable and send a copy of the traffic that passes through it to one or more other networked devices.

Monitoring IT controls: IT controls should be monitored on a continuous or periodic basis by assigned IT management, and all issues reported for action and resolution. Appendix 3 contains a 'Monitoring IT controls checklist' which could be used for this purpose. Other IT forms that may be used for management control and monitoring purposes are included in Appendix 4. This may be facilitated by following the monitoring and review activities management plan, presented in Chapter 1, and adding all relevant data to the IT management report (*as per Chapter 1*). It is the job of the CIO to ensure that the IT reporting mechanism is fed with the relevant data of this area.

The security audit programmes and checklists presented in Paragraph 6.9 of this chapter and the 'Security Incidents Log Form' (*see Appendix 4*) may be used for management control, system development and security monitoring and other quality monitoring purposes.

6.8 IT security performance measures

The complete integrated set of components of IT security, as described in this chapter, may be evaluated and improved by establishing and collecting performance data and by using the audit programmes and checklists (*see Paragraph 6.9*).

The typical IT security performance measures that may be used are shown in Table 8.

These performance measures could be based on a mixed system with two components: Component 1 would be an IT BSC (Information Technology Balanced Scorecard) Measurement System, described in Chapter 4; and Component 2, would be a Compliance Monitoring System for monitoring compliance to policies, procedures and related matters (e.g. budget issues).

All these data may be included in the IT management report issued by the CIO (*see Chapter 1*).

The IT management of the company, may, depending on various aspects of the organisation, analyse all this performance and compliance monitoring information to review, assess and improve the IT security elements of the IT function of the specific organisation.

IT Security Performance Measures
1. Number and types of incidents
2. Number and types of violations
3. Number and types of viruses eliminated
4. Number and types of obsolete accounts
5. Number of incidents that damaged the reputation of the organisation with the public
6. Number of developed and deployed systems where security requirements were not met
7. Number of access rights authorised, revoked, reset or changed; Number and types of violations (by IP Address, by port, by traffic type denied, etc.)
8. Access privileges maintenance response time
9. Number and types of external visitors
10. Number and types of maintenance visits
11. Number and types of access by remote calls
12. Security policies and procedures not crafted
13.Security policies and procedures not followed
14. Compliance with security policies and procedures

Table 8: IT Security Performance Measures

6.9 Review and audit tools and techniques

In order to ensure that the IT security governance controls are properly and effectively organised to serve the control needs of the specific corporate entity, guidelines and other tools may be necessary to aid the manager and other professionals (auditor, system development staff, IT security personnel, compliance officers, etc.) in discharging their duties.

The review and audit tools that may support IT managers and other professionals (IT auditors, IT consultants, internal auditors, external auditors, compliance officers, etc.) in establishing, evaluating, and improving the Enterprise Architecture controls described in this chapter, and which are offered for potential use, are: IT security audit programme, IT security policy checklist, and logical security controls checklist.

Guidelines and other tools are described in Appendix 3 (Monitoring IT controls checklist), Appendix 4 (Examples of IT forms), Appendix 5 (IT audit methodology), Appendix 6 (IT audit areas), and Appendix 7 (Internal audit report example).

The audit programme and checklists presented in this paragraph are not intended to be a complete management review or IT audit guide. IT managers and other professionals may choose to use only certain components of the checklists and audit programmes based upon the size, complexity, business needs and demands, IT maturity needs and expectations, nature of the organisation's business, and levels of deployment and utilisation of IT systems.

6.9.1 IT security audit programme

The objective of this audit programme is to support the process of constructing, reviewing, evaluating and improving the IT security controls identified.

This audit programme covers the following: basic management issues, human resource management, IT procurement procedure, contingency planning, IT legislation compliance, physical and environmental controls, system development and maintenance, data centre operations, and software and data security.

Basic management issues

1 Determine who has responsibility for IT security for the organisation and assess whether it is the right level of management.
2 Ensure that procedures for the preparation, approval and monitoring of IT strategic plans are implemented and that these plans are in alignment with the strategic plan of the organisation.
3 Examine the organisational security policy and compare it to the IT security policy to ensure that both of these serve the same purpose and needs.
4 Ensure that the IT security policy contains at least data classification and security penetration testing for all critical IT systems and services.
5 Assess the IT management reporting method to ensure that all IT issues are reported and monitored.
6 Assess the operation of the IT review mechanisms between end-users and IT, such as IT steering committee, user liaison group, IT project steering committee, etc.

7 Review the resolution procedures for security problems and ensure that these resolve all reported security incidents satisfactorily.

8 Ensure that all security issues are made known via written reports and discussions to higher levels of management, including the Board members.

9 Ensure that the evaluation of information security status is executed on the basis of self-assessments, on-site audit reviews, penetration testing, on-site technical evaluations, ethics assessments, data quality testing and best practice benchmarking.

Human resource management

10 Review the organisational charts and job descriptions to ensure that there is adequate segregation of duties in terms of security issues.

11 Review the training and education programmes and budget to ensure that all personnel have been given the approved training on security-related matters.

12 Assess the effectiveness of support provided by IT and other security mechanisms to the end-users on IT security issues.

IT procurement procedure

13 Review the IT procurement policy and procedures to ensure that all IT purchases are examined from the security perspective.

14 Review a good sample of IT purchase documentation to ensure that the formal IT policy and procedures are been implemented properly.

15 Review the major IT hardware and software contracts to ensure that the formal IT policy and procedures are been implemented properly.

16 Review the computer insurance policy of the organisation to ensure that major risks of IT hardware and software systems are covered adequately.

Contingency planning

17 Review the IT contingency plan and ensure that all critical IT systems are covered.

18 Ensure that this plan is reviewed and tested on a periodic basis.

19 Review the back-up policy and procedures to ensure that these are adequately implemented and monitored by IT management.

20 Review the back-up register to ensure that this is kept up to date.

21 Review both the on-site and off-site vault procedures.

IT legislation compliance

22 Determine which national and international laws and regulations pertaining to IT issues are relevant to the organisation.

23 Ensure that proper licences exist for all IT software and hardware purchased.

24 Test compliance with IT legislation, including data privacy and copyright issues.

Physical and environmental controls

25 Ensure that physical access controls are enforced in accordance with the corporate security policy and professional practices for the following: wholly owned buildings, shared buildings, central computer room and server rooms, personal computers and work stations, peripheral equipment, such as modems, routers, printers, etc. magnetic and other digital media, and technical manuals and documentation.

26 Ensure that management controls are enforced to protect buildings, personnel, equipment and media in accordance with the corporate security policy, vendor guidelines, and professional health and safety practices against the following: fire, flood, power fluctuations, static electricity, storms, and food and beverage accidents, etc.

System development and maintenance

27 Assess the system development and maintenance procedures to ensure that they are adequate in terms of security in all phases, such as analysis, design, construction, testing, implementation and support.

28 Review the system development and maintenance procedures to ensure that all phases are signed off by the key end-users.

29 Review the programming standards to ensure that they handle the security issues related to interfacing with other operating system software and application systems.

30 Review the program library maintenance procedures to ensure that all programs are fully tested and their movement to production status approved before they are transferred to the production library.

Data centre operations

31 Assess the adequacy of controls to ensure that the correct production files are used in all application systems running in the data centre.
32 Review all logs to ensure that all events are recorded and monitored.
33 Assess the adequacy of back-up and recovery procedures.
34 Assess the adequacy of external party maintenance and support procedures.

Software and data security

35 Ensure that general procedures and specific measures are implemented to protect against illegal access to the system, its utilities, the program libraries, the system and application software, the data files, etc.
36 Assess the adequacy of the general procedures and specific measures implemented to protect against illegal access to the system, its utilities, the program libraries, the application software, the data files, etc.
37 Ensure that passwords are used for each set of users and corresponding applications and for each class of actions (update, delete, read, remote access, etc.) and that these passwords are changed according to the corporate password policy.
38 Ensure that users cannot run their own programs to access production libraries and production data.
39 Ensure that IT personnel cannot access production data without specific authorisation.

6.9.2 IT security policy checklist

The objective of this checklist is to support the process of constructing, reviewing, evaluating and improving the controls identified in Paragraph 6.4 'IT security plans and policies'.

1 Is there a formal IT security policy? Consider: approval at Board level, objectives, scope and coverage, responsibility for monitoring or update, and distribution to staff.
2 Is the security policy supported by documented standards and procedures? Consider: responsibility for monitoring or update, internal audit involvement, areas covered e.g. information management, systems development, communications, personnel, logical access control, and distribution to staff.
3 Is there a security committee, or similar body, responsible for establishing, maintaining and reviewing security standards and guidelines? Consider: organisation chart, duties and responsibilities, training or experience, and segregation of administration and monitoring roles.
4 Is there a security administration function? Consider: organisation chart, duties and responsibilities, training or experience, and segregation of administration and monitoring roles.
5 Is there an end-user computing policy? Consider: software licensing or copyright, use of standard software, anti-virus procedures, security and distribution to staff.
6 Has a data ownership policy been established and issued to management and staff? Consider: objectives, appointment of data owners or data custodians, data

administration function, data classification defining levels of confidentiality, and access rights.

6.9.3 Logical security controls checklist

The objective of this checklist is to support the process of constructing, reviewing, evaluating and improving the controls identified in Paragraphs 6.5 and 6.7 'IT security procedures and practices' and 'Evaluation and monitoring controls of IT security').

1 Are data files, application programs and/or operating systems accessed and/or amended with appropriate authority?
2 Have sensitive data and applications been identified and classified?
3 Have appropriate security measures been implemented to restrict users' access to data and programs? Consider: user ID and passwords, menu facilities, and management approval of menu options.
4 Are development staff prevented from accessing data and software in the production environment? Consider: segregation of production and test environments, procedures for emergency changes e.g. documentation, review, etc.
5 Are unique user IDs assigned to each user? Consider: review a sample of user IDs to ensure they are authorised and unique for each user.
6 Are passwords changed regularly? (Note how often.)
7 Is there a procedure to ensure passwords are issued and changed in a controlled manner? (Explain this procedure.) Consider: management reports on current users and access rights, password changes e.g. system-generated, self-initiated changes, security advice,

avoidance of passwords which can be guessed easily, reuse of previous passwords and length of passwords.

8 Is there a procedure to ensure that user IDs or passwords are removed from the system when an employee leaves? Consider: obtaining a list of user IDs and determine if a sample or all individual users are still in employment.

9 Are employee access rights changed when they are relocated internally?

10 Is the password file encrypted? Consider: if not, who can access the file and are they authorised to do so?

11 Is the allocation, authorisation and use of powerful user IDs or passwords controlled and monitored? (Note to whom these passwords are assigned.)

12 Are there established procedures to be applied if and when the security officer is not available?

13 Are there adequate procedures to control the use of dial-up modems? Consider: dial-back facility, authorisation, operator connection requirements.

14 Are other logical access controls applied? Consider: restricted number of sign-on attempts, automatic password expiry facility, minimum length of passwords, logging unauthorised access attempts and restricted access to specific terminals.

15 Is an access control system(s) used? (Note the access control system and version.) Consider: obtaining specific control reports produced by the access control system, review selected reports, and client's procedures for reviewing reports and investigating violations.

16 Are end-users restricted from using utility programs capable of amending or deleting data?

17 Are development staff who have access to utilities for test purposes restricted from accessing live data? Consider: determine if the development staff, who have

access to the utilities, have access to production programs or libraries. Determine if development staff, who have access to utilities for test purposes, are restricted from accessing live data.

18 Is the use of utilities on live data authorised and documented? Consider: logging of the use of utilities, and review of log.

6.10 Conclusion

IT security means protecting data, information, information systems and other IT-related assets and elements of an organisation from unauthorised access, use, deployment, ownership, disclosure, disruption, modification or destruction.

IT security may be achieved, probably more efficiently and effectively, by implementing a suitable set of controls, such as the ones described in this chapter by reviewing, changing, adding, deleting, customising them, etc. to meet the needs, demands and operating mode of the given organisation, and operating them with continuous diligence. These controls, as we have seen, may include policies, practices, procedures, organisational structures and specialised hardware and software functions. These controls will need to be established to ensure that the specific IT security objectives of the organisation can be met.

Moreover, the main IT Security Controls and the audit and review programmes and checklists identified and revised to suit the needs of the organisation concerned protect the knowledge management framework of the organisation (*described in Chapter 1*), as they provide a safe and secure environment for its information collection, processing and knowledge reporting activities.

Further to the above, IT security controls, as practice has shown, are considerably cheaper and more effective if they are incorporated at the requirements specification and design stage of the IT systems, than later in implementation or during the operating phase.

In the fight to maintain IT security, organisations and managers will probably need to make compromises. Managers will have to make the choices that fit the needs of the organisation and balance between the advantages of enforced computer security and strong reliability, against the costs and disadvantages that tight security measures do, sometimes, have.

When efficient and effective IT security controls are exercised and executed in the best way, organisations, in the long run, are more protected and secure to serve their customers, stakeholders, community and greater society.

6.11 Review questions

This set of questions may be employed by those using the controls identified in this book to assess and double-check their own conceptual understanding and practical knowledge contained in this chapter.

1. What is the purpose of IT security controls?

Reference: Paragraph 6.2 'Purpose and main types of IT security controls'.

2. How is information security achieved?

Reference: Paragraph 6.2 'Purpose and main types of IT security controls'.

3. What are the main types of IT security controls?

Reference: Paragraph 6.2 'Purpose and main types of IT security controls'.

4. What are the usual IT security policies and plans?

Reference: Paragraph 6.4 'IT security plans and policies'.

5. What should the IT security policy cover?

Reference: Paragraph 6.4 'IT security plans and policies'.

6.What is the primary purpose of the privacy of information policy?

Reference: Paragraph 6.4 'IT security plans and policies'.

7. What is the purpose of the information sensitivity policy?

Reference: Paragraph 6.4 'IT security plans and policies'.

8. Which major actions should the IT security management plan include?

Reference: Paragraph 6.4 'IT security plans and policies'.

9. What is a 'cookie'?

Reference: Paragraph 6.4 'IT security plans and policies'.

10. What are the main activities of a computer security awareness and training programme?

Reference: Paragraph 6.4 'IT security plans and policies'.

11. What is the primary objective of the system development security plan?

Reference: Paragraph 6.4 'IT security plans and policies'.

12. What does separation of duties mean in an IT function?

Reference: Paragraph 6.5 'IT security procedures and practices'.

13. What steps does the process of end-user account management include?

Reference: Paragraph 6.5 'IT security procedures and practices'.

14. What does 'friendly termination' of end-users include?

Reference: Paragraph 6.5 'IT security procedures and practices'.

15. What is the reason why the password must not contain dictionary words from any language?

Reference: Paragraph 6.4 'IT security plans and policies'.

16. How should default passwords be controlled for system and database software?

Reference: Paragraph 6.4 'IT security plans and policies'.

17. How often should a password change?

Reference: Paragraph 6.4 'IT security plans and policies'.

18. How can a computer security incident result?

Reference: Paragraph 6.6 'Specialised IT security hardware and software protection controls'.

19. What are some of the hardware and software mechanisms for implementing security at the technical level?

Reference: Paragraph 6.6 'Specialised IT security hardware and software protection controls'.

20. What are some of the usual IT security performance measures?

Reference: Paragraph 6.8 'IT security performance measures'.

CHAPTER 7: DATA CENTRE OPERATIONAL AND SUPPORT CONTROLS

A man who had wasted his fortune had nothing left but the clothes he wore. On seeing a swallow one spring morning, he decided the weather would be warmer, so he sold his coat. The weather, however, turned colder the next day and killed the swallow. When the shivering man saw the dead swallow he moaned, 'Thanks to you I am freezing.'

(The meaning of this story is that one swallow does not make a summer. In other words, several IT operational controls are needed to work in co-operation with each other.)

Aesop (Ancient Greece: 6th century BC)

7.1 Scope

To run the IT application systems developed according to the IT strategy of the organisation and provide services across all levels and locations of the organisation and the wider community, including other interconnecting parties, you need to create and operate a physical infrastructure and obtain services from specialised external providers.

Controls at this level ensure that the IT facilities and equipment can remain in good operational status, and ensure the safe and successful operation of the IT infrastructure and systems for serving the business purposes of the organisation.

A set of main data centre operational and support controls are presented as follows: data centre design and infrastructural controls, data centre physical access controls, computer hardware management controls, IT contingency planning and disaster recovery controls. Examples of various methodologies and policies are shown in some cases.

In addition to these, a set of audit programmes and checklists are presented to support the CIO, the IT manager and other professionals (system development staff, end-users, IT auditors, internal auditors, IT consultants, external auditors, compliance officers, etc.) in executing and improving their duties and responsibilities.

7.2 Purpose and main types of data centre operational and support controls

A data centre is a facility used to house computer systems and associated components, such as telecommunications and storage systems. It generally includes redundant or back-up power supplies, redundant data communications connections, environmental controls (e.g. air conditioning, fire suppression) and security devices. A data centre can occupy one room of a building, one or more floors, or an entire building. Data centres need to be safe and secure, in order to enable the running of large and continuous IT operations.

Safety (construction that meets applicable industry design standards and codes) and security (protection from harm, intrusions, attacks, natural disasters, etc.) of data centres are provided by physical access controls and environmental management controls. Physical access and environmental management controls refer to the control of the environment of the workplace and computing facilities and may include monitoring and control access to and from such facilities (e.g. doors, locks, heating and air conditioning, smoke and fire alarms, fire suppression systems, cameras, barricades, fencing, security guards, cable locks, etc.).

Organisations may implement data centre operational and support controls based on policies, procedures and practices of the organisation considering and including the requirements of various compliance and legal requirements.

The objective of data centre controls is to ensure that the whole data centre and its support components operate in a reliable fashion in order for the IT systems to run effectively, efficiently and securely.

The main types of data centre operational and support controls are:

- data centre design and infrastructural controls
- data centre physical access controls
- computer hardware management controls
- IT contingency planning and disaster recovery controls
- monitoring and review controls
- IT operational performance measures.

7.3 Data centre design and infrastructural controls

Data centre design requires careful planning controls by management to make certain that the facility housing computing and network resources and the environment in which they operate will not adversely affect the data centre's reliability and security.

The designer of a data centre will need to view the continuous operation of the services provided by the data centre as paramount. The potential consequential losses and damage through failures or omissions, of any kind, could very quickly run into significant amounts of money and can be detrimental to the continued operation of an organisation.

Prolonged down time can be very costly and usually results in lost production, lost business, damaged image and good will, etc.

Data centre design and infrastructural controls are implemented to protect the facility housing system resources, the system resources themselves, and the facilities used to support their operation. In doing so, they can help prevent interruptions in computer services, physical damage, unauthorised disclosure of information, loss of control over system integrity, and theft.

The actual detailed data centre design and infrastructural controls may be developed and implemented by the IT manager in charge, sometimes with external support, overviewed by the IT committee, and ratified by the Board. The audit checklists in Paragraph 7.9 may be used to support the design, implementation and post-implementation review of these controls for the specific organisation.

The main controls in this area are:

- Guidelines for designing secure data centres
- Data centre environment management controls
- Data centre infrastructure test and review plan.

7.3.1 Guidelines for designing secure data centres

Building and protecting data centres is usually a job for specialists with expertise in designing and constructing data centres, running IT operations and electronic services, implementing physical security measures and establishing plans for business continuity.

The guidelines presented below are based on consulting experience and various industry, government and technical standards and guidelines.[50]

Physical location

The data centre is usually constructed some distance from corporate headquarters and at least over 300–500 metres from the main road.

It may not be built near refineries and other chemical plants, airports, chemical storage facilities, power plants, rivers, sea coast, dams, known earthquake zones, sandy sub-terrain, etc. as they are considered hazardous zones.

Landscaping may be used for protection. Trees, boulders and obscure security devices (like fences) help keep vehicles from getting too close.

It may be a good practice to keep a 100 to 200-metre buffer zone around the site, use crash-proof barriers for added protection, avoid putting up a 'data centre' sign anywhere

---

[50] For examples, see: (1) *EU Standards on Best Practices for Data Centres*, *http://re.jrc.ec.europa.eu/energyefficiency/html/standby_initiative_data_centers.htm*, (2) *The standards of the National Fire Protection Association*, *www.nfpa.org*, (3) *www.constructionweblinks.com/Industry_Topics/Building_Codes_and_Regulations/building_codes_and_regulations.html*, (4) The Design Guide of WBDG, www.wbdg.org/design/secure_safe.php, (5) *The standard for physical security of USA federal buildings*, *www.dhs.gov/files/committees/gc_1194977813020.shtm*, and (6) guidelines recommended in the article at *www.csoonline.com/article/220665/19-ways-to-build-physical-security-into-a-data-center*. These guidelines are only an example. Before their consideration for any potential use, they will need to be reviewed in detail, amended and customised to the corporate needs, compliance requirements and operating conditions applicable to the specific organisation. This is usually the task of a 'site design survey'.

on the road or include any information about its exact location in company reports, brochures, etc. and install and operate fire, heat, humidity and other contaminants protection systems.

Utilities

In order to reduce utility disruptions, management may consider having two sources for all utilities, such as electricity, water, voice and data.

Electricity sources should be traced back to two separate substations, and should be underground, entering the building at a different area than water or other lines. Electricity demands should be double the needed operational load. Management should plan to install a standby power generation (such as UPS) capability.

Water sources should be traced back to two different main lines, and water lines should be underground and should come into different areas of the building, with water lines separate from other utilities.

Walls and windows

Depending on the needs of the organisation and building codes and standards, concrete for external walls is probably required and may prove to be an effective barrier against the natural elements and explosive devices. Make sure internal walls run from the ceiling all the way to sub-flooring where wiring is usually housed. For extra security, use walls lined with special insulating and bomb-proof materials,[51] or build extra-high walls around the data centre. If you must have windows, limit them to the canteen or administrative area. In any case use bomb-resistant laminated glass.

Entry and exit points

Use retractable crash barriers at vehicle entry points.

Control access to the car park and loading dock with a security staffed guard station that operates the retractable doors or bollards.

Use mechanisms, such as a raised gate and a green light as visual cues that the bollards are down and the driver can go forward. When extra security is needed, have the barriers left up by default, and lowered only when someone has permission to pass through. Monitor all entrances and exits with cameras.

For data centres that are especially sensitive or possible targets, have guards use mirrors to check underneath vehicles for explosives, or provide portable bomb-sniffing devices. All vehicles should be checked regardless of who owns them – employees, visitors, suppliers, mail deliveries, police, others, etc.

Control access to the building by establishing one main entrance, plus a back one for the loading dock. For exits required by fire codes, install doors that don't have handles on the outside. When any of these doors are opened, a loud alarm should sound and trigger a response from the security command centre.

---

[51] See, for example, *www.gaffco.com.*

Surveillance cameras[52] should be installed around the perimeter of the building, at all entrances and exits, and at every access point throughout the building.

A combination of motion-detection devices, low-light cameras, zoom cameras and standard fixed cameras may also be used.

All surveillance data should be recorded digitally and stored off site.

Machinery protection

Make sure that the mechanical area of the building is always protected.

Environmental systems and uninterruptible power supply units should be strictly off limits. If generators are outside, use concrete walls to secure the area.

For both areas, make sure all external contractors and maintenance crews are accompanied by an authorised employee at all times.

Quality of air

Ensure the heating, ventilation and air-conditioning systems can be set to recirculate air rather than drawing in air (which may not be clean) from the outside.

This could help protect internal personnel, visitors and equipment if there were some kind of biological or

[52] See, for example, *www.video-surveillance-guide.com/surveillance-cameras.htm.*

chemical attack or heavy smoke spreading from a nearby fire.[53]

Put devices in place to monitor the inside air (or the air coming in) for chemical, biological or radiological contaminants.

Multiple security layers

Use standard access cards for entering offices and biometric and other sophisticated identification systems for access to sensitive areas of data centres. Ensure that anyone entering the most secure part of the data centre will have been authenticated at least as many times as needed, and their visits logged.

Restrict access to computer processing, network, cabling, telephone rooms, etc. on an as-needed basis, and separate these rooms as much as possible in order to control and monitor access.

Food and smoke control

Instruct and inform employees and visitors not to consume food and drinks in sensitive areas, such as network rooms, cabling areas, telephone centres, computer rooms, etc. The same rule should apply for smoking.

Provide a common area where people can eat, and smoke without getting smoke, food and drinks on computer equipment, cables, etc.

---

[53] See, for example, the *Occupational Safety & Health Administration Standards* of the US government: www.osha.gov.

Visitor toilets

Make sure to include toilets for use by visitors and delivery people who don't have access to the secure parts of the building.

Monitoring system

Security personnel should be able to monitor and control access to all areas from a central point and have remote monitoring without physically being in the data centre.

Attempts to access, whether successful or not, should be kept in the system.

Failure of supporting utilities

Systems, and the people who operate them, need to have a reasonably well-controlled operating environment. Consequently, failures of electric power, heating and air-conditioning systems, water, sewage and other utilities will usually cause a service interruption and may damage hardware. Organisations should ensure that these utilities, including their many elements, function properly.

Building structural collapse

Organisations should be aware that a building may be subjected to a load greater than it can support. Most commonly this is as a result of an earthquake, a snow load on the roof beyond design criteria, an explosion that displaces or cuts structural parts, or a fire that weakens structural parts, etc.

Protective measures are usually specified by building and other government regulations and codes.[54]

Constructing bioclimatic buildings

Organisations and their architectural teams, designing and building data centres, might also consider the 'bioclimatic design approach' in their data centre projects. This uses the following elements in building construction: solar systems for heating, shading, energy collectors, techniques for natural lighting, photovoltaic energy systems, water use reduction through rainwater collection and reuse, energy efficiency equipment, green roofs, etc.[55]

7.3.2 Data centre environment management controls

The objective of the following data centre environmental controls is to ensure that the whole data centre and its support components operate in a reliable fashion in order for the IT systems to run effectively, efficiently and securely.

Environmental controls

Computer areas should be properly cleaned and dusted. Facilities and equipment should be protected against the adverse effects of weather (sun, rain, snow, wind, etc.),

---

[54] See, for example, the code for earthquake protection www.buildingsmartalliance.org/index.php/bssc.

[55] For more, see: (1) 'Modeling energy efficiency of bioclimatic buildings', *Energy and Buildings*, Vol. 37, Issue 5, May 2005, Tzikopoulos AF et al (2005), (2) www.inbuilt.co.uk, (3) www.concept-bio.eu/bioclimatic-architecture-buildings.php, and (4) www.cres.gr.

plumbing leaks, and the calamitous result of a fire via the use of a fire-prevention system. While plumbing leaks do not occur every day, they can be seriously disruptive. An organisation should know the location of plumbing lines that might endanger system hardware and take steps to reduce risk (e.g. moving hardware, relocating plumbing lines and identifying shutoff valves).

Fire security controls

Building fires are a particularly important security threat because of the potential for complete destruction of computer hardware and data, the risk to human life and the pervasiveness of the damage. Smoke, corrosive gas and high humidity from a localised fire can damage systems throughout an entire building or data centre. Consequently, it is important to evaluate the fire safety of buildings that house systems.

Controls to reduce the damage caused by fire should include safes (for document and media storage with a four hour plus fire rating), computer facility protection measures (walls, floors and ceilings should have a two hour plus fire rating), fire alarms, on site and off site, fire-safety vaults (for critical documents and back-up media safe-keeping), smoke and ionisation detection, water detection, halon or other approved fire extinguishing system, and building code measures (computer facilities to be constructed according to approved building and cabling codes).

Radiation prevention controls

Computer equipment, the wiring and computer rooms themselves should be shielded to contain the radiation emanated by computers in order to avoid some external party from picking up all the critical communications and data transmitted from a distance from the data centre.

Other radiation prevention controls and guidelines are provided by international organisations,[56] governments, radiation prevention systems sold by vendors, etc.

Emergency power controls

A battery-based UPS (uninterruptible power supply) should be installed to provide continuous operation in case of a total or partial electrical power failure. This UPS may maintain power for a few minutes to several hours depending on the needs of the organisation. In many cases an independent power generator should also be installed and kept in good operational status for the operation of critical IT systems (banks, hospitals, airports, etc.).

7.3.3 Data centre infrastructure test and review plan

Failures of electric power, heating and air-conditioning systems, water, sewage, and other utilities will usually cause a service interruption and may damage hardware. Organisations should ensure that these utilities, including their many elements, function properly. This may be accomplished by the following plan:

Step 1: Have spare circuit boards and components for UPS units

Step 2: Check all electrical circuits (once a year)

---

[56] E.g.*www.ilo.org*, *www.ceessentials.net*, etc.

Step 3: Locate equipment not under sprinkler heads or water pipes

Step 4: Store extra critical computer motherboards, disks and controllers, and other devise and parts

Step 5: Test the fuel levels of standby generators (once every six months, etc.)

Step 6: Test smoke detectors (once a year)

Step 7: Change the passwords to the access door of the computer room every month (or so)

Step 8: Test the fire extinguishers once a year

Step 9: Lock the network and telecommunications rooms, at all times

Step 10: Record all tests and maintenance done.

These guidelines and controls may be considered to be used, customised, modified, etc. depending on the experience of management and other factors of the organisation. Usually, external experts are brought in to design, review and construct data centres, according to the needs, costs and benefits expected from the data centre of the organisation to its stakeholders and society.

The tests and reviews described above or required by the organisation can be executed by specialist teams on the basis of their experience, skills and knowledge, and according to industry codes and other government standards relevant in the location where the data centre exists and operates.

7.4 Data centre physical access controls

Physical access control is a process which enables an authorised person to control access to sensitive areas and resources in a given physical facility or office (e.g. data centre, computer room, network room, offices with access to computer-based information systems and services, etc.). This process may be seen as the second layer in the field of security of IT systems and services, while logical access controls (the policies, procedures and technical controls used in computerised information systems) may comprise the first level of security of these systems and services.

The possession of access control is of the most crucial importance when various persons seek to secure access to very important, confidential or sensitive information stored in IT systems, digital media and equipment.

Physical access control can be achieved by a human (a guard or receptionist), through mechanical means, such as locks and keys, or through technological means, such as computerised access control systems, biometric systems, video monitoring systems, etc.

The usual physical access controls of this control component include:

- IT physical security steering committee
- Physical access control policy.

7.4.1 IT physical security steering committee

Physical security of an IT environment can best be accomplished, in more organised companies and for better and more effective results, by a management committee and a policy.

The IT physical security steering committee is responsible for the identification and implementation of all approved physical access controls for the buildings and offices of the organisation. In order to do this they may employ security analysis, needs assessment and other techniques, as they consider necessary.

This process will probably include:

- Setting up a physical security team to conduct this task
- Identifying all physical and IT assets and IT operations to be protected
- Considering all relevant laws, regulations, policies, social and political environment, etc.
- Undertaking threat assessment by classifying most critical assets, identifying potential targets, defining potential threats, etc.
- Estimating relative security risks and probability of success
- Defining specific control measures
- Implementing approved physical control measures
- Training all employees
- Documenting findings and monitoring implementation.

7.4.2 Physical access control policy

The objective of this policy is to implement measures to prevent unauthorised physical access, damage and interference to its premises, prevent loss, theft or compromise of any information-holding assets or interruption of the organisation's normal IT activities.

Physical access control policy – example

1 The organisation may use and deploy personnel, traditional physical security methods, locks, security alarms, access control systems, biometric devices, surveillance video systems, and any other system or method considered appropriate, within the corporate culture and national legal framework.[57]

2 All employees of the organisation are responsible for their personal actions and should not carry out any activity, which is outside the relevant laws or in breach of the policies, procedures, work practices or codes of conduct, as defined by the organisation.

3 Authorised managers are responsible for authorising access to IT assets under their area of responsibility.

4 All accesses to IT assets, offices, rooms, facilities, terminals, systems, etc. should be authorised, recorded and reported.

5 All managers of the organisation are responsible for the implementation and monitoring of this policy within their areas of responsibility and for ensuring that those for whom they are responsible, including visitors, external consultants and maintenance contractors, are aware of and comply with this policy and associated physical access control guidelines.

6 Corporate security administration management is responsible for ensuring that all users are appropriately educated so that when they access IT assets, appropriate physical security measures are carried out.

7 All employees have the responsibility to report all potential or actual security breaches to the Corporate Information Security Officer.

8 All managers of the organisation are responsible for notifying Human Resources to ensure that employees leaving the organisation return all physical access control items (e.g. keys,

[57] Such as *US Physical Security Standards for Federal Facilities*: www.dhs.gov.

access cards, etc.).

9 An authorised staff member will co-ordinate building operating schedules and approve other individuals to access the building after normal business hours.

10 In the event of an emergency, all employees will need to contact their own management regarding access to their offices, building, etc. and follow the procedures documented under the business continuity policy.

11 All employees will be trained in the use of the physical security systems of the organisation.

12 All equipment should be located in a safe location, and that location should be locked after normal business hours.

13 Personnel working in the data centre, as well as authorised visitors, should be identified and recorded in a data centre visitors' log.

14 Visitors should be escorted while within the most sensitive areas. The same should take place for maintenance personnel (both internal and external).

15 Any breaches of this policy will be treated seriously and may be subject to disciplinary procedures or legal proceedings, up to and including dismissal, etc.

The traditional physical access controls and security industry is in rapid transition. New specialisations, systems and methods are on the rise. The management of organisations may need to consider these various methods and technologies as well as the above controls, and other corporate factors, in their efforts to improve their own physical access controls to very sensitive areas.

7.5 Computer hardware management controls

Computer hardware refers to mainframe or minicomputer servers, personal computers, mainframe computer printers, network printers, peripheral equipment, etc.

These may be located within the main computer room or in a network room, or in the offices of end-users.

Computer hardware needs to be managed effectively as other IT assets of the organisation using computer hardware management controls. Establishing these controls may be achieved by the IT manager in charge, sometimes with external support, overviewed by the IT committee, and ratified by the Board.

The audit checklists provided in Paragraph 7.9 may be used to support the design, implementation and post-implementation review of the personal computer controls for the specific organisation.

The main controls in this area are:

- Computer hardware controls
- Personal computers controls.

7.5.1 Computer hardware controls

The objective of computer hardware controls is to use the components of the computer hardware itself in order to protect the computerised application systems from unwanted, abrupt and unscheduled shutdowns.

These controls may include:

Fault-tolerant computer systems. These computer systems are built with redundant components. If one component fails, the other or others can provide a degraded, but effective, service until further improvement or safe system shutdown is accomplished.

Hardware locks. Locks for disk drives in personal computers and servers may be installed.

Hardware inventory register. A hardware inventory register should be maintained for all computer, network and related peripheral equipment of the organisation. See 'IT Asset Inventory Form' in Appendix 4 for such an example.

Food and smoking controls. Food and beverages should not be taken near any type of computer hardware. Smoking in computer and network rooms should not be allowed.

Consumables inventory register. A register of all consumables related to computers, printers, other peripheral equipment, etc. should be maintained.

Office equipment controls. Offline equipment, such as busters, decollators, printers, etc. should be located outside the main computer room.

Hardware maintenance log. A hardware maintenance log should be maintained, and the following should be recorded for each distinct hardware unit: errors, available time, productive time, non-productive time due to errors, scheduled down time, maintenance undertaken.

Hardware maintenance controls. Only authorised personnel (either internal or external) should maintain computer or other hardware and software. This maintenance should be recorded in a maintenance log and should be followed by whatever maintenance reports, slips, etc. are necessary. If remote maintenance (via an online modem) is carried out, this should also be authorised, recorded in a remote maintenance log, and the person who did the maintenance should file a maintenance report immediately after they finished the maintenance job.

7.5.2 Personal computers controls

The main purpose of controls in managing personal computers is to ensure that the end-users, especially when they are using personal computers to do their daily business tasks, are protected from harm, damage and errors.

These controls include:

Integrity and security of back-up digital media. All users should take periodic back-ups of their critical files. These should be securely stored in fire-safety office cabinets and a record of all the back-up contents should be kept in a back-up register.

Personal computers use policy. The organisation should create and communicate to all personnel a personal computers policy.

Personal computers use policy – example

This policy specifies what is and is not allowed as regards the personal computers of the organisation. The contents of such policy may include rules and guidelines for:

Organisation acceptable use of personal computers

Use of personal computers for personal reasons

Access to various unethical or illegal websites

Access to personal 'friendship' type social networks

Filing of electronic messages

Use of personal firewalls on individual PCs

Committing the organisation via the use of e-mail messages
Use of passwords for daily access to personal computers
Change of passwords on a predefined basis
Back up of critical department data and storing them (the back-up media) in a safe place
Documentation of all critical files kept in personal computers
Purchase of personal computers by a central organisational function (e.g. corporate purchasing department) and with the assistance of the IT function, purchase of software packages only by a central organisational function and with the assistance of the IT function
Housekeeping of personal computers and printers: cleaning, dusting, avoid drinking and eating near the computer hardware, storing digital media in clean drawers and fire-safety cabinets, etc.

Personal computer safe operations procedure. The organisation should create and communicate to all personnel a list of safe operation for their personal computers. This list should be part of a procedure and may include the following tips and guidelines:

- Turn off personal computer: Turning your computer off when you are not using it is both environmentally friendly and a good security practice. As long as your machine is running and connected to the network, it's a target, whether or not you are using it. Furthermore, it is normally a good idea to restart your computer every now and then to free up RAM and virtual memory that was not correctly reallocated after usage.
- Do not share any passwords: Remember, passwords are the 'keys' to your personal computer. Don't give them to anyone; and if you must, change them immediately afterwards.

- Maintain currency of anti-virus software: Anti-virus and anti-spyware programs rely on definition files that tell them what programs are bad. If you do not regularly update these definitions, your anti-malware applications will not recognise the new threats.
- Maintain currency of operating system (OS) and application software: Keep your OS and applications up to date. As new security vulnerabilities are discovered, operating system and application manufacturers release patches to correct them. All current operating systems (MS Windows, Apple OS, many LINUX distributions, and others) and many application vendors release patches to fix security vulnerabilities and performance flaws.
- Protect System Administrator account: You should always have a strong, complex password on the System Administrator or root account of your personal computer. Be aware of default Administrator accounts without a password. You will need to reboot your personal computer into safe mode in order to put a password on this account.
- Lock personal computer upon leaving: If you work in an office, then you should lock your personal computer whenever you leave it while it is running. Furthermore, you should set up a screen saver that locks the screen after a few minutes of inactivity.

IT management may consider using or changing or improving or even adopting other controls than the ones presented in this paragraph (above), depending on their needs, Board requirements, security control targets and corporate planning aspects of their organisation.

7.6 IT contingency planning and disaster recovery controls

All companies, enterprises, small and large businesses and organisations can experience a serious disaster, event or incident that can prevent them from continuing normal business operations. These can range from earthquakes, floods, fires, other natural phenomena, to explosions, strikes, serious software and hardware errors and malfunctions to IT security incidents. The statistics on business losses as the result of various disasters including IT failures are tremendous according to various sources.[58]

The management of the organisation have a responsibility to recover from such incidents in the minimum amount of time, with minimum disruption and at minimum cost. This requires careful preparation and planning.

In IT terms, disaster prevention and recovery is a well-documented process to design, install and test specific measures to enable the continued operation of an organisation as a result of a natural or man-made disaster or failure.

It may include planning for taking back-ups to a safe off-site location, locating redundant hardware at other external premises, and effective policy and procedures for protecting and restoring critical corporate information.

The purpose of controls in the area of IT contingency planning and disaster recovery is to ensure that critical IT assets, such as data centre facilities, computer hardware, operating system and database management system

---

[58] www.infoworld.com, www.computerworld.com, www.cio.com, www.fema.com, http://news.zdnet.com.

software, telecommunications lines, application systems (software and data), etc. can be recovered within a predefined time-frame in order to resume critical business operations after a disaster.

Establishing the actual detailed IT contingency planning and disaster recovery controls may be developed and implemented by the IT manager in charge, sometimes with external support, overviewed by the IT committee, and ratified by the Board. The audit provided in Paragraph 7.9 may be used to support the design, implementation and post-implementation review of the IT contingency planning and disaster recovery controls for the specific organisation.

These controls include the following:

- IT contingency planning methodology
- IT disaster recovery plan
- IT back-up procedure
- Vital records package procedure
- Off-site facility controls.

7.6.1 IT contingency planning methodology

The standard definition of 'methodology' is 'a body of methods, procedures, rules and techniques employed by a discipline in order to carry out a task'.

In terms of IT contingency planning, the methodology presented next is designed to be used for the single objective of creating an IT disaster recovery plan.

This methodology usually includes the following steps:

Step 1. Ensure management commitment: An effective contingency and disaster recovery plan requires management support at all levels.

Step 2. Conduct a business impact analysis: A good business impact analysis identifies the critical business functions of the organisation, the corresponding recovery time-frames, the recovery alternatives, the costs and benefits of each alternative, etc.

Step 3. Conduct an IT applications analysis: The critical IT applications that support the critical business operations to be recovered should be identified.

Step 4. Conduct a disaster site analysis: The various alternatives to recovering a data centre in case of disaster, such as 'hot site', 'cold site', 'warm site', 'dual data centre', etc. should be described, analysed and compared (costs and benefits, resource requirements, risks, difficulty factors, etc.). A hot site is a fully operational disaster recovery centre completely equipped with hardware, software, communications and on-site technical support personnel. This is a contingency alterative that may be used to recover from disaster, depending on the organisation's needs and requirements for resuming its business operations based on IT systems. A cold site is a contingency alternative to recovering from disaster, depending on the needs of the organisation. A cold site facility is wired and set up to operate computer and peripheral equipment supplied by the organisation recovering its IT systems. A warm site is a contingency alternative to recovering form disaster, depending on the needs of the organisation. A warm site is set up in such a way as to facilitate the remote processing of the IT systems of the organisation under recovery, at the recovery site. A dual data centre is a contingency alternative to recovering from disaster, depending on the needs of the organisation. A dual data centre is set up in such a way as to always have available a fully functioning data centre at a safe distance from the primary data centre.

Step 5. Develop a well-documented plan: A very well-documented plan will detail critical and vital business functions of the organisation, identify key resources (systems, funds, personnel, etc.), and list specific procedures for disaster recovery.

Step 6. Organise a vital records package: Identify everything that is critical to the functioning of the organisation.

Step 7. Notify insurance companies: Most insurance companies offer better rates for insured IT assets if they know that the specific organisation maintains a contingency and disaster recovery plan.

Step 8. Create a test plan: Establish the procedures for testing the IT disaster recovery plan. Describe the time-frames, training and resources required.

7.6.2 IT disaster recovery plan

The IT disaster recovery plan is the output of the IT contingency planning methodology presented above.

IT disaster recovery plan document – example

The IT disaster recovery plan document describes what must be done in order to recover from a predefined failure and resume operating an information system.

The contents of this plan should be:

1 Executive summary: A management overview and a summary statement of the contents of this document including a costs and benefits summary, also the critical business functions and the critical IT applications covered in this plan.

2 Resources required: Internal organisational conditions and resources required (legal, IT management, users, building facilities, administration, accounting, security), also external organisational resources required (insurers, vendors, alternate business processing personnel, telecommunications, public authorities, etc.).

3 Security issues: A detailed statement of the security issues regarding IT disaster recovery and how these should be implemented to facilitate the recovery process.

4 Risks covered: A detailed statement of the natural and other risks covered, such as rain, fire, storm, earthquake, etc.

5 Risk solutions analysis: A detailed statement of the recovery solutions covered by the document at the level of: recovery of data, recovery of the data centre, recovery of the network, recovery of end-user operations, recovery of the business function(s).

6 Recovery solution: A detailed statement of the recovery solution to be implemented, such as: hot site, warm site, parallel data centre, etc. For the solution to be implemented, all the hardware and software requirements and specifications should be documented as well.

7 Applications recovery list: A summary statement for each critical application to be recovered as per recovery solution.

8 Back-up procedure: A summary statement for the procedures executed, as per back-up procedure plan, and the set of back-up media required for the recovery of each critical application to be recovered.

9 Recovery invocation process: A detailed statement of the conditions triggering the recovery process, such as time period, impact of real or potential damage, production errors of the

application system, etc.

10 Recovery organisation: A detailed statement on the key personnel required, their organisation structure for recovery processes, their complete details (surnames, names, phone numbers, etc.) and the training that they have taken.

11 External support: A detailed statement of all external contractors, their contractual arrangements and their details (names, locations, phone numbers, etc.) required for the triggering and completion of the recovery process.

12 Recovery testing strategy: A detailed statement of the testing strategy for all elements of the recovery process and the resources required.

13 Return procedures: A detailed description of the procedures that have to be carried out for the successful return to the main data centre of the organisation after the recovery has taken place at the recovery location.

14 Insurance: Insurance coverage details should document what is covered (especially to cover any cost of moving data and operating in an alternative way) and what is not, as well as the necessary claims forms and procedures to be followed.

15 Plan maintenance procedure: A detailed description of the procedure to maintain this plan including all the required forms, such as history of changes log, testing schedule, change authorisation form, etc.

16 Appendix: The appendix may contain external support contracts for the recovery process, insurance contracts, insurance claims forms, and all other pertinent documentation required for the recovery process to be completed (e.g. distribution list, user comments form, glossary of recovery terms, vital records inventory list, systems and database software configuration lists, vehicles list for logistics support, the details (names, phone numbers) of back-up top management that must be present to authorise critical operations in case the assigned recovery management personnel are absent, etc.).

7.6.3 IT back-up policy and procedures

Recovery is only possible if proper back-ups are taken at predetermined time intervals, according to a set of IT back-up policy and procedures.

It is usually the job and responsibility of IT management to establish a back-up and restore policy and associated back-up and restore procedures.

The purpose of the back-up and restore policy is to standardise a means of backing up and recovering computer files. This policy contains statements in the following areas of information technology: daily and monthly data back-ups, network server back-ups, application back-ups, tape/media rotation schedule, delivering tapes and digital media off site, and job scheduling.

The following guidelines present an example of what the specific back-up policy and procedures might contain for a given organisation.

1 Back-up copies of operating system and database software, Enterprise Architecture software and data, application software and the data on all files and databases, should be taken on a predefined basis (daily, weekly, monthly, yearly, etc.), and should be stored both on site and off site.
2 Tapes and other back-up digital media (back-up media) must be stored on-site in a fireproof combination-lock safe on the company corporate offices.
3 Only the approved IT Support Manager or other authorised person will store and remove the tapes and other back-up digital media.
4 Back-up media are also stored off site in a secure bank safety deposit box. These are hand-delivered each week

by the IT Support Manager, who must sign in at the bank to enter the safety deposit box area. If the IT Support Manager is unavailable, the authorised person will deliver and remove the back-up media to the bank.

5 These back-up media should be tested as per the recovery test plan.
6 A log of all back-ups taken and their storage location should be maintained at all times.
7 All movement of back-up media should be authorised and logged in a storage log.
8 The volumes moved to an off-site storage facility should be securely stored until they arrive at their destination. An off-site storage log should be also maintained.
9 Corporate, business and IT management should set up a team to examine what should be contained in a vital records package, and take appropriate actions to execute what is required to put this into full implementation.
10 IT management should follow up and monitor these procedures.

7.6.4 Vital records package procedure

The IT contingency plan and the disaster recovery procedures, as well as the disaster site alternative, will be effectively worthless unless the organisation has taken measures to ensure that a copy of its vital records (the vital records package) exist in an off-site safe location, to enable full disaster recovery.

It is usually the job and responsibility of corporate and IT management to establish the procedure to ensure that a vital records package is put into operation for the specific organisation.

The vital records package usually includes copies of:

- all application programs, systems software (including networking software and database management systems), and Enterprise Architecture components (including the Enterprise Architecture repository)
- recent application data
- documentation of all applications, and the Enterprise Architecture framework information
- contracts (purchasing, maintenance)
- licences
- a small stock of pre-printed stationery
- system software books (vendor manuals)
- a small stock of digital storage media (flash disks, diskettes, DVDs, CD-ROMs, tapes, printer cartridges, etc.)
- a list of key personnel and their details (addresses, phone numbers, etc.), documentation of corporate policies, procedures and standards
- employment contracts for critical staff (managers, IT, finance, etc.)
- corporate performance printed reports for the last years, depending on the regulatory framework, such as balance sheets, transaction listing, budgets, etc.
- escrow passwords (escrow passwords are passwords that are written down and stored in a secure location (like a safe) that are used by emergency personnel when privileged personnel are unavailable)
- financial transactions on digital media for the last years (corresponding to corporate performance reports).

The vital records package should be taken to a safe off-site location according to a schedule and authority outlined in the back-up and recovery policy and procedures.

7.6.5 Off-site storage review procedure

The IT contingency plan, the vital record package, the disaster recovery procedures, as well as the disaster site alternative, will be effectively of no added value unless the organisation has taken measures to ensure that the off-site storage location is properly maintained.

It is usually the job and responsibility of corporate and IT management, with support from internal audit (in some organisations) to establish and carry out these controls.

For the better and more effective use of the off-site storage facility of the organisation, the following procedural controls may be designed and implemented at the off-site storage facility:

- Review of the fire-detection and alarm system
- Review of the temperature and humidity monitoring system
- Review of the physical security procedures
- Review of the physical location to ensure that it is not subject to flooding, earthquakes or power fluctuations
- Review of the back-up power facilities
- Review of the fire-safe storage cabinet space.

IT management may consider using or changing or improving or even adopting other IT contingency controls that the ones presented in this paragraph, depending on their IT needs, Board requirements, security control targets and corporate business continuity planning aspects of their organisation.

7.7 Monitoring and review controls

Monitoring, according to COSO (*www.coso.org*), applies to all components of internal controls of organisations: risk assessment, control environment, control activities, and information and communication. Controls, both corporate and IT, that are not monitored and reviewed, are not improved and deteriorate, as a result, over time.

The purpose of monitoring and review controls, in the area of data centre operational and support controls, is to ensure that the IT controls designed and implemented for this area serve both the purposes of the organisation and the IT function.

Establishing the specific detailed monitoring and review controls of this area may be carried out by the formal IT committee, or the IT management and its senior staff, or some other corporate work team or group, or a combination of these. It would be useful, however, and as it has been proved in practice, to have these controls approved by the Board or senior management executive committee of the said organisation. All the audit programmes and checklists contained in Paragraph 7.9 may be used to support the formulation execution of these monitoring and review controls.

The typical controls in this area are:

- Computer operations processing controls
- Daily activities review controls
- Surveillance and eavesdropping detection controls.

These controls may also be facilitated by following the monitoring and review activities management plan, and all the performance data included in the IT management report (*see Chapter 1*).

7.7.1 Computer operations processing controls

For the efficient and effective running of IT systems and services in a data centre, the management of the computer operations department will need to carry out various actions and implement processing controls:

1 Operations manuals for the computerised applications running in the data centre must be strictly followed.
2 All jobs run by the operations personnel should be recorded in a jobs processing log.
3 Console logs recording all system messages and operator instructions should be kept both in printed form and on magnetic media for a definite time period (at least six months).
4 All additions and removals of equipment within the computer and network rooms should be authorised and recorded in the equipment log.

7.7.2 Daily activities review controls

It is of paramount importance that IT management monitors and reviews the implementation of all data centre controls. Carrying out this review process, on a daily basis, includes the following:

- Reviewing visitors log (recording entry and exit of visitors on a daily basis)
- Reviewing daily work activities log (recording transactions processed, enquiries served, customers served, units produced, etc.)
- Reviewing problem log (recording problems solved by date, description of problem, description of solution, who solved the problem, who tested the solution of the problem, etc.)

- Reviewing the relevant performance indicators (*see also Paragraph 7.8*)
- Conducting periodic vulnerability scans of the computer access control system, and reviewing the reports with all relevant management levels
- Checking with the security personnel to ensure that they monitor, document and review all entries and exits to the data centre
- Reviewing computer jobs schedule (recording data processing jobs executed per day of operation, etc.).

These logs and schedules should be monitored and reviewed at the appropriate level of IT management. Various other Internet log reports may be produced and reviewed[59] by IT management.

Examples of various IT journals and logs, and other IT forms that may also be used for management control, system development and security monitoring and other quality monitoring purposes are included in Appendix 4.

7.7.3 Surveillance and eavesdropping detection controls

Depending on the type of data an IT system processes, there may be a significant risk if these data are intercepted in some way. Organisations, corporate and IT management, and security specialists should be aware that there are three usual routes of data interception:

- direct observation

---

[59] See examples of log reports by SANS www.sans.org, 'SANS Top 5 Essential Log Reports'.

- interception of data transmission by various surveillance and eavesdropping devices located within the premises of the organisation
- electromagnetic interception (by remote means).

Physical security controls may protect against intercepting data by direct observation (*see Paragraph 7.4*). Protecting data against electromagnetic interception may be accomplished by other means beyond the scope of this book (e.g. TEMPEST Shielding, special applications, such as RINT, data scrambling, etc.).

Interception of data transmission by surveillance and eavesdropping devices can be controlled by various procedures, one of which is described later on in this paragraph.[60]

Interception of data transmission by various surveillance and eavesdropping devices located within the premises of the organisation may be prevented or eliminated all together (potentially) by carrying out the steps of the following process (Electronic Interception Detection (EID) Process):

Step 1. Organise and appoint an EID Committee with a chairperson and other corporate staff, specific terms of reference, a mission and a budget.

---

[60] See also (1) 'When competitors really bug you (industrial espionage)', *Security Management*, pp. 44–47, Jones P (1990); (2) 'Clear the air with TSCM (technical surveillance countermeasures survey)', *Security Management*, pp. 54–59, Calhoun J (1992); (3) 'Espionage 101and much more', *Security Management*, pp. 106–114, Murray KD (1995); (4) 'Countering the threat of espionage', *Security Management*, pp. 35–37, O'Connell EP (1994); and (5) 'Developing a counterintelligence mind-set', *Security Management*, pp. 54–56, Pavucek L (1992).

Step 2. Hire professional experts (from outside) and select inside technical personnel to form a Surveillance Countermeasures Review (SCR) team.

Step 3. Sign a non-disclosure agreement with all external experts, as a standard part of their assigned work contract.

Step 4. Appoint an SCR project team manager.

Step 5. Provide the SCR team with all relevant organisational drawings and schematics, such as floor plans, wiring diagrams, vendor manuals of the heating, ventilation, fire safety, air conditioning systems, etc.

Step 6. Review and approve the team's list of the EID equipment, which should be state of the art.

Step 7. Ensure that the planned EID is only known to very few people.

Step 8. Execute the EID at a time period so as not to interfere with normal daily operations.

Step 9. Review the EID results and take appropriate action.

Step 10. Document the EID results and close the project.

7.8 IT operational performance measures

The complete integrated set of controls of data centre operational and support services, may be evaluated and improved by establishing and collecting performance data and by using the audit programmes and checklists (*see Paragraph 7.9*).

The usual IT operational performance measures that may be used are depicted in Table 9.

Number	Performance Measure
1	Online response time
2	Number of pages printed
3	Number of operational hours
4	Number of idle hours
5	Number of transactions processed
6	Number of processing errors
7	Mean time to back up
8	Mean time to recover
9	Average time of error correction
10	Average availability (percentage) of applications
11	Average availability (percentage) of hardware/communications/software
12	Data centre policies and procedures not followed

Table 9: IT operational performance measures

These performance measures could be based on a mixed system with two components: Component 1 would be an IT BSC (Information Technology Balanced Scorecard) Measurement System, described in Chapter 4, and Component 2, would be a Compliance Monitoring System for monitoring compliance to policies, procedures and related matters (e.g. data centre procedures not crafted, data centre budget not followed, etc.).

The IT management of the company, may, depending on various aspects of the organisation, analyse all this performance and compliance monitoring information to review, assess and improve the data centre operational and support elements of the IT function.

7.9 Review and audit tools and techniques

In order to ensure that the data centre operational and support controls are properly and effectively organised to serve the control needs of the specific corporate entity, guidelines and other tools may be necessary to aid the manager and other professionals (auditor, system development staff, IT security personnel, compliance officers, etc.) in discharging their duties. Those offered for potential use are checklists for reviewing: physical security controls, environmental issues, production environment issues, data centre management, back-up and recovery, IT disaster recovery, and personal computers.

Additional guidelines and other tools are described in Appendix 3 (Monitoring IT controls checklist), Appendix 4 (Examples of IT forms), Appendix 5 (IT audit methodology), Appendix 6 (IT audit areas), and Appendix 7 (Internal audit report example).

The checklists presented in this paragraph are not intended to be a complete management review or IT audit guide. IT managers and other professionals may choose to use only certain components of the checklists and audit programmes based upon the size, complexity, business needs and demands, IT maturity needs and expectations, nature of the organisation's business, and levels of deployment and utilisation of IT systems.

7.9.1 Physical security controls checklist

The objective of this checklist is to support the process of constructing, reviewing, evaluating and improving the data centre environmental management controls identified in this chapter.

1 Does the site have a perimeter fence erected?
2 Is access to the site controlled and monitored? Consider: security gate house, guards on duty for 24 hours a day or only normal working hours, regular patrols, CCTV, use of identity badges.
3 Are staff and visitors prevented from parking close to the computer room? Consider: controlling access by visitors and suppliers, allocated parking spaces for permanent staff.
4 Is the security of the building appropriate to the activities of the organisation? Consider: security guards present, regular security patrols, guards on duty for 24 hours a day or only normal working hours, burglar alarm system, CCTV, window locks, use of identity badges.
5 Is a record maintained of all visitors?
6 Are there any unattended access points? Consider: goods entrance(s), rear entrance(s), fire exit(s).
7 Are there control procedures to restrict access from unattended access points?
8 Are there control measures in place to ensure that only members of staff or authorised visitors are on the premises? Consider: staff and visitors required to carry visible identification badges, procedures controlling the issue of passes or badges to visitors, requirement for

visitors to be accompanied by a permanent member of staff, security awareness of staff, i.e. to challenge unescorted visitors.

9 Is specific authority required for staff to remove computer equipment or media from the building?

10 Is access to the computer room(s) restricted to authorised persons? Consider: record of visitors (including system engineers, cleaners, etc.), use of access control devices (e.g. card keys), controls to prevent misuse of the card access system, different access levels, allocation of cards, record of violations, investigation of violations, access restrictions to different areas, requirement for visitors to be accompanied.

11 Is access to particularly sensitive areas (e.g. telecommunications area) further restricted? Consider: access authorisation procedures, record of access, review of access log.

12 Are there procedural controls to restrict or monitor access to sensitive areas?

13 Are the windows to the computer area protected? Consider: toughened glass, opaque glass, use of screens, curtains, etc. burglar alarm system, use of window locks.

14 Is it possible to easily locate the computer area (i.e. by observation)?

15 Are master system consoles and other critical terminals (e.g. SWIFT terminals) located within the computer area? Consider: restriction of access.

16 Is access to the mains power supply in the building restricted to authorised personnel only?

17 Is there an alternative power supply? Consider: uninterruptible power supply, standby generator, access restricted only to authorised personnel.

18 Are there controls to prevent the loss or disruption of communications (e.g. secure cable pits, locked PABX room)?
19 Is access to cable risers, distribution boards, PABX rooms, etc. controlled?
20 Are service maintenance visits scheduled, authorised and, as far as possible, monitored?
21 Are cleaners and service staff required to sign in/out of the building and computer area(s)?
22 Are cleaners accompanied when in the computer area(s)?

7.9.2 Environmental issues checklist

The objective of this checklist is to support the process of constructing, reviewing, evaluating and improving the data centre environmental management controls identified in this chapter.

1 Have appropriate environmental controls been implemented both within the building and within the computer area? Consider: fire prevention or detection systems, air conditioning, humidity controls, false floor.
2 Are there fire precautions and instructions on what to do in the event of a fire posted in all departments?
3 Are fire drills (practices) regularly held? (Note date of last practice.)
4 Is fire-fighting equipment regularly serviced? (Note date of last service.)
5 Are staff trained in the use of fire-fighting equipment?
6 Is fire-fighting equipment available to prevent both an electrical and paper fire?
7 Are all catering or kitchen facilities located away from the computer room to reduce the risk of fire or water

damage causing loss or disruption of computer service and/or data?

8 Is computer data, media and documentation adequately secured? Consider: fire-proof storage for magnetic media, off-site storage, restriction of access, physical access controls.

7.9.3 Production environment issues checklist

The objective of this checklist is to support the process of constructing, reviewing, evaluating and improving the monitoring and review controls identified in this chapter.

1 Are all program updates to the production environment specifically authorised by IT management? Consider: management approval on program change forms.

2 Are development staff prevented from implementing new program versions into the production environment?

3 Is there a facility or software to determine if unauthorised changes have occurred to operational programs? Consider: object compare software, management review, logging of changes.

4 Is automated change control software used? Consider: coverage of all program changes, responsibility for supporting this software.

5 Is there a procedure to ensure previous versions of software are made inactive and only current versions are operative?

6 Are there established procedures for controlling any emergency changes made by systems development staff? Consider: approval by appropriate level of IT operational management, recording of all such changes, testing, retrospective approval by senior IT management, security officer.

7 Are separate libraries assigned for development, test and production activities?
8 Is a formal sign off (end-users, IT management, etc.) required after system testing and before transferring application software to production? Consider: approval by appropriate level of end-user and IT management, recording of all such changes, testing, retrospective review by IT auditing, and security officer.
9 Is regression testing carried out when production failures have been rectified?

7.9.4 Data centre management checklist

The objective of this checklist is to support the process of constructing, reviewing, evaluating and improving the IT contingency planning and disaster recovery controls identified in this chapter.

1 Is there an inventory of hardware, software and peripheral equipment? Consider: make, model and location of all computer hardware, communications network plan, software versions.
2 Are there any special processing requirements? Consider: use of special stationery, stock of special stationery.
3 Is there a computer equipment maintenance contract? Consider: contracted response times.
4 Is there adequate physical security to prevent accidental or malicious damage to the computer equipment?
5 Have environmental controls been implemented to minimise the damage arising from, for example, fire and flood? Consider: fire detection equipment, fire-fighting equipment, air conditioning, location of canteens and restaurant facilities, etc. humidity controls.

6 Is there an alternative power supply? Consider: uninterruptible power supply, standby generator.
7 Have access requirements to the computer systems been defined and are they complied with? Consider: data classification, system access controls, use of access control software, procedures to establish or delete user IDs or passwords.

7.9.5 Back-up and recovery checklist

The objective of this checklist is to support the process of constructing, reviewing, evaluating and improving the IT contingency planning and disaster recovery controls identified in this chapter.

1 Are back-up copies of data files, system software and application programs taken regularly? (Note the back-up cycle.) Consider: data at end of day, week, month, year, programs taken once a modification is implemented.
2 Are back-up copies held in a secure location remote from the computer site? Consider: data files, programs, systems software, systems documentation, operating procedures, user procedures, disaster recovery plan, environmental or physical security.
3 Are back-up versions taken off site regularly?
4 Has off-site storage been tested to ensure that the back-up data is reusable? Consider: records maintained of the physical location of tapes, other digital media, and disks and their contents, off-site copies of systems documentation, effectiveness of back-up procedures, timeliness of receipt of tapes, etc. from off-site storage, practical experience(s) of recalling and use of tapes, etc. from off-site storage.

5 Is access to the back-up copies limited to specified responsible individuals? (Note who they are.)
6 Is access to the back-up copies available 24 hours a day? Consider: authorisation requirements.
7 Are similar back-up controls applied to data stored on microcomputers (PCs, servers, etc.) e.g. on floppy disk or other digital media?
8 Is a complete back-up copy of the database taken regularly?
9 Are back-up copies of the database kept off site?
10 Are there fully documented back-up and restore procedures for the database?
11 Are the back-up and restore procedures regularly tested?

7.9.6 IT disaster recovery checklist

The objective of this checklist is to support the process of constructing, reviewing, evaluating and improving the IT contingency planning and disaster recovery controls identified in this chapter.

1 What is the risk that the business will not be able to resume effective operations (within a reasonable period of time) in the event that their existing IT (systems, communications, infrastructure, etc.) processing facilities were not available? Consider: risk management policy and procedure (corporate and IT).
2 Are risk analysis reviews carried out, as part of a disaster avoidance exercise, to minimise the likelihood of a major business disturbance occurring? Consider: scope of reviews, date of last review.
3 Have the organisation's critical systems been identified? Consider: How long could the organisation operate

effectively without their critical computer systems (e.g. hours, days, etc.)?

4 Are all application systems tested and approved before they are put into productive operational use?

5 Are there procedures to prevent unauthorised modification to operational and systems software?

6 Is the system software (including operating system, database and communications) version installed fully supported by the vendor or supplier?

7 Is comprehensive system documentation maintained and secured?

8 Are job processing procedures fully documented and secured?

9 Are user clerical procedures fully documented and secured?

10 Are back-up procedures documented and in full operating mode?

11 Has a disaster recovery plan been developed, documented and tested? Consider: adequacy of plan to ensure that in the event of disruption or loss, recovery can be achieved with minimal disruption to the business, regular review and update of the plan (note when it was last updated), periodic testing (note when last tested).

12 Have users specified their recovery requirements? Consider: levels of disruption (e.g. one hour, half a day, etc.), recovery of critical applications only, recovery of all applications, alternative clerical procedures, if appropriate, length of time alternative processing arrangements will last for, etc.

13 Have the users developed alternative working practices (as part of their recovery procedures) to take effect if normal processing is interrupted?

14 Is there a formal contract with a disaster recovery company? Consider: terms of contract, details of tests carried out.
15 Are there other areas of the business, in addition to IT, which require recovery arrangements to be developed? (Note details.)
16 Have business recovery arrangements or plans been developed for all critical business areas?
17 Are all contractual obligations with third parties satisfied? Consider: software licences, use of micro software, record of all licences.

7.9.7 Personal computers controls checklist

The objective of this checklist is to support the process of constructing, reviewing, evaluating and improving the computer hardware management controls identified in this chapter.

1 Are there adequate controls with regard to the security of information through end-user use of PCs, terminals, printers, and/or workstations? Consider: policy for end-user computing, security guidelines and responsibilities, authorisation rules, etc.
2 Have end-user guidelines been developed and distributed? Consider: security requirements, authorised software, authorised hardware, programming requirements, testing and documentation.
3 Are authorisation procedures in place for the purchase and introduction of new hardware and software? Consider: evaluation of new hardware and software prior to being placed onto the authorised software list, evaluation of hardware and software to ensure

compatibility between existing hardware and software packages.

4 Are hardware and software purchases recorded?
5 Is the removal or transfer of hardware and software controlled?
6 Has virus detection or vaccine software been installed?
7 Are procedures in place to inform users of what actions to take in the event of their PC being infected by a virus?
8 Is the information or data classified to restrict access and mode of access to the data or information?
9 Is there security or access control software in place to control the access of sensitive information?
10 Is access to sensitive data controlled and monitored?
11 Are there procedures in place to ensure the proper and secure disposal of commercially sensitive data on magnetic, other digital and/or paper media?
12 Is personal information registered in terms of the National Data Protection Act?
13 Are regular back-ups taken of the PC or workstation files?
14 Are similar controls applied to data stored on microcomputers as that on the mainframe (e.g. control over floppy disks)?
15 Is new software installed by suitably qualified or trained personnel?
16 Is a log maintained of all hardware and software errors and the action taken to resolve the errors?
17 Is there access control software in place to prevent unauthorised access to any PC, workstation or terminal?
18 Does the length of password required conform to the industry's accepted standard or the organisation's requirements?

19 Is data downloaded from mainframe systems? Consider: identification of data, access rights.
20 Is data uploaded to the central computer systems? Consider: identification of data, access rights.
21 Are controls in place to ensure that access to production programs and data files cannot occur in an unauthorised manner?
22 Are file controls in place to prohibit update of production files and programs except under controlled authorised conditions?

7.9.8 Personal computers management checklist

The objective of this checklist is to support the process of constructing, reviewing, evaluating and improving the computer hardware management controls identified in this chapter.

1 Does IT have responsibility for PC management?
2 Do procedures exist for requirements approval and is there a link between the needs for PC and the IT strategy?
3 Is a hardware/software list maintained?
4 Are all PC developed applications approved by management and properly documented?
5 Do procedures exist to protect PCs from theft, damage and environmental hazards?
6 Do adequate controls exist to ensure that software and data cannot be stolen or copied without authorisation?
7 Are diskette drives removed?
8 Is anti-virus software installed?
9 Are security issues monitored?
10 Are levels of authority specified?

11 Do technical support procedures exist for hardware, software and user problems?
12 Do job descriptions of staff providing PC support exist?
13 Is training given to IT users adequate?
14 Are all media maintained in safe storage?
15 Is there a log for all problems?
16 Is end-user developed software adequately protected?
17 Is there an application list maintained and is support by IT available on the following:

- Word processing?
- Spreadsheets?
- Personal Computer hardware?
- Database systems?
- Electronic mail?
- PC Accounting packages?
- PC link to fax?
- Telex?
- Desk top publishing?
- Time planning systems?
- Project management?
- Graphical presentation systems?
- Design support tools?
- Access to external databases?
- Internet access?

18 Do problem logging and reporting procedures exist for handling user problems?
19 Are data back-ups taken regularly?
20 Are back-ups safely stored?
21 Is there a list of back-up media maintained?

7.10 Conclusion

IT operations are a crucial aspect of most current organisations. One of the main concerns is business continuity; organisations rely more and more on their information systems and ITC (Information Technology and Communications) to run their operations. If an IT system and its related operations become unavailable, everyday business operations may be impacted greatly, or impaired or even stopped completely.

It is therefore necessary to provide a reliable infrastructure for IT operations, in order to minimise any chance of disruption. Information security is also a great concern, and for this reason a data centre has to offer a secure environment which minimises the chances of a security breach.

A data centre must therefore keep high performance standards for assuring the integrity and functionality of its hosted computer environment.

One of the key elements of data centre operations, besides defending the IT systems and infrastructure against internal and external intrusions and attacks, is to prevent data modifications and alterations in such a way that whenever an attack on an IT system and its services has been successful, you will still have software and data and be able to restore the systems, services and facilities to full productive functionality and proper business use.

Studies have shown that half of the businesses affected by data loss disasters have never recovered and most have been closed shortly after, unless they had excellent back-up and recovery strategies and an effective IT disaster plan.

In the fight to uphold efficient and effective IT operations in data centres, we may have to make compromises. We have to make the choices that fit us and our organisations and balance between the advantages of enforced computer security and strong data centre reliability, against the disadvantages that tight security measures and data centre procedures might have.

If we are aware about the risks of operating IT operations in data centres and the proper measures that can be taken to prevent these risks from becoming actual damage, then we are able to ensure that the data centre will continue to operate normally, and recover from contingencies.

The data centre operational and support controls presented in this chapter may be the instrument by which the achievement of the goals and the critical and significant facts, strategies, policies, procedures and results of data centre operations are accomplished. These controls may be reviewed, changed, added, deleted, customised, etc. to meet the needs, demands and operating mode of the given organisation, and must be operated with continuous diligence. These controls, as we have seen, may include policies, practices, procedures, organisational structures and specialised tools.

These controls will need to be established to ensure that the specific data centre operational and support services objectives of the organisation can be met.

Moreover, the main data centre operational and support controls and the audit and review programmes and checklists identified and presented in this chapter, and customised accordingly, facilitate the knowledge management framework (*outlined in Chapter 1*), as they support the infrastructural components housing and operating IT systems and services, the life-blood of both organisations and the knowledge management framework.

When these controls are exercised and executed in the best way, organisations run their IT operations more efficiently and effectively, and in the end, are more profitable and beneficial to its stakeholders, to society at large, and to the national and international economy.

7.11 Review questions

This set of questions may be employed by those using the controls identified in this book to assess and double-check their own conceptual understanding and practical knowledge contained in this chapter.

1. What do data centre operational and support controls ensure'?

Reference: Paragraph 7.1. 'Scope'.

2. What is the purpose of data centre operational and support controls?

Reference: Paragraph 7.2 'Purpose and main types of data centre operational and support controls'.

3. What are the main types of data centre operational and support controls?

Reference: Paragraph 7.2 'Purpose and main types of data centre operational and support controls'.

4. What are the main data centre controls?

Reference: Paragraph 7.3 'Data centre design and infrastructural controls'.

5. What is the role of radiation prevention controls of computer equipment, wiring and computer rooms?

Reference: Paragraph 7.3 'Data centre design and infrastructural controls'.

6. What types of utility failures will cause service interruptions?

Reference: Paragraph 7.3 'Data centre design and infrastructural controls'.

7. Which usual elements and actions are included in data centre infrastructure controls?

Reference: Paragraph 7.3 'Data centre design and infrastructural controls'.

8. What are the three routes of data interception?

Reference: Paragraph 7.7 'Monitoring and review controls'.

9. What are the main daily activities controls?

Reference: Paragraph 7.7 'Monitoring and review controls'.

10. What data should be recorded in an IT visitors log?

Reference: Paragraph 7.7 'Monitoring and review controls'.

11. What is the objective of hardware controls?

Reference: Paragraph 7.5 'Computer hardware management controls'.

12. What is the purpose of controls in the area of IT contingency planning?

Reference: Paragraph 7.6 'IT contingency planning and disaster recovery controls'.

13. How is a 'disaster' defined in IT terms?

Reference: Paragraph 7.6 'IT contingency planning and disaster recovery controls'.

14. What is a definition of the term 'hot site' in terms of disaster recovery?

Reference: Paragraph 7.6 'IT contingency planning and disaster recovery controls'.

15. What is a definition of the term 'cold site' in terms of disaster recovery?

Reference: Paragraph 7.6 'IT contingency planning and disaster recovery controls'.

16. What is a definition of the term 'warm site' in terms of disaster recovery?

Reference: Paragraph 7.6 'IT contingency planning and disaster recovery controls'.

17. What is a definition of the term 'dual data centre' in terms of disaster recovery?

Reference: Paragraph 7.6 'IT contingency planning and disaster recovery controls'.

18. What are some of the contents of a personal computers policy?

Reference: Paragraph 7.5 'Computer hardware management controls'.

19. What are some safe operation tips for personal computers?

Reference: Paragraph 7.5 'Computer hardware management controls'.

20. What are some of the usual IT operational performance measures?

Reference: Paragraph 7.8 'IT operational performance measures'.

CHAPTER 8: SYSTEMS SOFTWARE CONTROLS

A mouse bit a bull on the nose and slipped into a hole in a wall before the bull could react. The bull charged at the wall without making any impression time and again until he had worn himself out, at which the mouse darted out and bit the exhausted bull on the nose again. The bull could do nothing except fume with anger. 'You big ones don't always win,' squeaked the mouse from his hole, 'Sometimes we little ones come off best.'

(The meaning of this story is that the stronger do not always win.)

Aesop (6th century BC)

8.1 Scope

IT application systems, whether developed by IT in house, or acquired from an external party, are normally run in a secure data centre facility.

These systems are made up of application software which cannot be run alone, but must have system software upon which they achieve their tasks.

System software, such as database management systems, data communications and network software, etc. must be installed, configured and controlled. Controls at this level ensure that the operating system, database and data communications software can remain in good operational status, and ensure the safe and successful operation of the IT infrastructure and systems for serving the business purposes of the organisation.

A set of main systems software controls, such as: systems operating environment controls, database controls, data communications controls, audit trail controls, and monitoring and review controls are presented. Examples of various procedures, measures and forms are noted. In addition to these, a set of audit programmes and checklists are provided to support the CIO, the IT manager and other professionals (system development staff, end-users, IT auditors, internal auditors, IT consultants, external auditors, compliance officers, etc.) in executing and improving their duties and responsibilities.

8.2 Purpose and main types of systems software controls

Systems software is computer software designed to operate the computer and network hardware and to provide, enable, support and maintain a platform for running application software. Systems software usually includes diagnostic tools, compilers, servers, windowing systems, utilities, language translators, data communication programs, data management programs, database management systems software, and more. The purpose of systems software is to insulate the applications programmer as much as possible from the details of the particular computer and network platform being used.

Various controls are required to be implemented in the area of systems software to ensure the safe, efficient and effective operation of IT systems and services.

The main purpose of systems software controls, is to ensure that the operating system and the main components required for the safe and secure operation of the data centre and the computerised applications running in it, are managed in a disciplined manner to support the most optimal IT operations of the organisation.

The main types of systems software controls are:

- Systems software operating environment controls
- Database controls
- Data communications controls
- Audit trail log file controls
- Monitoring and review controls.

These controls may be considered for use, customised, modified, etc. depending on the experience of corporate and IT management, and other costs, benefits, corporate and IT culture and resource factors of the organisation.

8.3 Systems software operating environment controls

In order for systems software to allow the efficient and effective operation of application software, they both (systems software and application software) must function in a safe and properly controlled environment.

The main purpose of systems operating environment controls is to ensure that the operating system, and its main parts (nucleus, kernel, shell, etc.), the data communications software, the database management system software, the utilities of the operating system, the libraries containing system, database, application and network software, the security files, the various control files, and whatever other components are needed for the safe and secure operation of the data centre and the computerised applications running in it are in full productive status.

The actual detailed systems software operating environment controls may be developed and implemented by the IT manager in charge, sometimes with external support, overviewed by the IT committee, and ratified by the Board.

The audit programmes and checklists contained in Paragraph 8.9 may be used to support the design, implementation and post-implementation review of the systems software operating environment controls for the specific organisation.

The main controls in this area are:

- Production environment controls
- Systems software change management controls
- Systems software job description controls.

8.3.1 Production environment controls

The production environment in a computer room of a small IT function or a large data centre operation houses, is made up of computer and network hardware, test and production data, and test and production software libraries. These are operated, managed and supported by computer operations personnel, systems software support staff and maintenance contractors.

The main controls in this area are:

Production data and libraries access controls

Access to production data stored in any kind of file (flat file, database, etc.) and to the programs stored in production program libraries should not be allowed to systems software personnel without explicit written authorisation both by the IT manager and the user manager of the application data. All such authorised accesses should be properly documented by the system programmers immediately after they have completed their assigned tasks.

Computer room access controls

Systems programming personnel should not have free and easy access to the systems console and carry out testing or other tasks without written and well-justified authorisation. All actions carried out should also be documented and properly reported.

Software suppliers maintenance procedure

As software suppliers (operating system, database, application software package, etc.) tend to release minor and major changes to the supplied software very regularly, it is paramount also that these changes are controlled properly.

The mechanism for minor changes is the software suppliers maintenance procedure. This should contain the following:

- Authorising all systems software changes
- Documenting all changes (*see Appendix 4* 'Software Suppliers Minor Changes Form')
- Testing all changes before they are moved to production
- Keeping a log of all changes
- Backing up the complete system software and its environment before the changes are implemented
- Having a recovery plan prepared in case the implemented changes create errors and problems when they are moved to the production environment.

See also Paragraph 8.3.2 'Systems software change management controls' for major changes.

Various IT forms that may be used for management control, system development and security monitoring and other quality monitoring purposes are included in Appendix 4.

Segregation of duties

One system programmer should not design, test and implement changes to production systems. These tasks should be split between two or more personnel, and if this is not possible, all work should be carefully planned out, executed correctly and supervised by IT management in all work phases. Application programming personnel and computer operations personnel should review all changes to system software before these are implemented.

Documentation controls

All work carried out to systems software by systems programming personnel should be properly authorised, recorded by the use of specialised forms, reviewed by all stakeholders and maintained in a software changes file.

These forms are the following:

- Systems software change installation control form
- Systems software installation authorisation form
- Systems software review procedure control form
- Systems software emergency update form.

In addition to these, all changes should be appended with a narrative description of the changes carried out by the systems programming personnel.

An example of a form that may be customised by each organisation's IT department for controlling system software is presented in Appendix 4 'Systems Personnel Changes Form'.

8.3.2 Systems software change management controls

The major changes to systems software (operating system, database, application software package, etc.), may be managed and controlled more effectively by the following process.

The purpose of this process and related controls is to describe the procedures that must be followed for the: request, approval, initiation, implementation and testing of major changes in existing systems software, database management systems and data communications software systems.

Each major change should be documented, approved and managed as a project, with phases falling to both IT and end-user personnel.

Systems software management process

Project initiation phase: The purpose of this phase is to define and document the nature and scope of the change to confirm and develop among interested parties a common understanding of the project scope and how it relates to other projects within the overall IT-enabled investment programme. The definition should be formally approved by the senior management before project initiation.

Requirements analysis phase: If necessary, the business requirements and initial plan should be documented and forwarded to the IT manager who will identify the feasibility of the change with respect to existing infrastructure, the impact of the change to the IT budget and company's investment, and upon initial approval of the plan the IT manager should conduct a risk assessment to identify the impact of the amended application/system to the existing infrastructure.

System design phase: In the design phase, the IT manager forwards the plan to the technical support personnel for review and clarifications. The detailed system plan is produced including information, such as milestones, resources required, manpower and man-hours required.

The Security Officer should verify together with the IT manager whether they conform to the risk assessment performed and the security policies of the organisation.

System implementation phase: The system implementation phase includes the following procedures: installation of the changed application or system to the test environment of the organisation, and development of the test scenarios and test scripts in co-operation with the third-party vendor to identify conformance to business requirements of the organisation.

System testing and approval phase: System testing and approval should be performed by the business users that have requested and approved the change (especially when it concerns a software package). The results of the user acceptance test should be formally documented and forwarded to the IT manager, who will be responsible to perform the migration of the application or system to the production environment.

The 'Systems Software Major Changes Form' (*see Appendix 4*) may also be used.

Various other IT forms that may be used for management control, system development and security monitoring and other quality monitoring purposes are included in Appendix 4).

8.3.3 Systems software job description controls

As was described previously both the test and production environments of the IT function of any organisation are usually supported by both systems software staff and maintenance contractors. Some IT administration and personnel controls were described in Chapter 2 and in the paragraphs above.

All these controls, however, can only be properly implanted by the tool of 'job description', i.e. the formal assignment of duties and responsibilities for IT staff. In terms of systems software the following job descriptions may act as the needed controls in this area.

Systems programmer

The main responsibilities of a systems programmer usually includes the support of systems software to enable application software and IT services to be developed and run in a safe and secure environment.

In more detail, a systems programmer has the following responsibilities:

- Provide system-level support of multi-user operating systems, database and data communications software, hardware and software tools, including installation, configuration, monitoring, maintenance and support of these systems
- Identify alternatives for optimising computer and network resources
- Collect information to analyse and evaluate existing or proposed systems software

- Research, plan, install, configure, troubleshoot, maintain and upgrade operating systems, network and database software
- Research, plan, install, configure, troubleshoot, maintain and upgrade hardware and software interfaces with the operating system
- Analyse and evaluate present or proposed business procedures or problems to define IT processing needs and services
- Prepare detailed flow charts and diagrams outlining systems capabilities and processes
- Research and recommend hardware and software development, purchase and use
- Troubleshoot and resolve hardware, software and connectivity problems, including user access and component configuration
- Record and maintain hardware and software inventories, site and/or server licensing, and user access and security
- Write and maintain system software documentation
- Conduct technical research on system software upgrades to determine feasibility, cost, time required and compatibility with current system
- Document system software problems and resolutions for future purposes.

The knowledge, skills and capabilities of a systems programmer include:

- Knowledge and practical experience of several computer programming languages (e.g. Fortran, COBOL, PL/1, Assembler, Java, C, etc.), web technologies and tools, and particularly the languages and web platforms used in the IT function of the organisation

- Knowledge of the use and limitations of computer and network processing equipment
- Knowledge and experience of the design, execution and operation of systems software, such as operating systems, database management and database communications systems
- Ability to learn the programming languages used in operating systems or software packages
- Ability to evaluate technical proposals and to communicate effectively with user personnel and others on technical issues, both orally and in writing.

The minimum qualifications of a systems programmer are: university degree in computer science; additional experience of four years as a computer programmer, and two or more years as a systems programmer; trained or certified in the systems software operating in the data centre of the organisation; and holder of a professional accreditation title from a valid international professional association.

Web applications developer

The main responsibilities of a web applications developer usually includes the support of web applications development.

In more detail, a web applications developer has the following responsibilities:

- Design, create, produce and maintain web pages using relevant software packages
- Discuss ideas with end-users to get a clear understanding of their web requirements
- Develop the website content of the organisation

- Manage the image and copyrights of the organisation on the Internet
- Develop custom programs to extend the function of the website of the organisation
- Maintain the website once it is completed by adding new content, icons, illustrations or features and co-ordinate other people, such as programmers and analysts, to help maintain the website.

The knowledge, skills and capabilities of a web applications developer include:

- Knowledge of several computer programming languages (e.g. Fortran, COBOL, PL/1, Assembler, Java, C, etc.), web technologies and tools, and particularly the languages and web platforms used in the IT function of the organisation
- Knowledge and experience of the design, execution and operation of web applications and services
- Ability to learn the web programming languages and tools used in the data centre of the organisation
- Ability to evaluate technical proposals and to communicate effectively with user personnel and others on web technical issues, both orally and in writing.

The minimum qualifications of a web applications developer are: university degree in computer science; additional experience of four years as a computer programmer, and two or more years as a web applications programmer; trained or certified in the web platform and software operating in the data centre of the organisation; and holder of a professional accreditation title from a valid international professional association.

Network support analyst

The main responsibilities of a network support analyst usually includes the support of the network environment of the organisation.

In more detail, a network support analyst has the following responsibilities:

- Plan, design, analyse and provide technical support for the data communications network of the organisation
- Conduct research and evaluation of network technology and recommend purchases of network equipment
- Consult with users and evaluate requirements, recommend designs, provide cost analyses, plan projects and co-ordinate tasks for installation of data networks
- Analyse and resolve technical problems for established networks
- Plan, test, recommend and implement network, file server, mainframe, and workstation hardware and software
- Provide network documentation, training and guidance to computing system clients and programmers
- Serve as technical specialist and resolve network problems and emergencies
- Recommend network solutions for strategic purposes
- Install, upgrade and configure network printing, directory structures, user access, security, software and file services
- Establish user profiles, user environments, directories, and security for networks being installed
- Work as a team member with other technical staff to ensure connectivity and compatibility between systems

- Document network problems and resolutions for future reference.

The knowledge, skills and capabilities of a network support analyst include:

- Knowledge of several computer programming languages (e.g. Fortran, COBOL, PL/1, Assembler, Java, C, etc.), web and network technologies and tools, and particularly the network software and platforms used in the IT function of the organisation
- Knowledge and practical experience of the design, execution and operation of network applications and services
- Ability to evaluate technical proposals and to communicate effectively with user personnel and others on network technical issues.

The minimum qualifications of a network support analyst are: university degree in computer science; additional experience of four to six years in network support; trained or certified in the network platform and software operating in the data centre of the organisation; and holder of a professional accreditation title from a valid international professional association.

8.4 Database controls

A database consists of an organised collection of data for one or more uses. One way of classifying databases involves the type of data model or data architecture used to organise, store and retrieve data. The most common model is the relational model. Other models in some use are the hierarchical, the network and the object-oriented model. A database management system (DBMS) consists of software that organises the storage of data. A DBMS controls the creation, maintenance and use of the database storage structures of application systems and of their users. It allows organisations to place control of organisation-wide database development in the hands of specialists, such as database administrators (DBAs) and data analysts.

Most commercial DBMSs execute their functions (database development, interrogation, application development and database maintenance, etc.) by a set of components, such as interface drivers, software for organising and storing data, software for transaction processing and searching, metadata management, etc.

The establishment, design, implementation and utilisation of databases require, usually, special skills, methods and disciplined management. All these define a set of required controls for managing the database environment more efficiently and effectively.

The objective of database controls is to protect all resources of database systems (application software, database management system software, data dictionary, databases and users) from potential harm or damage, and to keep them in excellent operational mode and of the highest quality.

The actual detailed database controls may be developed and implemented by the IT manager in charge, sometimes with external support, overviewed by the IT committee, and ratified by the Board. The audit checklists 'Data management checklist', 'Database and data communications checklist' and 'Database management system checklist' (*see Paragraph 8.9*) may be used to support the design, implementation and post-implementation review of the database controls for the specific organisation.

The main controls in this area include: data custodian, data owner, data privacy officer, database administration, database analyst, data dictionary controls, database integrity checking, audit trail, database testing controls, data concealment controls, database purging, and data warehousing controls.

Data custodian

The data custodian role for all, or specific, data of the organisation must be assigned to a specific person (or persons) within the organisation. This person (usually within the IT department, but could also be an end-user) ensures that the data are managed properly, that they are backed up as per the back-up policy, archived, purged, etc. In some installations this role is exercised by the database administrator. The point is that data stored in end-user computers and applications, sometimes outside the control of IT, should not be forgotten.

Data owner

All data of the organisation, whether computerised or not, should have data owners. Data owners should have ownership rights over the particular data. The IT staff should implement access controls over these computerised data only when these accesses are authorised by the data owners. The data of the organisation belongs to business functions, not the IT department. The IT committee should ensure that this role is set up and exercised at all times.

Data privacy officer

Some large organisations establish a data privacy officer (or Chief Privacy Officer) position. The responsibilities of a data privacy officer might, in some cases, be specified by national laws and international guidelines.

The usual responsibilities of a data privacy officer are to ensure that the confidentiality of the data of the organisation is protected at all times. Other responsibilities are also specified by legislative rules and guidelines issued by national governments and parliaments.

Some more detailed responsibilities include:

- Providing development guidance and assists in the identification, implementation and maintenance of organisation information privacy policies
- Performing initial and periodic information privacy risk assessments and conducts related ongoing compliance monitoring activities in co-ordination with the entity's other compliance and operational assessment functions
- Working with legal counsel and management, all departments and committees to ensure the organisation has and maintains appropriate privacy policy and procedures
- Directing or ensuring delivery of privacy training and orientation to all employees
- Establishing with management a mechanism to monitor access to protected corporate information, within the framework of the organisation and as required by law
- Establishing and managing a process for receiving, documenting, tracking, investigating and taking action on all complaints concerning the organisation's privacy policies

- Ensuring compliance with privacy practices and consistent application of sanctions for failure to comply with privacy policies for all individuals in the organisation's workforce.

Database administration

The database or databases of the given organisation usually hold data which are common to a number of users. The fact that different departments of the organisation are using the same data may cause political and technical problems in the organisation. Therefore, it is important that a database administration function within the IT department is set up.

A database administrator (DBA) is basically responsible for the performance, integrity and security of a corporate database. Additional role requirements are likely to include planning, development and troubleshooting.

Additional detailed responsibilities may include some or all of the following:

- Establishing the needs of corporate end-users and monitoring end-user access and security
- Monitoring and reviewing database performance
- Managing performance parameters to improve database performance
- Defining the physical and logical database designs
- Carrying out database reorganisation
- Installing and testing new versions of the database management system (DBMS)
- Maintaining data standards, including compliance to the Data Protection Act

- Maintaining database documentation, including data standards, procedures and definitions for the data dictionary
- Controlling database access permissions
- Developing and testing database back-up and recovery plans
- Co-operating effectively with IT project development managers, database programmers and web application developers
- Communicating continuously with technical, systems development applications and operational staff to ensure database integrity and security
- Controlling the subschema of the database
- Implementing access controls to individual programs updating the organisational databases
- Maintaining the integrity of the database environment
- Implementing the data ownership and data deletion procedures, especially on common data laying down
- Monitoring data documentation standards, setting up and maintaining the data dictionary, setting standards of data back-up and recovery.

Database Analyst

A Database Analyst is basically responsible for the management and organisation of the end-user requirements for a database application system.

Additional detailed responsibilities may include some or all of the following:

- Use specialised tools and techniques to maintain the data model

- Provide advice and support for data analysis and application
- Train and educate users
- Provide data administration advice to application programmers
- Implement data administration solutions, methods and standards
- Define data access rules and metadata
- Manage data policies, security and standards across the organisation
- Provide expertise to multiple database projects
- Provide support on new and innovative data administration techniques and tools.

Data dictionary controls

In a database system, the data dictionary[61] is usually a part of the DBMS software, and is designed to hold standard information about data items and application programs updating the databases, and of the supporting programs which update and control the data dictionary. Therefore, this should be controlled accordingly.

Some of the particular controls include:

- Access to the data dictionary should be monitored
- The data validation rules of the application programs updating the database added or updated in the data dictionary should be well documented

---

[61] See also 'Why Use a Data Dictionary/Directory', *Guide Conference Proceedings*, June 5–8, 1984, Kyriazoglou J, London, England, pp. 281–284.

- The data dictionary should be backed up on the same basis as the database application programs
- All changes to the data dictionary should be authorised and documented in a changes log.

Database integrity checking

Periodically, all databases should be read sequentially and their records and key values checked, such as record counts, totals of certain important fields, etc. These values should be checked against the control total fields maintained in the databases (assuming of course that these are maintained within the databases). All databases should also be checked for the existence of noise, as this will imply that some legal or illegal modification of fields in a database, while preserving its aggregate structure, has occurred, and therefore the databases must be corrected and their original data reinstated.[62]

Audit trail

In very sensitive databases, such as the financial database systems, audit trails should be used to record the contents of the databases before and after each update. When errors and other potential frauds occur, the audit trail may be investigated to ensure that no fraud has taken place and to recover from errors. More details on audit trail controls are presented in Paragraph 8.6.

---

[62] For more on database integrity checking, see (a) *Principles of Database Management*, Martin J, Prentice-Hall (1976) and (b) *Concurrency Control and Recovery in Database Systems*, Bernstein P et al (2008), www.database-books.us.

Database testing controls

Testing of systems and applications containing databases is very critical to the success of any IT development effort. In order to attain a successful systems implementation, all aspects of the testing phase require to be reviewed to incorporate not merely the software but also the IT elements, such as databases. Testing for the databases of any system should be performed through the system development process on the basis of an IT testing standard and methodology, an IT application test plan and a set of testing tools. These controls are described in detail in Chapter 4.

Data concealment controls

Data concealment controls denote the use of a concealment system whereby the confidentiality of very sensitive data and information is achieved by hiding the data and the information and embedding them in irrelevant data.

Database purging

Controls should be established to ensure that the removal of sensitive or old data from the databases of computerised information systems, computer storage devices, or peripheral devices with storage capacity, at the end of a processing period, are properly exercised. All purging operations should be authorised by the data owners, reported to the Board, logged in a formal register, and the pertinent files copied before the purging operation is carried out.

Data warehousing controls

A data warehouse (DW) is, in general terms, a systematic collection of integrated operational data (current and historical) of the organisation. Usually these data are stored in corporate databases and other sources and are transferred by a DW process into the corporate DW.

The data in the DW are not updated. A DW is designed to support managerial decision-making and problem-solving functions. The DW may contain both very detailed current and summarised historical data related to various categories, subjects, topics, transactions or areas, depending on how it (the DW) has been organised.

The security and integrity requirements of the DW environment are not unlike those of other database applications. Therefore, having an effective control process to endure the confidentiality, integrity and availability of data in a DW environment is of the most paramount importance.

This process may include the following steps:

- Step 1: Data identification
- Step 2: Data classification
- Step 3: Assessment of the value of data
- Step 4: Carrying out a risk assessment of the security of data
- Step 5: Establishing the security cost–benefit analysis for data protection
- Step 6: Selecting and implementing security controls
- Step 7: Review and evaluation of the effectiveness of the whole process.

8.5 Data communications controls

Data communications technical controls[63] refer to your computer's configuration, software settings and specific security applications you may be running, all designed to make your data communications system and information less vulnerable. The objective of controls in this area is to protect all resources of online system (network servers and software, application software, data communications software, transmitted data and network users) from potential harm or damage, and to keep them in excellent operational mode and of the highest quality.

The establishment, design, implementation and utilisation of data communications for organisations require, usually, special skills, methods and disciplined management. All these define a set of required controls for managing the data communications environment more efficiently and effectively.

The actual detailed data communications controls may be developed and implemented by the IT manager in charge, sometimes with external support, overviewed by the IT committee, and ratified by the Board. The audit checklists 'data networking audit programme', 'database and data communications checklist', and 'data communications checklist' (*see Paragraph 8.9*) may be used to support the design, implementation and post-implementation review of the data communications controls for the specific organisation.

---

[63] See also (a) *Principles of Voice and Data Communications*, Bates RJ and Bates M, McGraw-Hill (2006), and (b) *Understanding Data Communications* (2nd Edition), Friend GE; Fike JL, Charles Baker H, Bellamy JC, Howard W. Sams & Company, Indianapolis (1988).

The main controls in this area include: data communications management plan, data communications security controls, data communications personnel controls, intrusion detection system, EDI controls and specialised security application.

8.5.1 Data communications management plan

A data communications management plan is a formal, approved document that defines how the data communications project is executed, monitored and controlled. The objective of this plan is to define the approach to be used by the project team to deliver the intended project management scope of the data communications project.

This plan may be formulated, usually, before any decisions are made on data communications issues. The typical activities of this management plan are:

1 Establish a data communications project with resources and a project manager
2 Carry out a needs analysis for data communications of the organisation
3 Carry out data centre and network site planning
4 Search for network providers, vendors and technical support companies
5 Decide on network equipment and related elements (policies, procedures, EDI business transactions, work stations, servers, connections, routers, bridges, cabling types, cryptography, etc.)
6 Decide on network topology and protocols (wireless networks, etc.)

7 Decide on which operating system, data communications and application software should be obtained
8 Study and decide all network and data communications security options
9 Obtain data communications lines from network providers
10 Obtain all network components (hardware, software, firewalls, intrusion detection systems, etc.)
11 Build data centre and network sites
12 Lay out the cabling systems in all locations
13 Install all network components
14 Test the data communications system on a pilot basis
15 Deploy and operate the data communications network by the use of proper methods, policies, procedures and staff (web administrators, architects, etc.).

This plan is usually carried out by a project team and various purchase and construction activities, as noted above, and by implementing the following controls.

8.5.2 Data communications security controls

Network security controls must be designed and implemented to improve the security and management control aspects of data communications. These controls include (usually): network cryptographic controls, line and transmission controls, firewalls, wireless network controls, eavesdropping controls, login controls, penetration tests, and network segregation.

Network cryptographic controls

The objective of cryptographic controls is to ensure, at a reasonable level, the confidentiality, integrity and authenticity of digital information being transmitted, while providing non-repudiation by the sender. These controls include:

- Encryption: encryption is designed to ensure the confidentiality of the data being transmitted
- Hashing: the main objective of hashing is to ensure that electronic data transmitted to a receiver has not been modified in any way or detected (wholly or partly). This is implemented by various mathematical formulae that use the electronic message as its input and create a block of data called a message digest. These are subsequently checked by the receiver to ensure that the proper data has been received
- Digital signatures and digital certificates: these ensure the authenticity of electronic data transmissions and the non-repudiation of the transmissions by the creators.

Line and transmission controls

Communications security controls should be instituted to prevent unauthorised individuals from tapping, modifying or otherwise intercepting data transmission. These controls include:

- Line security (restricting access to the communications lines connecting the various parts of the computer system)
- Cryptosecurity (the security or protection resulting from the proper use of technically sound cryptosystems)
- Transmission security (preventing unauthorised interception of communications)

- Emission security (preventing the interception of radio frequency waves, without wires, by unauthorised personnel)
- Physical security of communications security material and information
- Security modems (modems with password and callback features).

Firewalls

A firewall is a piece of hardware, software or both that will examine inbound, and sometimes outbound, network traffic, and based on a set of configurable rules and techniques (e.g. packet filters, application gateways, proxy servers, etc.), will decide to let the traffic pass, or will try to block the traffic.

A firewall can consist of an application that you install on your PC or a server, or it can be a dedicated hardware appliance that protects an entire enterprise network. Multiple layers of firewalls can add more protection, especially for Internet users, as these users should not have direct access to customer and other corporate sensitive data, and should only be allowed to access publicly accessible information.

Wireless network controls

As wireless network access points (APs) and wireless network adapters become cheaper and more prevalent, many organisations allow users to access their systems via wireless networks.

While these systems and devices deliver great convenience, they also pose a significant security risk. Most access points or routers are not 'secured' by default, leaving your network traffic and computer vulnerable to a variety of attacks. A wireless control system with specialised hardware and software may be required to give the organisation added protection against potential intruders. Some additional controls may include:

1 Change the manufacturer's default identifier on your router
2 Change your router's preset administration password to your own strong password (*see Chapter 6* for more details)
3 Use anti-virus, anti-spyware and intrusion detection software, and a firewall
4 Use encryption software and techniques to scramble communications over the network
5 Turn off 'broadcasting' in the wireless routers
6 Turn off your wireless network when you are not monitoring
7 Allow only specific computers to access your wireless network. Particularly public hot spots may not have effective security controls in place. This means that it may be best to avoid sending or receiving sensitive information over that network.

Eavesdropping controls

There are various wiretapping methods and devices that allow intruders to access your data remotely. If your data is not encrypted, anyone with the right software can capture and read your transmissions right off the air. They could be in the lounge, out in the car park, or in the next building, etc. One control that may be used is that of steganography. With this method a user encodes one file inside another file which makes the original file essentially impossible to access by anyone without the right protocol to access it.

Login controls

After three invalid login attempts, the user should be locked out of the system, and must be reset by the organisation's web administrator.

Penetration tests

The IT department should perform regular (monthly, quarterly, etc. depending on the needs of the organisation) vulnerability scans of its websites to ensure that no known vulnerabilities exist. In addition, they may have to engage with a reputable third party or external consultant to perform an independent vulnerability scan and penetration tests every six or twelve months. The tests may be staged, with either a vulnerability or penetration test performed every quarter. A vulnerability test scans for known vulnerabilities. A penetration test is performed by a group of highly skilled network security employees that attempt to compromise the website.

Network segregation

Networks may also be made more secure by segregating them, adding additional layers of firewalls, honeypot diversion devices and trapping mechanisms, etc. to protect critical data from publicly available data of the organisation. Honeypots and honeynets are mechanisms (hardware, software) that create an environment where the tools and behaviour of 'blackhats' (the most dangerous hackers) can be captured and analysed further.[64]

8.5.3 Data communications personnel controls

The data communications network is managed by the proper web-specialised staff, such as the ones noted below:

Web administrator

Only authorised web administrators (or data communications administrators) should be allowed to manage, allocate, monitor and control specific web resources.

The web administrator will need to have:

- General knowledge and understanding of networking infrastructures, including Internet, local area or wide area or web networking technologies, platforms and protocols
- Expert knowledge, skills and capabilities of managing of web and network technologies
- Thorough knowledge of web client/server technical architectures
- General knowledge of desktop software and hardware technologies
- Expert knowledge of applications development processes and tools

---

[64] For more on honeypots and honeynets, see (a) *www.cert.org*, (b) *www.honeypots.net*, (c) The Honeynet Project (*http://project.honeynet.org*), and (d) *Honeypots, Tracking Hackers*, Spitzner L, Addison-Wesley (2003).

- Expert knowledge of database technologies.

Web systems engineer

The responsibilities (in summary) of a web systems engineer usually include:

- Establish the architecture, implementation and administration of a large network according to the needs of the organisation
- Recommend expandable advanced technologies and methods to integrate web systems with existing corporate systems
- Enable the creation of new web services for expanding existing business into the electronic commerce area
- Lead the upgrade of various technologies and platforms (e.g. Linux, Windows, web servers, etc.)
- Plan, design and develop all required web architecture elements
- Plan, design, implement and support the network infrastructure for an ever-expanding business of the organisation
- Manage, configure and tune the elements of network infrastructure including firewalls, routers, switches, and load balancers, etc.

8.5.4 Intrusion detection system

In addition to the data communication controls mentioned above, an intrusion detection system (IDS) may improve further the security aspect of the data communications network of the organisation.

An IDS is a system (hardware and software) that monitors data network and system traffic for potential or actual malicious activities, irregular messages and file transfers, exceptional transactions or policy violations, and produces reports to a reporting system (terminal, file, application, etc.).

Monitoring traffic is only one aspect of control; acting on what has been reported is the second aspect. This is usually carried out by an action plan, which includes (as an example) the following steps:

Step 1: Identify and understand the problem.

Step 2: Document the problem by collecting all evidence.

Step 3: Limit or stop the damage immediately.

Step 4: Activate the corporate crisis team, if necessary.

Step 5: Confirm the problem diagnosis and determine the other effects that occurred due to the damage reported.

Step 6: Restore the system to a previous safe status.

Step 7: Take any legal or disciplinary action, if necessary.

Step 8: Deal with the cause in terms of long-term effects and take extra protection.

Step 9: Acquire new systems, or upgrade existing systems, to implement extra security policies, procedures and monitoring controls.

Step 10: Review and train staff in new monitoring techniques.

8.5.5 EDI controls

Networks may be used by organisations for electronic data interchange (EDI) transactions. EDI systems are ready-made computerised application systems designed to provide for capture, storage, retrieval and presentation of images, documents, forms, etc. of real or simulated objects. EDI systems usually rely on digital image processing systems.

When organisations use such EDI systems and technologies to communicate with each other and transmit via computers and communications business data, documents and transactions (invoices, purchase orders, customer orders, fund transmittal orders, payments, research and development work, etc.), they need a set of specific controls. These controls are necessary in order to improve accuracy, reduce errors, avoid potential fraud and abuse, and avoid legal hassles. These controls are both administrative and IT-oriented controls. Examples of these IT controls are: digital signatures, data encryption, IT security measures, passwords, expert systems for customer profiling, firewalls, etc.

The administrative controls pertain to whether the data, documents, transactions, etc. sent were received correctly by the other party, who is responsible for the integrity of the information, who implements security mechanisms, how errors are corrected, what are the penalties for non-compliance, etc.

These types of issues are usually handled by a legal agreement, which should be authorised, agreed and ratified by the Boards of all parties concerned, and should be put into operation accordingly. An example of the EDI contract standard clauses[65] usually includes the clauses of: Purpose and area of application, Definitions, Contract enforcement, Receipt of EDI messages as evidence, Processing and confirmation of EDI messages, EDI message security, Confidentiality and protection of private data, Recording and storing of EDI messages, EDI operational requirements, Technical specifications and requirements, Responsibilities of parties, Resolution of differences, Applicable laws, Period of contract validity, modifications and applicability of clauses.

8.5.6 Specialised security application

In addition to the above data communication controls, a separate ready-made security application may be purchased and put into productive use to manage and control access to various entities of the organisation, such as the online critical corporate and customer financial data and transactions, online programming facilities, computer and network resident software and data files, sensitive system transactions, other significant system software, and various system facilities and utilities. A specialised security application protects all these entities by default from everyone by various methods which are specified by the given security application, purchased and deployed in an organisation.

[65] According to UN EDIFACT standard and the various EU guidelines (86/361, 87/372, 88/301, 90/387, 90/388, 90/544, 91/250, 92/100, 93/98, 94/820, 200/1999, etc.

8.6 Audit trail log file controls

Log files record events that take place in running the systems software (operating system, database management system, data communication system, etc.). These may be defined as audit trails.

Audit trails maintain a record of system (operating system, database management system, data communications system, firewall, IDS, WEB, etc.) activity by system or application process and by user activity.

In conjunction with appropriate mechanisms, software tools and procedures, audit trails provide a means to help accomplish several security-related and fraud prevention objectives, including individual accountability, reconstruction of events, intrusion detection and problem identification.

An audit trail must include sufficient information to establish what event occurred and who (or what) caused them. The scope and contents of the audit trail will balance security needs with performance needs, privacy and costs.

At a minimum the contents of the audit trail record must contain: type of event, when the event or transaction occurred (time and day), user ID associated with the event or transaction, program or command used to initiate the event or transaction, copy of the transaction, and copy of the database record before and after the update process.

An indicative set of detailed audit controls include:

Individual user accountability: The audit trail should support accountability by providing a trace of user actions. While users cannot be prevented from using resources to which they have legitimate access authorisation, audit trail analysis can be used to examine their actions.

Reconstruction of historical events and problem analysis: The audit trails should support after-the-fact investigations of how, when and why normal operations ceased. Audit trails should be used as online detection tools to help identify problems other than intrusions as they occur. This is often referred to as real-time auditing or continuous monitoring.

Intrusion detection: The organisation should design and implement their audit trails to record appropriate information to assist in intrusion detection. Intrusions can be detected in real time, by examining audit trails as they are created or after the fact, by examining audit records in a batch process.

Audit trail security: The organisation should protect the audit trail from unauthorised access by controlling access to online audit logs, by separation of duties between security personnel who administer the access control function and those who administer the audit trail, and by undertaking audit reviews.

8.7 Monitoring and review controls

After you have established the protection mechanisms on your systems software, you will want to be sure that your protection mechanisms actually work. You will also want to observe any indications of misbehaviour or other problems. This process is known as monitoring and reviewing.

The actual detailed monitoring and review controls may be developed and implemented by the IT manager in charge, sometimes with external support, overviewed by the IT committee, and ratified by the Board. The audit checklists 'systems software management audit programme', 'system software acquisition checklist', and 'systems software operation checklist' (*see Paragraph 8.9*) may be used to support the design, implementation and post-implementation review of the systems software controls for the specific organisation.

Three of the most common monitoring and review controls in this area are file integrity checks, review of system log files and review of audit trails by internal audit.

File integrity checks: There are basically three approaches to detecting changes to files. The first approach is to use comparison copies of the data to be monitored and cross check their contents. The second approach is to monitor metadata about the items to be protected. This includes monitoring the modification time of entries as kept by the operating system, and monitoring any logs or audit trails that show alterations to files. The third approach is that you may use some form of signature of the data to be monitored, and periodically recompute and compare the signature against a stored value.

Review of system log files: This process includes reviewing the logs for:

- users logging in at strange hours
- unexplained reboots and unexplained changes to the system clock
- unusual network, system, server or database error messages
- failed login attempts with bad passwords
- users logging in from unfamiliar sites on the network
- changes in network access files and start-up files

- change to configuration files
- hidden files and directories and unowned files
- new network services.

Audit trail review: Review of the audit trails may be carried out by internal audit according to the audit programme, review guidelines and schedule (at least annually, unless a potential fraud has been reported or detected). Search-automated tools should also be utilised to execute reviews of the audit trails.

This may also be facilitated by following the monitoring and review activities management plan and all the data included in the IT management report (*see Chapter 1*).

8.8 IT technical performance measures

The complete integrated set of control components of systems software controls, as described in the previous paragraphs, may be evaluated and improved by establishing and collecting performance data and by using the audit programmes and checklists (*see Paragraph 8.9*).

The usual IT technical performance measures that may be used for this purpose are depicted in Table 10.

These performance measures could be based on a mixed system with two components: Component 1 would be an IT BSC (Information Technology Balanced Scorecard) Measurement System, described in Chapter 4, and Component 2, would be a Compliance Monitoring System for monitoring compliance to policies, procedures and related matters (e.g. budget issues).

Number	Performance Measure
1	Mean time between system repairs
2	Change controls not followed
3	Operating system, database management system and communications software not kept current
4	Security controls for operating system, database management system and communications software not followed
5	Documentation controls for operating system, database management system and communications software not followed
6	Authorisation controls for operating system, database management system and communications software not kept
7	Audit trail controls not maintained
8	Average availability of operating system, database management system and communications software

Table 10: IT technical performance measures

The IT management of the company, may, depending on various aspects of the organisation, analyse all this performance and compliance monitoring information to review, assess and improve the systems software elements of the IT function of the specific organisation.

8.9 Review and audit tools and techniques

In order to ensure that the systems software controls are properly and effectively organised to serve the control needs of the specific corporate entity, guidelines and other tools are necessary to aid the manager and other professionals (auditor, compliance officers, etc.) in discharging their duties.

Guidelines and other tools are described in Appendix 3 (Monitoring IT controls checklist), Appendix 4 (Examples of IT forms), Appendix 5 (IT audit methodology), Appendix 6 (IT audit areas), and Appendix 7 (Internal audit report example).

The following audit programmes and checklists may also be used: systems software management audit programme, system software acquisition checklist, systems software operation checklist, data management checklist, database and data communications checklist, database management system checklist, data networking audit programme, and data communications checklist.

8.9.1 Systems software management audit programme

The objective of this audit programme is to support the process of constructing, reviewing, evaluating and improving the systems software controls identified in this chapter.

This audit programme covers the following issues: software asset inventory review, maintenance contracts review, program library maintenance, problem fixing, security review, system documentation review, segregation of duties assessment, performance monitoring, and change management.

Software asset inventory review

1 Obtain copies of original purchases, invoice and maintenance contracts for all purchased or used systems software (operating system, database, utilities, security package, network, etc.).
2 Obtain copy of system documentation for software products and licences.
3 Obtain report (from computer system) on what software is installed.
4 Ensure that all changes are documented.

Maintenance contracts review

5 Review all vendor maintenance contracts.
6 Access vendor support.
7 Review all media, licences and documents to ensure compatibility.

Program library maintenance

8 Review management control process for changes and revisions to system software.

Problem fixing

9 Review system log, maintained by the system manager, on system software problems, how they are fixed and how they are reported and controlled.

Security review

10 Check to see that access is restricted to system programmer.
11 Ensure that all changes to the systems are fully tested before installation or modification.
12 Try to access the system software libraries by using the passwords of programmers, operators, simple users and super users and vendor personnel if applicable (e.g. remote maintenance).

System documentation review

13 Get copy of the documentation for the management of the computer system.
14 Ensure that the documentation contains sections on: system diagram, disk storage contents, user accounts, back-up procedure, recovery procedure, reorganisation procedure, queue management, security management and network management.

Segregation of duties assessment

15 Review role, responsibilities and job description of system programmer to ensure segregation of duties.
16 Check training taken by the systems programmer to ensure that he/she is adequately trained.

Performance monitoring

17 Review performance monitoring and capacity planning activities and procedures of system programmer.

18 Check to see that performance monitoring is executed and reported regularly.

Change Management

19 Review change management activities and procedures of system programmer.
20 Check to see that all amendments are approved prior to testing and implementation.

8.9.2 System software acquisition checklist

The objective of this checklist is to support the process of constructing, reviewing, evaluating and improving the systems software controls identified in this chapter.

1 Are all system software upgrades properly tested and authorised before they are implemented? Consider: impact assessment, extent of testing and upgrade co-ordination.
2 Is appropriate system documentation prepared in terms of the design and content of system software? Consider: maintenance procedures, currency, completeness and off-site copy.
3 Are appropriate versions of system software used? Consider: currency of current versions, vendor support or supplier maintenance contact, staff training/experience and use of system exits/modifications.
4 Is an appropriate record maintained of system software installed and in operation? Consider: all system software installed, all internally generated modifications or extensions, and all system software problems encountered.

5 Are all programs and data files (compilers, assemblers, link editors, macro libraries, source libraries, etc.) used to construct and maintain system software adequately protected? Consider: identification of protected datasets, use of access control software and update authorisation procedures.
6 Is appropriate control exercised over the use of system utility programs? Consider: access by users, reporting of access (datasets accessed, changes made) and security over datasets directly.

8.9.3 Systems software operation checklist

The objective of this checklist is to support the process of constructing, reviewing, evaluating and improving the systems software controls identified in this chapter.

1 Is the integrity of the system software controlled through authorised amendments?
2 Is the system software adequately secured through back-up copies?
3 Is there a specialist function responsible for maintaining system software? Consider: organisation structure, segregation of duties, job descriptions.
4 Are security requirements clearly defined? Consider: IT security policy, classification of sensitive systems and data, quality control, independent review.
5 Have adequate operational and access control procedures been implemented to restrict access to the operating system? Consider: change management, problem handling, access control over specific datasets, system software upgrades.

6 Has the need for protecting various types of resource, e.g. important files (including those holding system software) and transactions been identified and specified?
7 What are the sensitive system software features and libraries and how are they controlled? Consider: library protection, user exits control, system initialisation parameters.
8 Is there a systems software maintenance plan?
9 Is a record maintained of all system software upgrades? Consider: supplier updates, internally written modifications.
10 Are all system software upgrades tested before they are implemented?
11 Are all system software upgrades properly authorised?
12 Is system documentation prepared in terms of the design and content of system software? Consider: maintenance procedures, currency, completeness, off-site copy.
13 Are all programs and data files (compilers, assemblers, link editors, macro libraries, source libraries, etc.) used to construct and maintain system software adequately protected? Consider: identification of protected datasets, use of access control software, update authorisation procedures.
14 Are current versions of system software in use? Consider: vendor support or supplier maintenance contact, staff training, staff recruitment.
15 Is a record maintained of all system software installed?
16 Is a record maintained of all internally generated system software modifications or extensions?
17 Is a record maintained of all system software problems encountered?
18 Are there system programs with special authorities? (Note the program names.)

19 Are there critical components of the operating system? (Note the critical components.) Consider: identify and locate ‘libraries’ where certain sensitive code is stored (e.g. supervisor calls and exits) and determine level of access control over the above, and the function of the above routines.
20 Is use made of the system logging facilities? Consider: hard copy production, log retention policy, system log (audit trail), run log (job accounting), maintenance log (system component performance).
21 Is control exercised over the use of system utility programs?
22 Are back-up revisions of the system software taken? Consider: frequency, completeness, off-site storage.
23 Does the degree of integration of communication systems, if appropriate, allow the system software and applications to be run in isolation?
24 In a disaster recovery situation is there a single system software pack (i.e. a bootstrap version)?
25 Are monitoring reviews of the system operation carried out to ensure that system resources are being used most effectively?

8.9.4 Data management checklist

The objective of this checklist is to support the process of constructing, reviewing, evaluating and improving the database controls identified in this chapter.

A. Review data modelling/management

1 Is data modelling done as part of strategic planning?
2 Do metadata exist (especially for data warehouses)?

3 Are integrity rules contained in the metadata definitions?
4 Have interviews with the users been conducted as to what data are critical for operations and decision making?
5 Is the corporate data model agreed by user management?
6 Is capacity planning determined due to data modelling?
7 Are access rights to database agreed by data owners?
8 Does an experienced database administrator exist?
9 Does the DBMS have a built-in integrity checking mechanism?
10 Are all DBMS changes authorised by management?
11 Is all down time to the database recorded?
12 Is the database fully backed up?
13 Are users adequately trained?
14 Is there a DBMS log and audit trail facility (auditing, recovery)?
15 Are logs ever checked for inconsistencies?
16 Is the data dictionary adequately controlled?
17 Is database performance monitored?

B. Database procedures review

18 Do database administration procedures (formal or informal) exist and are the following areas covered: back-up, recovery, space management (reorganisation), data retention, data growth, data integrity (editing/validation rules), data dictionary, security, naming conventions?

C. Security assessment

19 Are security mechanisms effectively applied for the protection of:

- database software
- data on files
- information segregation for the critical data (if applicable)?

8.9.5 Database and data communications checklist

The objective of this checklist is to support the process of constructing, reviewing, evaluating and improving the database and data communications controls identified in this chapter.

1 Are database and data communications operating procedures appropriately documented? Consider:
   - Processing requirements/schedule
   - Recovery or restart procedures
   - Emergency changes
   - Incident reporting
   - Housekeeping
   - Program interdependencies.

2 Are database and data communications operations functions adequately supervised? Consider:
   - Supervisory procedures
   - Experience
   - Training
   - Operating procedures documentation
   - Review of processing logs
   - Operations activities performed by users.

3 Are there appropriate procedures in place to provide for reliability and continuity of network transmissions? Consider:
   - Network capacity and performance monitoring

- o Network security
- o Alternative routing
- o Physical security of network components
- o Documentation of physical/logical network.

4 Are job processing procedures appropriately documented? Consider:
- o Job scheduling
- o Authorisation procedures
- o Online processing requirements
- o Batch processing requirements
- o Back-up and restart or recovery procedures
- o Job overrides or emergency changes
- o Housekeeping
- o Output distribution.

5 Are database and data communications operations effectively monitored? Consider:
- o Analysis of errors/problems
- o Capacity review
- o Performance monitoring
- o Review of bottlenecks
- o Network capacity review.

8.9.6 Database management system checklist

The objective of this checklist is to support the process of constructing, reviewing, evaluating and improving the database controls identified in this chapter.

1 Is the database properly maintained (data confidentiality, integrity and availability)?

2 Is there a DBMS in use? (Note which.) Consider: relational, hierarchical, object, central or distributed

model, also when (how many years ago) the database software was obtained, and if there are any database replacement plans.

3 Are there controls to ensure consistency of distributed databases is maintained?

4 Is there a database administration (DBA) function?

5 Is the DBA function segregated from application programming?

6 Are the duties and responsibilities of the DBA defined in writing?

7 Does the DBA maintain records of, for example, persons who have access to the database, programs which can access the database, response and performance statistics?

8 Are all DBMS software amendments logged and reviewed by the DBA?

9 Are there data dictionary standards covering development and maintenance?

10 Is a copy of the data dictionary stored at an off-site secure location?

11 Is the DBA responsible for the security classification of individual data elements?

12 Does the DBA regularly review the dictionary to ensure that only required data items are accessed by application programs?

13 Is access to application program functions restricted, e.g. by use of menus specific to user IDs or groups?

14 Is the use of inherent database access control software effective in restricting access to the database?

15 Is access control software used to restrict access to the database?

16 Are violation reports produced and reviewed by the DBA or security administrator?

17 Is the database area containing passwords restricted to the DBA only?

18 Have known data corruptions been corrected, and the corrections checked and authorised by users?

19 Is there user-written software to check record integrity and data integrity? Consider: note what it is and how often it is run.

20 Is there proprietary database integrity checking software? Consider: note what it is and how often it is run.

21 Is there non-transaction-based amendment software available to correct corrupt data? Consider: authorisation of use and record of usage.

22 Is this database amendment software password protected?

23 Is a complete back-up copy of the database taken regularly? Consider: how often (daily, weekly, monthly, yearly, etc.), incremental copying, disk shadowing and mirroring, transaction logging, off-site storage, documentation and testing of restore procedures, procedure to inform the users on database problems, etc.

8.9.7 Data networking audit programme

The objective of this audit programme is to support the process of constructing, reviewing, evaluating and improving the data communications controls identified in this chapter.

This audit programme covers the following issues: network design review, maintenance contract review, and problem resolution and support.

Network design review

1 Obtain a network diagram for the (voice and) data network.
2 Obtain a diagram for the cabling infrastructure of the building physical (vertical, horizontal) network (including a floor plan if applicable).
3 Ensure that all network purchases are subject to commercial technical evaluation procedures.

Maintenance contract review

4 Obtain a copy of the maintenance contract of the voice network for the buildings examined.
5 Obtain a copy of the maintenance contract of the data network for the buildings examined.
6 Check to see that industry standard hardware and software clauses are used.
7 Assess any mobile, radio, telex, satellite, microwave ramifications.

Problem resolution and support

8 Ensure that network facilities are covered in contingency planning.
9 Check to see that the following are recorded in the problem log: voice problems, data problems, mobile and other problems, cabling problems.
10 Review how the voice and data networks are supported both by outside parties and by IT.
11 Check to see that documentation to users is available regarding the network facilities to be used.

8.9.8 Data communications checklist

The objective of this checklist is to support the process of constructing, reviewing, evaluating and improving the data communications controls identified in this chapter.

1 Is the security over data communications adequate? Consider: data confidentiality, integrity and availability.
2 Is the overall network plan fully documented? Consider: local area networks, wide area networks, wireless networks, data that is transmitted.
3 Is responsibility assigned for management and control of the network? (Provide name and position of person.) Consider: integration of network planning and development with the IT plan, network control and monitoring of utilisation, performance and security.
4 Has a review of network security been carried out and the potential risks identified and evaluated? Consider: the time the organisation could survive without communications e.g. an hour, day or month, contingency plan, date of last review.
5 Are there adequate recovery procedures for a loss of communications links? Consider: internal audit involvement, steps taken to minimise the risks highlighted by the review.
6 Is important data encrypted when being transmitted over communications links to ensure its integrity and confidentiality? Consider: type of encryption e.g. private key system (i.e. DES) or public key system, authentication of the sender as genuine, protecting the data from unauthorised access and browsing, error detection (e.g. checksum), management of the keys used for encryption (e.g. generation and distribution).

7 Do modems which are attached to the computer have security facilities installed, such as encryption or dial-back to verify the caller's location?

8 Are there adequate access controls over users' access to the network? Consider: smart cards for identification and authentication of network users, limiting users access to data and other resources, authorisation of transactions, using digital signatures, verifying the occurrence of a transaction, etc.

9 Is the risk of uncontrolled access from external parties minimised? Consider: communications processor, X25 network, modems – dial up facility, total of external lines, network control facilities.

10 Is access restricted to the communications centre?

11 Is all communications equipment secured within the communication centre? Consider: access restriction to equipment (e.g. line analysers), access restriction to control documentation.

12 Are there alternative procedures available in the event of disruption to the communications network? Consider: storage of data for batch processing, alternate communication lines, agreement with software vendor to provide a new controller, PABX.

13 Is there an alternate network?

14 Does the disaster recovery plan include network contingency procedures? Consider: update for network upgrades and regular testing.

15 Are data communications security policies and procedures in place? Consider: the data security policy should protect all data being interchanged or used to validate or initiate interchange, security over messages from initiation to taking action is adequate, considering features available within: operating system and

application level security, communications media (service type e.g. dial-ups vs. dial-back), communications protocol, EDI security facilities within message standards including controls provided by EDI service providers, a declaration by users as to confidentiality, improper use of computer systems and responsibilities.

16 Is there adequate back-up, recovery and restart capability to ensure system and network continuity in the event of an in-house system or network failure?

8.10 Conclusion

There are many corporate governance and legal requirements that require the safe, secure and proper operation of IT systems and services.

Crucial to this is also the continuous and effective functioning of the systems software elements upon which these IT systems and services run.

Any disruptions of any type to the systems software environment will impact, if not damage tremendously, the full operation of IT systems and services.

Lately, more and more, organisations will need to protect their systems and infrastructure against new types of frauds (e.g. electronic fraud, impersonation, etc.), omissions, invasion of privacy, electronic processing errors and improper intrusions.

New methods and techniques (e.g. computer forensics) are coming into the foreground and will require serious consideration before they are implemented. Managing systems software requires better controls.

These systems software controls, may be reviewed, changed, added, deleted, customised, etc. to meet the IT needs, demands and operating mode of the given organisation, and must be operated with continuous diligence. These controls, as we have seen, may include policies, practices, procedures, organisational structures and specialised tools to ensure that the specific IT systems software objectives of the organisation can be met.

Moreover, the main systems software controls and the audit and review programmes and checklists identified and presented in this chapter, customised and improved accordingly, enable and facilitate the knowledge management framework of organisations (*outlined in Chapter 1*) as they may provide a safer and more manageable technical infrastructure for developing and running IT systems and services, the life-blood of both the organisations and their knowledge management framework.

When systems software controls are instituted, exercised and executed in the best way, organisations use IT systems containing databases and data communications more efficiently and effectively, and in the end, in a more profitable beneficial way to achieve its strategic goals.

8.11 Review questions

This set of questions may be employed by those using the controls identified in this book to assess and double-check their own conceptual understanding and practical knowledge contained in this chapter.

1. What components are a typical web (Internet) application made up of?

Reference: Paragraph 8.2 'Purpose and main types of systems software controls'.

2. What do systems software controls ensure?

Reference: Paragraph 8.2 'Purpose and main types of systems software controls'.

3. What are the main types of systems software controls?

Reference: Paragraph 8.2 'Purpose and main types of systems software controls'.

4. What is the main purpose of systems software controls?

Reference: Paragraph 8.2 'Purpose and main types of systems software controls'.

5. What actions are required to manage the changes to systems software supplied by systems software suppliers?

Reference: Paragraph 8.3 'Systems software operating environment controls'.

6. Which forms are used for documenting systems software changes by systems programming personnel?

Reference: Paragraph 8.3 'Systems software operating environment controls'.

7. What is the objective of controls in the area of database?

Reference: Paragraph 8.4 'Database controls'.

8. What are the main database controls?

Reference: Paragraph 8.4 'Database controls'.

9. What is the responsibility of an appointed database administrator?

Reference: Paragraph 8.4 'Database controls'.

10. What are the main actions of a database purging operation?

Reference: Paragraph 8.4 'Database controls'.

11. What is the objective of data communications controls?

Reference: Paragraph 8.5 'Data communications controls'.

12. What are the main data communications controls?

Reference: Paragraph 8.5 'Data communications controls'.

13. What are the main network cryptographic controls?

Reference: Paragraph 8.5 'Data communications controls'.

14. What is a firewall?

Reference: Paragraph 8.5 'Data communications controls'.

15. How are networks segregated?

Reference: Paragraph 8.5 'Data communications controls'.

16. What do audit trails do?

Reference: Paragraph 8.6 'Audit trail log file controls'.

17. What are the minimum contents of audit trail records?

Reference: Paragraph 8.6 'Audit trail log file controls'.

18. What is the purpose of change management controls?

Reference: Paragraph 8.3 'Systems software operating environment controls'.

19. What does the system testing and approval phase of change management controls entail?

Reference: Paragraph 8.3 'Systems software operating environment controls'.

20. What are the usual IT technical performance measures?

Reference: Paragraph 8.8 'IT technical performance measures'.

CHAPTER 9: IT APPLICATION CONTROLS

The north wind and the sun argued which was the stronger. On seeing a traveller they agreed a suitable test would be to strip him of his cloak. First the wind blew with all his might, but the more he blew, the more than man wrapped the cloak tightly around himself. When the sun's turn came, he gently beamed at the man, who loosened the cloak. The sun shone brighter still, and the man threw off his cloak.

(The meaning of this story is that persuasion is better than force.)

Aesop (Ancient Greece: 6th century BC)

9.1 Scope

IT application systems are made up of individual programs that receive data of occurring business transactions, check them for errors, process and store them in computerised files, and provide reports and results to all approved users of these systems. As these programs need to accomplish their tasks with the highest level of accuracy, quality and safety, effective management controls must be exercised.

Controls at this level ensure that the computer programs of a particular computerised application, process the business transactions according to a set of predefined rules, and store the processed data in computerised files and databases, in a safe and secure way.

A set of main IT application controls, such as: input controls, processing controls, output controls, database controls, change controls, etc. are presented next. Examples of various procedures, measures and forms are also noted.

In addition to these, a set of audit programmes and checklists are presented to support the CIO, the IT manager and other professionals (system development staff, end-users, IT auditors, internal auditors, IT consultants, external auditors, compliance officers, etc.) in executing and improving their duties and responsibilities.

9.2 Purpose and main types of IT application controls

In almost all types of organisations, both private and public, corporate controls denote the set of policies, procedures, techniques, methods and practices to manage and control their business operations.

Within this corporate controls governance framework IT controls are specific actions, usually specified by policies, procedures, practices, etc. performed by persons, hardware or software with the main objective to ensure that specific business objectives are met.

The overall guiding aim of IT controls relate to the secure processing, confidentiality, integrity and availability of data and the overall management of the IT function of the organisation.

IT controls are commonly described in two categories according to various sources:[66] IT general controls and IT application controls.

IT general controls (*see Chapters 1 to 8*) are those controls that are applicable to all IT activities (systems, services, issues, processes, operations, etc.) and data for a given organisation or IT systems environment. They include

---

[66] www.isaca.org, www.theiia.org, www.itpi.org.

controls over such areas as the strategy for IT, systems development, data centre operations, database and data communications infrastructure, systems software support and maintenance, IT security, and ready-made application systems acquisition, development and maintenance.

IT application controls are those controls that are appropriate for transaction processing by individual computerised subsystems, such as financial accounting, personnel administration, customer sales, inventory control, payroll or accounts payable, etc. and individual computer programs.

They relate to the processing and storing of data in computer-based files by individual IT applications and computer programs, and help ensure that business transactions occurred, are authorised, and are completely and accurately recorded, stored, processed and reported.

IT application controls are mainly built into the computer software of the specific application to prevent and deter crime and potential fraud and to minimise if not eliminate errors. They are also instituted outside the given application at the entry and exit points of the system.

The actual detailed IT application controls may be developed and implemented by the IT development manager, sometimes with external support, supervised by the IT executive, overviewed by the IT committee, and ratified by the Board. The audit programmes 'computerised application controls audit programme', 'computerised application quality audit programme', 'computerised application audit programme', and 'post-implementation review audit programme' (*see Paragraph 9.8*) may be used to support the design, implementation and post-implementation review of the IT application controls for the specific organisation.

The main types of IT application controls typically include:

- Input, processing and output controls
- IT application database, operation, change and testing controls
- End-user computing controls
- Monitoring and review controls.

9.3 Input, processing and output controls

9.3.1 Input controls

The main objective of input controls is to prevent the entry of erroneous, incomplete or otherwise improper data into the computerised information system. They also ensure that each transaction is authorised, processed correctly and processed only one time.

This is because imputing of data is the area where significant risks and exposures for abuse, crime and errors exist. These controls must, therefore, ensure accuracy of data, completeness of input and validation of input.

Accuracy of data: In order to ensure accuracy of data, information systems developers should:

- Design both the documents and the screens so as to minimise the number of errors which could be made by the data entry personnel, especially when data are keyed from documents.
- Include check digits in the codes that identify transactions and other entities which enable the

computer application software to check whether a code has been entered correctly.

- Display a message on the screen (for online systems) to remind data entry personnel that all input transactions should be authorised (i.e. the original documents should be checked). For batch systems, the check for authorisation should be visual.

Completeness of input: In order to ensure completeness of input, information systems developers should provide instructions and software code in the system developed so that:

- For batch systems, all transactions entered into the system, should be compared against the count for the batch produced by the computer program of the information system. Financial totals for the batch, when financial data are involved, should be compared between what has been inputted and what exists on the input documents.
- For online systems, 'logical' batches may be created by each data entry clerk on some time-period basis (e.g. hourly or daily, etc.). Again the manual count of what has been entered can be compared to the count kept by the computerised application system. Financial totals can also be compared (as explained above for the batch systems).
- For both batch and online systems, the approach of 'dual read' may be applied, especially for very critical financial or other transactions. This means that the data are inputted twice, once by person A, the second by person B, and the input is accepted only when both actions (input by person A and input by person B) are the same.

Validation of input: In order to ensure validation of input, information systems developers should write software code to perform a variety of checks, such as:

- Format checks: Character validation tests should check input data fields to see if they contain alphanumerics (upper or lower case letters and numbers), when they are supposed to have only numerics (arabic numerals: 0, 1, 2…9) and so on. For example, if a customer's name contains digits, the format is improper. If special characters (for example, punctuation or symbols ([};"!$=) are in the input data field, the format is improper.
- Reasonableness checks: These checks compare input data to expected values by testing logical relationships, or checking whether an upper limit has not been exceeded. For example, employee weekly hours should not be automatically processed if the sum of regular and overtime hours per individual exceeds 80. Another example can be with dates, when a birth date entered is greater than today's date or less than the current year. If such a difference occurs, then the data may have to be corrected and inputted again.
- Code checks: The system can compare the code entered, beyond its digit code, with valid codes exiting in the corporate or other database.

The result of all validations is an error file, a valid transactions file and an error report for subsequent human inspection and correction.

Input controls may make good use of business rules stored and maintained in an Enterprise Architecture Repository (*see Chapter 3*) or of the rules documented in corporate procedures and policies manuals.

9.3.2 Processing controls

The main objective of processing controls is to ensure that transactions entered into the computerised application system are valid and accurate, that external data are not lost or altered, and that invalid transactions are reprocessed correctly.

Processing controls include:

- Crossfooting tests: Crossfooting tests means the execution of logical tests for information consistency. This presupposes that two independent computations of a total figure can be made and compared. For example, in a payroll processing program, control totals may be calculated for net salary, deductions and gross salary of all personnel. At the end of the payroll processing run, gross salary should equal net salary plus reductions.
- Reasonableness checks: Reasonableness checks compare processed data to a set of predefined values or against an upper or lower limit before updating the corporate database. For example, computer salary deductions should not be greater than 50% of gross salary.
- Functional checks: Functional checks ensure that invoices for zero or negative amounts are not printed. Funds are not transferred or paid beyond some upper of preset limit per customer account.
- Rounding-off checks: Correct rounding off of financial data can avoid a possible 'salami' attack where very tiny sums (e.g. one pence) are deposited into an account of the defrauder for every financial transaction processed. This may amount to several hundreds or millions of pounds (or euros) in a financial institution in a given year stolen and defrauded.

- Parity checks: The addition of a parity bit (i.e. make all '1' bits even or odd) in a set of data to be processed, assures that bits are not lost during computer processing and prevents data corruption.
- Sequence checks: Sequence checks are used to check for missing items either within the given transaction or in a predefined set of transactions.

Processing controls may make use of business rules stored and maintained in an Enterprise Architecture Repository (*see Chapter 3*) or of the rules documented in corporate procedures and policies manuals.

9.3.3 Output controls

The main objective of output controls is to authenticate the previous other controls (input and processing), i.e. to ensure that only authorised transactions are processed correctly and that reports, screens and other output (e.g. magnetic media) are of the highest quality, complete and available only to authorised personnel.

Output controls include:

- Schedule checks: Schedule checks ensure that reports, media and documents are produced and printed according to schedule.
- Distribution checks: Distribution checks ensure that all printed output is distributed according to the rules of security (e.g. for cheques or payroll reports), and that electronic output (media, etc.) is also sent to the authorised recipients.
- Balancing checks: Balancing checks confirm that output figures balance back to inputs from which they are derived. This is a must in order to check the

reasonableness of financial figures, and to perform a variety of spot checks on the printed information (e.g. review all printed cheques to verify that cheques beyond an upper limit have not been printed, that there is only one cheque per recipient, that dates are of the valid format, etc.).

- Report quality checks: Report quality checks ensure that all printed output is of the highest quality, such as: timely (available when needed), complete (includes the stated user needs), concise (does not include elements not required by the users), relevant (is directly relevant to the situation), accurate (has no errors), precise (offers exact and quantitative information), and appropriate in form (with the correct level of detail, tabular versus graphics, etc. and as predefined report quality guidelines).
- Output log: The output log is used to record manually all the outputs produced, printed and distributed. This may serve as evidence for historical purposes, especially when disputes have to be settled and for auditing purposes.

Output controls may make use of business rules stored and maintained in an Enterprise Architecture Repository (*see Chapter 3*) or of the rules documented in corporate procedures and policies manuals.

9.4 IT application database, operation, change and testing controls

9.4.1 IT application database controls

The main purpose of IT application database controls is to ensure information system files and databases are protected from destruction, improper access or modification.

IT application database controls may include the following: file updated report, critical transactions report, application-specific access authorisation, application-specific back-up and recovery, database health checks, and application audit trails.

File updated report

A report may be prepared showing the master file before and after each update. For online systems, especially if they operate around the clock, reports may be issued on a daily basis, etc.

Critical transactions report

A report may be produced automatically and sent to a list of authorised staff (management, auditors, etc.) for transactions of high value to the organisation (e.g. transmittal of millions of dollars, financial reports, etc.).

Application-specific access authorisation

In certain very critical systems (e.g. income tax processing, payroll data updating, etc.) a certain level of security check by the specific application is sometimes required and implemented. These application-specific security checks may include: authorisation rules at the level of each user and the level of each data category, data encryption, digital signatures, limit checks for financial data at the level of the user, etc.

Application-specific back-up and recovery

The primary aim of this control is to be able to recover a file or a database maintained by the given computerised application in case of a system or other failure. This is addressed by a back-up and recovery policy, both at the organisational level (for all IT systems) and at the level of the specific application.

For example, at the level of the application, a version of the file or database from some prior time and a log of transactions (changes to the files and the database) from that time on may be used to recover one or all the files and the database.

In a batch system, the master file, prior to the transaction file being run off against it, serves as an excellent back-up file. In an online system, it is necessary to dump (copy to tape, for example) the database periodically to create such a back-up file.

To recover from the failure of the database (for example, as the result of a disk crash), logged transactions are run off against the previous version or against the dump. It is common for organisations to maintain multiple back-up versions (dumps) of their database with the corresponding transaction files, some of them in vaults on highly secure remote sites (bank vaults, other data centres, etc.).

Database health checks

These checks involve writing and executing software code to read all records in application classical files and databases and navigate all the paths of the tree or other structure of the databases, and printing a summary report with details of what records, data and figures exist in the files and the databases.

Application audit trails

Application program security may be defined as the system, policies, methods, tools and procedures that protect an application program from improper activities. Application programs usually implement security through the platforms and facilities of systems software, database management systems and data communications technologies.

Application-specific audit trails can be used to enhance security for certain very sensitive applications. These audit trails maintain a record of the application system activity by application process, transaction and user activity.

These audit trails maintain a record of the events and transactions interacting with the specific application, and can be used to reconstruct events, solve problems and detect potential frauds.

An application audit trail must include sufficient information to establish what event occurred and who (or what) caused them. The scope and contents of the audit trail will balance security needs with performance needs, privacy and costs.

At a minimum the contents of the application audit trail record must contain:

- type of event
- when the event or transaction occurred (time and day)
- user ID associated with the event or transaction
- program or command used to initiate the event or transaction
- copy of the transaction
- copy of the database record before and after the update process.

The audit trail should support accountability by providing a trace of user actions. While users cannot be prevented from using resources to which they have legitimate access authorisation, audit trail analysis can be used to examine their actions.

The audit trails could also support after-the-fact investigations of how, when and why normal operations ceased. Audit trails should be used as online detection tools to help identify problems other than intrusions as they occur.

Audit trails can be reviewed easier if the audit trail records can be queried by user ID, device ID, application name, date and time, or some other set of parameters to run reports of selected information.

Review guidelines should be developed by application owners, business data owners, system administrators and the internal audit department, as to how much review of audit trail records is necessary, and the time to be expended on these activities, based on the importance of identifying unauthorised activities.

IT application database controls may also make use of business rules stored and maintained in an Enterprise

Architecture Repository (*see Chapter 3*) or of the rules documented in corporate procedures and policies manuals.

9.4.2 IT application operation controls

The main purpose of IT application operation controls is to ensure the adequacy of both manual and automated controls over data input, validation and editing, and that error handling procedures enable and facilitate the timely and accurate resubmission of all corrected data.

These controls usually include the following:

- End-user transaction controls
- Computer operations controls
- Output review controls
- IT application rules, policies, procedures and forms controls.

End-user transaction controls

End-user transaction controls are used by the end-user function to ensure that their business transactions have been processed accurately, completely and at the right time, by either batch or real-time processing by the IT application.

The end-user transaction controls may include the following:

- Documented procedures must specify the method for handling any erroneous data entered into the application. These procedures should include how to identify, correct and reprocess rejected data.

- Source documents should be balanced to input data processed by the use of record counts, batching techniques, control totals, or some other type of logging.
- All input documents containing appropriate data for the application must be approved by authorised end-users, usually at the supervisory level of management. The levels of authorisation of the assigned approving officers should also be reviewed (periodically) to determine if they are reasonable.
- Passwords should be used to control access to the IT application by end-users. There should be a policy specifying that all passwords should be changed periodically. These passwords must be deleted when end-users, employees and other approved parties do not offer services to the organisation, or they do not need access to the specific IT application.
- Segregation of duties should be enforced as regards the IT application. Management should ensure that no one individual performs more than one of the following operations without management review and explicit approval: origination of data, input of data into the IT application, processing the data, distribution of the output, and reporting on the processed and stored data.

Computer operations controls

Computer operations controls are used to ensure the accuracy, completeness and timeliness of data during either batch or real-time processing by the IT application.

The computer operations controls may include the following:

- Documentation for the IT application should exist. This must explain the processing of data through the given IT application, diagrams and narratives on how the application processes data, processing flowcharts, an explanation of computer system and IT application or error messages, etc. For an example of IT application documentation, *see Chapter 5*.
- IT job scheduling rules should be documented for the running of the specific IT application. These must specify whether the IT application runs on a regular basis, which day of the week or month, the functions to be accomplished (process data, update data warehouses, reporting, file validity, etc.), triggering rules (manual submission, or automatic), the duration and results, etc. The controls to be exercised should be documented.
- All IT application runs should be recorded in a computer jobs processing log. This log should be used to document any errors or problems encountered during each execution of the IT application. The information that should be considered for recording purposes include descriptions of any errors encountered, dates and times identified, any codes or messages associated with transaction inputting, data validations, or archival and storage errors, any corrective action taken, date and times corrected, etc. Examples of logs are included in Appendix 4.
- Application audit trails (*see Paragraph 9.4.1*) should be generated during the processing phase of an IT application. These application audit trails should contain the necessary information about each transaction. For example, data that should be included are: who initiated each of the transactions, the data and time of the

transactions, the location of the transaction origination, the name of the user, the application program, etc.

Output review controls

Output review controls are used to ensure the integrity and quality of output and the correct and timely distribution of any output produced by the specific IT application. Output can be in printed form, digital media, files used as input to other systems, or information available for online viewing.

These controls can be exercised by either end-users or IT or both, depending on the mode of IT processing (batch, online, mixed, etc.), and other organisational conditions.

The output review controls may include the following:

- Balancing or reconciling output to input, and correcting output errors identified, should be done after every processing phase. This should be done according to the instructions and methods contained in the IT application user guide or other documentation. Management must ensure that adequate separation of duties is enforced for the balancing or reconciliation procedure.
- Printed output should be reviewed for general acceptability, quality, accuracy and completeness, including any control totals produced by the IT application. Electronic output should be examined to see that the files produced can be opened, read, etc.
- All output error reports should be recorded in a log kept of output errors. This log should contain information, such as: a description of problems and errors, date, and time identified, corrective action taken, etc. Examples of logs are included in Appendix 4.

- All output files (reports, digital media, electronic files, etc.) should follow the back-up and recovery policy and procedures of the organisation. Archiving or deletion of these files will need to follow the relevant corporate guidelines and procedures applicable for all assets of the organisation.

IT application rules, policies, procedures and forms controls

The IT application rules, policies, procedures and forms controls support the other input, processing and output controls, as they are fundamental to their good operation.

In corporate terms, the design, writing and implementation of the policies, procedures and forms of an organisation should be based on business rules and external regulations and must be controlled (for management and efficiency purposes) by a central corporate administration function.

The general aspects of administering IT policies, procedures and forms are described in Chapter 2.

All these rules, policies, procedures and forms are usually kept in an Enterprise Architecture Repository (*see Chapter 3*).

In terms of achieving the better operation, however, of the particular IT application, the rules, policies, procedures and forms relevant to the running of the given IT application controls may be kept in a separate electronic file for the use of running and controlling this IT application.

This may also be complemented by having a printed copy of these rules, policies, procedures and forms readily available and for easy reference purposes to support the error management process of the operation of IT applications.

The stock of pre-printed sensitive forms (e.g. cheques, invoices, etc.) used by the given IT application should be strictly controlled and managed.

9.4.3 IT application change controls

The main objective of application change controls is to safeguard the integrity of the IT application system by establishing standard procedures for making modification to the system. These standards should apply to all the IT systems of the organisation.

At the level of each IT application, each change should be recorded on a changes request. Each change might need to go through a problem analysis process in order to document the change that is required to solve a particular problem.

This process would have the following steps:

1 Problem identification.
2 Definition and representation of the problem.
3 Examination of several alternate strategies for problem solution, such as structured analysis, working backward approach, CSF factors analysis, etc.
4 Use of all the required tools (e.g. 'MIND TOOLS') for preparing a solution to the problem, such as fishbone diagram, five whys approach, decision tree analysis, force field analysis, requirements analysis techniques, Delphi Technique, brainstorming, mind mapping, focusing, abductive/inductive reasoning, assumption reversal, lateral thinking (Edward de Bono's technique), root cause analysis, etc.
5 Carry out the action plan for the solution of the problem.

6 Review and evaluate the actual results.
7 Document the results for each problem solved.

After the problem analysis, the changes to be implemented should be recorded, as would be all the applied changes to the specific IT application system.

For an example of a form to record changes, see Appendix 4 'Application Change Request Form'.

9.4.4 IT application testing controls

IT application testing controls ensure that reliance can be placed on the application system before the given system is put into full production status. The strategy of testing controls is defined in the general testing standards for information systems of the organisation.

At the level of each IT application, these tests should be customised and designed to be applied to the very specific environment of the application tested, on the basis of its own application-specific data, files, copy of production database, the set of security rules to be applied, application documentation, etc.

The main controls in this area are:

- Test methodology
- Test plan
- Organisational structure for application software testing.

Various other IT forms that may be used for management control, system development and security monitoring and other quality monitoring purposes are included in Appendix 4.

Test methodology – example

The test methodology should have the following steps:

Step 1: Organise test project.

Organising the test project involves creating a system test plan, a schedule and test approach, and requesting and assigning resources.

Step 2: Design and build system tests.

Designing and building system tests involves identifying test cycles, test cases, entrance and exit criteria, expected results, etc. In general, test conditions and expected results will be identified by the test team in conjunction with the project business analyst or business expert. The test team will then identify test cases and the data required. The test conditions are derived from the business design and the transaction requirements documents.

Step 3: Design and build test procedures.

Designing and building test procedures includes setting up procedures, such as error management systems and status reporting, and setting up and loading the test database tables.

Step 4: Execute tests.

This involves executing unit, subsystem, operations acceptance and integrated tests, as described in the test plan.

Step 5: Sign-off.

Sign-off involves getting the approval of the users on the basis of the tests executed previously.

Test plan – example

The contents of a test plan should be:

Objectives and scope

Roles and responsibilities

Test scenarios and cases

Acceptance criteria

Test results

Test approvals

Application software testing forms

Examples of the forms to execute and document the tests are included in Appendix 4.

Organisational structure for application software testing

For the support of the activities of IT application software testing the organisational structure for testing should have the following roles and responsibilities:

Test project manager: Overall responsibility for managing, and organising testing, obtaining, co-ordinating and allocating the required resources, providing technical guidance, performing quality reviews and inspections, undertaking and managing risks, and maintaining the test library.

Test designer: Produces, categorises and files test scenarios.

Tester: Executes test scenarios, documents the results and documents any required changes.

System test administrator: Establishes and maintains the required technical environment for application testing.

Conclusion

The final product of all these controls (input, processing, output, database, testing, etc.) is a well-tested and managed IT application, ready for the next phase in the system development process.

IT applications are usually developed and deployed by the classical IT function, with possibly the assistance and support of external parties.

Lately, however, with all the currently available office productivity tools (such as databases, spreadsheets, etc.), end-users have the opportunity, and many times exercise it, to develop their IT office applications by themselves.

Controls are, therefore, required for preventing and avoiding decision-making errors, potential fraud issues, information presentation errors and other statistical miscalculations.

9.5 End-user computing controls

End-user computing is changing the fundamental nature of IT office applications and the way such applications are being developed and used in different business environments.

As the risks of incorrect information entered, processed and presented by these applications are not well understood by the end-users themselves, various controls are usually developed and implemented to minimise, if not avoid altogether, these risks.

The end-user computing controls may include the end-user computing policy and the end-user office applications development controls.

9.5.1 End-user computing policy

The end-user computing policy may contain guidelines to cover the following issues and topics:

- Definition of what can be done and what is not allowed
- Segregation of duties and access control
- Documentation required
- Accuracy of information processing (e.g. data integrity)
- Input/output control
- Safeguarding of records (e.g. critical spreadsheets and databases, monitoring of controls, etc.)
- Standards for the development, acquisition, documentation, security, maintenance and operation of end-user computing applications
- Security guidelines for authorised software, authorised hardware, programming requirements, testing and documentation
- Evaluation of new software prior to being placed onto the authorised software list, and evaluation of software to ensure compatibility between software packages.

9.5.2 End-user office applications development controls

Office applications, like spreadsheets and databases, based on personal computers and developed by end-users (e.g.

professional staff, knowledge workers, managers, analysts, experts, etc.), are often used to accomplish various management and reporting tasks.

The output of these tasks is to provide critical data or complex calculations related to financial reporting, various risk areas, simulation studies, etc. offering significant flexibility and immediate results to several management problems.

However, with flexibility and power comes the risk of errors, an increased potential for fraud, and potential abuse for critical spreadsheets and databases not following the usual software development life cycle (e.g. design, develop, test, implement).

To manage and control office applications (spreadsheets, database, etc.), organisations may implement controls, such as:

- Documentation must exist for all applications, containing calculation formulas, data used, information flows, tests done, error handling, to which corporate decisions or processes this application is contributing.
- Passwords must be used for all users accessing these applications.
- Each application must have an owner, a person maintaining it, and a higher level manager to approve access, changes and distribution of the results of this application.
- All applications should be supported by the IT function of the organisation.
- Back-ups should be taken by both the end-users and IT as per the back-up and recovery policy.

- Each application developed must adhere to the budget process.
- Adequate training must be given to all users of the applications.
- All application runs and their results must be recorded in a log.

Responsibility for management control over office applications is usually a shared responsibility with the end-users and IT. The IT function is typically concerned with providing a secure personal computer environment for storing the data of the spreadsheets, databases, etc. and for data back-ups. The end-user personnel are responsible for the remainder of the activities.

9.6 Monitoring and review controls

Establishing IT monitoring and review controls for this area may be achieved by the IT management report, the performance measures of IT applications and the audit review tools and techniques described later in this chapter.

This may also be facilitated by following the monitoring and review activities management plan and all the data included in the IT management report (*see Chapter 1*).

The following may be monitored, reviewed and included in the IT management report:

- Application input controls not used
- Application processing controls not used
- Application output controls not used
- Application database controls not used
- Audit trail controls not used
- Application change controls not used

- Authorisation controls for application software not kept
- Application software not kept current
- Security controls for application software not followed
- Documentation controls for application software not followed.

It is the job of the CIO to ensure that the IT reporting mechanism is fed with the relevant performance and compliance data of this area.

9.7 IT application performance measures

The complete integrated set of control components of IT application controls, may be evaluated and improved by establishing and collecting performance data and by using the audit programmes and checklists (*see Paragraph 9.8*).

The usual IT application performance measures that may be used for this purpose are depicted in Table 11.

These performance measures could be based on a mixed system with two components: Component 1 would be an IT BSC (Information Technology Balanced Scorecard) Measurement System, described in Chapter 4, and Component 2 would be a Compliance Monitoring System for monitoring compliance to policies, procedures and related matters (e.g. documentation standards not drafted, testing plan not followed, etc.).

The IT management of the company, may, depending on various aspects of the organisation, analyse all this performance and compliance monitoring information to review, assess and improve the IT application operational elements of the IT function of the specific organisation.

Number	Performance Measure
1	Mean time between application failures
2	% Application changes correctly implemented
3	% Application errors resolved within budget and time constraints
4	% End-users satisfied with particular application
5	% End-user applications operating without errors
6	% Applications without quality errors reported
7	% Applications without audit trails implemented
8	Average application availability
9	% Applications with no user acceptance
10	Number of backlog changes
11	Application testing procedures not followed
12	Rules for input, output and processing not documented

Table 11: Computerised application performance measures

9.8 Review and audit tools and techniques

In order to ensure that the IT application controls are properly and effectively organised to serve the control needs of the specific corporate IT application, guidelines and other tools are necessary to aid the manager and other professionals (auditor, compliance officers, etc.) in discharging their duties.

Guidelines and other tools are described in Appendix 3 (Monitoring IT controls checklist), Appendix 4 (Examples of IT forms), Appendix 5 (IT audit methodology), Appendix 6 (IT audit areas), and Appendix 7 (Internal audit report example).

The following audit programmes and checklists may be used: computerised application controls audit programme, computerised application quality audit programme, computerised application audit programme, post-implementation review audit programme, end-user security checklist, end-user application development and operation, web-based applications checklist, and monitoring IT application controls checklist.

The checklists and audit programmes presented are not intended to be a complete management review or IT audit guide. IT managers and other professionals may choose to use only certain components of the checklists and audit programmes based upon the size, complexity, business needs and demands, IT maturity needs and expectations, nature of the organisation's business, and levels of deployment and utilisation of IT systems.

9.8.1 Computerised application controls audit programme

The objective of this audit programme is to support the process of constructing, reviewing, evaluating and improving the IT applications controls identified in this chapter.

This audit programme covers the following issues: data preparation, source document design and control, clerical procedures, screen design, file validity, testing, logging, etc.

1 Review data preparation:
   - o Identify documents used for each type of input.
   - o Ensure valid data are entered in each source document.
   - o Identify personnel responsible for input preparation, review of source documents, and authorisation of input.
   - o Assess data preparation control functions performed prior to submitting data for processing.

2 Review source document design:
   - o Determine if source documents are pre-numbered.
   - o Determine if, for each type of transaction, the source document used provides a unique code or identifier.
   - o Determine if source documents are specially designed to guide the initial recording of data in a uniform format.
   - o Determine if source documents have a cross-reference to the transactions used by the given IT system.

3 Review source document controls:
   - o Are source documents stored in a secure location?
   - o Are source documents released on two signatures?
   - o Are source documents retained long enough (to allow reconstruction)?
   - o Are source documents destroyed as per security procedures?
   - o Is the retention period recorded on each source document?
   - o Is only one person responsible for the origination, authorisation and control of each source document?

4 Review clerical procedures to ensure that all input documents are stamped to prevent duplicate entries, all rejected items are properly controlled, and that all input documents are attached to the computer (printout) entries.

5 Review verification of online input and determine whether program data checks are adequate (per transaction/field) and that they contain the following controls: check digits, format checks, reasonableness checks, limit checks, sequence checks, value of one field depends on other field, date checks, (not higher than today's date or other value, etc.), checks on partial update to given parts of files or databases, and any automatic transactions created checks.

6 Review screen and report design per application program and ensure that each screen and report have: screen ID, report ID, company name, application name, date and time, program number, help menu, error or message line, and totals line.

7 Review file validity (per file). Consider: are files properly set up?

- o Initially (record counts, conversion checks)?
- o Sequence checks (duplicate records, sorted)?
- o Retention (period to be specified)?
- o Run to run checks (are control figures produced to verify actions taken – especially in batch runs, etc.)?

8 Review system testing strategy and determine whether all critical application functions are tested and the results documented, and whether the system testing strategy is well documented.

9 Review source code documentation (per application program) and determine whether: the source code is well documented, the source code is readable, if any logic

bombs exist within the source code, if comments exist within the source code, and if there are logic loops for the source code reviewed.

10 Review output handling. Do retention and security procedures exist for handling critical reports and computer output (on disk/tape)?

11 Review the use of data manipulation utilities:

- Are users allowed to use data utilities? If so, for what reason (database update, data extraction)?
- Is the use properly authorised and controlled?
- Is there a log of these activities?
- Is this log retained?
- Are IT staff (programmers, systems support) allowed to use data manipulation and extraction utilities and for what reason (database update, data extraction)?
- Is the use properly authorised and controlled?
- Is there a log of these activities?
- Is this log retained?

12 Review batch processing for databases and assess if any application batch programs are run on online databases (for what reason, under what controls, by which staff (IT, users)?).

13 Review data dictionary and ensure that it contains: field names/synonyms, field sizes/descriptions, data descriptions, data origins per field, database update/security rights, field edit rules, relationships to other data, and log of changes.

14 Review database health. Consider: access all database structures and tables to ensure that all access paths are accessible and that all the data are properly stored.

15 Review audit trail:

- Are transactions traced back to the same document?

- o Review the types of logs available (e.g. system log, database log, application log, operating system log).
- o Are the following recorded: username, date/time, update before image, update after image, database name, program number, terminal number, transaction ID, network node location?

16 Review continuity of application in case of ready-made software package and determine: vendor financial stability, support contract, escrow account for source code, IT support staff properly trained, and vendor staff on call issues.

17 Review software quality and determine whether the package or home software exhibits the following qualities: maintainability, testing ability, portability, reliability, accuracy of results and data, efficiency and usability.

9.8.2 Computerised application quality audit programme

The objective of this audit programme is to support the process of constructing, reviewing, evaluating and improving the IT applications controls identified in this chapter.

This audit programme covers the following issues: application design, maintenance and operation.

A. Application design

1 Input and output data controls: Determine whether adequate controls exist for inputting data into the application and for outputting data from the application. Consider:

   - What is provided (no or one to two minor controls, over three controls, a set of over five controls, a full set of logical controls, too many controls) at the time of the evaluation?
   - What is expected by the organisation?
   - How important is this to the organisation?
2. Accuracy of results produced: Determine whether accurate results are produced by the application. Consider:
   - How accurate are the results (1% to 3% errors, 4% to 6% errors, 7% to 10% errors, 11% to 50% errors, over 50% errors) at the time of the evaluation?
   - What is expected by the organisation?
   - How important is this to the organisation?
3. Compliance with quality standards and procedures: Determine whether the application complies with the system development standards of the organisation as regards quality. Consider:
   - How compliant is the application (not at all, only up to 20%, only up to 50%, only up to 80%, fully compliant, i.e. 100%) at the time of the evaluation?
   - What is expected by the organisation?
   - How important is this to the organisation?
4. Data security: Determine whether the application contains effective security mechanisms to avoid fraud, omissions and illegal access to sensitive elements of the application. Consider:
   - Whether effective mechanisms exist in the application (none at all, only a small number, a small somewhat satisfactory logical number, a larger somewhat satisfactory number, a very satisfactory and effective number) at the time of the evaluation.

- o What is expected by the organisation?
- o How important is this to the organisation?

5 Interfacing capability: Determine whether the application contains effective interfacing mechanisms to other applications. Consider:

- o Whether effective mechanisms exist in the application (none at all, quite impossible, only under very specific conditions, very easy, extremely easy) at the time of the evaluation.
- o What is expected by the organisation?
- o How important is this to the organisation?

6 Response: Determine whether the application responds to queries by end-users in a satisfactory way. Consider:

- o Whether the application has effective responses (slow response, fast response, very fast response) at the time of the evaluation.
- o What is expected by the organisation?
- o How important is this to the organisation?

7 Availability: Determine the availability of the application. Consider:

- o How available is the application during the specified production time-frame (not at all, only up to 20%, only up to 50%, only up to 80%, fully available, i.e. 100%) at the time of the evaluation?
- o What is expected by the organisation?
- o How important is this to the organisation?

8 Easy to use: Determine how easy to use is the specific application by its end-users. Consider:

- o How easy to use (ergonomic, help line exists, documentation exists) is the application during the specified production time-frame and for its functions (not at all easy, easy for 20% of the functions only, easy for 50% of the functions only, easy for 80% of the functions only, easy for all its functions, i.e. 100% easy) at the time of the evaluation?

- What is expected by the organisation?
- How important is this to the organisation?

9 Alignment of application to business functions: Determine whether the application is aligned to the business processes of the organisation. Consider:

- How aligned the functions of the application are to the business processes (less than 20% alignment, up to 30% alignment, up to 50% alignment, up to 80% alignment, up to 100% alignment) at the time of the evaluation.
- What is expected by the organisation?
- How important is this to the organisation?

10 Understanding of results produced: Determine whether the results produced by the application are understood by its business users. Consider:

- How much the results produced by the application are understood by the business (end-) users (less than 20% of the results are understood, up to 30% of the results are understood, up to 50% of the results are understood, up to 80% of the results are understood, up to 100% of the results are understood) at the time of the evaluation.
- What is expected by the organisation?
- How important is this to the organisation?

B. Application maintenance

11 Analysis comprehension: Determine whether the application contains effective tools and documentation for understanding its logic. Consider:

- o Whether it is easy to comprehend the logic, find errors, solve problems and read the documentation of the analysis of the application (none at all, quite impossible, only under very specific conditions, very easy, extremely easy) at the time of the evaluation.
- o What is expected by the organisation?
- o How important is this to the organisation?

12 Maintenance of changes: Determine whether the application is easy to maintain. Consider:

- o Whether it is easy to maintain and make changes to the logic of the application (impossible to maintain, not easy to maintain at all, only easy to maintain under very specific conditions, very easy to maintain, extremely easy to maintain) at the time of the evaluation.
- o What is expected by the organisation?
- o How important is this to the organisation?

13 Data for application testing: Determine whether proper data were provided to the application for effective testing. Consider:

- o Whether the data provided for testing were adequate (no data provided, some data provided but with low quality, some data provided with good quality, enough data provided with good quality, enough data provided with excellent quality).
- o What is expected by the organisation?
- o How important is this to the organisation?

14 Testing methodology for application testing: Determine whether a proper testing methodology was used by the developers of the application for effective testing. Consider:

- o Whether the methodology for testing was adequate (no methodology used, a standard methodology was used for only up to 20% of the tests, a standard methodology was used for only up to 50% of the tests, a standard methodology was used for only up to 80% of the tests, a standard methodology was used for up to 100% of the tests).
- o What is expected by the organisation?
- o How important is this to the organisation?

15 Cost of application maintenance: Determine the cost of application maintenance. Consider:

- o Whether the resources used are recorded and charged out.
- o Whether the costs are very high, medium, or low for a given time-frame.
- o What is expected by the organisation?
- o How important is this to the organisation?

C. Application operation

16 Operational easiness: Determine whether the application is easy to run. Consider:

- o Whether it is easy to run the application without the involvement of the developers (not possible to run at all, sometimes easy to run, only easy to run under very specific conditions, very easy to run, extremely easy to run) at the time of the evaluation.
- o What is expected by the organisation?

- o How important is this to the organisation?

17 Operational reliability: Determine whether the application is reliable. Consider:
- o Whether the application is reliable and can run without problems (not reliable at all, sometimes reliable, only reliable under very specific conditions, very reliable, extremely reliable) at the time of the evaluation.
- o Record the most critical factors affecting its reliability (hardware, software, network, controls, etc.).
- o What is expected by the organisation?
- o How important is this to the organisation?

18 Application vendor reliability: Determine whether the vendor of the application is reliable. Consider:
- o Whether the vendor of the application is reliable and financially stable problems (not reliable at all, not enough data exist for evaluation, somewhat reliable, very reliable and financially stable).
- o Record the most critical factors affecting their reliability (support, profit, network, hardware, software, training, problem solution, etc.).
- o What is expected by the organisation?
- o How important is this to the organisation?

9.8.3 Computerised application audit programme

The objective of this audit programme is to support the process of constructing, reviewing, evaluating and improving the IT applications controls identified in this chapter.

1 Obtain computerised application documentation.
2 Study and review application documentation.

3 Review technical design and architecture of application with system developers.
4 Study key functions of the software by monitoring actual business transactions supported by the application.
5 Prepare test runs and test scenarios.
6 Run through the various menus, features and options of the application via the use of a test system.
7 Record all tests, errors and cases of non-conformance to business rules and practices.
8 Validate all system inputs against the applicable criteria (e.g. numeric validations, date checks, range checks, upper and lower limit checks, etc.).
9 Verify access controls in application software.
10 Verify how errors and exceptions are handled.
11 Evaluate the production environment of the application by conducting a security review of the operating system and database software.
12 Run a security penetration test, if possible.
13 Review tests and results with both IT staff and users.
14 Prepare draft audit report.
15 Review draft report with IT management and users.
16 Incorporate IT and user feedback into the audit report.
17 Finalise and issue audit report to authorised IT, user and executive level management.

9.8.4 Post-implementation review audit programme

The objective of this audit programme is to support the process of constructing, reviewing, evaluating and improving the IT applications controls identified in this chapter.

This audit programme covers the following issues: IT steering committee issues, application functionality, user expectations, training and support, documentation, administration and change control issues, and application stability, and maintenance agreement.

IT steering committee issues

1 Review IT steering committee minutes and other relevant application documentation to ascertain that the critical issues related to all aspects of the application (feasibility, analysis, design, etc.) were reviewed by this committee.
2 Review all documentation to ensure that the committee did provide guidance and instructions on all issues referred to it, before the application went live.

Application functionality

3 Review business case, feasibility study and project initiation documentation and determine (by questionnaire, group discussion, critical success factors analysis, and individual interview (as appropriate)), with the Board project sponsor, end-users and IT development staff, whether the computerised application, as installed and implemented, varied significantly to the initial proposal and scope of work.
4 Review change control documentation to ascertain level and scope of changes to original specification of needs and requirements.

User expectations

5 Review and determine with the end-users whether their expectations have been met and up to what level.

6 Review and determine with the IT development staff whether their expectations have been met and up to what level.

7 Review and determine with the Board project sponsor whether Board expectations have been met and up to what level.

8 Review and determine with the project stakeholders whether their expectations have been met and up to what level.

Training and support

9 Review and determine whether users received training, whether the training was timely, adequate and pertinent, and whether users received take-away material and workbooks.

10 Review and determine whether IT operational staff and system administrators received training, whether the training was timely, adequate and pertinent, and whether they received take-away material and workbooks.

11 Review and determine whether effective processes are in place to identify deficiencies in training (e.g. constant calls from users and system administrators for advice on how to perform basic functions).

Documentation

12 Review and determine whether end-users have user guides, whether these guides are available to all, whether these are adequate and whether they are kept up to date.

13 Review and determine whether system administrators have technical guides, whether these guides are available

to all, whether these are adequate and whether they are kept up to date.

14 Review and determine whether IT development staff have technical guides, whether these guides are available to all, whether these are adequate and whether they are kept up to date.

Administration and change control issues

15 Review and determine whether relevant records are kept of down time, application issues, faults and errors, maintenance of user profiles, documentation changes, access rights changes, other performance statistics, etc.

16 Determine whether all changes from the original specification have been logged and authorised.

Application stability

17 Review and determine whether:

- The application has proved robust.
- The down time has been minimal.
- The users have expressed concern over the system (speed, durability, poor outcomes, etc.).
- There are substantial outstanding issues with the vendors.
- There are ongoing problems with the maintenance of the system (software/hardware/peripherals).
- Upgrades have been provided in accordance with contractual obligations.

Maintenance agreement

18 Review and determine whether:

- o There is a maintenance agreement with an external vendor.
- o Service levels for support and maintenance have been met.
- o The agreement has proved adequate and satisfactory.

9.8.5 End-user security checklist

The objective of this checklist is to support the process of constructing, reviewing, evaluating and improving the end-user IT applications controls identified in this chapter.

1. Has responsibility for the security of end-user computing been assigned to a specific official with the necessary authorisation?
2. Has virus detection or virus prevention software been installed?
3. Are procedures in place to inform users of what actions to take in the event of their PC being infected by a virus?
4. Is the data classified to restrict access to unauthorised staff?
5. Is there security or access control software in place to control the access of sensitive information?
6. Is access to sensitive data controlled and monitored effectively?
7. Are there procedures and controls in place to ensure the proper and secure disposal of commercially sensitive data on digital, video, film, magnetic or paper media?
8. Is personal information registered in terms of the National Data Protection Act?
9. Is there access control software in place to prevent unauthorised access to any PC, workstation or terminal?
10. Does the length of user password comply with the password policy of the organisation?

9.8.6 End-user application development and operation checklist

The objective of this checklist is to support the process of constructing, reviewing, evaluating and improving the end-user IT applications controls identified in this chapter.

1 Are installation standards in place to control the implementation of new software?
2 Are regular back-ups taken of the PC or workstation files? Consider: regular back-ups taken of key models and data, and record maintained of back-ups.
3 Is new software installed by suitably qualified IT personnel?
4 Is a log maintained of all hardware and software errors and the action taken to resolve the errors?
5 Are controls in place to monitor and authorise the development of spreadsheets, databases and applications?
6 Is the documentation for programs, spreadsheets and models adequate? Consider: central guidelines, quality control, peer reviews, formula coding, etc.
7 Is access to programming languages and tools controlled?
8 Are changes to programs, models, etc. authorised and controlled?
9 Are models and programs sufficiently tested before going into production status?
10 Are procedures in place for the creation of secure models?
11 Can the various models, spreadsheets, databases, etc. interface satisfactorily with other software to avoid rekeying of data?

12 Are procedures in place to control the migration of programs from development on end-user PCs to production?

13 Is data transferred (downloaded/uploaded) to/from mainframe systems to PCs in a secure manner? Consider: identification of data, access rights, file controls to ensure that access to production programs, data, files cannot occur in an unauthorised manner, file controls in place to prohibit update of production files, programs except under controlled authorised conditions, recording of all data transfers, balancing controls, etc.

9.8.7 Web-based applications checklist

The objective of this checklist is to support the process of constructing, reviewing, evaluating and improving the IT applications controls identified in this chapter.

This checklist covers the following issues: input processing, application security, web server software, web host, network environment and website management.

Input processing

1 Is unnecessary disclosure of information avoided? Consider:

- o Review the source of HTML, JavaScript and other client-side scripting languages to ensure that these do not contain unnecessary information that could be observed and exploited by potential attackers, such as: names and other details of development personnel, disabled functionality, details about Common Gateway Interface functions and parameters, third-party tools in use, etc.

- o Review error messages returned by the web-based application to ensure that they do not reveal undesirable information.

2 Has a robust logon process been implemented?
3 Are sessions appropriately tracked?
4 Are session timeouts implemented?
5 Are GET/POST operations carefully implemented?
6 Are hidden form fields restricted?
7 Are cookies carefully controlled?
8 Is user input properly validated?
9 Are scripts carefully constructed?
10 Do all CGI scripts record in a log what they have done?

Application security

11 Has security of the application, web server and web host been checked before going into production?
12 Is the application architecture secure?
13 Does back-end connection to a database avoid use of privileged user IDs?
14 Does connection to a database avoid use of hard-coded passwords?
15 Are any hard-coded passwords held in obscure places?
16 Are hard-coded passwords lengthy and in a cryptic format?
17 Are hard-coded passwords held and on files adequately protected?
18 Is the web server run on a physically different server from the back-end application server?
19 Is sensitive customer data (e.g. bank account data, credit card details, etc.) encrypted?

Web server software

20 Are web servers containing sensitive pages run on alternate ports and is access restricted by the packet filter?
21 Is any sensitive information removed from public web servers?
22 Are sensitive pages secured by password or access list?
23 Are known server bugs removed?
24 Are users appropriately authenticated?
25 Are FTP services carefully implemented?
26 Is logging of access to web pages enabled and are logs reviewed?

Web host

27 Has hardware been carefully sized?
28 Is actual usage of the resources over time monitored?
29 Is resilience built in?
30 Is physical security adequate?
31 Are all user accounts except for the web server account(s), web master accounts and authorised administrator account removed?
32 Are different root directories for the web server and server documents used?
33 Are packet filters installed to restrict connections from known hosts or services and to log incoming service requests?
34 Are all sensitive files protected from access through the web?
35 Are robust server administration practices implemented?
36 Are log failures and successes of administration operations, log-ins, security configuration changes and server initialisations and shutdowns monitored?

Network environment

37 Have bandwidth requirements been estimated?
38 Have network services been restricted?
39 Have networks been carefully configured?

Website management

40 Has a capacity monitoring process been implemented?
41 Are potential security problems identified?
42 Is a workable and reliable change control process with event logging, documentation and reporting procedures established to ensure that updates are made in a safe and timely manner?
43 Are changes managed effectively (hardware, software and content)?
44 Is security monitored?
45 Is an effective logging process implemented?
46 Is intrusion detection implemented?
47 Is incident management effectively implemented?
48 Are all outsourcing issues considered before the decision to award this task is made? Consider:
   - establishing security targets and linkage to a risk/reward policy
   - identifying how security monitoring will be conducted and reported
   - assessing the security of the third party's network architecture
   - assessing the third party organisation's security practices and culture
   - identifying the third party's ability to respond to new vulnerabilities

- o identifying the third party's ability to respond to security incidents
- o identifying data back-up and disaster recovery requirements
- o implementing secure mechanisms for remotely updating website content
- o establishing the right to conduct security tests and reviews.

9.8.8 Monitoring IT application controls checklist

The objective of this checklist is to support the process of constructing, reviewing, evaluating and improving the IT applications controls identified in this chapter.

1 Does the IT strategic plan describe all IT applications serving the given organisation?

2 Is there a mechanism by which the business community articulates expected events (transactions, new locations, etc.) to IT so that IT can adequately plan?

3 Are IT policies and procedures developed, approved and centrally maintained for key IT processes and application systems?

4 Are the policies and procedures reviewed and updated at least annually?

5 Are IT performance measures (including an IT budget) used to monitor system performance and output?

6 Is there an acceptable used policy regarding company IT assets that all personnel are required to acknowledge?

7 Are IT compliance issues fully understood by all IT staff?

8 Does the IT function appear to be adequately staffed?

9 Is there a mechanism to monitor the productivity of IT personnel?

10 Are IT personnel required to attend certain training or obtain certain qualifications?
11 What is the average length of service for IT personnel?
12 Are there policies that expressly prohibit the usage of company programs or data for purposes other than work?
13 Are all third party services properly managed and monitored?
14 Is the IT asset inventory properly managed and its elements monitored?

9.9 Conclusion

Expectations are increasing steadily among regulatory authorities, corporate and IT managers, IT professional staff, external and internal auditors, customers and other stakeholders regarding the protection of corporate data against information processing errors, security, invasion of privacy, fraud, sabotage, erroneous decision making, etc.

These concerns apply both to applications running in the data centre and in the end-user area of responsibility.

Spending on IT controls and best practices continues to rise. However, IT executives want to see a strong business case for spending on IT audit and IT control activities, as per IT Process Institute.[67]

ITPI's groundbreaking study of top performers shows that IT audit and control related activities are not just a necessary cost but actually improve operating performance!

---

[67] www.itpi.org/, 4/2010.

IT application controls are mainly built into the computer software of the specific application to prevent and deter crime and potential fraud and to minimise if not eliminate errors. They are also instituted outside the given application at the entry and exit points of the system.

The cost of errors has been determined to be: four times greater if controls are introduced into the application after the specifications phase, eight times greater after the programming phase, 12 times greater after the testing phase, and 16 times greater after the implementation phase.

The IT application or program controls presented in this chapter are performed automatically by the systems and are executed manually by both the end-users and IT. These are designed to ensure the complete and accurate processing of data, from input through processing, output, storage and reporting.

These are general type IT application controls and will need to be customised to suit, among other things, the given organisation's needs, IT standards on system development and security, business operating model, compliance requirements, regulatory expectations and business control maturity levels.

Moreover, the main IT application controls and the audit and review programmes and checklists identified and presented in this chapter, modified and customised accordingly to operate for the specific organisation, contribute to the better operation of the knowledge management framework, as they improve the quality and reliability of processed data and reported information of this framework, for the purposes of the given organisation.

9.10 Review questions

This set of questions may be employed by those using the controls identified in this book to assess and double-check their own conceptual understanding and practical knowledge contained in this chapter.

1. What is the main purpose of computerised application controls?

Reference: Paragraph 9.2 'Purpose and main types of IT application controls'.

2. What are the main types of computerised application controls?

Reference: Paragraph 9.2 'Purpose and main types of IT application controls'.

3. Why are computerised application controls built into the computer software of the specific application?

Reference: Paragraph 9.2 'Purpose and main types of IT application controls'.

4. What do input controls of computerised application controls ensure?

Reference: Paragraph 9.3.1 'Input controls'.

5. What are some of the checks written into the software code to ensure validation of input?

Reference: Paragraph 9.3.1 'Input controls'.

6. What are some of the checks and tests included in processing controls?

Reference: Paragraph 9.3.2 'Processing controls'.

7. What do 'reasonableness checks' do?

Reference: Paragraph 9.3.2 'Processing controls'.

8. What is the main objective of output controls?

Reference: Paragraph 9.3.3 'Output controls'.

9. What do output controls include?

Reference: Paragraph 9.3.3 'Output controls'.

10. What do report quality checks ensure and in what terms?

Reference: Paragraph 9.3.3 'Output controls'.

11. What do database controls include?

Reference: Paragraph 9.4.1 'IT application database controls'.

12. What do database health checks involve?

Reference: Paragraph 9.4.1 'IT application database controls'.

13. What is the main objective of change controls?

Reference: Paragraph 9.4.3 'IT application change controls'.

14. Which are the main testing controls?

Reference: Paragraph 9.4.4 'IT application testing controls'.

15. What should the contents of a test plan be?

Reference: Paragraph 9.4.4 'IT application testing controls'.

16. What is the responsibility of a test project manager?

Reference: Paragraph 9.4.4 'IT application testing controls'.

17. What are some of the usual computerised application performance measures?

Reference: Paragraph 9.7 'IT application performance measures'.

18. What should be done to review source document design?

Reference: Paragraph 9.8 'Review and audit tools and techniques'.

19. What should be done to review source code?

Reference: Paragraph 9.8 'Review and audit tools and techniques'.

20. How is application stability determined?

Reference: Paragraph 9.8 'Review and audit tools and techniques'.

CHAPTER 10: USING IT CONTROLS IN AUDIT AND CONSULTING ASSIGNMENTS

If you wish your conduct to be good and to save yourself from all evil, resist the opportunity of greed. It is a sore disease of the worm, no advance can come of it.

From The Teachings of Ptahhotep: The Oldest Book in the World. First published around 2388 BC.

10.1 Scope

The IT strategic and operational controls contained in the previous chapters have been applied in establishing and reviewing IT controls, and in auditing and evaluating controls of IT application systems, networks and IT infrastructure, in several organisations (private and public), in various countries and corporate cultural environments.

10.2 Purpose

The purpose of this chapter is to give the reader an idea of how the controls presented have been used in actual practice. This is attempted by three case studies, one IT audit assignment and one IT policies and procedures review assignment.

The names of the private companies and public organisations and their operational data and other industry and economic sector characteristics have been withheld for confidentiality and privacy reasons. The titles of the applications, the audit or review findings and recommendations, as well as the computing environments presented are purely coincidental.

10.3 Retail operation: IT strategy case study

This case study uses mainly the IT controls (policies, procedures, practices, methods, etc.), audit programmes and checklists identified in Chapters 1 (IT organisation), 3 (Enterprise Architecture), 4 (IT strategy), 5 (Systems development) and 7 (Data centre support) and Appendix 3 (Monitoring IT controls checklist) in providing a practical solution to a critical concern about IT activities posed by the Board of Directors of a retail operation.

In addition, the audit programmes and checklists contained in Chapter 1 of the Addendum were used.

Background information

'ABCXXX' (fictitious business entity) is a European retail operation with over 700 employees. The Board of Directors of this company decided that they wanted more structure and discipline applied to their IT practices and operations, because of the problems presented next.

Until now, the various business departments, such as: administration, personnel, payroll administration, sales, retail operations, logistics, inventory control, production services, customer services, etc. have been able to approach anyone in the IT market and obtain computer hardware and IT applications to suit their particular purposes.

These applications were maintained by either the software suppliers or the central IT department, or both, depending on the priority of the production problem and the timing aspects of the request.

The central IT department, with only limited staff, developed and operated financial systems in the central computer facility of the company.

All these applications were not connected to each other in any way at all.

Many times, critical reports were produced and detailed corporate data were provided by these application systems to senior management for strategic purposes and compliance issues, which did not agree with each other.

These resulted in erroneous decisions made and other embarrassing experiences.

A previous study by the corporate finance committee did not rectify the situation as it recommended a complete IT outsourcing solution. This was found to be inappropriate by the Board as the various costs, benefits and stakeholder needs and expectations were not considered in depth.

This resulted in hiring an external consultant with the mandate to come up with a quick method to provide a framework to resolve this situation caused by the plethora of IT systems working on their own.

Result of external consulting assignment

The new management consultant, using strategic analysis tools, such as the Critical Success Factor Analysis Technique, GAP Analysis, etc. (*see Chapter 4*) posed the following questions to each senior business manager and to each key user of the IT applications deployed in the organisation.

Question 1: What were the short-term as well as the long-term business goals of the organisation, from the Board perspective?

Question 2: How did the Board perceive and expect the role, contribution and support by IT systems and services of both the short-term as well as the long-term business goals of the organisation?

Question 3: How did the present IT systems and services support and enable the organisation to provide products and services on the basis of the existing operating model of the organisation?

Question 4: Are there any efforts or future plans to change the current operating model of the organisation?

Question 5: How did the present IT systems and services contribute to corporate decision making?

Question 6: How much did the present IT systems and services cost, both to each business function and to the overall organisation?

Question 7: What were the short-term as well as the long-term business goals of the organisation, from the business function perspective?

Question 8: How did the specific business function perceive and expect the role, contribution and support by IT systems and services of both the short-term as well as the long-term business goals of the function?

Question 9: How did the present IT systems and services support and enable the function to provide products and services on the basis of the existing operating model of the organisation?

Question 10: Are there any efforts or future plans to change the current operating model of the function?

Question 11: How did the present IT systems and services contribute to corporate decision making of the function?

Question 12: What were the constraints and enabling factors driving the operations of the organisation, from both the perspectives of external regulatory authorities, market sector, customers, community and industry?

The management consultant, from the data collected during the above process, and upon reviewing the current IT controls of the organisations in all business departments and their future demands from IT, recommended that the company resolve the IT practices issue, improve on this and plan for the future, by implementing the actions identified next:

1 **Establish an implementation process**: An implementation process is required for the effective management of all the recommended actions of this effort (Actions 2 to 7). This will be achieved by establishing a project team with adequate resources (manager, staff, users, etc.), funds and practices. The Board and the IT committee will need to sponsor, supervise, ratify, review, monitor and improve all of their related activities and implementation efforts.

2 **Improve the IT function**: Improve the present organisation of the IT department by staffing it with resources which possess modern skills, technical capabilities and business knowledge of the functions of the organisation. IT management will need to develop the required IT policies, standards and procedures and obtain senior management for their effective implementation.

3 **Craft an effective IT strategy**: Formulate an IT strategy for hardware, system software, applications, technological platforms, etc. to provide short-term flexibility and suit the long-term strategic and operating needs of the organisation.

4 **Build a data centre**: Design and build a new data centre facility with adequate capacity to house and operate from a central location both the present and the future IT applications and services of the organisation. This includes obtaining and installing to full production status all the required new hardware, systems software and technological platforms, networks, etc. to operate all IT applications and services. The data centre will be managed by IT, and end-users will have access to their applications on the basis of an authority scheme.

5 **Improve IT applications**: This will be accomplished by:

- the design of a new, integrated with full business functionality, information architecture plan
- the transfer of all applications running in the business functions of the organisation to run in full productive mode in the central data centre facility, or the modification or even the scrapping of some of these, depending on various problems technical and operational considerations
- the development or purchasing or leasing of new applications to support existing or new needs
- the linking of all these applications on the basis of a new information architecture plan.
- a separate action plan must be created and executed depending on the problems of transferring the applications to the new data centre, the issue of obtaining or developing the new applications, etc.

6 **Prepare for IT disaster**: This will be achieved by the design of an IT contingency strategy, plan, resources, procedures and a disaster team. This planning effort should be based on the corresponding business continuity plan of the organisation, as a whole.
7 **Manage changes**: This will be achieved by designing and executing a change management programme to enable senior management, business end-users, IT and external providers, etc. to interact and operate efficiently and effectively in the new IT-enabled environment.

Conclusion

This plan was implemented effectively, with some small variations. The results of this process were reviewed and evaluated by both the Board and the original management consultant on a monthly basis, with the needed adjustments made as the project was being implemented.

10.4 Trading company: applications controls case study

This case study uses mainly the IT controls (policies, procedures, practices, methods, etc.), audit programmes and checklists identified in Chapters 3 (Enterprise Architecture), 4 (IT strategy), 5 (Systems development) 7 (Data centre support), 8 (Systems software), 9 (Application controls) in providing a practical solution to a critical concern about information quality issues posed by the Board of Directors of a trading operation.

In addition, the audit programmes and checklists contained in the Addendum were used.

Background information

'ABCDEF' (fictitious business organisation) is a commercial trading operation with over 300 employees, and several large-scale application systems operating in a data centre. The Board of Directors of this company decided that they wanted more structure, controls and disciplined methods applied to their IT applications, because of various data quality errors appearing in the management reports submitted to them. These management reports were produced by the central IT applications, and by end-users with the use of spreadsheet applications.

Until now, the various business departments recommended the checks to be included in the application systems designed and developed by IT for their operational activities, on the basis of the rules applied to their business function. The spreadsheet applications were not documented as there were no standards regarding this issue.

These business rules were given to IT in a written form, or in interviews, or even orally.

The IT systems development section did not keep a separate computerised file of these business rules. The corresponding checks and validations were written inside the application programs themselves.

This resulted in hiring an external consultant with the mandate to come up with a quick method to provide a framework of needed application controls to resolve this situation efficiently and effectively.

Result of external consulting assignment

The new management consultant, upon reviewing the situation, recommended the implementation of the following set of controls to the IT applications environment. These were:

1 Design, develop and make full use of a system to record and maintain the business rules relevant to each of the applications operating in the data centre, in a computerised repository, such as data dictionary, Enterprise Architecture repository, etc.
2 Institute a policy on end-user application development especially for spreadsheet applications. This policy should define what can and cannot be done by the end-users, authorisation procedures for using these applications, documentation procedures for all spreadsheets, support by the IT department of all end-user developed applications, testing applications developed by end-users with several sets of data, and in a very strict and disciplined way, and keeping an inventory of all of these by IT.
3 Design and implement an IT application controls plan to streamline and manage better the specific controls written within the application programs. This plan would contain, for each application, the required application control objectives, and, for each objective, the corresponding IT application controls. The control objectives would be:
   - input validity
   - completeness of inputs and file updates
   - accuracy of inputs and updates
   - effectiveness of operations
   - security of resources.

4 **IT controls for input validity** might be: (a) encryption, (b) digital certificates, (c) data coding schemes, (d) training in correcting errors, and (e) other controls identified in Chapter 9.
5 **IT controls for completeness of inputs and file updates** might be: (a) enter data close to the source, (b) immediate interactive feedback checks, (c) update rejection procedures, (d) data quality procedures, (e) file health check routines, (f) audit trails, and (g) other controls identified in Chapter 9.
6 **IT controls for accuracy of inputs and updates** might be: (a) enter data close to the source, (b) data coding schemes, (c) pre-formatted screens and forms, (d) online prompting, (e) programmed edit and logic checks, (e) file health check routines, (f) file trial balances, (g) monitoring of audit trails, and (h) other controls identified in Chapter 9.
7 **IT controls for effectiveness of operations** might be: (a) enter data close to the source, (b) pre-formatted screens and forms, (c) online prompting, (d) programmed edit and logic checks, and (h) other controls identified in Chapter 9.
8 **IT controls for security of resources** might be: (a) logical access controls (user identification, strong passwords, etc.), (b) digital signatures, (c) monitoring of audit trails and operations logs, (d) incident intrusion and prevention system and (h) other controls identified in Chapter 9.

Conclusion

These controls were implemented by the organisation over a one-year plan. The results of this process were reviewed and evaluated by both the executive committee and the management consultant on a quarterly basis, with the needed adjustments made as the controls were being implemented.

10.5 Public organisation: IT security case study

This case study uses the IT controls identified in all chapters of the book in providing a practical solution to a critical concern about IT security activities posed by the executive committee of a public organisation.

In addition, the audit programmes and checklists contained in Chapters 1 and 7 of the Addendum were used.

Background information

The senior executive committee of the organisation, faced with several security issues and concerns, hired a high-level security consultant to study the situation and provide guidance. This person recommended various technical controls on the basis of protecting the following security dimensions of IT resources:

- availability
- integrity
- confidentiality
- possession
- authenticity
- utility
- quality.

The implementation of the recommended technical controls was carried out by the organisation itself (IT team). This implementation did not rectify the situation as the identified security problems were not resolved satisfactorily.

This resulted in hiring an external consultant with the mandate to come up with a quick method to provide a framework of needed IT controls to resolve this situation better.

Result of external consulting assignment

The new management consultant, upon reviewing the situation, recommended the implementation of the following IT controls, per security dimension identified by the security consultant. These are:

1 **IT controls for availability**: (a) e-business integrated testing, (b) security penetration testing, (c) back-up procedures, (d) firewalls and anti-virus protection, and (e) audit trails.
2 **IT controls for integrity**: (a) systems development with security controls, (b) application controls within the specific application programs, (c) implementation of corporate ethics and information security policies, (d) fair treatment of employees and external contractors, (e) operation of an intrusion detection system, (f) analysis of traffic and transactions on the basis of logs, (g) audit trails, and (h) review of source code for 'logic bombs'.
3 **IT controls for confidentiality**: (a) physical access controls for installations, offices, digital media, back-up copies, (b) logical access controls for software, end-users, applications, data, (c) cryptography, (d) training in avoiding 'social engineering' techniques, and (e) audit trails.

4 **IT controls for possession**: (a) physical access controls for installations, offices, digital media, back-up copies, (b) logical access controls for software, end-users, applications, data, (c) cryptography, (d) inclusion of 'copyright statement' in developed application programs according to the relevant copyright laws, (e) segregation of duties, (f) archival and deletion procedures, (g) assigning ownership rights for each application, (h) inventory register, and (i) configuration management.
5 **IT controls for authenticity**: (a) personnel controls (segregation of duties, vacation policy, rotation of duties, etc.), (b) IT application controls, (c) digital certificates, (d) password controls, and (e) original licences for software.
6 **IT controls for utility**: (a) IT application controls, (b) IT auditing, and (c) customer satisfaction surveys.
7 **IT controls for quality**: (a) IT application development on the basis of a systems development life cycle methodology, (b) end-user acceptance testing, (c) security testing, (d) technical and end-user documentation, and (e) a data quality management process.

Conclusion

These controls were implemented by the organisation over a two-year plan. The results of this process were reviewed and evaluated by both the executive committee and the management consultant on a quarterly basis, with the needed adjustments made as the controls were being implemented.

10.6 IT audit assignment for organisation 'ABCXYZ'

'ABCXYZ' is a European multinational organisation with operations across many countries. This is their audit report, which is the result of an IT audit assignment of their central IT operations. The IT audit methodology used for this audit is described in Appendix 5.

The areas audited were:

- IT organisation: The overall audit objective for reviewing the area of IT organisation was to determine the quality and effectiveness of the organisation's management of information technology. The IT audit programmes and checklists described in Chapter 1 were used.
- IT administration: The overall audit objective for reviewing the area of IT administration was to determine the quality and effectiveness of the organisation's administrative support of information technology. The IT audit programmes and checklists described in Chapter 2 were used.
- IT strategy: The overall audit objective for reviewing the area of IT strategy was to determine the quality and effectiveness of the organisation's strategic support of information technology. The IT audit programmes and checklists described in Chapter 4 were used.
- Systems development: The overall audit objective for reviewing the area of systems development was to determine the quality and effectiveness of the organisation's systems development process in designing, developing and deploying information systems. The IT audit programmes and checklists described in Chapter 5 were used.

- IT security: The overall audit objective for reviewing the area of IT security was to determine the quality and effectiveness of the organisation's IT security policies, procedures and practices in designing, developing and deploying information systems and services. The IT audit programmes and checklists described in Chapter 6 were used.
- Data centre operational and support services: The overall audit objective for reviewing the area of data centre operational and support services was to determine the quality and effectiveness of the organisation's data centre operations, and policies, procedures and practices used in running information systems and services. The IT audit programmes and checklists described in Chapter 7 were used.
- Systems software: The overall audit objective for reviewing the area of systems software was to determine the quality and effectiveness of the IT management process of systems software. The IT audit programmes and checklists described in Chapter 8 were used.

Additional programmes and checklists that may also be of some use are provided in the Addendum.

The following report presents the results of a detailed IT audit of the IT policies and procedures of this fictitious company. It describes gaps and omissions found during the audit review process, and makes several recommendations to resolve these findings. It proposes a prioritised roadmap for addressing them. Any similarities to an actual company or computing environment are purely coincidental.

IT AUDIT REPORT FOR 'ABCXYZ' (example only)

1 Scope of IT audit coverage

During this IT audit, as per the internal audit annual plan and further to the agreement with the audit committee, we reviewed and evaluated the controls of the following areas of IT activities of company 'ABCXYZ'.

These areas are:

- IT organisation
- IT administration
- IT strategy
- Systems development
- IT security
- Data centre operational and support services (computer room, IT contingency planning and disaster recovery, back-up and recovery procedures, and personal computers)
- Systems software.

The area of Enterprise Architecture and operating specific IT applications in the data centre or in end-user personal computers will not be examined. Testing in a test environment with real or 'dummy' transactions, scanning the facility for eavesdropping devices, and security penetration testing will not be undertaken.

The audit findings and recommendations per area audited, both in summary and in detailed form, are presented next.

2 Summary of audit findings and recommendations

Our recommendations are presented according to an audit priority scheme. 'High' priority means that these recommendations should be considered first for implementation, because their impact level is deemed to be of the highest importance to the specific IT operations. 'Medium' priority denotes that these may be examined for implementation next, as their impact level may be important, but not as important as the impact level of 'High' priority recommendations. Finally, 'Low' priority does not mean that these should be disregarded altogether, but may be implemented, as the last step.

IT management and other corporate officers (e.g. CEO, compliance officer, risk officer, chief finance officer, etc.) may change this priority, should they wish. The important thing here is to set priorities and do what is right to rectify and improve the situation.

'High' priority recommendations

There are 11 audit recommendations of 'High' priority value listed next. Each recommendation number below is the recommendation number identified in the 'Detailed Recommendations' section of this report.

No. 1: Formal IT Steering Committee required.

No. 2: Creation of a CIO position required.

No. 6: Segregation of duties of IT personnel requires improvement.

No. 7: Formal IT strategic plan required.

No. 8: Application systems development standards required.

No. 11: Formal IT security policy and related procedures required.

No. 12: Access controls on production elements by IT personnel require improvement.

No. 13: Password controls require improvement.

No. 14: Computer room access controls require improvement.

No. 16: IT contingency and disaster recovery plan required.

No. 19: Critical forms require improved control.

'Medium' priority recommendations

There are 5 audit recommendations of 'Medium' priority value listed next. Each recommendation number below is the recommendation number identified in the 'Detailed Recommendations' section of this report.

No. 9: Formal application testing procedures required.

No. 10: End-user documentation requires improvement.

No. 15: Safe off-site storage for back-ups required.

No. 17: Personal computers policies and procedures required.

No. 18: System software changes require improved control.

'Low' priority recommendations

There are 4 audit recommendations of 'Low' priority value listed next. Each recommendation number below is the recommendation number identified in the 'Detailed Recommendations' section of this report.

No. 3: Job descriptions need formalisation.

No. 4: Vacation policy needs to be made mandatory.

No. 5: Training of IT personnel requires improvement.

No. 20: Review of logs may assist in problem solutions.

3 Analysis of detailed audit findings and recommendations

The detailed audit findings and recommendations are presented next, by IT area audited.

3.1 IT organisation area: audit findings and recommendations

The following types of IT organisation controls were reviewed during the audit process, to ascertain both their use and potential effectiveness, at this organisation: IT department functional description controls, IT organisational controls, IT vision, mission and values statements, IT control frameworks, monitoring and review controls.

The following audit findings and recommendations for resolving these findings are included:

- Audit recommendation 1: Formal IT steering committee required

- Audit recommendation 2: Creation of a CIO position required.

Audit recommendation 1: Formal IT Steering Committee required

Title of area reviewed: IT Steering Committee.

Audit findings: IT Steering Committee duties, responsibilities and guidelines necessary for managing the IT function on a continuous and effective basis have not been adequately defined by the Board.

Audit evaluation: This has resulted in approved corporate objectives going unfulfilled or extending them far beyond estimated schedules and budgets. The present informal IT Steering Committee consists of senior executives and is not in a position to assume responsibilities at the operational or strategic levels or monitor accountability and IT results.

Audit recommendation: We recommend that duties and responsibilities of the IT Steering Committee should be clearly defined in a formal charter and should include the review and approval for: major changes in hardware or software, the results of any IT project cost–benefit analysis, software application development or acquisitions, IT project priorities, emergency procedures, contingency and physical security plans, budgets and plans pertaining to the IT function, etc.

Management response: Management will take this up with the Board for a permanent solution to be established.

Audit recommendation 2: Creation of a CIO position required

Title of area reviewed: IT management.

Audit findings: There is no formal definition of a CIO position of the IT function within the organisation's current structure. The Chief Finance Officer (CFO) currently manages the IT operations while also performing his duties as Finance Executive.

Audit evaluation: A specific CIO position for managing IT operations will enhance the accountability of the IT function as well as provide a more effective system of internal control.

Audit recommendation: We recommend that the Board of the organisation consider and create a full-time CIO position as soon as it is possible and beneficial to do so. Until such a position is created, we recommend that controls surrounding the dual role of the current Finance Executive be monitored by the Board on a more disciplined manner.

Management response: Audit Committee members and the CFO will take this up with the Board for a permanent solution to be established.

3.2 IT administration area: audit findings and recommendations

The following types of IT Administration controls were reviewed during the audit process, to ascertain both their use and potential effectiveness, at this organisation: IT standards, policies and procedures, IT budget, IT asset controls, IT personnel management controls, IT personnel job descriptions, IT purchasing controls, monitoring and review controls, and IT administration performance measures.

The following audit findings and recommendations for resolving these findings are included:

- Audit recommendation 3: Job descriptions need formalisation
- Audit recommendation 4: Vacation policy needs to be made mandatory
- Audit recommendation 5: Training of IT personnel requires improvement
- Audit recommendation 6: Segregation of duties of IT personnel require improvement.

Audit recommendation 3: Job descriptions need formalisation

Title of area reviewed: IT job descriptions.

Audit findings: Most IT job descriptions are either non-existent or do not contain responsibilities necessary for effective internal control.

Audit evaluation: Written job descriptions are a useful mechanism to communicate responsibilities, accountabilities and reporting lines of authority. They also provide an objective means of measuring job performance, since IT employees must know what is expected of them if they are to perform adequately and according to the standards of the organisation.

Audit recommendation: We recommend that job descriptions for all IT positions should be established and communicated to all IT staff. These job descriptions should be accepted and signed by both corporate management and IT staff. These should be maintained throughout the employment cycle of each IT employee.

Management response: IT management will look into this and take the proper actions with support from the human resources department.

Audit recommendation 4: Vacation policy needs to be made mandatory

Title of area reviewed: IT vacation policy.

Audit findings: The organisation does not have a mandatory vacation policy for IT personnel.

Audit evaluation: Requiring employees in sensitive IT positions to take annual vacations is a good control that reduces the risk of an employee undertaking and continuing a fraud scheme and being able to conceal it over a long period of time.

Audit recommendation: We recommend that consideration be given to the establishment of a vacation policy that would require all IT employees to take their vacation within a calendar year (and preferably consecutively). Exceptions should be approved by the CIO and the senior manager of human resources and properly documented.

Management response: IT management, with support from human resources, will look into this and take the proper actions.

Audit recommendation 5: Training of IT personnel requires improvement

Title of area reviewed: IT training.

Audit findings: IT employees have not been adequately trained on the latest ITC issues on the basis of what technologies are currently used by IT and upon reviewing the IT budget (planned and actual expenditures) over the last year.

Audit evaluation: Adequate IT training may improve programming practices and therefore result in fewer errors, reduced system implementation times resulting in reduced development costs, and fewer operational and other labour costs.

Audit recommendation: We recommend that a formal IT training programme be developed for each employee, which will address methods and techniques required to improve the use of technologies for the organisation and bring the performance of the particular IT personnel in line with corporate strategic and operational objectives.

Management response: IT management will look into this in relation to budget constraints and take the proper actions.

Audit Recommendation 6: Segregation of duties of IT personnel require improvement

Title of area reviewed: IT segregation of duties.

Audit findings: The CFO (acting as a CIO), the IT section managers and most of the programmers and analysts have unrestricted access to computer programs and corporate application production data. Further, we noted that there are no management controls to prevent or detect unauthorised changes to the production programs library.

Audit evaluation: The combination of these duties makes it possible for errors to occur and remain undetected for significant periods of time. With this type of environment, any individual can undertake actions that might prove irregular without being detected on a timely basis.

Audit recommendation: We recommend that segregation of duties should be put into practice for all critical activities of IT. For example, the CIO, once appointed, should concentrate their efforts in managing the data centre, review all program changes and control the production program library, and the programmers should concentrate their efforts on programming responsibilities and should not serve as a back-up computer operators and must never have access to the production program library without prior CIO authorisation (emergency cases only).

Management response: IT management will look into this and take the proper actions.

3.3 IT strategy area: Audit findings and recommendations

The following types of IT strategic controls were reviewed during the audit process, to ascertain both their use and potential effectiveness, at this organisation: IT strategic process controls, IT strategy implementation and monitoring controls, and IT strategic performance management controls.

The following audit findings and recommendations for resolving these findings are included:

Audit recommendation 7: Formal IT strategic plan required

Title of area reviewed: IT strategy.

Audit findings: During our review, we noted that no long-term IT strategic plan has been developed. The current planning horizon is a short-term one and only examining the IT issues for the next year. Application systems have accordingly evolved over time and are not integrated at all. Senior management from the end-user community have not been consulted about their business objectives and strategic goals and their future user requirements for information technology products and services.

Audit evaluation: Effective long- and short-term IT strategic planning is essential for the IT function of the organisation to ensure that its information resources will support established business strategic goals and operational objectives.

Audit recommendation: We recommend that the organisation develop a written three- to five-year strategic IT plan that is based on the organisation's long-term corporate strategic or business plan. This plan should be a working document that addresses such key issues as: hardware requirements, systems software requirements, communications, application development, budgeting, emergency procedures and contingency plans, and review of relationships with outside IT vendors, etc.

Management response: IT management will look into this and take the proper actions.

3.4 Systems development area: audit findings and recommendations

The following types of IT strategic controls were reviewed during the audit process, to ascertain both their use and potential effectiveness, at this organisation: application development controls, IT systems testing methodology, end-user application development controls, audit trails, software package controls, and system development quality controls.

The following audit findings and recommendations for resolving these findings are included:

- Audit recommendation 8: application systems development standards required
- Audit recommendation 9: Formal application testing procedures required
- Audit Recommendation 10: End-user documentation requires improvement.

Audit recommendation 8: application systems development standards required

Title of area reviewed: Application systems development.

Audit findings: We noted during our review that application system development standards including documentation standards are informal and not ratified by the IT steering committee or other senior executive body of the organisation.

Audit evaluation: The use of formalised application system development standards when properly customised and implemented by the IT staff of the organisation ensures, as much as possible that: (a) controls within each application system and program are suitably designed and maintained, (b) development of application systems and related program changes satisfy management objectives, (c) the implemented controls operate in accordance with specifications of the internal corporate controls framework, (d) application systems and related program changes are adequately tested, and (e) potential production errors are corrected before they occur.

Audit recommendation: We recommend that IT selects a standard system development methodology, customises it to suit the organisation's needs and uses it to develop its own systems.

Management response: IT management will look into this and take the proper actions.

Audit recommendation 9: Formal application testing procedures required

Title of area reviewed: Application testing procedures.

Audit findings: We noted during our review that the organisation does not have formalised standards which govern the testing of new IT applications, either at the overall system level or at the individual application program level. Programmers test application systems and specific programs to the extent they deem necessary and appropriate. End-user involvement is not required or thought as a must in a testing process. In addition, documentation of application testing procedures and results is not carried out.

Audit evaluation: The risk to the organisation is that new application systems and the revised application programs may not operate as designed initially and may not meet the information needs and business functional requirements of the intended end-users.

Audit recommendation: We recommend that in order to achieve the maximum benefit from application test procedures, end-users should be involved in the whole process of application systems testing. Application systems testing procedures and data should be designed so as to simulate all conditions which will occur under normal processing conditions. Program changes and new programs should be tested in accordance with a predetermined user approved application system test plan and test standards. Documentation of application systems testing procedures should include: specific objectives of the application system test, types of transactions to be tested, test data used, expected test results, the actual test results, reported errors and the comparison to the predicted results, etc.

Management response: IT management will look into this and take the proper actions.

Audit recommendation 10: End-user documentation requires improvement

Title of area reviewed: End-user documentation.

Audit findings: End-user manuals for most application systems are not being kept up to date. Systems X, Y and Z have very little documentation. Many sections of the documentation of systems A and B are incorrect or incomplete and other sections are missing completely.

Audit evaluation: The end-user application system manuals usually contain sufficient information to enable the users to understand, interact, control and operate the specific application system. If the manual is incomplete, incorrect or written in such a way that the end-users cannot understand how to interact with it, the end-user will do things by trial and error. Procedures developed by trial and error will probably disregard, in the long run, certain functions of the application system and may result in incomplete and inaccurate information in the computerised files of the given application systems.

Audit recommendation: We recommend that all end-user application system manuals be brought up to date. Minimum documentation and procedures necessary for an end-user application system manual may include: system narrative, applications system features and constraints, explanation of input fields, samples of all screens and forms, end-user related codes and formulas, report samples, report descriptions defining field sources and calculations, balancing procedures, explanation of data error messages, other controls, etc.

Management response: IT management will look into this and take the proper actions.

3.5 IT security area: audit findings and recommendations

The following types of IT security controls were reviewed during the audit process, to ascertain both their use and potential effectiveness, at this organisation: IT security governance guidelines, standards, and legal frameworks, IT security plans, policies and procedures, personnel security management controls, specialised IT technical protection controls, etc.

The following audit findings and recommendations for resolving these findings are included:

- Audit recommendation 11: Formal IT security policy and related procedures required
- Audit recommendation 12: Access controls on production elements by IT personnel require improvement
- Audit recommendation 13: Password controls require improvement.

Audit recommendation 11: Formal IT security policy and related procedures required

Title of area reviewed: IT security.

Audit findings: The organisation has not published an IT security policy for all of its employees and managers which defines the responsibilities of all end-users for maintaining the confidentiality and integrity of all company data. Neither management nor staff are required to sign a non-disclosure and confidentiality statement at the point of joining the company and every year thereafter which defines their duties towards the company, the data maintained and other security considerations. Moreover, procedures have also not been documented regarding all IT security issues (such as password administration, etc.) which would have to be identified in the security policy.

Audit evaluation: Without formal IT security standards, a policy and related procedures, management and employees of the organisation do not have clear guidelines and instructions regarding IT security matters.

Audit recommendation: We recommend that the Board assign the task of developing IT standards and a security policy to a corporate committee (e.g. IT Steering Committee). Security procedures should also be documented to provide guidance to the persons managing security functions and to ensure that security responsibilities are defined for all users of IT systems.

Management response: IT management will look into this and take the proper actions.

Audit recommendation 12: Access controls on production elements by IT personnel require improvement

Title of area reviewed: Logical access controls.

Audit findings: During our review, we noted that application programmers, systems programmers and systems analysts have unrestricted access to all information systems in production mode. These may even be in conflict with their assigned functions to specific information systems.

Audit evaluation: When effective access controls are placed on production programs and data files, changes can be made in a controlled way, thus avoiding both intentional and accidental errors. The opposite, which is what we observed, results in abuse of critical resources of both time and manpower in finding and correcting the errors, and may potentially increase costs and reduce the level of performance of the whole IT function.

Audit recommendation: We recommend that all IT personnel (programmers, analysts, system programmers) should be restricted, by default, to have only that access to computer resources, information systems and production data that is necessary to perform their jobs effectively and efficiently. This should be done to minimise the risk of unauthorised or fraudulent access to sensitive information systems and corporate data.

Management response: IT management will look into this and take the proper actions.

Audit recommendation 13: Password controls require improvement

Title of area reviewed: Password controls.

Audit findings: During our review, we noted that the end-users of all information systems as well as the IT staff maintaining these systems and the environment are not required to change passwords on a regular basis. No officer monitors the access of employees even when they are moved to another position within the organisation for which no access to information systems is required. Furthermore, no policy, system, procedure or manual controls are established to guide or enforce users to monitor password changes and in fact change their passwords regularly.

Audit evaluation: The practice of not monitoring and not changing passwords regularly may allow the initiation of fraudulent acts, data abuse and information processing errors, and intrusion by unauthorised internal and external parties easier to achieve.

Audit recommendation: We recommend that IT management craft and implement a policy and related procedures to enforce changing all user passwords (end-user, IT) on a regular basis and when personnel terminations occur or employees change job duties and responsibilities.

Management response: IT management will look into this and take the proper actions.

3.6 Data centre operations: audit findings and recommendations

The following types of data centre operational and support controls were reviewed during the audit process, to ascertain both their use and potential effectiveness, at this organisation: Data centre design and infrastructural controls, data centre physical access controls, computer hardware management controls, IT contingency planning and disaster recovery controls, etc.

The following audit findings and recommendations for resolving these findings are included:

- Audit recommendation 14: Computer room access controls require improvement

- Audit recommendation 15: Safe off-site storage for back-ups required
- Audit recommendation 16: IT contingency and disaster recovery plan required.

Audit recommendation 14: Computer room access controls require improvement

Title of area reviewed: Computer room access.

Audit findings: During our review, we noted that all employees of the organisation, whether users of the information systems or not, entered the computer room by the use of their employee access card, without any controls whatsoever. External maintenance personnel and other visitors entered this computer room just by calling the operators, or knocking on the computer door.

Audit evaluation: Almost free access to the computer room is prone to result in damage or loss or theft or misallocation to hardware, reports, digital media, tape files, documentation, consumables, pre-printed forms (such as invoices, cheques), etc.

Audit recommendation: Only computer operations personnel and authorised management should be allowed access to the computer room. Any visitors, regardless of their role or function, should be approved by IT management, escorted when they enter the computer room, and recorded in the computer room visitors' log.

Management response: IT management will look into this and take the proper actions.

Audit recommendation 15: Safe off-site storage for back-ups required

Title of area reviewed: IT disaster recovery.

Audit findings: We noted during our review that there is no back-up documentation for applications, and that software and data back-ups are not stored in a safe off-site location.

Audit evaluation: Back-ups of software, data and IT documentation are very critical for IT operations, and should be stored off site to cover cases where the prime back-ups are not available.

Audit recommendation: In order to ensure the integrity, and completeness of the corporate information systems of the organisations, we recommend that the organisation obtains a safe, off-site location where back-up copies of system documentation, software and data can be stored safely. These procedures will significantly enhance the company's ability to reconstruct computer-based systems in the event of disaster or other damage.

Management response: IT management will look into this and take the proper actions.

Audit recommendation 16: IT contingency and disaster recovery plan required

Title of area reviewed: IT disaster recovery.

Audit findings: We noted during our review that the company does not have a formal IT contingency and disaster recovery plan to document how the organisation would recover in the event of an extended disruption in IT processing services provided by the data centre.

Audit evaluation: A formal IT contingency and disaster recovery plan is crucial in order to ensure the continuity of processing critical IT applications and services and to minimise the potential financial impact of an extended disruption of IT services in the event of a disaster. While we are sensitive to the Board's and operating management's concerns for controlling costs, we believe that the benefits of such a formal plan far outweigh the development costs.

Audit recommendation: We recommend that a comprehensive contingency plan be developed, documented and periodically tested to ensure continuity in data processing services as needed in the event of a disaster. The plan should describe at least the following:

- objectives and scope of the plan
- assumptions and recovery strategies including a business interruption impact assessment, and critical application analysis
- recovery timing
- procedures for damage assessment
- plan activation procedures
- notification procedures
- emergency recovery team's roles and responsibilities
- insurance coverage
- written vendor agreements
- back-up processing facilities
- off-site storage procedure
- back-up procedures and data recovery procedures
- vendor contact list
- inventory of forms, etc.
- testing procedures
- plan maintenance responsibilities, etc.

Management response: IT management will look into this and take the proper actions.

3.7 Personal computers: audit findings and recommendations

The following audit findings and recommendations for resolving these findings are included:

Audit recommendation 17: personal computers policies and procedures required

Title of area reviewed: Personal computers environment.

Audit findings: During our review we noted that the organisation is increasingly using personal computers in almost all business areas. End-users develop various spreadsheet applications and use them widely, without any control. No written policies and procedures have been developed for controlling personal computers and the development and use of spreadsheet applications by end-users.

Audit evaluation: Comprehensive policies and procedures for the use of personal computers and the development of spreadsheet applications by end-users will ensure that the environment will be controlled better., and that data entered into these applications will likely produce more accurate results.

Audit recommendation: We recommend that the organisation develops formal policies and procedures for the control personal computers and the development of end-user applications.

Management response: IT management will look into this and take the proper actions.

3.8 Systems software area: audit findings and recommendations

The following types of systems software controls were reviewed during the audit process, to ascertain both their use and potential effectiveness, at this organisation: systems operating environment controls, database controls, data communications controls, audit trail controls, and monitoring and review controls.

The following audit findings and recommendations for resolving these findings are included:

Audit recommendation 18: System software changes require improved control

Title of area reviewed: Systems software control.

Audit findings: We noted during our review that a formal procedure for controlling changes to the computer's system software (operating system, network software, DBMS, etc.) does not exist. Changes are implemented without authorisation by IT management and without a record of the changes maintained.

Audit evaluation: A formal procedure for the authorisation, implementation, approval and documentation of system software changes is necessary to ensure that unauthorised changes will not damage the operation of the whole system and possibly result in unnecessary shutdowns and operational problems to the application systems of the organisation.

Audit recommendation: We recommend that an appropriate set of policies and procedures for controlling changes to the systems software be implemented in a timely manner and consistently applied in all cases.

Management response: IT management will take appropriate actions to remedy this situation.

3.9 IT applications operation: audit findings and recommendations

The area of IT applications operation is not within the agreed scope of this IT audit, and therefore, no full review was conducted of the relevant controls related to operating computerised applications in the data centre of the organisation at the time of this audit.

However, we noted the following for which we make the corresponding recommendations:

Audit recommendation 19: Critical forms require improved control

Title of area reviewed: Forms control.

Audit findings: We noted during our review that critical forms, such as invoices, accounts payable cheques, purchase orders, etc. are not properly controlled (e.g. are not stored in a locked area, they are released with no authorisation, etc.).

Audit evaluation: The risk that a potential fraud will go unnoticed is very great. The risk that critical business activities will be delayed is quite apparent.

Audit recommendation: We recommend that all critical forms should be under the control of an authorised manager, and should be released to authorised personnel only.

Management response: IT management will take appropriate actions to remedy this situation.

Audit recommendation 20: Review of logs may assist in problem solutions

Title of area reviewed: Logs control.

Audit findings: We noted during our review that the various computer operations logs are not examined by the relevant computer manager responsible for the jobs running in the data centre.

Audit evaluation: By reviewing computer operations logs on a regular basis, problems or unauthorised use of application systems, files and utilities can be detected.

Audit recommendation: We recommend that the company computer operations manager regularly review all applications logs to identify possible production problems and potential breaches of security.

Management response: IT management will take appropriate actions to remedy this situation.

10.7 IT policies and procedures review for company 'ABCXXYX'

'ABCXXYX' is a large manufacturing concern with operations across many countries. This is their report of findings, which is the result of a review of IT policies and procedures of their IT practices. This company had several commercial off-the-shelf applications running for most of their business functions (administration, payroll, finance, sales, marketing, engineering, research and development, plant, etc.) and small informal IT groups within the business departments serving them and their applications.

The policies and procedures of the following areas were agreed to be reviewed: internal controls system, IT organisation, IT strategy, application systems, IT back-up procedures, IT security, IT disaster recovery, IT legislation and IT vendor support.

The IT audit programmes and checklists, described in Chapter 1 of the Addendum and of Chapters 1, 4, 5, 6, 7, 8 and 9 of the book, were used.

The following report presents the results of a detailed review of the IT policies and procedures of this fictitious company. It describes gaps and omissions found during the review process only. It does not make any recommendations to resolve these findings, as this was not within the scope of work, for various reasons. For the same reasons, it does not propose a prioritised scheme for addressing the findings of the review process. Any similarities to an actual company or computing environment are purely coincidental.

IT REVIEW REPORT FOR 'ABCXXX' (example only)

1 Scope of IT review

During this review process, as per the agreement between an external IT management consultant with the Board of the company, we reviewed and evaluated the controls of the following areas of activities of company 'ABCXXX'.

These areas are:

- Internal controls system
- IT strategy
- IT organisation
- Application systems
- IT back-up procedures
- IT security

- IT disaster recovery
- IT legislation
- IT vendor support.

The operation of specific IT applications in the data centre or in end-user personal computers may be examined. However, testing any applications in a test environment with real or 'dummy' transactions, scanning the facility for eavesdropping devices, and security penetration testing will not be undertaken.

In preparing our report, we relied in substantial part upon the accuracy and completeness of information provided to us by the client management. We could not ascertain whether this information was indeed correct and complete, as there was no application testing done on the existing policies and procedures and on the IT application systems operating at the client sites and offices. Our review did not pertain to any scanning activities of the facility for eavesdropping devices, and security penetration testing of any kind.

2 Findings of review

2.1 Findings of the review of internal controls system

Background: The Board of Directors of the company has full responsibility to ensure that a system of management with the appropriate policies, procedures and controls is used effectively to manage all operations and functions of the company for the good of its shareholders, employees and other stakeholders. This whole framework is usually termed 'corporate governance'. The medium through which corporate governance is exercised throughout the whole company is the internal controls system. This system is usually made up of a set of policies, procedures, techniques, methods, practices, organisation, staff and control mechanisms, and its main purpose is to control all functions, systems and operations, in the most proper way. This is crucial so that: (a) assurance is provided to the Board that all functions, activities and operations are managed appropriately, (b) all property assets are safeguarded, (c) operational and financial risks are minimised and (d) effective controls are in place to avoid potential misappropriation and abuse.

Review findings: The company does not have a formally established internal controls system of any kind. The internal audit function is deemed to provide this service according to several senior managers of the company, but this not their role and duty, and it is not accepted by the internal audit staff.

Review remarks: The risk of not having a formally established internal controls system to control and guide the company's operations is very high. The lack of a formal integrated set of management controls can result in major management problems, crises on various issues, operational ineffectiveness and potential revenue losses.

2.2 Findings of the review of IT organisation

Background: The IT function is normally established to support the IT needs of the given enterprise. The essence of the IT unit is to ensure that IT systems and associated infrastructural components are managed and controlled most appropriately. The IT unit may be structured to serve the company and its divisions: as a separate division, as a part of another division, interfacing with an outsource entity, shared service among several departments, a combination of the above, etc. The technology coverage that it should provide may consist of the following: mainframe and micro hardware platforms, operating systems, database management technologies, information systems, data centre, personal computers, office systems and applications, Internet, networking (cabling, hubs, WAN, LAN, intranet), data transmission with external parties and protocols, voice and data communications, etc.

Review findings: The company does not have a formal centrally located IT function in place. There are no standard IT policies and procedures developed or formalised. Every IT group does things by their own experience and how they see fit.

Review remarks: The risk of not having a well-established IT function to provide support to the company's operations, especially in the next years where a market increase for the company's products and services are expected, is very high. Managing IT systems by small IT groups in the end-user areas, and under the direct influence of the end-users themselves, can result in major management control crises, wrong decisions, operational ineffectiveness and potential revenue losses. Some of the problems that may be encountered are: (a) incorrect data entered and maintained in the application systems, (b) data and procedural errors, (c) erroneous reports produced, (d) new functions not designed, implemented and supported by the application systems, (e) unresolved hardware and network problems, (f) security problems with access levels, etc.

2.3 Findings of the review of IT strategy

Background: IT strategic planning is not only about IT. It is about the business activities of the company and how these are enabled by the use of IT systems and services. The essence of IT strategic planning is to ensure that: (a) IT systems and network services deliver to all levels of management and users, appropriate solutions to their stated business requirements and problems, (b) provide competitive advantages for the organisation, (c) accurately target the corporate critical success factors to make the company successful in the long run, and (d) enable the company to achieve its corporate tactical, operational and strategic goals and specific objectives in the most cost-effective way. Long-term information systems planning is achieved through the formulation of an IT strategy.

An IT strategy is a plan to meet the organisation's information needs over three to five years through the development of application systems and related services, such as automation, network services, online access to customers, etc. The IT strategy includes a hardware and application systems development plan but also the business needs and goals that must be satisfied including the issues that must be addressed in support of a primary process of the business delivered through IT. Good corporate governance also supposes that an effective IT strategy is co-ordinated with the goals and strategic directions incorporated in the company business plan.

Review findings: The company does not have a formal IT strategy in place. Some discussions have taken place from time to time, but without a definite target or time-frame. The business model of the company, part of the company's strategic planning process, is in the process of being finalised at the time of the review.

Review remarks: The risk of not having an IT strategy to suit the company's operations, especially in the next 1–5 year period, is very high. The lack of management commitment and resources (funds, personnel, methods, strategic direction, etc.) and the existence of old, inadequate and ineffective IT systems for the new needs and requirements, can result in major management control crises, operational ineffectiveness and potential revenue losses.

2.4 Findings of the review of application systems

Background: Application systems are the life-blood of IT. Their first reason for existence is to ensure that timely, accurate and quality information is delivered to all levels of management and users, appropriate solutions are applied to the stated business requirements and problems of the area they support, and operational and strategic objectives are met in the most cost-effective way. Good corporate governance also supposes that the operation of effective application systems match extremely well with the goals, operational objectives and strategic directions incorporated in the company business plan.

Review findings: Application systems exist and support the functional requirements of invoicing, accounts payable, general ledger, payroll, production and logistics support, and customer support. All these were provided by different external parties. These applications were interfacing with many problems. Their maintenance contracts had different clauses, depending on the parties providing the IT solutions. Written business procedures do not exist for any of the functions supported by these application systems.

Review remarks: The risk of not having up-to-date information, provided by effective application systems, and the related IT strategy to suit the company's operations, especially in the next one to five year period, is very high.

The lack of standard maintenance contracts will lead to ineffective systems and potential over-invoicing issues. The fact that these contracts are not managed by one central function, such as the IT department, will probably result in major management control crises, application and business operational ineffectiveness and potential corporate revenue losses.

2.5 Findings of the review of IT back-up procedures

Background: Back-up relates to copying, storing and retrieving of computer data and computer software (operating system, database management system, network system, office applications, business applications, various utilities, etc.). In relation to data, back-up can provide for: disaster recovery, retention of transactions for regulatory purposes, maintaining ongoing computer operations, subsequent data analysis or interrogation, and recovery, in case of errors. In relation to software (operating system, database management system, network system, application, office systems), back-up can provide for: disaster recovery (rebuild operational environment), supporting the production versions of software, retaining earlier versions of programs to enable going back to previous proven software, maintaining and supporting the system development environment analysis or interrogation and software version control, and resetting the point of processing in case of software errors.

Review findings: The company staff, running the various applications, execute IT back-up procedures on a regular basis for each of the applications operating in the user departments. The back-up media are kept locked in a regular storage cabinet in one location, and some copies are in another office location. A formal, written and Board-approved back-up policy does not exist. A back-up log documenting all the relevant details was not maintained locally by each user, and also was not maintained at a central location for management control purposes. Dedicated fire-proof vaults do not exist at each user location or site for storing, in a safe and environment-controlled facility, only the back-up media. The back-up media were not taken to a proper off-site storage facility (e.g. bank vault). The recovery procedure related to the back-up media of each business computerised application and the related operating system could not be verified as to its completeness and effectiveness. Copies of the keys of the existing storage cabinets were not kept at a designated management office for management control purposes.

Review remarks: The risk of allowing the end-users to run the IT back-ups on their own authority and not having an IT unit to manage, oversee and control the IT back-up process and maintain the proper recoverability of the current IT systems to suit the company's operations is very high. Managing the back-up process for the IT systems by the users themselves, can result in major data and software losses, inability to recover after a disaster, wrong decisions, operational ineffectiveness and potential revenue losses.

2.6 Findings of the review of IT security

Background: The purpose of IT security is to protect an organisation's valuable resources, such as information, data, installations, facilities, resources, hardware, infrastructural components and software from a wide range of threats in order to ensure business continuity, minimise business damage and maximise return on investments and business opportunities. Through the selection and application of appropriate safeguards, security helps the organisation's mission by protecting its physical and financial resources, reputation, legal position, employees, and other tangible and intangible assets. IT security is achieved by implementing a suitable set of controls, which may include policies, practices, procedures, reward and compliance mechanisms, organisational structures, physical access control processes and software functions. These controls need to be established to ensure that the specific security objectives of the organisation can be met. In this respect, information security controls are considerably cheaper and more effective if incorporated at the requirements specification and design stage. Good corporate governance also supposes that an effective IT security is absolutely necessary so that the goals and strategic directions incorporated in the company business plan are executed.

Review findings: The company does not have a formal IT security framework in place. A formal, written and Board-approved IT security policy does not exist and was not in the process of being completed. Very simple passwords are used at present to access and maintain the running applications; these, however, are not changed regularly as there is no policy for this. Full physical access controls to the end-user offices where IT applications function for the company's operations are not in place. Copies of the keys of the storage cabinets containing back-up media and other materials were not kept at a designated management office for management control purposes.

Review remarks: Not having an IT security framework in place, run, managed and controlled by authorised IT personnel and audited by the internal audit function (both do not exist) to face the company's operational risks, could prove very damaging. The lack of management co-ordination and commitment to IT security issues can result in major asset, software and data losses, management control crises, operational ineffectiveness and potential revenue losses. Without formal IT security standards, a policy and related procedures, management and employees of the organisation do not have clear guidelines and instructions as to what to do in IT security matters.

2.7 Findings of the review of IT disaster recovery

Background: IT disaster recovery planning refers to the policies, plans and procedures in place to counter a prolonged down time at the company's central IT data centre (where major IT applications are operating) or at critical user locations at which computerised applications support essential business operations of the company. The purpose of IT disaster recovery planning is to ensure that an organisation's valuable resources, such as information, data, installations, facilities, resources, hardware, infrastructural components, systems and software can recover and restart operating, within the minimum time period, after some major catastrophe. The IT disaster recovery planning will have to match and co-ordinate very well with the associated business disaster recovery and business continuity planning process in order to ensure proper business continuity, minimise business damage and maximise return on investments and business opportunities.

Review findings: A formal IT disaster recovery plan is not in place. The company does not have a business disaster recovery and business continuity framework in operation.

Review remarks: The risk of not having an IT disaster recovery plan to activate in cases of major catastrophes to the company's operations and IT facilities is very high. The lack of required management planning, commitment and resources (funds, personnel, methods, strategic direction, etc.) to set up and test such an IT disaster recovery plan, can result in major operational shutdowns and major revenue losses to the company.

2.8 Findings of the review of IT legislation issues

Background: The purpose of IT legislation is to protect an organisation's valuable IT resources, such as information, data, installations, facilities, resources, hardware, infrastructural components, software and personnel, from a wide range of legal threats (e.g. copyright law compliance, data privacy law compliance, pirate hardware and software, consequential damages, etc.). It is the job of management to ensure that the company complies with all the relevant IT laws and state regulations.

Review findings: The review of the IT legislation issues identified several issues, such as: (a) Data Privacy Declaration: a required application and filing of the relevant details regarding the data maintained and other information according to the Privacy Act, has not been made to the relevant state authority, and (b) licences for purchased software were missing.

Review remarks: The risk of the company not controlling the procurement process in a formalised way and managing fully all issues related to complying with the relevant IT legislation is quite high and can lead to fines and bad image for the company's market plans.

2.9 Findings of the review of IT vendor support

Background: The purpose of IT vendor support is to ensure that the company's computer facilities, hardware equipment and software systems are up and running, and that any malfunctions are corrected quickly and effectively, in order to ensure business continuity and minimise potential business damage and thus maximise return on IT investments. IT vendor support is achieved by implementing a suitable set of controls, which may include policies, practices, procedures, and IT maintenance contracts.

Review findings: Maintenance contracts are in effect for all the IT application systems operating in the user departments. Support problems related to the provided services were not mentioned by the users. The review of the maintenance contracts, however, identified several issues, such as: (a) the maintenance contract for Package 'ABX' does not have a confidentiality clause, no software upgrades have been provided for the last 5 years, and a capability for the provision of documentation (user, technical) and training does not exist, (b) for Package 'ABCX' maintenance contract, a confidentiality clause for remote access does not exist, and (c) for the 'TTTXX' Package, the termination clause allows the vendor to cancel its services by giving 2 months' notice to the company, and an escrow account for the source code of the vendor for the application systems purchased by the company does not exist.

Review remarks: The risk of allowing the end-users to manage the IT vendors on their own authority and not having an IT unit to manage, oversee and control this and maintain the proper recoverability of the current IT systems to suit the company's operations is very high. Managing the vendor process for the IT systems by the users themselves, can result in major management control crises, wrong decisions, operational ineffectiveness, and potential additional payments for maintenance not required or not properly executed by the vendors.

3 Recommendations

Our immediate recommendations on the basis of our review comments are presented next. This list does not impose any 'High', or 'Medium' or 'Low' priority on each recommendation as these issues will need to be reviewed both with Board members and the management of the company before an action plan is drafted and implemented.

1 Design, develop and implement an internal controls system.
2 Establish a central IT organisation.
3 Craft an IT strategy for the long term (next 5 to 10 years).
4 Appoint a team to write business procedures and link them with the IT applications.

5 Formalise IT back-up procedures for both data and software, and assign responsibility to IT.
6 Establish and implement a formal IT security framework (plan, policies, procedures, practices, persons, organisational structure, etc.).
7 Devise and maintain a formal IT disaster recovery plan.
8 File the relevant Data Privacy Declaration to the state authorities.
9 Obtain licences for purchased software from the original suppliers.
10 Review and standardise maintenance contracts of all IT applications, and assign responsibility to IT.

Other issues, such as setting up a data centre, hiring and training additional IT staff, upgrading the IT applications on the basis of the new IT strategy, etc. require further cost–benefit analysis before any concrete recommendations can be made.

10.8 Final conclusion

The main purpose of IT controls is to ensure the safe and secure operation of information systems and the protection from harm or other potential damage of the organisation's IT assets and data maintained by these systems. These objectives are achieved by a set of policies, procedures, practices, methods, techniques and technological measures, collectively called 'controls'.

IT systems and infrastructure controls are classified as general IT controls, i.e. controls applying to the whole of an organisation's Information Systems activity, and as IT application controls, which are specific to a given application, such as payroll processing, general ledger accounting, accounts receivable, etc. Both of these types of controls, within any type of organisation must operate within the greater framework of corporate governance and internal controls system, to fulfil their purpose to the fullest.

Sometimes the boundary line between these control types is rather arbitrary, particularly in client/server, web-based and cloud computing applications, most of which may run on several computers.

What is important and crucial is for IT management, systems development professionals and other stakeholders (auditors, fraud examiners, etc.) to realise that a comprehensive and effective combination of both of these control types are required to ensure, as much as possible, an adequately safe and secure processing environment. We need to be proactive, plan and prepare both ourselves and our organisations for possible attacks, frauds committed, and errors occurring to information systems, disasters to IT facilities and unusual events.

We should probably note that modern intruders to IT systems and networks do not publish their tools, successful or failed attacks or profits. They act with anonymity, quietly, in a step-by-step approach, from both inside and outside the organisation, across the planet, and they usually cover their trail.

'The players now include terrorists, white collar criminals, hackers, open source. The global underground cyber criminal community is actually trying to do better than what we do ... Earlier (1998) people sold you user IDs and passwords. Now the menu includes your CVs, ATM and credit cards with pin numbers, whole e-mail inboxes. They will ship information to anywhere in the world for money,' according to a latest report.[68]

There is an army of them with new skills and capabilities:

- mappers
- scanners
- hackers
- crackers
- password sniffers
- readers and shooters with van Eck tools
- programmers who write code to enter network and application systems without leaving a trail
- moles (personnel) employed to work in an organisation before it is attacked
- vendors who sell illegal and improper hardware and software
- social engineers who get passwords and other sensitive information by various means, etc.

They need to be controlled by society on the one hand, by the enactment of rules, regulations, laws, ethics codes, etc. and by organisations on the other hand, by devising and implementing overall corporate and detailed IT controls.

Corporate and IT control issues are quite complex and may be included in corporate and business strategic and operational concerns, rather than on their own ground, as such. Detailed IT controls require far more than the latest methods, practices and software tools or technology. Organisations must understand very precisely what IT entities, data, media, systems, services and assets they are

---

[68] See Computer Crime Research Center: www.crime-research.org, March 31, 2010.

trying to protect, and why, before selecting any general or specific IT control solutions.

IT management, IT professionals, IT auditors, internal auditors, fraud experts, etc. must be always on their guard to protect their organisations, the data stored and reported by their IT systems, and the greater society, by using, implementing and improving IT controls and methods in a most efficient and effective way.

As a recent international report[69] points out vividly: 'Data privacy and protection shortcomings can do irreparable harm to companies' balance sheets, not to mention their brands, credibility and customer trust and relationships'.

IT controls, operating within the greater IT governance practices framework, can create value for an organisation.[70]

Moreover, the most recent IT disasters[71] more than prove the point that IT controls are here to stay, to be reviewed and to be improved.

It is our mission, moral duty, responsibility and job to do this. IT application systems are the life-blood of organisations. Quick dissemination of correct and timely information drives forward, enables and facilitates our national and global economies, benefiting everyone across the globe.

---

[69] See 'How Global Organisations Approach the Challenge of Protecting Personal Data', Accenture, 2009: *www.accenture.com.*

[70] See 'How IT Governance Drives Improved Performance', IT Process Institute, 2009: *www.itpi.org.*

[71] London Underground failure due to IT problems, as per *www.computerworld.com,* April 7, 2010, McDonald's $170 million ERP disaster, as per *www.infoworld.com,* EDS and UK child support problems due to IT, as per *http://news.zdnet.com,* etc.

We need to work hard to achieve effective and working IT controls. We need to both plan and act. We must be persistent in reaching the goal of controls, and last but not least, we must be disciplined in our approach.

APPENDICES: EXAMPLES OF POLICIES, GUIDELINES, FORMS AND METHODOLOGIES

Science is organized knowledge

Herbert Spencer (1820–1903)

Appendix 1: Examples of IT security policies

This appendix contains the following policies (as generic examples):

- General IT security policy
- Privacy of information policy
- Information sensitivity policy.

General IT security policy

Introduction

The corporate information security policy of 'ABCX Corporation' (fictitious company) contains high-level overall statements describing the general objectives of the company with regard to the control, protection and security of its critical information assets, such as information systems, information technology and application software, operating systems and database management system software, buildings, computer rooms, cabling, network and computer facilities, other related installations and technical infrastructures, data, back-up media and archived files, and information resources in general.

Basic definitions

The term 'systems' shall refer to all computerised information systems and their databases, classical files, other digital files and media processed and stored by them, the operating and application software, and the computer operations within the given organisation, including, but not limited to, computer mainframes, mid-range systems, minis, local, wide area and information networks, personal desktop and laptop computers, workstations and servers, telecommunications (routers, bridges, etc.), any new technologies currently under development, and any other specialised computers residing in functional (business) areas where data is transmitted, distributed or processed via electronic, telecommunications, satellite, microwave or other media. All these and all data residing in them are deemed to be company property and must be protected as such by all personnel.

Purpose and objectives

The purpose of the company's IT security policy is to provide the essential guidelines and controls for secure, efficient and effective data collection and processing operations, electronic transaction processing and information reporting services, management information systems, and appropriate customer information capabilities for company management and the Board of Directors to effectively operate and manage the company.

The objectives of this policy are: managing risk, ensuring business continuity of the company's computing environment, defining responsibilities, expectations and acceptable behaviours, discharging fiduciary duty and complying with any regulatory requirements, protecting the company from liability and ensuring information integrity and confidentiality.

Management responsibility

It is the responsibility of the company's management (top operational management, Board of Directors, senior management committee, IT steering committee, etc.) to manage the company's computing and telecommunications systems. The president of the company (or other officer authorised by the Board) shall establish an operating structure that effectively runs and optimises the company's system capabilities and information assets consistent with sound business, industry and regulatory practices.

The various systems and infrastructural IT components will be monitored on a continuous basis to ensure that they function properly, and that they have the ability to meet the current and future needs and requirements of the company. The authorised management staff shall be responsible for and direct the feasibility studies regarding the procurement of IT solutions and the development, implementation, system and data conversion, system review, system operation and training of personnel for all systems of the company.

It is also management's responsibility to ensure that procedures are in effect for these systems to operate in case of disasters or other calamities.

IT solutions procurement and system development

The company's IT solutions procurement and development/operation of the systems, maintenance services, application systems, consulting support, IT training, etc. shall be managed by the authorised management of the company and/or designated individuals or functional entities, and the steps identified below shall be followed for the attainment of these.

The computing and telecommunications systems of the company shall be constantly monitored, and should a current and/or future need for change or improvement be identified, the company should again follow the system development life-cycle (SDLC) approach as follows: business needs scoping analysis, requirements analysis, feasibility study, review of alternative solutions, system analysis and design, system development, system testing, system and data conversion, system operation, and system post-implementation review.

Equipment, software and other physical installations

The management of the company is authorised to install all the necessary equipment and software, (servers, terminals, printer, modems, rooters, bridges, etc.) and supervise the design and completion of all the physical installations (buildings, cabling, computer rooms, network rooms, etc.) that may be required for the computing and telecommunications systems of the company. Users of these systems are not allowed to install any devices and/or software on any personal computers or workstations assigned to them by the company. Transfer of any company files and/or data in any way, into or out of company premises, facilities and systems is not allowed.

General IT and application systems controls

The establishment, development, maintenance and review of a complete security programme covering computing and telecommunications systems and related infrastructures is the responsibility of the president or other authorised management staff of the company. The systems, infrastructural components and related information will be safeguarded, protected and provided a safe operating environment. The controls and security that shall exist include, but are not limited to, the following:

- Administrative controls: Administrative controls aim to ensure that the entire control framework is instituted, continually supported by management, and enforced with: a published controls policy, formal systems development standards and procedures, employment contracts and confidentiality clauses, personnel screening, continuous personnel supervision, separation of duties, and disaster recovery planning for computing and telecommunications systems.
- Physical protection of data centres: Normal operating condition should be ensured with environmental controls (air conditioning, air filtering, humidification, dehumidification, etc), protection against fire and flooding, emergency power supply, radiation shielding, etc.
- Operations controls: The company shall establish operations controls (policies, procedures and technology) to ensure that data centres are operated in a reliable fashion. These controls include: controls over

personnel access to the data centre, control over operations personnel, control over computer and telecommunications equipment maintenance, and control over archival media and storage facilities, etc.

- Information and communication security: The company shall maintain integrity and security controls for the protection of all computing and telecommunication systems and information. These controls are also indented to address the risks arising from the potential misuse of the resources of the computing and telecommunication systems. The establishment of these controls shall include, but not limited to, the following: logical access controls (operating system, database system, application software), network and local access security, identification and authentication of users, firewalls, cryptographic controls (encryption, hashing etc.), message transmission controls (e-mail, telecommunications, etc.), an information resource classification method, retention and disposal of information, and a security incident monitoring and resolution mechanism.
- System development and maintenance controls: The management of the company will ensure that auditing procedures are established and are put into continuous use to ensure that all systems are developed and maintained through the SDLC methodology identified in this document and in the company's IT standards. These audits should also ensure that only authorised personnel perform approved changes and improvements to the systems, and that the administrative controls are also in effect (segregation of duties, screening and supervision of personnel, etc), and audit mechanisms are established

for the periodic review of the source code of applications in escrow.

- Application controls: The authorised management staff of the company will ensure via various mechanisms (e.g. IT audit) that all application systems are developed and operated by having the following indicative controls to ensure information accuracy: input controls, processing controls, database controls, telecommunications controls and output controls.
- Data centre controls: It shall be the responsibility of the authorised management of the company (e.g. IT division manager) to ensure that the following operational procedures are in effect. These may include: biometrics to determine access to facilities, back-up and recovery procedures, system (operating, database, network) performance monitoring, problem management and resolution, application health check and integrity control procedures, off-site storage procedures, IT disaster plan testing procedures, and security incident monitoring and reporting procedures.

IT systems continuity

The company management shall ensure that proper back-up systems and procedures are established and operated for all the computing and telecommunications systems. These back-up systems shall be established to protect the company in the event of an unforeseen breakdown or major catastrophe. The company shall develop and maintain a plan that addresses the risk that such events can occur and this shall require planning for alternate computing systems processing options (facilities, equipments, procedures, etc.). All these are to ensure that the company can provide for business continuity. The requirements for IT systems continuity may include, as a minimum, the following: critical application systems identification, alternate processing facilities evaluation, documented back-up and recovery plans, test procedures, contingency evaluation procedures, off-site storage procedures, computer data recovery and equipment, and a computer insurance policy.

Security standards

Information systems security standards define the minimum criteria, rules and procedures established by senior company management and ratified by the Board of Directors, which are required to be implemented to help ensure the achievement of the corporate information security policy. These are implemented by various staff (e.g. security manager, system security administrator, end-users, IT divisional managers, system development staff, etc.) under the direction of management. These should specify in detail the specification of each procedure and/or control to be implemented.

Applicability and compliance

This security policy applies to all locations, premises, equipment, installations, systems, networks, personnel and external contractors of the company. Information disclosure to any unauthorised parties is not allowed without written approval. Personal use of all these systems, facilities, equipment, etc. (as defined in the introductory paragraph and in the various parts of this policy) are not allowed without written management approval at the appropriate level. Company management shall not make any commitments of any kind via the use of electronic media and network software facilities without written management approval. Any breach of this policy and/or related procedures, and/or related laws, whether voluntary or involuntary, will be dealt with according to the laws of the country where the office of the company is located. All personnel shall maintain secrecy for all passwords, access procedures and related controls. Cases involving company personnel directly or indirectly may bring immediate dismissal of these staff, other disciplinary and/or legal actions as the national laws or the company regulations dictate.

Privacy of information policy

Purpose

The primary purpose of the privacy of information policy is to provide guidelines for the privacy issues of information activities (collection, use, disclosure, monitoring, etc.) of the organisation.

Collection of information

The company considers the protection of the privacy of customer data to be of utmost importance and is committed to providing all customers with a personalised service that meets your requirements in a way that safeguards your privacy. This policy explains how we may collect information about you, and then use it in order to satisfy your particular requirements. It also outlines some of the security measures that we take in order to protect your privacy, and gives certain assurances on things that we will not do. When we first obtain personal information from you, or when you take a new service from us, we will give you the opportunity to indicate if you do or do not (as applicable) wish to receive information from us about other services or products. Normally this will be done by way of a tick box on an application form or contract. You may revise the choice that you have made at any time by writing to us informing us of the change. Some of the personal information we hold about you may be sensitive personal data within the meaning of the Data Protection Act and other relevant laws. We may collect personal information about you from a number of sources, including: (a) from you when you agree to take a service from us in which case this may include your contact details, date of birth, payment method and possibly bank details, (b) from you when you contact us with an enquiry or in response to a communication from us, in which case this may tell us something about your preferences, etc.

Use of information

Information you provide or we hold about you (whether or not under our contract(s) with you) may be used by us to: (a) identify you when you make enquiries, (b) help administer, and contact you about improved administration of, any accounts, services and products provided by us previously, now or in the future, (c) carry out marketing analysis and customer profiling (including with transactional information) and create statistical and testing information, (d) help us to prevent and detect fraud or loss, and (e) contact you by any means (including mail, e-mail, telephone or text or multimedia messages) about other services and products offered by us, and selected partners. We will only contact you in this way if you have previously indicated your consent. In some circumstances, we may do certain credit checks with licensed credit reference agencies when you apply to take a service or product. If this is applicable, then it will be stated in our terms and conditions of business.

Disclosure of information

We may disclose information only where legitimately requested for legal or regulatory purposes, as part of legal proceedings or prospective legal proceedings.

Monitoring

You should also note that communications with you (including phone conversations and e-mails) may be monitored and recorded by us for security, quality assurance, legal, regulatory and training purposes.

Protection of information

We maintain strict security measures in order to protect personal information. This includes following certain procedures, for example to check your identity when you telephone us, encrypting data on our websites and in order to ensure compliance with all applicable legal requirements.

The Internet

If you communicate with us via the Internet, then we may occasionally use e-mail to contact you about our services and products. When you first provide personal information to our website we will normally give you the opportunity to indicate whether you would prefer us not to contact you in this way. However, you can always send us an e-mail at any time to change your preferences. Please be aware that communications over the Internet, such as e-mails, are not secure unless they have been encrypted. Your communications may route through a number of countries before being delivered. We cannot accept responsibility for any unauthorised access or loss of personal information that is beyond our control. We may use 'cookies' to monitor website user traffic patterns and site usage. This helps us to understand how our customers and potential customers use our websites so that we can develop and improve the design, layout and functionality of the sites. You can normally alter the settings of your browser to prevent acceptance of cookies. If you do not want us to deploy cookies in your browser, you can set your browser to reject cookies or to notify you when a website tries to put a cookie on your computer. However, rejecting cookies may affect your ability to use some of the products and/or services at our website.

Information sensitivity policy

The primary objective of the information sensitivity policy is to provide guidelines for the data classification issues of information collected and processed by information systems activities of the organisation.

Purpose

The information sensitivity policy of the company or organisation (referred to as Company from now on), is intended to help employees determine what information can be disclosed to non-employees, as well as the relative sensitivity of information that should not be disclosed outside of <Company> without proper authorisation. The information covered in these guidelines includes, but is not limited to, information that is either stored or shared via any means. This includes: electronic information, information on paper, and information shared orally or visually (such as telephone and video conferencing).

Definitions

All <Company> information is categorised into two main classifications: <Company> public, or <Company> confidential.

<Company> public information is information that has been declared public knowledge by someone with the authority to do so, and can freely be given to anyone without any possible damage to < Company>.

<Company> confidential contains all other information. It is understood that some information is more sensitive than other information, and should be protected in a more secure manner. This information includes: trade secrets, development programmes, potential acquisition targets and other information integral to the success of our company. Included in <Company> confidential is information that is less critical, such as telephone directories, general corporate information, personnel information, etc. which does not require as stringent a degree of protection.

Responsibility of personnel

All <Company> personnel are encouraged to use common sense judgement in securing <Company> confidential information to the proper extent. If an employee is uncertain of the sensitivity of a particular piece of information, they should contact their manager.

Sensitivity guidelines

The sensitivity guidelines below provides details on how to protect information at varying sensitivity levels.

Minimal sensitivity: General corporate information:

- Access: <Company> employees, contractors, people with a business need to know.
- Distribution within <Company>: Standard interoffice mail, approved electronic mail and electronic file transmission methods.
- Distribution outside of <Company> internal mail: national mail and other public or private carriers, approved electronic mail and electronic file transmission methods.
- Electronic distribution: No restrictions except that it be sent to only approved recipients.
- Storage: Keep from view of unauthorised people; erase whiteboards, do not leave in view on tabletop. Machines should be administered with security in mind. Protect from loss. Electronic information should have individual access controls where possible and appropriate.
- Disposal/destruction: Shred and deposit outdated paper information in specially marked disposal bins on <Company> premises. Electronic data should be destroyed by the use of special devices.

- Penalty for deliberate or inadvertent disclosure: Up to and including termination, possible civil and/or criminal prosecution to the full extent of the law.

More sensitive: Business, financial, technical, and most personnel information:

- Access: <Company> employees and non-employees with signed non-disclosure agreements who have a business need to know.
- Distribution within <Company>: Standard interoffice mail, approved electronic mail and electronic file transmission methods.
- Distribution outside of <Company> internal mail: Send via national mail or approved private carriers.
- Electronic distribution: No restrictions to approved recipients within <Company>, but should be encrypted or sent via a private link to approved recipients outside of <Company> premises.
- Storage: Individual access controls are highly recommended for electronic information.
- Disposal/destruction: Shred and deposit in specially marked disposal bins on <Company> premises. Electronic data should be destroyed by the use of special devices.
- Penalty for deliberate or inadvertent disclosure: Up to and including termination, possible civil and/or criminal prosecution to the full extent of the law.

Most sensitive: Trade secrets and marketing, operational, personnel, financial, source code, and technical information integral to the success of <Company>:

- Access: Only those individuals (<Company> employees and non-employees) designated with approved access and signed non-disclosure agreements.
- Distribution within <Company>: Delivered direct – signature required, envelopes stamped confidential, or approved electronic file transmission methods.
- Distribution outside of <Company> internal mail: Delivered direct. Signature required. Use approved private carriers.
- Electronic distribution: No restrictions to approved recipients within <Company>, but it is highly recommended that all information be strongly encrypted.
- Storage: Individual access controls are very highly recommended for electronic information. Physical security is generally used, and information should be stored in a physically secured computer.
- Disposal/destruction: Destroy and deposit in specially marked disposal bins on <Company Name> premises.
- Penalty for deliberate or inadvertent disclosure: Up to and including termination, possible civil and/or criminal prosecution to the full extent of the law.

Enforcement

Any employee found to have violated this policy may be subject to disciplinary action, up to and including termination of employment.

Business connections

<Company> computer use by competitors and unauthorised personnel must be restricted so that, in the event of an attempt to access <Company> corporate information, the

amount of information at risk is minimised. Connections shall be set up to allow other businesses to see only what they need to see. This involves setting up both applications and network configurations to allow access to only what is necessary.

Encryption

Secure <Company> sensitive information in accordance with the acceptable encryption policy. International issues regarding encryption are complex. Follow corporate guidelines on export controls on cryptography, and consult your manager and/or corporate legal services for further guidance.

Appendix 2: Example of IT ethics code

This appendix contains the commandments of the (USA) Computer Ethics Institute Code (listed with the permission of the Computer Ethics Institute).

These commandments are:

1. THOU SHALT NOT USE A COMPUTER TO HARM OTHER PEOPLE.
2. THOU SHALT NOT INTERFERE WITH OTHER PEOPLE'S COMPUTER WORK.
3. THOU SHALT NOT SNOOP AROUND IN OTHER PEOPLE'S COMPUTER FILES.
4. THOU SHALT NOT USE A COMPUTER TO STEAL.
5. THOU SHALT NOT USE A COMPUTER TO BEAR FALSE WITNESS.
6. THOU SHALT NOT COPY OR USE PROPRIETARY SOFTWARE FOR WHICH YOU HAVE NOT PAID.
7. THOU SHALT NOT USE OTHER PEOPLE'S COMPUTER RESOURCES WITHOUT AUTHORISATION OR PROPER COMPENSATION.
8. THOU SHALT NOT APPROPRIATE OTHER PEOPLE'S INTELLECTUAL OUTPUT.
9. THOU SHALT THINK ABOUT THE SOCIAL CONSEQUENCES OF THE PROGRAM YOU ARE WRITING OR THE SYSTEM YOU ARE DESIGNING.
10. THOU SHALT ALWAYS USE A COMPUTER IN WAYS THAT INSURE CONSIDERATION AND RESPECT FOR YOUR FELLOW HUMANS.

Appendix 3: Monitoring IT controls checklist

IT ethics management

1 Do senior executives set a day-in, day-out example of high integrity and ethical behaviour in both corporate and IT issues?
2 Is there a written code of ethics for all employees?
3 Is the code of ethics reinforced by training, top-down communications and periodic written statements of compliance from key IT and end-user employees?
4 Is it clear that fraudulent IT reporting at any level and in any form will not be tolerated?
5 Are IT ethics woven into criteria used to evaluate individual and IT department performance?
6 Does IT management react appropriately when receiving bad news from IT subordinates?
7 Does a process exist to resolve close IT ethical calls?

IT risk management

1 Are IT and business risks identified and candidly discussed with the Board of Directors and IT management?
2 Is relevant, reliable internal and external information timely identified, compiled and communicated to those positioned to act?
3 Are controls in place to ensure IT management decisions are properly carried out?
4 Does IT management routinely monitor controls in the process of running the organisations operations?
5 Are periodic, systematic evaluations of IT control systems conducted and documented?

IT strategic management

1 Is there an IT strategic plan?
2 Is there a mechanism by which the business community articulates expected events (transactions, new locations, etc.) to IT so that IT can adequately plan?
3 Are IT policies and procedures developed, approved and centrally maintained for key IT processes and application systems?
4 Are the policies and procedures reviewed and updated at least annually?
5 Are IT performance measures (including an IT budget) used to monitor system performance and output?
6 Is there an acceptable used policy regarding company IT assets that all personnel are required to acknowledge?
7 Are IT compliance issues fully understood by all IT staff?
8 Does the IT function appear to be adequately staffed?
9 Is there a mechanism to monitor the productivity of IT personnel?
10 Are IT personnel required to attend certain training or obtain certain qualifications?
11 What is the average length of service for IT personnel?
12 Are there policies that expressly prohibit the usage of company programs or data for purposes other than work?
13 Are all third party services properly managed and monitored?
14 Is the IT asset inventory properly managed and its elements monitored?

Data management

1 Is there a data dictionary (usually provided by the standard DBMS package) of data identified as critical?
2 Is it clear who is formally responsible for data integrity?
3 Is DBA access to databases restricted to the authorised personnel only?
4 Is all database activity logged and monitored?
5 Are sensitive data (e.g. credit card numbers, social insurance numbers, etc.) encrypted or masked in the databases?
6 Are the data transferred to the corporate data warehouse properly controlled?
7 Is ownership of the data in and access to the data warehouse appropriately defined and controlled?
8 Are all data removed from laptops or workstations prior to their disposal?
9 Has the flow of key corporate (e.g. financial, compliance, production, customer, etc.) reporting or other key critical data been documented so that all computer programs are properly identified?

Data centre operations

1 Does IT management monitor the performance and capacity levels of the systems and internal corporate network?
2 Does IT management monitor the formal problem management and help desk process?
3 Does IT management review and monitor the average length of time to close reported problems?
4 Are changes to programs or systems documented, formally approved and monitored by IT management?
5 Is there a formal process to handle emergency requests?

6 Are all changes initiated by business needs and requirements?
7 Is the operation and testing of the uninterrupted power supply for the data centre monitored?
8 Is the operation of the non-liquid fire suppression system for the data centre monitored?

Corporate applications development

1 Is there a system development life cycle (SDLC) model that is utilised (e.g. waterfall, rapid application development, spiral, agile, etc.) and monitored?
2 Are test results approved and monitored?
3 Is there a committee (end-users and IT) that monitors the progress of each project?
4 Is the source code protected through copyright and is this monitored?
5 Is the source code placed in escrow and is this monitored?
6 Does the IT management monitor that an inventory has been performed of applications and databases that support business processes and that these are in alignment with Sarbanes-Oxley?
7 Is there a formal process, including documentation, by which users are provided with access to the application?
8 Is there immediate communication from human resources regarding employee termination that results in the timely removal of user accounts?
9 Is security, including segregation of duties, considered and monitored during the development cycle?
10 Are interfaces between systems subjected to an SDLC process that includes retention of test results and approvals?

11 Are there separate development, quality assurance and production environments and are these monitored?
12 Is the access by development staff to the production environment monitored?
13 Is there a monitoring mechanism to track the labour involved during the development cycle so that those costs can be capitalised?
14 Is there an ongoing monitoring process to manage segregation of duties conflicts?
15 Are company-wide licences utilised and monitored for standard software packages?
16 Is the company up to date on all vendor released patches and is this monitored by IT management?
17 Are there user-approved written specifications for new systems and modifications to existing application systems?
18 Are there written procedures to test and implement new systems and modifications to existing application systems?

End-user application development

1 Is the inventory of spreadsheets that are relevant to financial reporting or other high-risk processes maintained and monitored?
2 Has the logic in all spreadsheets been verified and tested by somebody other than the creators of the spreadsheets?
3 Is access to key spreadsheets restricted via a password mechanism?
4 Are each of these spreadsheets backed up periodically and is this monitored?

Computerised applications operation

1 Is the IT function independent from the accounting and other operating functions (e.g. administration, production, sales, etc.) for which it processes data?
2 Do controls exist over preparation and approval of input transactions outside the IT function?
3 Is the IT function prohibited from initiating transactions?
4 Does the user exercise control procedures over input to ensure that all approved input is processed correctly, and only once through the system?
5 Are controls over entry of data in online systems and restricting access to terminals and data entry to authorised employees monitored?
6 Do online systems controls exist that prevent documents from being keyed into the system more than once, and that permit tracing from computer output to data source and vice versa?
7 Do controls exist over changes to master files, such as requiring preparation of specific forms indicating data to be changed, approval by a supervisor in the user department, and verifying against a printout of changes?
8 Do user controls exist over rejected transactions through the use of a computerised suspense file of rejected transactions or an auxiliary manual system?
9 Does user department management reconcile output totals to input totals for all data submitted, reconcile the overall file balances, and review outputs for reasonableness?
10 Do procedures exist within the data processing function that ensure that data is properly controlled between the user and the IT functions?
11 Do controls exist over data entry, for example, that include adequate supervision, up-to-date instructions,

key verification of important fields and self-checking digits?

12 Do program controls exist over entry of data into online systems?

13 Is input data edited and validated?

14 Do data processing controls exist over rejected transactions?

15 Do controls exist for balancing transactions and master files?

16 Do procedures exist within the data processing control function concerning review and distribution of output?

17 Do controls exist over changes to systems software?

18 Do controls exist over use and retention of tape and disk files, including provisions for retention of adequate records to provide back-up capabilities?

19 Do procedures exist to protect against a loss of important files, programs or equipment?

20 Are IT equipment, application programs and data files covered by insurance?

Security and disaster recovery management

1 Are access rights at the application and operating system level periodically monitored, reviewed and confirmed?

2 Is there an intrusion detection system and are all incidents monitored?

3 Are external vulnerability scans (security penetration tests) performed periodically and monitored by management?

4 Is access to IT assets (e.g. data centre assets), appropriately restricted, monitored and controlled?

5 Is there a formal disaster recovery plan and are its activities (tests, off-site areas, alternate sites, etc.) monitored?
6 Are the formal back-ups taken for databases, application software and end-user data monitored according to a plan?

Operating system and network software

1 Are all system and network elements and activities monitored?
2 Is each operating system currently supported by its manufacturer?
3 Is each operating system up to date with patches provided by the manufacturer?
4 Are there any users with unsupported operating systems on their laptops or workstations that transmit data into the network?
5 Is there a formal process, including documentation, by which users are provisioned with access to the operating systems(s)?
6 Is there a topology diagram of the network hardware?
7 Is wireless traffic encrypted?
8 Is each point of entry protected by a firewall?
9 Is each VPN or other remote access to the network protected?

IT personnel control procedures

1 Does appropriate segregation of duties exist within the IT function for systems development (design and programming), technical support (maintenance of systems software) and computer operations?

2 Do the personnel policies of the IT function include such procedures as reference checks, security reviews, rotation of duties and terminated employee security measures that enhance segregation of duties and otherwise improve controls?
3 Are controls that limit access to data processing equipment, tapes, disks, digital media, system documentation and application program documentation to authorised employees monitored?
4 Is a job accounting system used to ensure that scheduled programs are processed and proper procedures followed and that supervisory personnel know that only required programs have been processed?
5 Are IT department employees supervised for all work shifts?
6 Are procedures to be followed by computer operators documented and monitored?
7 Are all critical systems documented such that the organisation could continue to operate if important IT employees leave?

Outsourcing services review

1 Are there appropriate formal policies and procedures for obtaining third party services? Consider:
   - o objectives of IT outsourcing
   - o approval by Board
   - o definition of responsibilities
   - o feasibility study authorised
   - o existing agreements reassessed
   - o new opportunities explored.

2 Does the organisation have policies and procedures for monitoring the external supplier performance? Consider:

- o continuous performance evaluation
- o fees payment approval cycle
- o cost–benefit analysis.

3 Are existing agreements with third parties comprehensively drawn up? Consider:

- o description of goods/services
- o time/place of delivery (including timetables)
- o penalties for delays/defaults
- o acceptance tests
- o price, terms of payment and cost of living
- o duration of contract, termination and renewal
- o warranties
- o protection against copyright/patents infringement
- o licensing (use by other group companies)
- o transfer rights (to other group companies)
- o supplier's liability
- o actions to be performed by customer
- o confidentiality/information disclosure protection
- o security terms/conditions (also for remote access)
- o escrow account requirements for source safe-keeping
- o 'do not hire' personnel clause
- o insurance (professional liability, civic damages, data reconstruction)
- o tax liability
- o rights to new ideas/inventions
- o parental guarantee (especially for software distributors)
- o disputes settlement procedure
- o force majeure terms/conditions
- o law applicable
- o minimum level service

- o performance guarantee
- o internal/external auditors review
- o rights, responsibilities/liabilities of both parties
- o ownership of data/documents/programs developed
- o description of deliverables (source, object, documentation, diskettes, digital media, etc.)
- o training
- o documentation
- o contingency for data and software developed
- o record retention for data
- o processing priorities for both normal and emergency situations (including response windows)
- o vendor responsible for keeping software current
- o incorporation of regulatory changes
- o cancellation, termination and bankruptcy changes
- o description of disaster recovery procedures
- o prohibition against the assignment of the contract by the vendor to another party with the consent of the client
- o vendor financial evaluation capability
- o capability to transfer system to alternate facility due to contingency (e.g. disaster).

4 Does the organisation have a clear understanding of the nature and extent to which it is dependent on each third party? Consider:

- o known to the IT steering committee
- o precautions to limit exposure
- o financial stability
- o vendor reputation.

5 How does the organisation ensure the quality of service that third party delivers? Consider:

- o cost management

- o quality of contacts/personnel
- o standards, ISO accreditation
- o size of market
- o history
- o back-ups and off-site storage
- o on-site audit and audit reports.

6 Has the organisation appropriate in-house IT controls to monitor and review controls exercised by third party or compensate for missing or ineffective controls. Consider:

- o overall controls over data accuracy and completeness
- o logical security
- o review/reconciliation of billings.

Appendix 4: Examples of IT forms

Information Asset Register Form

INFORMATION ASSET REGISTER FORM	
Information Entity	Field names and contents
Payroll	<File name>, <Format: Word, Excel, hard copy, database, etc.>, <application system maintaining this information>, <File location>, <Officer responsible for the quality of this information>, <data classification category: secret, public, etc. according to corporate policy>
Accounting	As above
Xxx	As above

Test Case Form

TEST CASE FORM
System name:
Test case number:
Tester name:
Hardware required:
Software required:
Other test case dependency:
Brief description of the test case:
Inputs required:
Outputs expected:

Test Scenario Form

TEST SCENARIO FORM
System name:
Test scenario title:
Project name:
Work package:
Unit:
Tester:
Date:
Number:
Test cases:
Set-up instructions:
Start instructions:
Proceed instructions:
Performance measures:
Stop instructions:

Test Case Execution Log Form

TEST CASE EXECUTION LOG FORM
System name:
Test case number:
Project:
Tester:
Date:
Pass/fail:
Actual results (for fail):
Error log number (for fail):
Approval:

Error Log Form

ERROR LOG FORM
System name:
Error no:
Description:
Severity:

IT Activities Journal Form

IT ACTIVITIES JOURNAL FORM	
<Organisation>: <page no>:	
<IT department location>:	
Seq. No	Data to be recorded
1	<date>, <time>, <procedure>, <transaction name>, <work done>, <success: yes/no>, <comments>, <name of staff>, <IT system involved>
2	As above
…	As above

IT Visitor's Log Form

IT VISITOR'S LOG FORM	
<Organisation>: <page no>:	
<IT department location>:	
Seq. No	Data to be recorded
1	<date of entry>, <time of entry>, <date of exit>, <time of exit>, <location visited>, <visitor's particulars (name, identification no, etc.)>, <escort's name and phone no>, <visitor's signature>, <escort's signature>
…	As above

IT Security Incidents Log Form

IT SECURITY INCIDENTS LOG FORM	
<Organisation>: <page no>:	
<IT department location>:	
Seq. No	Data to be recorded
1	<date reported>, <time reported>, <name of person who reported the incident>, <incident particulars (description, what location or system affected, etc.)>, <person's name responsible to resolve incident>, <actions taken>, <date and time incident successfully resolved>
2	As above
...	As above

IT Problems Log Form

IT PROBLEMS LOG FORM	
<Organisation>: <page no>:	
<IT building location>:	
Seq. No	Data to be recorded
1	<date and time reported>, <name of person who reported the problem>, <problem particulars (description, what location or system affected, etc.)>, <person's name responsible to resolve problem>, <actions taken>, <date and time problem successfully resolved>, <date and time resolution of problem reported to affected person/function, etc.>
2	As above
…	As above

Software Suppliers Minor Changes Form

SOFTWARE SUPPLIERS MINOR CHANGES FORM	
No	Data to be noted
1	Change no
2	Change request date
3	Change requestor
4	Change urgency
5	System or application affected
6	Description of change
7	Requestor signature
8	Impact of change
9	Signature of IT manager

Systems Personnel Changes Form

SYSTEMS PERSONNEL CHANGES FORM	
No	Data to be noted
1	Change no
2	Change request date
3	Change requestor
4	Change urgency
5	System software affected
6	Description of change
7	Requestor signature
8	Impact of change
9	Signature of IT manager
10	Signature of stakeholder

Systems Software Major Changes Form

SYSTEMS SOFTWARE MAJOR CHANGES FORM	
No	Data to be noted
1	Change no
2	Change request date
3	Change requestor
4	Change urgency
5	System/application software affected
6	Description of change
7	Requestor signature
8	Impact of change
9	Signature of IT manager
10	Signature of stakeholder
11	Signature of DBA
12	Signature of security manager

Application Change Request Form

APPLICATION CHANGE REQUEST FORM
The following data should be recorded:
1. Change number: 2. Date of change request:
3. Name of requester:
4. Priority: (indicate which: Low, Medium, High)
5. Name of computerised application affected: (Indicate which. If more applications are affected, these should also be noted.)
6. Description of requested change: (Note a short description of the requested change. Give an estimate of the human resources required and the intended impact on time period, new or modification of existing deliverables, schedule, budget, modification to business function, new forms, new inputs, etc.)
7. Rationale for change: (Document the reasons for which the change is required. For example: new laws, changes to regulatory framework, new business function, customer demand, enhance business or system performance, auditing requirement, etc.)
8. Business impact: (Describe the expected impact of the implemented change, such as: additional human and other technical resources, business structural changes, new data and information, business function or procedures, etc.)
9. Expected benefits: (Describe the expected benefits of the implemented change, such as: reduction of business transaction cost, improved performance, improved customer satisfaction, satisfaction of auditing requirements, etc.)
10. Signature of the requester: 11. Signature of the manager:
THE FOLLOWING DATA ARE NOTED ONLY BY THE IT FUNCTION
12. Impact on the specific computerised application: (Describe

the expected impact of the requested change on the existing systems, such as: new procedures, temporary application shutdown, implementation difficulties, testing difficulties, etc.)

13. Cost of change: (Describe the financial and non-financial expenses required to implement the change, such as: programming staff cost, design and printing of new or revised existing forms, change testing cost, etc.)

14. Approval by IT manager:

15. Signature of owner of computerised application:

16. Signature of IT security official:

17. Test date and signature:

18. Acceptance date and signature:

Minutes of Meeting Form

MINUTES OF MEETING FORM	
Meeting subject:	
Editor(s):	
Meeting date:	
Meeting place:	
Attendees:	

ITEMS DISCUSSED	
Number	Item description and summary of points
1	<item title>, <summary of points made>
2	
3	
…	

Actions				
No	Item	Responsible	Action description	Deadline
1				
2				
…				

Activities Journal Form

ACTIVITIES JOURNAL FORM	
<Organisation>: <page no>:	
<Department/Division/Function>:	
Seq. no	Data to be recorded
1	<date>, <time>, <procedure>, <transaction name>, <work done>, <success: yes/no>, <comments>, <name of staff>, <IT system involved>
...	As above

IT Mail Log Form

IT MAIL LOG FORM	
<Organisation>: <page no>:	
<IT department location:	
Seq. no	Data to be recorded (for both incoming and outgoing mail)
1	<date arrived>, <time arrived>, <name of sender>, <name of recipient>, <type of mail received or sent (book, report, magnetic media, parts, electronic message, etc.)>, <date and time delivered>, <mail service type> (courier, national mail, personal messenger, etc.)
...	As above

Visitor's Log Form

VISITOR'S LOG FORM	
<Organisation>: <page no>:	
<Building/Department/Division/Function>:	
Seq. no	Data to be recorded
1	<date of entry>, <time of entry>, <date of exit>, <time of exit>, <location/function visited>, <visitor's particulars (name, identification no, address, etc.)>, <escort's name and phone no>, <visitor's signature>, <escort's signature>
...	As above

Security Incidents Log Form

SECURITY INCIDENTS LOG FORM	
<Organisation>: <page no>:	
<Building/Department/Division/Function>:	
Seq. no	Data to be recorded
1	<date reported>, <time reported>, <name of person who reported the incident>, <incident particulars (description, what location or system affected, etc.)>, <person's name responsible to resolve incident>, <actions taken>, <date and time incident successfully resolved>
...	As above

IT Asset Inventory Form

IT ASSET INVENTORY FORM	
<Organisation>: <page no>:	
<Department/Division/Function>:	
Seq. no	Data to be recorded
1	<date asset obtained>, <serial number of asset>, <type of asset (hardware, software, etc.)>, <date of last maintenance>, <location>, <success: yes/no>, <comments>, <name of IT staff responsible>, <IT system involved>, <supplier name>
2	
...	

Standard Software Test Plan

1 INTRODUCTION

This section summarises the test plan.

2 TEST CONSIDERATIONS

This section describes the issues that influence the test plan that need to be addressed or resolved before attempting to execute the tests.

Assumptions: Any assumptions about the project not explicitly contained in the test plan but which may affect the understanding or execution of this plan should be recorded here.

Risks: Describe the issues, conditions or limitations pertaining to the project that may interfere with the ability to test the product and/or the goals for testing. A contingency plan should accompany each risk.

Impact items: Describe the items, elements, properties or resources that are available that might positively influence testing of the software.

3 TESTING STRATEGY

This section describes the overall testing strategy and the project management issues that are required to properly execute effective tests.

Features to be tested: Describe the features and functions that will be tested during the project. This should include functional and non-functional requirements. If appropriate, list which items are in scope for testing. This could include items, such as the entire application, individual components, source files, etc.

Features not to be tested: Identify and explain why certain features and combinations of features will not be tested. If appropriate, list any applicable items that will not be available to the testing team. This could include items, such as source code to third party applications, requirements documents from other companies, etc.

Test procedure: Describe the testing approach the project will use. This includes the test life cycle, types of testing, test objectives and test criteria.

Unit testing: The strategy for unit testing of individual subsystems is described. This includes an indication of the subsystems that will undergo unit tests or the criteria to be used to select subsystems for unit test. Test cases are NOT included here.

Integration testing: The integration testing strategy is specified. Describe the tests that will be performed in order to verify the interfaces between the subsystems of the software system. This section includes a discussion of the order of integration of subsystems. Test cases are NOT included here.

Acceptance testing: The strategy for testing the software once it has been installed on the user site is specified. This section includes a discussion of the order of acceptance by software function. Test cases are NOT included here.

4 RESOURCES

This section describes the resources needed to fulfil the test plan described in the previous sections, such as personnel, hardware, data, budget, time schedule, etc.

Personnel: The required, available and necessary personnel for each type of testing (unit, integration, acceptance, etc.), for both IT and end-user areas, must be defined and obtained. The standard test personnel may include: test project manager, test designer, tester, system test administrator, and end-user tester. The test project manager is the overall person responsible for managing and organising testing, obtaining, coordinating and allocating the required resources, providing technical guidance, performing quality reviews and inspections, undertaking and managing risks, and maintaining the test library. The test designer produces, categorises and files test scenarios. The tester executes test scenarios, documents the results and documents any required changes. The system test administrator establishes and maintains the required technical environment for application testing. The end-user tester undertakes their own testing to ensure the given application performs according to their business requirements and expectations.

Hardware: The required hardware equipment (servers, network facilities, accounts, data communications lines, special web (IP) addresses, personal computers, bar coding devices, firewalls, routers, etc.) must be defined and made available to the testing team for the duration of the tests.

Data: The necessary data, sometimes good copies of real production application data, must be defined, located and loaded into the testing application files and databases, so that they can be used for all types of testing without impacting the real production environment.

Budget: A testing budget must be established for testing along the lines of the normal IT budget. This budget must be managed, approved by senior management, revised (as needed), followed and reported by the CIO.

Time schedule: A specific time schedule with the test milestones of the test project, time allocated for each phase of testing, dependencies, etc. must be established and used.

Other related resources: In some very special cases, specialised resources must be allocated to the test effort (e.g. chemical application software), such as production equipment (petrol loading automated equipment), lab facilities, simulation software, etc.

Appendix 5: IT audit methodology

Scope of IT audit methodology

The scope of this IT audit methodology[72] is to ensure the most successful organisation and completion of auditing ITC (Information Technology and Communications) systems and infrastructural components for any organisation. To this effect, this audit methodology may, at least, cover some of the following issues:

- Assess the risks of ITC systems and ensure appropriate risk management systems and procedures are in place.
- Enable the optimal use of all ITC resources (equipment, operational and communication infrastructure, resources, operating systems, database and other application software, network maintenance and administrations systems, data files, personnel, etc.).
- Ensure that improvement of the integrity of information and knowledge sources is apparent and exercised effectively throughout the organisation.
- Ensure that protection and deterrence mechanisms are in place for the ITC assets of the organisation.
- Minimise (if not avoid) the potentiality of fiscal and operational fraud.
- Improve the protection of ITC resources from both internal and external probable intrusion(s).

---

[72] This methodology has not been verified by any scientific or other method, and is offered as an example only. If it is considered in any way, it must be changed, amended and customised to suit the needs and requirements of both the auditors executing the audit work and the organisation being audited.

Methodological approach

This methodological approach is based on actual IT audit experience and on some of the most recent developments in the area of audit planning, risk assessment, IT systems development and project management approaches, including the Information Systems Audit and Control Association's (ISACA) COBIT methodology. It focuses on assessing the structure of the relationships and processes which are employed to direct and control the IT operation of the organisation in order to ensure the attainment of the organisation's strategic goals, balancing carefully the inherent risks with their expected returns within the overall ITC framework.

The approach proposed for ITC audit comprises of the following principal phases and stages:

- Phase A: Audit planning
  - Stage 1: Annual audit planning
  - Stage 2: Management and key users review
  - Stage 3: IT audit objectives planning
  - Stage 4: Data collection and review
  - Stage 5: Risk assessment.
- Phase B: Audit execution
  - Stage 1: Audit each IT area
  - Stage 2: Evaluate and record findings
  - Stage 3: Review findings with personnel audited.
- Phase C: IT audit reporting
  - Stage 1: Issue initial draft report
  - Stage 2: Review draft report
  - Stage 3: Revise draft report
  - Stage 4: Issue final IT audit report.
- Phase D: IT audit project management

- Stage 1: Administration of audit project
- Stage 2: Documentation of audit work notes.

Phase A: Audit planning

Stage 1: Annual audit planning

During this stage the internal audit management of the organisation will meet extensively with the senior management, Board members and the audit committee in an attempt to collect all the necessary information regarding the audits that should be carried out in all business activities, including IT, during the next year.

The primary activities of this stage are:

1. Conduct in-depth interviews with Board members.
2. Conduct in-depth interviews with audit committee members.
3. Conduct in-depth interviews with senior management.
4. Conduct in-depth interviews with key stakeholders.
5. Review, organise and evaluate information.
6. Prepare annual internal audit plan (including IT audit activities).
7. Obtain approval for annual audit plan.

Stage 2: Management and key users review

During this stage, the audit team will meet extensively with company management, conducting in-depth interviews and group workshops in an attempt to collect all the necessary information regarding management's view on:

- Management's vision and goals for the company's ITC systems vis-à-vis the services they are deemed to offer to the end-users.

- Management's strategic goals and their correspondence to deployed ITC systems, processes and personnel.
- The company's ITC strategy, policies, standards and procedures as they are currently designed and implemented.
- Management's view on inherent corporate strategic risks, including their views on respective significance and potentiality of existence for the IT area.

The primary goal of this stage is to identify the key IT audit issues according to company management as well as those operational areas on which the IT audit process will eventually focus, without discounting the possibility of adding further focal points as mandated by the information as it will be collected in the subsequent audit stages and activities.

The primary activities of this stage are:

1 Conduct in-depth interviews with company management.
2 Organise and evaluate information.
3 Conduct workshops with key users of ITC services.
4 Organise and evaluate information.
5 Establish initial focal areas.
6 Determine company's management needs.

Stage 3: IT audit objectives planning

The IT audit required within the context of the internal audit activities must aim to provide quick and effective results on the basis of an efficiently organised schedule, resource allocation, budget and implementation planning. Additionally, it should focus on the company's critical business functions and its corporate objectives and should have as its most important dimension the assurance that the company's ITC assets and data are properly controlled and protected. Furthermore, it must ensure that effective and efficient management controls are deployed for the whole organisation, in order to avoid problems pertaining to potential ITC systems abuse and fraud.

The main activities of this stage are:

1 Establish management strategic goals.
2 Select IT areas to be audited (*see Appendix 6* for a full list).
3 Define IT audit project scope and objectives.
4 Define IT audit project limits and boundaries.
5 Organise and plan IT audit project: schedule, resources, IT test environment, test data, test transactions, audit programmes, audit checklists, etc.

Stage 4: Data collection and review

During this stage, all the necessary documentation pertaining to the design, deployment and operation of the company's ITC systems will be collected and reviewed in order for the existing resources, facilities, information, data, transactions and test environments to be identified.

As an indication, some of the information which will be collected are:

- Reports: annual (and other relevant) corporate reports, previous internal audit reports, management reports, Board of Directors reports, ITC studies and relevant reports, customer and user satisfaction surveys, performance benchmarks, etc.
- Technical drawings: system diagrams, network schematics, work flow process charts, information flowcharts, etc.

- Corporate operational transactions: financial transactions, purchase order contracts, maintenance agreements, insurance policy agreements, etc.
- Strategic plans: corporate and IT strategic plans, production and other functional plans, corporate and IT budget and action plans, mission and vision statements, long- and short-term objectives, etc.
- Standards, policies and procedures: corporate handbook (working terms and policies), security policies and procedures, performance management policies, corporate governance framework and guidelines, internal audit standards and procedures, Enterprise Architecture framework, ITC systems development standards, procurement policies, computerised systems operational standards, etc.
- Resources: personnel available for support and assistance during the auditing process, list of existing ITC vendors, ITC vendor personnel availability, corporate management availability, IT personnel availability, etc.

The main activities of this stage are:

1 Collect basic information.
2 Evaluate basic information.
3 Collect additional information.
4 Review and evaluate all collected information.
5 Prepare final audit programmes and checklists.

Stage 5: Risk assessment

An effective comparative risk evaluation is essential for the completion of the ITC audit of the company's systems. The audit approach focuses on three specific elements:

- Complete analytical recording of all potential risks according to their respective subject areas (information and telecommunication systems, organisation, final user participation, documentation, project definition and management) as they relate to the ITC audit project.
- Grading of all recorded risks in a predefined scale (one to 10 – one being the lowest possible risk and 10 being the highest) and assigning respective probability of occurrence for each risk on a similar scale.
- Aggregation of the end result for each identified danger according to the aforementioned grading.

This approach enables and facilitates the quicker, more objective and more efficient assessment and classification of identified inherent risks facing the company's ITC systems, according to their relative significance for the organisation.

The main activities of this stage are:

1 Review corporate risk register.
2 Record any new or additional risks.
3 Assign risk importance.
4 Assign risk potentiality.
5 Evaluate risks.

Phase B: Audit Execution

Stage 1: Audit each IT area

The audit of each specific IT area selected will involve:

- Identification of the correspondence of the company's strategic goals to the objectives and processes of each identified IT area.

- The examination of the risks within each process and their impact on the company's ITC strategy and overall operation.
- The evaluation of the controls deployed to minimise or avoid these risks.

The significant amount of work required to accurately and effectively complete this stage requires the complete and timely co-operation of all organisational members involved in the IT audit project (including IT, end-users and general management).

The main activities of this stage are:

1. Prepare a list of areas to be audited.
2. Ensure that the test environment is ready for the use of the IT audit team.
3. Prepare the final audit programmes and checklists.
4. Prepare the test transactions.
5. Execute the audit tests (both manual and computerised).

Stage 2: Evaluate and record findings

During this stage the audit team will evaluate, grade and document all initial findings and comments, and issue a draft report.

The main activities of this stage are:

1. Complete collection of necessary evidential information.
2. Record initial findings in work notes.
3. Evaluate initial findings.
4. Prepare draft audit report with initial findings.
5. Issue draft audit report with initial findings.

Stage 3: Review findings with personnel audited

During this final stage of the audit project, the audit team will review extensively the initial findings with the personnel audited at their respective management levels, ensuring the best possible feedback from all operational and organisational levels within the company, as well as the IT department.

The main activities of this stage are:

1 Present findings to personnel audited.
2 Review findings with personnel audited.
3 Review findings with the respective management levels.
4 Evaluate comments and observations.
5 Incorporate comments into draft audit report.
6 Present draft audit report to management.
7 Review draft audit report and management suggestions.

Phase C: IT audit reporting

Stage 1: Issue initial draft report

Complete reporting, with an appropriate focus, is critical to ensure the highest possible effectiveness of the IT audit within any organisation. During this stage, the audit team, with the assistance of key audited personnel, will compile the initial draft report containing:

- The audit's main findings across all IT operational and strategic levels in the company.
- The principal ITC processes and their identified associated risks.
- List of all deployed controls and an initial assessment of their respective effectiveness.

- The potential impact of various adverse scenarios in the company's ITC operations and processes.
- Proposals for the design and implementation/improvement of additional controls.

The main activities of this stage are:

1. Prepare draft audit report (see also internal audit report example in *Appendix 7*) with summaries for management.
2. Prepare draft audit report with details for personnel audited.
3. Issue draft reports to the appropriate management levels.

Stage 2: Review draft report

During this stage, the audit team will assess the validity of its initial assessment results by:

- presenting them to the participating auditees
- discussing the results in depth
- collecting comments and suggestions.

The purpose of this stage is to incorporate the feedback of the personnel audited and additional suggestions into the final report, thereby offering management a clearer and more functional view of the company's audited ITC operations.

The main activities of this stage are:

1. Present draft audit report to senior management.
2. Present draft audit report to auditees.
3. Collect comments and suggestions.

Stage 3: Revise draft report

Utilising all comments, suggestions and observations into the final report ensures the full and complete participation of all key ITC personnel and management in the most effective implementation of the ITC audit.

The main activities of this stage are:

1 Incorporate the more constructive comments into the report.
2 Revise initial draft audit report.
3 Review the revised draft audit report with the audit committee.

Stage 4: Issue final IT audit report

Upon completion of all required revisions and updates, the audit team will issue a complete report to company management, incorporating, in addition to those elements mentioned before, the opinion of the audit team on:

- appropriateness of deployed IT controls
- business and IT strategic process effectiveness and functionality
- effectiveness of controls of ITC systems
- security of ITC systems and networks
- any other relevant issues identified during the audit process.

The main activities of this stage are:

1 Incorporate the comments of the audit committee into the final report.
2 Incorporate management's action plans to audit findings into the final report.
3 Present the final audit report to audit committee members and the Board.
4 Issue the final audit report to auditees, audit committee and senior management.

Phase D: IT audit project management

Stage 1: Administration of audit project

This stage will be effectively implemented throughout the duration of the audit project. Its purpose is to ensure the best possible allocation both of internal audit resources as well as key users involved.

The main activities of this stage are:

1 Conduct regular meetings with the management of the personnel audited.
2 Review the progress of the audit team and its activities.
3 Establish and ensure quick and accurate communications.
4 Resolve any identified issues and problems arising during the audit process.

Stage 2: Documentation of audit work notes

To ensure that the company's internal IT audit personnel can continue to develop further the processes and controls required to maintain the highest possible level of IT audit functionality, the audit project team will document in detail all project phases, with their corresponding findings and results.

Appendix 6: IT audit areas

1 IT organisation and administration

- IT department organisation
- Company and CIO business plan
- Budget/costing
- Management reports
- Performance monitoring and capacity planning
- IT service performance management
- Inventory control
- Project management
- Problem management
- Auditing report
- IT procurement
- Customer service agreements
- Vendor management
- Computer insurance.

2 IT strategy

- Strategy process
- Strategic management
- EDI (Electronic Data Interchange) strategy.

3 IT security

- Management of information security issues
- Information security policy
- Hardware security

- Magnetic media control
- Physical access security
- Operating system and database management
- Application systems
- Networks
- Personnel ethics (IT, users)
- Controls over data and files
- Data protection rules
- Data classification system.

4 Contingency planning

- Preliminary planning for critical applications
- Identification of various processing alternatives
- Contingency plan deliverables
- Escrow agreement audit
- Alternate facility review
- Alternate computer vendors review.

5 Software and computerised data – back-up process

- Back-up policy review
- On-site back-up safe vault review
- Off-site back-up safe vault review
- Recovery testing plan review
- Data back-up media archival/recycling review
- Application software media archival/recycling review.

6 IT legislation compliance

- Legislation review

- Licences review
- Data privacy review.

7 Health and safety controls

- Fire protection policy review
- Health and safety legislation review
- Health and safety controls review (for personnel, equipment, media, documentation).

8 System development and maintenance

- Management review
- Standards and methodologies review
- Software specifications review
- Error correction procedures
- Software package evaluation
- Program library maintenance
- Program and system testing
- User documentation review
- System documentation review
- Emergency procedures review
- Application data retention policy review
- Training plans review
- Audit trail review
- Conversion review.

9 Data centre operations

- Operations standards review
- Operations log review
- Consumables review

- Massive/sensitive reports printing
- Media library control
- Media access control.

10 Systems software maintenance

- Software asset inventory review
- Maintenance contracts review
- Program library maintenance
- Problem fixing
- Security review
- System documentation review
- Segregation of duties assessment
- Performance monitoring.

11 Data and database management

- Scope of data management (identification, classification, ownership, distribution, protection, integrity)
- Controls review (management, corporate data model, data-driven methodology, normalisation of database structure, synchronisation)
- Assessment (data modelling, database procedures, security, DBA personnel, user training, performance monitoring, database integrity).

12 Personal computers

- Management control and procedures review
- Security review
- Technical support audit
- Software development review

- Office applications support/review.

13 User support

- User satisfaction assessment
- Help desk support
- Data back-up review.

14 Telecommunications and networking

- Strategic planning and design review
- Network security review
- Maintenance contract review
- Problem resolution and support
- Change and performance management.

15 Application controls and testing

- Processing controls assessment
- Transaction audit trail review
- Data integrity controls review
- Application related integrity controls review (data element validity, file validity, audit trail, network transmission, concurrent updating, feasibility, quality)
- Continuity of application processing
- Transaction tests (as per worksheets).

Appendix 7: Internal audit report example

<COMPANY LOGO>
<TITLE OF AUDIT>

1. EXECUTIVE SUMMARY
Introduction:
Objectives:
Scope:
Overall opinion:

2. DETAILED RECOMMENDATIONS
Detailed Recommendation 1
Title of area reviewed or risk:
Rationale:

Recommendation:
Management response:

Detailed Recommendation 2
Title of area reviewed or risk:
Rationale:
Recommendation:
Management response:

Detailed Recommendation N
Title of area reviewed or risk:
Rationale:
Recommendation:
Management response:

3. MANAGEMENT ACTION PLAN				
Ref	Agreed action	Responsibility	Impln date	Status

FURTHER RESOURCES

Maintain the knowledge you have by studying, and what you do not have, by research.

Isocrates, Ancient Greek Writer (436–338 BC)

Books and articles

Abernethy, M.A. and Brownell, P. 'The role of budgets in organisations facing strategic change', *Accounting, Organisations and Society*, 24:3, pp. 189–204 (1999).

Abrams, M., Jajodia, S. and Podell, H. (eds) *Information Security – An Integrated Collection of Essays*, CA, USA: IEEE Computer Society Press (1995).

Ackoff, R.L. *The Art of Problem Solving: Accompanied by Ackoff's Fables*, New York: John Wiley & Sons (1978).

Adams, J.L. *Conceptual Blockbusting. A Guide to Better Ideas*, Reading, Massachusetts: Addison-Wesley Professional (1986).

Adler, M.D. *Cost-Benefit Analysis, Legal, Economic and Philosophical Perspectives*, Chicago: University of Chicago Press (2001).

Adrion W.R., Branstad M.A. and Cherniavsky J.C. *Validation, Verification, and Testing of Computer Software*, USA: NBS Special Publications (1981).

Aghili, S. 'A six sigma approach to internal audits', *Strategic Finance* (February 2009), pp. 38–43.

Albrecht, W.S. and Albrecht, C.O. *Fraud Examination and Prevention,* Tennessee: South-Western Educational Publishing (2004).

Allen, D. 'Take a good look at yourself: how to make IS performance self-examination more thorough', *ComputerWorld* (February 15, 1993), pp. 90–91.

Anderson, R.H. et al *Universal access to e-mail. Feasibility and Societal Implications,* RAND Corporation Report (No. MR-650-MF) (1995).

Ansoff, I. *Corporate Strategy*, New York: McGraw Hill (1965).

Anthony, R. and Govindarajan, V. *Management Control Systems*, 12th edn, New York: McGraw-Hill (2007).

Applegate, L.M., Austin, R.D. and McFarlan, F.W. *Corporate Information Strategy and Management: Text And Cases*, 6th edn, New York: McGraw-Hill Companies (2003).

Arnold, J.D. *The Complete Problem-Solver. A Total System for Competitive Decision Making*, New York: John Wiley & Sons (1992).

Arredondo, L.A. *Telecommunications Management for Business and Government*, New York: Telecom Library (1980).

Aristotle *Athenian Constitution. Eudemian Ethics. Virtues and Vices*, Cambridge, Mass: The Loeb Classical Library, Harvard University Press (1935).

Aristotle *Nicomachean Ethics,* Cambridge, Mass: The Loeb Classical Library, Harvard University Press (1934).

Aristotle *On Man In The Universe (Metaphysics, Ethics, Politics, Ethics, Poetics*), USA: Walter J. Black (1943).

Avgerou, C. *Information Systems and Global Diversity*, Oxford: Oxford University Press (2002).

Avison, D. and Fitzgerald, G. *Information Systems Development*, 3rd edn, Maidenhead: McGraw-Hill (2003).

Bacon, F. *Essays and New Atlantis*, New York: Walter J. Black (1942).

Bancroft, N.H., Henning, S. and Sprengel, A. *Implementing SAP R/3: How to Introduce a Large System into a Large Organization*, 2nd edn, Greenwich, Connecticut: Manning Publications Company (1998).

Banks, I.D. 'Internal control of on-line and real-time computer systems', *Management Accounting* (June 1977), pp. 28–30.

Bass, L., Clements, P. and Kazman, R. *Software Architecture in Practice*, Reading, Massachusetts: Addison-Wesley Professional (1998).

Berners-Lee, T. *Weaving the Web*, USA: Texere Publishing (2000).

Bernus, P., Nemes, L. and Schmidt, G. (eds) *Handbook on Enterprise Architecture*, Heidelberg: Springer Verlag (2003).

Berscheid, E. and Walster, E.H. *Interpersonal Attraction*, Reading, Massachusetts: Addison-Wesley Educational Publishers, Inc. (1969).

Bodnar, G.H. 'Internets and intranets: network accounting', *Journal of Cost Management* (November/December 1999), pp. 33–37.

Bolter, T.D. *Turing's Man: Western Culture in the Computer Age*, Chapel Hill: University of North Carolina Press (1984).

Bristow, N. and Sandberg, S.J. *The Corporate Culture Audit,* Devon: Cambridge Strategy Publications (1998).

Bryson, J.M. *Strategic Planning for Public and Nonprofit Organizations*, San Francisco: Jossey-Bass (1995).

BS 7649:1993 Guide to the Design and Preparation of Documentation for Users of Application Software, London: British Standards Institution (1993).

BS 7799 Code of practice for information security management, London: British Standards Institution (1998).

Burton, R.N. 'Discussion of information technology-related activities of internal auditors', *Journal of Information Systems* (Supplement), pp. 57–60 (2000).

Business Intelligence Unit *Building a Strategic Balanced Scorecard*, (www.business-intelligence.co.uk).

Butler, J. *Contingency Planning and Disaster Recovery Strategies*, USA: Computer Technology Research Corporation (1994).

Canadian Bible Society *The Bible*, London: Collins Clear Type Press (1952).

Carr, N.G. *The Big Switch: Re-wiring the World*, New York: W.W. Norton & Co (2008).

Castells, M. *The Rise of the Networked Society: The Information Age*, Cambridge Mass: Blackwell Publishers (1996).

Chadwick, H. *Saint Augustine Confessions*, Oxford: Oxford University Press (1998).

Chaffee, E. 'Three models of strategy', *Academy of Management Review*, Vol. 10, No. 1 (1985).

Chambers, A. and Rand, G. *Auditing the IT Environment*, Spilsby: Management Audit Ltd (1997).

Chao, J.C. 'Interception controls of data communications systems', *Journal of Information Systems* (Spring 1990), pp. 69–80.

Cheney, G. 'Cyberfraud and computer crime', *Strategic Finance* (November 1999), pp. 38–43.

Chorafas, D.N. *Implementing and Auditing the Internal Control System*, Basingstoke, Hampshire: Palgrave Macmillan (2001).

Christansen, J.A. *Building the Innovative Organisation*, Basingstoke, Hampshire: Palgrave MacMillan (2000).

Commission of the European Communities *Information Technology Security Evaluation Criteria (ITSEC), Provisional Harmonised Criteria: Version 1.2*, Luxembourg: Office for Official Publications of the European Communities, Luxembourg, June 1991.

Conti, T. *Building Total Quality*, London: Chapman & Hall (1993).

Cortada, J.W. *EDP Costs and Charges*, Upper Saddle River, New Jersey: Prentice-Hall (1980).

Covey, S.R. *Principle-Centred Leadership*, revised edition, New York: Simon and Schuster, Inc. (1999).

Crosby, P. *Quality is Free*, New York: McGraw Hill (1979).

Currie, W. *The Global Information Society*, Chichester: John Wiley & Sons (2000).

Currie, W. *Management Strategy for IT*, London: Pitman (1995).

Currie, W.L. and Galliers, B. (eds) *Rethinking Management Information Systems*, Oxford: Oxford University Press (1999).

Dale, B.G. *Managing Quality*, Upper Saddle River, New Jersey: Prentice Hall (1994).

David, R. and Brierley, J.E.C. *Major Legal Systems in the World Today*, 3rd edn, London: Stevens and Sons (1985).

Demi, H. *Buddha*, New York: Henry Holt & Company (1996).

Deming, W.E. *Quality, Productivity and Competitive Position*, Massachusetts: MIT Centre for Advanced Engineering Study (1982).

Department of Defense Standard, *Department of Defense Trusted Computer System Evaluation Criteria (TCSEC)*, DOD 5200.28-STD, GPO 1986-623-963, 643 0, December 26, 1985.

Descartes, R. *Meditations on First Philosophy*, tr. Laurence J. LaFleur, Indiana: Bobbs-Merril (1960).

Donaldson, G. and Lorsch, J,. *Decision Making at The Top: The Shaping of Strategic Direction*, New York: Basic Books (1983).

Doty, E.A., Sen, A. and Wang, S.C. 'Effect of internal controls in database design', *Journal of Information Systems* (Spring 1989), pp. 70–91.

Douglas, I.J. *Audit and Control of Mini- and Microcomputers*, Manchester: NCC Publications (1983).

Douglas, I.J. *Audit and Control of Systems Software*, Manchester: NCC Publications (1983).

Douglas, I.J. *Security and Audit of Database Systems*, Manchester: NCC Publications (1980).

Dudik, E.M. *Strategic Renaissance*, USA: AMACOM (2000).

Duncan, W.J. *Great Ideas in Management*, San Francisco: Jossey-Bass (1990).

Dunn, C.L., Gerard, G.J. and Worrell, J.L. 'Evaluation of network operating system security controls', *Issues in Accounting Education* (August 2003), pp. 291–306.

Earl, M.J. *Management Strategies for Information Technology*, London: Prentice-Hall (1989).

Ehrmann, H.W. *Comparative Legal Cultures*, Englewood Cliffs, NJ: Prentice Hall (1976).

EU Directive on Electronic Commerce, *European Law Journal*, p. 363 (2000).

EU Guidelines on Cyberspace Issues (86/361, 87/372, 88/301, 90/387, 90/388, 90/544, 91/250, 92/100, 93/98, 94/820, 200/1999, etc.).

Feigenbaum, A.V. *Total Quality Control*, New York: McGraw-Hill (1991).

Fields, K.T., Sami, H. and Summers, G.E. 'Quantification of the auditor's evaluation of internal control in database systems', *Journal of Information Systems* (Fall 1986), pp. 24–47.

FitzGerald, J. and Eason, T.S. *Fundamentals of Data Communications*, New York: John Wiley & Sons (1978).

Fitzsimmons, J.A. and Fitzsimmons, M.J. *Service Management, Operations, Strategy, and Information Technology*, New York: McGraw-Hill (2001).

Galbraith, J. and Kazanjian, R. *Strategy Implementation: Structure, Systems and Process*, 2nd edn, St. Paul, Minnesota: West Publishing Company (1986).

Galliers, R.D. and Baker, B.S.H. *Strategic Information Management*, Oxford: Butterworth Heinemann (1994).

Gelinas, U.J., Sutton, S.G. and Otam, A.E. *Accounting Information Systems*, Cincinnati, Ohio: South-Western College Publishing (1988).

Gilb, T. *Software Metrics*, Cambridge, Massachusetts: Winthrop Publishers (1977).

Gluck, F.W., Kaufman, S.P. and Wallek, A.S. 'Strategic management for competitive advantage', *Harvard Business Review*, (July–December 1980), pp. 154–161.

Grindley, K. *Managing IT at the Board Level*, 2nd edn, London: FT Pitman Publishing (1995).

Groomer, S.M. and Murthy, U.S. 'Continuous auditing of database applications: an embedded audit module approach', *Journal of Information Systems* (Spring 1989), pp. 53–69.

Groomer, S.M. and Murthy, U.S. 'Monitoring high-volume on-line transaction processing systems using a continuous sampling approach', *International Journal of Auditing* (Spring 2003) 7, pp. 3–19.

Hall, J.A. *Information Systems Auditing and Assurance*, Cincinnati: South-Western Publishing (2000),

Harper, R.M. Jr 'Internal control of microcomputers in local area networks', *Journal of Information Systems* (Fall 1986), pp. 67–80.

Harrington, H.J. *Business Process Improvement*, New York: McGraw-Hill (1991).

Hill C.W.L. and Jones G.R. *Strategic Management*, 5th edn, Orlando: Houghton Mifflin (2001).

Hindle, J. *Guide to Management Ideas*, London: Profile Books (2000).

Howard, W.J. *The Cost of Quality Audit*, Cambridge: Cambridge Strategy Publications (1998).

Hoyle, D. *ISO 9000 Quality Systems Handbook*, Oxford: Butterworth-Heinemann (1994).

Humphrey, W.S. *The Software Process*, Reading, Massachusetts: Addison-Wesley (1990).

Humphrey, W.S. *A Discipline for Software Engineering*, Reading, Massachusetts: Addison-Wesley (1995).

IBM *A Management System for the Information Business*, USA: IBM (1981).

IBM *Management Planning Guide for a Manual of Data Processing Standards*, USA: IBM (1980).

ISACA *CoBIT Methodology on IT Auditing*, USA: Information Systems Audit and Control Association (2000).

Juran, J.M. *Juran on Planning for Quality*, New York: The Free Press (1988).

Juran, J.M. *Juran on Quality*, New York: The Free Press, (1992).

Juran, J.M. 'The Quality Trilogy', *Quality Progress*, 9:8 (August 1986), pp. 19–24.

Kaplan, R.S. and Norton, D.P. 'Linking the Balanced Scorecard to Strategy', *California Management Review*, Vol. 39, No. 1, pp. 53–79 (1996).

Kaplan, R.S. and Norton, D.P. 'Putting the Balanced Scorecard to Work', *Harvard Business Review*, September–October 1993, pp. 134–147.

Kaplan, R.S. and Norton, D.P. 'The Balanced Scorecard – Measures That Drive Performance', *Harvard Business Review*, January–February 1992, pp. 71–79.

Kaplan R.S. and Norton, D.P. 'Using the Balanced Scorecard as a Strategic Management System', *Harvard Business Review*, January–February 1996, pp. 75–85.

Kelly, C., Kocourek, P., McGaw, N. and Samuelson, J. 'Deriving values from corporate values', The Aspen Institute and Booz Allen Hamilton Inc, USA (2005).

Kennedy, A.J. *The Rough Guide to the Internet*, London: Rough Guides (2001).

Kyriazoglou, J. 'Methodology on systems testing of database information systems', 1st Panhellenic Computer Congress & Conference Proceedings, Greece, April 1984.

Kyriazoglou, J. 'Dictionary – Directory of information systems', 1st Panhellenic Computer Congress & Conference Proceedings, Greece, April 1984.

Kyriazoglou, J. 'Why use a Dictionary – Directory', European GUIDE, England, June 1984.

Kyriazoglou, J. 'Information quality standards in computerised systems', *Information Management Journal*, UK: IDPM Society (1995).

Kyriazoglou, J. 'Management information systems and network', COPISEE Conference, Greece (1980).

Laudon, K.C. and Laudon, J.P. *Management Information Systems: Managing the Digital Firm*, 7th edn, New Jersey: Prentice Hall (2002).

Lessig, L. *The Future of Ideas: The Fate of the Commons in a Connected World*, New York: Random House (2001).

Li, D.H. *Controls in a Computer Environment: Objectives, Guidelines, and Audit Procedures*, USA: EDP Auditors Foundation (1983).

Lindsay, J. *The Technology Management Audit*, Cambridge: Cambridge Strategy Publications (1998).

March, J.G. *The Pursuit of Organisational Intelligence*, Massachusetts: Wiley-Blackwell (1999).

Martin, J. *Principles of Data-Base Management*, Englewood Cliffs, New Jersey: Prentice-Hall (1976).

Matthews, D.Q. *The Design of the Management Information System*, New York: Auerbach Publishers (1971).

McLuhan, M. *The Man and his Message*, Colorado: Fulcrum, Inc. (1989).

Mintzberg, H. and Quinn, J.B. *The Strategy Process*, Harlow: Prentice-Hall (1988).

Mintzberg, H., Ahlstrand, B. and Lampel, J. *Strategy Safari: A Guided Tour Through the Wilds of Strategic Management*, New York: The Free Press (1998).

National Computer Security Centre *Trusted Network, Glossary of Computer Security Terms*, NCSC-TG-004, October 1988.

Negreponte, N. *Being Digital*, New York: Alfred A. Knopf (1995).

Naughton, J. *A Brief History of the Future*, 2nd revised edn, London: Phoenix Press (2000).

NCC *Guidelines for Computer Managers*, UK: NCC (1981).

Neumann, P.G. *Computer-Related Risks*, New York: ACM Press (1995).

OECD *OECD Principles of Corporate Governance* www.oecd.org (2007).

Olins, W. and Selame, E. *The Corporate Identity Audit*, Cambridge, Cambridge Strategy Publishers. (1995).

Page, S.B. *Establishing a System of Policies and Procedures*, Mansfield, Ohio: Bookmasters (1998).

Pearson, A.E. (1989). 'Six Basics for General Managers', *Harvard Business Review*, July–August 1989.

Perks, C. and Beveridge, T. *Guide to Enterprise IT Architecture*, New York: Springer (2003).

Pfleeger, C. *Security in Computing*, 4th edn, New Jersey: Prentice Hall (1996).

Plato *Five Great Dialogues (Apology, Crito, Phaedo, Symposium, Republic)*, tr. B. Jowett, New York: Walter J. Black (1942).

Plato *Charmides*; *Timaeus and Critias*; *Laches*; *Laws*; *Phaedrus*; *Protagoras*; *Republic*; *Theaetetus*, The Loeb

Classical Library, Cambridge, Mass: Harvard University Press.

Purvis, R.L. and McCray, G.E. 'Project assessment: a tool for improving project management', *Information Systems Management*, Vol. 16, No. 1, Winter 1999.

Putman, J. *Architecting with RM-ODP*, New Jersey: Prentice Hall (2001).

Rae, K., Subramaniam, N. and Sands, J. 'Risk management and ethical environment: Effects on internal audit and accounting control procedures', *Journal of Applied Management Accounting Research* (Winter 2008), pp. 11–30.

Ruthberg, Z.G. and McKenzie, R.G. *Audit and Evaluation of Computer Security*, Washington: NBS Special Publication (1977).

Sahlman, W.A. 'How to write a great business plan', *Harvard Business Review*, July–August 1997.

Sarbanes, P. and Oxley, M.G. *The Sarbanes-Oxley Act of 2002*, USA: Publication of the Library of Congress (2002).

Sarker, S. and Lee, A.S. 'IT-enabled organisational transformation: a case study of BPR failure at TELECO', *The Journal of Strategic Information Systems*, March 1999, Vol. 8, No. 1, pp. 83–103.

Sauders, C.S. and Williams Jones, J. 'Measuring performance of the information systems function', *Journal of Management Information Systems* 8, No.4, pp. 63–82 (1992).

Scheer, A-W. *ARIS – Business Process Frameworks*, Berlin: Springer (1998).

Schwartau, W. *Information Warfare*, New York: Thunder's Mouth Press (1994).

Scott Morton, M.S. *The Corporation of the 1990s: Information Technology and Organisational Transformation*, Oxford: Oxford University Press (1991).

Shapiro, C. and Varian, H. *Information Rules*, Boston: Harvard Business School Press (1999).

Singh, I. et al *Designing Enterprise Applications with the J2EETM Platform*, New York: Addison-Wesley (2002).

Singh, J. *Great Ideas in Information Theory, Language and Cybernetics*, New York: Dover Publications (1962).

Sommerville, I. *Software Engineering*, New York: Addison-Wesley (1998).

Spewak, S.H. *Enterprise Architecture Planning. Developing a Blueprint for Data, Applications and Technology*, New York: John Wiley & Sons (2000).

Thomas, R.R. *Telecommunications for the Executive*, New York: Petrocelli Books (1984).

Thomas, A.J. and Douglas, I.J. *Audit of Computer Systems*, Manchester: NCC Publications (1981).

Toffler, A. *The Third Wave*, New York: Bantam Books (1980).

Walsham, G. *Interpreting Information Systems in Organizations*, Chichester: Wiley (1993).

Walsham, G. *Making a World of Difference: IT in a Global Context*, Chichester: Wiley (2001).

Ward, J. and Griffiths, P. *Strategic Planning for Information Systems*, 2nd edn, Chichester: Wiley (1996).

Ward, J. and Peppard, J. *Strategic Planning for Information Systems*, 3rd edn, New York: John Wiley & Sons Ltd. (2002).

Watad, M.M. and Herlihy, M. 'Implementing distributed solutions', *Information Systems Management*, Vol. 16, No. 1, Winter 1999.

Weber, R. *Information Systems Control and Audit*, New York: Prentice Hall (1998).

Weil, P. and Broadbent, M. *Leveraging the New Infrastructure: How Market Leaders Capitalize on Information Technology*, Boston: Harvard Business School Press (1998).

Weiss, I.R. 'Auditability of software: a survey of techniques and costs', *Management Information Systems Quarterly*, Vol. 4, No. 4, 12/1980, p. 39.

Wigmore, J.H. *Panorama of the World Legal Systems*, 2nd edn, Florida: WM. W.Gaunt & Sons, Inc. (reprint 1992) (1928).

Woolf, E. *Auditing Today*, London: Prentice-Hall (1994).

Zachman, J.A. 'A framework for information systems architecture', *IBM Systems Journal*, Vol. 26, No. 3, pp. 276–292 (1987).

Zachman, J.A. 'Enterprise Architecture: the issue of the century', available at the Zachman International website *www.zachmaninternational.com*.

Zuboff, S. *In the Age of the Smart Machine*, New York: Basic Books (1988).

Zwass, V. *Foundations of Information Systems*, New York: McGraw-Hill (1998).

Other resources

Association for Operations Management.

Balanced Scorecard Collaborative: *www.thepalladiumgroup.com/pages/welcome.aspx.*

Balanced Scorecard Institute: *www.balancedscorecard.org*.

British Standards Institute: *www.bsi-global.com.*

Canada/Alberta Province Performance Measurement: *www.finance.gov.ab.ca*.

Conference Board, Canada: *www.conferenceboard.ca*.

Canadian Institute of Chartered Accountants, Canada: *www.cica.ca*.

Center for Democracy & Technology: *www.cdt.org.*

Center for Ethics (University of Tampa, Florida, USA): *www.ut.edu.*

Centre for Business Performance: *www.cranfield.ac.uk.*

Contingency Planning & Recovery Institute, USA.

COSO/Treadway Commission: *www.coso.org*.

Electronic Commerce Europe: *ec.europa.eu/internal_market/e-commerce/index_en.htm*, www.semper.org.

European Corporate Governance Institute: *www.ecgi.org.*

European Court of Auditors: *http://eca.europa.eu*.

European Management Association: *www.europeanmanagement.org*.

European Operations Management Association.

Federal Computer Incident Response Capability, USA: *http://csrc.nist.gov*.

Forrester Research: *www.forrester.com.*

Foundation for Performance Measurement: *www.fpm.com.*

Gartner Group: *www.gartner.com.*

Information Systems Audit and Control Association: *www.isaca.org*.

Institute of Operations Management (UK).

Institute of Supply Management: *www.ism.ws.*

Institute of Value Management: *www.ivm.org.uk.*

International Auditing and Assurance Standards Board: *www.ifac.org/IAASB.*

International Data Corp: *www.idc.com.*

International Organization for Standardization (ISO).

Management Centre Europe: *www.mce-ama.com.*

MIT Technology Review: *www.technologyreview.com.*

National Institute of Standards and Technology, USA: *www.nist.gov.*

Performance Measurement Association: *www.performanceportal.org*.

Production and Operations Management Society.

RAND Corporation: *www.rand.org*.

SANS: *www.sans.org*.

Society for Human Resource Management: *www.shrm.org*.

Society of Competitive Intelligence Professionals: *www.scip.org*.

University of Cambridge, Institute for Manufacturing, Centre for Strategy and Performance: *www.ifm.eng.cam.ac.uk.*

Yankee Group: *http://yankeegroup.com*.

Zachman International: *www.zachmaninternational.com*.

ITG RESOURCES

IT Governance Ltd. sources, creates and delivers products and services to meet the real-world, evolving IT governance needs of today's organisations, directors, managers and practitioners. The ITG website (*www.itgovernance.co.uk*) is the international one-stop-shop for corporate and IT governance information, advice, guidance, books, tools, training and consultancy.

http://www.itgovernance.co.uk/it_governance.aspx is the information page on our website for IT governance resources.

Other Websites

Books and tools published by IT Governance Publishing (ITGP) are available from all business booksellers and are also immediately available from the following websites:

www.itgovernance.co.uk/catalog/355 provides information and online purchasing facilities for every currently available book published by ITGP.

www.itgovernanceusa.com is a US$-based website that delivers the full range of IT Governance products to North America, and ships from within the continental US.

www.itgovernanceasia.com provides a selected range of ITGP products specifically for customers in South Asia.

www.27001.com is the IT Governance Ltd. website that deals specifically with information security management, and ships from within the continental US.

Pocket Guides

For full details of the entire range of pocket guides, simply follow the links at *www.itgovernance.co.uk/publishing.aspx.*

Toolkits

ITG's unique range of toolkits includes the IT Governance Framework Toolkit, which contains all the tools and guidance that you will need in order to develop and implement an appropriate IT governance framework for your organisation. Full details can be found at *www.itgovernance.co.uk/products/519*.

For a free paper on how to use the proprietary Calder-Moir IT Governance Framework, and for a free trial version of the toolkit, see *www.itgovernance.co.uk/calder_moir.aspx*.

There is also a wide range of toolkits to simplify implementation of management systems, such as an ISO/IEC 27001 ISMS or a BS25999 BCMS, and these can all be viewed and purchased online at: *http://www.itgovernance.co.uk/catalog/1*.

Best Practice Reports

ITG's range of Best Practice Reports is now at *www.itgovernance.co.uk/best-practice-reports.aspx*. These offer you essential, pertinent, expertly researched information on a number of key issues including Web 2.0 and Green IT.

Training and Consultancy

IT Governance also offers training and consultancy services across the entire spectrum of disciplines in the information governance arena. Details of training courses can be accessed at *www.itgovernance.co.uk/training.aspx* and descriptions of

our consultancy services can be found at *http://www.itgovernance.co.uk/consulting.aspx.*
Why not contact us to see how we could help you and your organisation?

Newsletter

IT governance is one of the hottest topics in business today, not least because it is also the fastest moving, so what better way to keep up than by subscribing to ITG's free monthly newsletter Sentinel? It provides monthly updates and resources across the whole spectrum of IT governance subject matter, including risk management, information security, ITIL and IT service management, project governance, compliance and so much more. Subscribe for your free copy at: *www.itgovernance.co.uk/newsletter.aspx.*